CASTLEREAGH COLLEGE F.E.

A-Z
HEALTH
&
SOCIAL
CARE
h a n d b o o k

the complete

A-Z
HEALTH
&
SOCIAL
CARE

h a n d b o o k

Judy Richards

Specialist editors
Hilda Haws and Carole Rees

Hodder & Stoughton

A MEMBER OF THE HODDER HEADLINE GROUP

British Library Cataloguing in Publication Data
A catalogue entry for this title is available from the British Library

ISBN 0–340–70557–4

First published 1999
Impression number 10 9 8 7 6 5 4 3 2 1
Year   2003 2002 2001 2000 1999

Copyright © 1999 Judy Richards

Typeset by GreenGate Publishing Services, Tonbridge, Kent.

Printed and bound in Great Britain for Hodder and Stoughton Educational, a division of Hodder Headline plc, 338 Euston Road, London NW1 3BH, by Redwood Books, Trowbridge, Wilts.

HOW TO USE THIS BOOK

The A–Z Health and Social Care Handbook is an alphabetical glossary designed for easy use. As you can appreciate, health and social care covers a wide subject area and the major concepts which you will come across in your health and social care studies have been included. This handbook therefore constitutes an important reference work which will help you to understand the basic requirements for your study. Government legislation and reports which have been responsible for structural changes within health and social care services are included to support your research – numbered references within the text refer you to a comprehensive list of the relevant legislation and reports at the back of the book.

Each entry begins with a definition. This should help you to gain some understanding of what you are looking for. The length of an entry usually depends on how relevant the content is to the caring concepts within health and social care. Entries therefore try to provide some guidance or introduce you to the major points. Illustrations and tables have been provided to help you to understand the entry.

To support your research, you can make use of the cross-referenced entries. These are to be found in *italics* either in the main body of an entry or at the end of the entry. These cross-references direct you to related subjects.

This A–Z is a **glossary** which will aid your study of health and social care; it is important to recognise that it is **not** a textbook. This means that you will need to carry out further reading to complete your grasp of the subject but the A–Z will provide you with a handy reference source, when you come across terms of which you are unsure.

Samples of organisations have been included to support you and increase your understanding of the scope of voluntary organisations. These include the umbrella organisations in Northern Ireland, Scotland and Wales.

To help you in your revision, lists of terms have been provided at the end of the book. I have used the most popular GNVQ Advanced level to structure these lists.

Finally, I hope that you enjoy using the A–Z on a daily basis and that you find it is an invaluable resource in your studies. I have certainly enjoyed compiling it.

Judy Richards

ACKNOWLEDGEMENTS

This has been an enormous task which I could not have achieved without my invaluable supporters. I wish to thank my husband Jeff, my daughters Jessica and Helen who kept my spirits up during the research, Doreen Rowe whose expertise at the keyboard was such an asset, and my specialist editors who edited the entries, Hilda Haws and Carole Rees.

To friends and colleagues Esther, Pat, Sarah R, Marg, Lyn (T), Jan, Barbara, Vee, Donna, Milicia, Anthea, Wendy, Chris and Jenny Giles.

My past and present students who continue to be my inspiration.

Finally, thanks to Tim Gregson-Williams, Clare Smith, Sarah Dobson at Hodder & Stoughton and Ian Marcousé, the series editor.

Different organisations have given invaluable information. A special note to students: if you contact any of these organisations for information then **please do not** forget to enclose an A4 size envelope with a stamp to the value of £1.00.

ABC of resuscitation: a method of *resuscitation* which can be applied in an emergency.

- A is for **airway** – tilting the casualty's head back and lifting the chin will 'open the airway'. The tilted position lifts the casualty's *tongue* from the back of the throat so that it does not block the air passage.
- B is for **breathing** – if a casualty is not breathing, another person can breathe for him or her and so oxygenate the *blood*, by giving 'artificial ventilation', blowing their expired air into the casualty's *lungs*.
- C is for **circulation** – if the *heart* has stopped, 'chest compressions' can be applied to force blood through the heart and around the body. These must be accompanied by artificial ventilation so that the blood is oxygenated (St. John Ambulance 1997)[57]. (See *artificial respiration, AVPU Code.*)

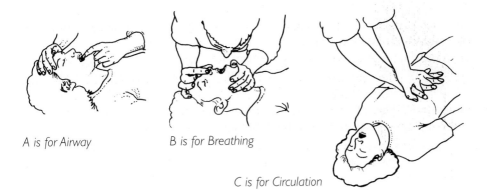

A is for Airway   B is for Breathing

C is for Circulation

abdomen: the region of the body that contains all the internal organs except the *heart* and *lungs*. The abdomen is separated from the thorax by a partition called the *diaphragm*. The abdomen is lined with a membrane called the peritoneum.

abnormal behaviour is *behaviour* that does not conform to what is considered to be normal or the 'norm' by certain groups of people in society. An example of this would be a person shouting obscenities at passers-by in the street, oblivious to the effect he may be having, and the fear and uncertainty he may be promoting through this type of behaviour. (See *challenging behaviour.*)

abortion is the termination of *pregnancy*. Abortion can be either by natural means (spontaneous abortion), commonly known as *miscarriage*, or by artificial or surgical means. Abortion is increasingly viewed as the termination of an unplanned and unwanted pregnancy. Since 1967, following the *Abortion Act,* it is legal to terminate a pregnancy up to 24 weeks in duration. However, most abortions are carried out in the first 12 weeks of pregnancy, via either the *National Health Service* or private medicine. There are different views on abortion; for example:

- 'Pro-life' groups believe that abortion limits the life choices of the growing foetus. They believe that the foetus has a right to be born and a right to life.
- 'Right to Abortion' groups support women's rights. They believe that women have a choice; that a planned abortion is an appropriate medical intervention in an unwanted pregnancy, or a pregnancy where the unborn child may have a genetic *disability.*

Because of the issues involved regarding the rights and choices of the individual, abortion is a controversial subject.

Abortion Act 1967: an Act of Parliament which enables a woman to terminate an unwanted and unplanned *pregnancy.* Under this Act, two *doctors* must agree to the abortion on the grounds of:

- 'risk' to the life of the pregnant woman
- 'risk' to the lives of her existing children
- 'risk' of abnormality in the *foetus.*

Under the Act the woman's emotional, psychological, social and physical *well-being* are taken into account by the doctors. The introduction of the Abortion Act in 1967 was a means whereby 'backstreet abortions' were greatly reduced and women were given the chance to seek proper medical attention. The Act was amended in 1996 with regard to the grounds on which a pregnancy may be terminated. The meanings of the terms 'risk' and 'serious' which are mentioned in the 1967 Act, were clarified. The Act does not extend to Northern Ireland (HMSO 1967 and 1996).[2]

abuse is a deliberate and intended injury to another person or way of treating an individual so as to cause them harm. Such acts of abuse can be:

- Physical – 'actual or likely physical injury to a child or individual or failure to prevent physical injury or suffering to a child'. It includes deliberate poisoning, suffocation and *Munchausen's syndrome* by proxy (HMSO 1992)[16]. Examples of physical abuse are hitting and smacking in anger, burning with a cigarette and beating with a stick or belt.
- *Neglect* – 'the persistent or severe neglect of a child or individual or the failure to protect a child from exposure to any kind of danger'. This includes cold or starvation and extreme failure to carry out important aspects of care, such as giving a child a *diet* which leads to *malnutrition, vitamin* deficiency and *failure to thrive* (HMSO 1992)[16]. Examples of neglect may involve leaving a child, elderly person or disabled client alone, unsupervised and not providing for these clients the basic needs such as *food,* clothes, *warmth* and medical care.
- *Sexual* – 'actual or likely sexual exploitation of a child, adolescent or other. The child may be dependent and/or developmentally immature' (HMSO 1992)[16]. Examples of sexual abuse includes intercourse with a child or with a person against their will. Other examples are activities such as fondling, masturbation, oral sex, anal intercourse and violating a child's or person's intimate and personal privacy.
- Emotional – 'actual or likely adverse effect on the emotional and behavioural development of a child caused by persistent or severe emotional

ill-treatment or rejection. All abuse involves some emotional ill-treatment. This category should be used where it is the main or sole form of abuse.' (HMSO 1992)[16]. Examples of emotional abuse include verbal threats, shouting, screaming and persistently telling the child or individual how hopeless, stupid or ugly they are. This may have a damaging, long lasting effect on the *self-esteem* of an individual.

- Self harm – in which the abuse is directed at oneself. An individual may scratch or cut themselves or try to injure themselves in some way. Examples include cutting their wrists, pulling their hair out.

Groups of people who are most vulnerable to abuse are children (see *child abuse*) women (see *domestic violence*) and elderly people (see *elderly abuse*).

Access to Health Records Act 1990: an Act of Parliament giving individuals the right to recorded health *information* about themselves. This involves information which is not already covered by the rights of access to computerised records under the *Data Protection Act 1984*. Section 5 of the Access to Health Records Act sets out three cases where access is not given to the whole of a health record. These are when:

- in the opinion of the holder of the record, giving access would disclose information likely to cause serious harm to the physical or *mental health* of the *patient* or of any other individual
- giving access would, in the opinion of the holder of the record, disclose information relating to, or provided by, an individual other than the patient who could be identified from that information
- the relevant part of the health record was made before the commencement of the Act on 1st November 1991 (HMS0 1990)[3].

access to information: the right that clients, patients and service users have to all information concerning their personal lives (see *Access to Health Records Act 1990, Access to Medical Reports Act 1988, Access to Personal Files Act 1987* and the *Patient's Charter*). Health and social care providers have different methods of storing *information*. These can be manual and/or computerised *records*. For example, the records which individual *GPs* maintain with regard to their patients and their different visits may be hand written. The *drugs* and personal details of a patient would however be fed into a computer system. Some agencies may have a limit on the length of time that they maintain an individual's records. (See also *NHS – new information technology*.)

Access to Medical Reports Act 1988: an Act of Parliament which deals with requests from employers or insurance companies who want medical reports on *clients*. Such requests cannot be met without the *consent* of the *client* or *patient*.

Access to Personal Files Act 1987: an Act of Parliament which reinforces the *Data Protection Act 1984* and gives individuals the right to *access* their personal records. For example, individuals have the right to make a written request for access to manually held personal information within *housing* and *social service departments*. These organisations must reply within 40 days. (HMSO 1987)[4]

access to services: clients and service users are entitled to treatment and therapy provided through the *National Health Service* and *social services*. Under the *Patient's Charter 1992* patients have rights to:

- receive health care on the basis of their clinical need, not on their ability to pay, *lifestyle* or any other factor
- be registered with a *GP* and be able to change their GP easily and quickly if they want to
- have access to emergency medical treatment at any time through their GP, the *ambulance* service and *hospital accident and emergency* departments
- be referred to a consultant acceptable to them, when their GP thinks it necessary, and to be referred for a second opinion if they and their GP agree this is desirable (see *referral to health care services, NHS performance*).

Patients can expect the NHS to make it easy for everyone to use its services, including children, *elderly people* and those with physical or mental *disabilities*. For example, if a child needs to be admitted to hospital, parents can expect the child to be cared for in a children's ward under the supervision of a consultant *paediatrician*. Exceptionally, when a child has to be admitted to a ward other than a children's ward, a parent can expect a named consultant paediatrician to be responsible for advising on their care. (See also *barriers of access to health and social care services, Platt Report, Audit Commission.*)

accident: an unpredictable injury which affects a person at any time and which may require medical treatment. There are groups of people who are more at risk from accidents. They are:

- young children – because they are less aware of danger
- disabled people – because different impairments lead to vulnerability
- *elderly people* – because of diminishing mobility, or mental awareness.

Any individual can be at risk at certain times, for instance, a preoccupied adult may leave a toddler to wander out into a garden with a fish pond. The toddler does not have a sense of danger but is full of curiosity about the goldfish in the pond. She/he may lean over and fall in and within a matter of moments be in danger of drowning. As a result of an accident of this kind at a *nursery* in Lancashire, the government is reviewing its regulations for local authority inspection procedures for early years provision. Under the present system, *local authorities* are required to undertake one visit a year (see *accident book*). Accidents are identified in the *national health targets*.

accident and emergency: a special department at a *hospital*, which deals with accidents and acute illness; sometimes known as the 'A and E Department' or 'casualty'.

accident book: a method of recording *accidents* which occur in all *organisations* including those in health and social care. Information recorded should include:

- the name and address of the injured person
- the date and time of the accident
- details of the accident
- the type of injury
- the treatment given or action taken
- details of who was informed
- a signature of the person in charge at the time of the accident.

The accident book is often a requirement of the health and *safety* policy of a health and social care provision. This book should be accessible to all the members of staff (see *Regulations for Reporting of Injuries, Diseases and Dangerous Occurrences (RIDDOR) 1985*).

accommodation – child protection: a service which a local authority provides to the parents of children in need and to their children. The child is not in care when she/he is being provided with accommodation; nevertheless the local authority has a number of duties towards children for whom it is providing accommodation, including the duty to discover the child's wishes regarding the provision of accommodation and to give them proper consideration (HMSO 1991)[67].

accommodation – in health and social care provision is a type of *residential care* which can be offered to *clients*. It can be *statutory, voluntary, private* or *informal* care provision for:

- children – e.g. *children's homes* or in families through *fostering* and *adoption*
- clients with a disability – e.g. *hostels, sheltered housing*
- *elderly people* – e.g. *residential homes, nursing homes, sheltered accommodation,* family homes.

accommodation – of the eye: the ability of the eye to change focus so that both near and distant objects can be seen clearly. When a person looks at a distant object the rays of the light are bent (refracted) by the *cornea* and the lens and are focused on the retina. If the object is brought closer, the light rays have to be refracted more if they are to remain focused. This is done by contraction of the ciliary muscles which change the shape of the lens so that it becomes more convex.

accountability: professional responsibilities between *health authorities, primary care groups* and *primary care trusts*. This process reviews the ways in which *primary care trusts* work within the *health improvement programme* to ensure that financial discipline and probity are maintained. In addition to this, the health authorities and the primary care group agree targets for improving health, health services and value for money. These are set out in an annual accountability agreement.

acid-fast bacilli (AFB) are *bacteria* which are able to retain dyes even after treatment with *acid*. The process is a method of identifying organisms which can be the cause of disease. An example of this type of bacterium is *Mycobacterium tuberculosis* which causes tuberculosis.

acids are chemicals that release hydrogen ions when dissolved in *water.*

acquired disorder: a *disease* or *disability* which is contracted after *birth*. It is not *inherited* or *congenital*. An example of an acquired disease would be an *infection* such as *meningitis* which is the inflammation of the meninges of the *brain* caused by a viral or bacterial infection.

acquired immune deficiency syndrome (AIDS): a *disease* which is caused by the human immune deficiency *virus* (HIV). This virus attacks the immune system and therefore alters the body's response to infection. HIV is transmitted:

- through sexual contact via infected body fluids such as semen and vaginal fluid
- by injecting *drugs* – i.e. using previously infected needles
- by *artificial insemination* – introducing infected semen into the vagina or uterus of the female to induce conception
- through *blood transfusion* – using blood which is infected with HIV
- from a mother who is HIV-positive to the unborn child – the HIV virus can

pass from the mother through the placenta to the *foetus*; the HIV virus is also present in the breast milk of an HIV-positive mother

It is important to remember that *not* every person who is infected with the HIV virus will get full blown AIDS. Full blown AIDS usually occurs after the following four stages have been completed. There is no set period of time for each stage.

- Stage 1 – symptomless stage, the person is infected with the HIV virus, but is producing antibodies to combat the infection and appears quite healthy. They can still infect others so health and safety precautions should continue to be taken, e.g. protected sex using a condom.
- Stage 2 – persistent generalised lymphadenopathy (swollen glands). This is the first sign that the immune system is breaking down, highlighted by swollen lymph glands in the neck, groin and the *axillae.*
- Stage 3 – AIDS-related conditions such as weight loss, night sweats, fever, lack of resistance to disease, a general feeling of tiredness or fatigue and feeling unwell.
- Stage 4 – the immune system shows signs of failing and the lack of resistance can lead to different infections affecting the body. These include chest infections, brain infections causing blindness, loss of speech and tremors, *skin* diseases causing ulceration, boils, ringworm, *cancer* of the tongue and genital areas. This stage leads to death.

There are health and safety precautions which should be applied when working with people with HIV such as wearing gloves when attending to *wounds.*

active immunity: a type of resistance to *disease* in which individuals manufacture their own *antibodies.* This may or may not be the result of a natural *infection.* It is possible for the body to produce antibodies without suffering from the illness. This kind of immunity can be induced by the process of *vaccination.*

active listening skills are *listening skills* which are used during *interaction* between the *client* and the *carer.* There are two types of active listening:

- paraphrasing – this is a way of summarising what the *client* has said and feeding back to the client for confirmation that what they have said has been understood. For example a carer could say to a client 'what you have just told me has raised these points, is that right?' Paraphrasing is an important way of checking for accuracy that what has been said has been understood by the carer. It also gives the client the feeling that the carer has been listening and is making an effort to understand their conversation. It is a means by which the carer can communicate that they want to care for the client. Often, this is the first step in building up an effective client and *carer* relationship.
- reflective listening – concentrates on what is being said. The carer will either repeat what a client has said or use non-verbal messages and positive body language with space and silence for the client to respond further.

activities of daily living are daily tasks and activities associated with the process of living. They include washing, *toileting* and dressing. Activities for daily living can be categorised into:

- self care skills – personal care such as eating, drinking, washing, *bathing*, dressing, hair and skin care.
- home care skills – caring for the home environment such as cooking and kitchen skills, gardening, washing, ironing, cleaning, budgeting and shopping skills.
- employment skills – identifying skills which would be suitable for employment such as communication and computer skills.
- *mobility* skills – using the body for daily tasks such as washing, dressing, shopping, housework.
- social skills – making relationships such as friendships.

Understanding the activities of daily living is a vital part of assessing a client and the way in which they are able to cope with life. Development of these skills can be written into a client's individual *care plan*. Supporting clients with their daily living activities can be:

- short term – clients need support because they have had an *accident*, surgical operation or are suffering from a temporary debilitating *disease* or *disorder*
- long term – clients need continuing support because the disorder, *dysfunction* or disease suffered restricts *their mobility*.

In some cases specialist aids or equipment are necessary in order to maintain the *health and safety* of both the *client* and the *carer*. (See also *aids and adaptations, Disabled Living Foundation, occupational therapy*.)

activity based interaction comprises the different activities which *clients* and *carers* can carry out together. These activities are designed to develop and promote their *communication* and *interpersonal* skills. Activities which can be provided to develop these skills include:

- 'one to one', e.g. discussion, practical tasks
- small group activities, e.g. discussion, debate, practical tasks
- large group activities, e.g. oral presentations, discussions, practical tasks.

(See also *interaction*.)

acupressure: an *alternative method* of treatment which is a combination of *acupuncture* and *massage*. It is used to relieve pain, produce anaesthesia or regulate a body function. In this treatment the thumbs and fingertips apply pressure and massage along the same points at which needles are inserted during acupuncture.

acupuncture: an *alternative method* of treatment which originated in China. It is a relatively painless treatment which involves the insertion of fine needles at specific points on the skin. Acupuncture has been found to enhance *health* and the *immune system* as well as addressing specific symptoms. To qualify as an acupuncturist may involve full-time training lasting three to four years, or three to five years part-time.

acute: a disease or condition which is of quick onset. It is often short and severe. An example is appendicitis which involves inflammation of the *appendix*. The signs and symptoms are severe right-sided abdominal pain, sickness and high temperature. The treatment is immediate surgical removal of the appendix.

acute services: medical and surgical treatment and care mainly provided in *hospitals*.

addiction: the way in which an individual can become dependent physically, intellectually, emotionally and psychologically on a substance or activity, e.g. nicotine addiction, *heroin* or *alcohol* addiction.

adenosine diphosphate (ADP) is a high *energy* compound found in cells. Its function is energy storage and transfer. When extra energy and phosphate are added it forms *adenosine triphosphate* (ATP).

adenosine triphosphate (ATP) is a compound with a high level of *energy* found in cells. Its function is energy storage and transfer. It can be broken down so that ADP and phosphoric acid are formed. Energy is released in this process. Some of the energy is lost as heat, but a proportion of it can be used for biological activities. (See *glycolysis*.)

adipose tissue consists of cells containing fat which group together to form a protective layer under the *skin*. Extra layers of fat surround the organs of the body in order to provide protection and insulation.

administration consists of the procedures involved in managing services or organisations. These procedures usually relate to business management. They may be applied to health and social care organisations in the following ways:

- human resourcing, which includes staffing and personnel issues, e.g. employment of *carers* and client/staff ratios
- accounting and finance; budget issues such as costing of care packages and necessary resources to support the *caring* process
- marketing and product sales, for example advertising different caring services especially in the private or *independent* sector
- operations management; this includes reviewing the product and its production, for example *care management* which may involve setting up *care plans*, monitoring and evaluating the process.

Admiral Nurse Service is an example of a *voluntary organisation* which supports carers of people with a *dementia* illness. It aims to:

- provide *information* about the nature of dementia and the progress of the *disease*
- assist the *carers* in organising practical help
- enhance, increase and support the skills of carers in *caring* for a person with a dementia illness
- enhance the skills needed to deal with the *stress* and *anxiety* that may arise during the care process
- provide the carer with emotional *support* to reduce the sense of isolation and feeling of loss associated with the experience of bereavement and to continue to provide on-going support after *bereavement*
- provide *advice* to other agencies and individuals in contact with people with a dementia illness and their care-givers, and to support efforts to meet their needs
- act as a training resource for *informal carers* such as family members.

(For further information contact The Dementia Relief Trust, Pegasus House, 37–43 Sackville Street, London W1X 2DL.)

admission is entry into *hospital* or residential care. The admission may be planned from a *waiting list*, or be an emergency via the hospital *accident and emergency* department. Admissions can also be arranged via the hospital outpatient department. Individuals may also be admitted to hospital under the *Mental Health Act 1983*. This procedure is called sectioning.

adolescence: the period of development starting with *puberty* and ending in *adulthood*.

adoption: the legal transfer of an *infant* or child from their birth family to another family. Adoption was introduced under the Adoption of Children Act in 1926. This was amended in terms of statutory rules and procedures through the Adoption Act 1976, Adoption Rules 1984, the Adoption Regulations 1983, the *Children Act 1989* and the Adoption Amendment Rules 1991. Legislation with regard to adoption is currently under review. Couples who want to adopt children should apply to their local social services adoption and *fostering* ('family finders') department. When they apply formally to become available for adoption parents are screened to see whether they are suitable. When a child is chosen, there is a settling-in period during which the child and his or her potential parents will take time to get to know each other before the legalities are completed. Adoption enables the new parents to have full parental rights over the child (*parental responsibility*). The natural parents or the birth families no longer have legal rights over the child, although there may be some cases where some informal contact is arranged. (See *British Agencies for Fostering and Adoption*.)

adoption agency: an organisation which undertakes adoption services. The adoption agency must be validated and approved by the *Secretary of State for Health*. An adoption agency will set up the adoption process which will include:

- selecting prospective parents
- placing children
- providing counselling for both prospective parents and for birth parents who have given up their children for adoption.

Adoption agencies can be found in *social services departments*, charitable organisations such as *Barnados* and church organisations such as the Catholic Children Society.

Adoption Contact Register: a register of names of children who are available to be contacted by their natural parents or families. The register is a means by which children who have been adopted and have reached the age of 18 years are able to make contact with their natural parents.

adoption hearing: the legal procedure which involves an application by a couple for the *adoption* of an infant or child or young person. This takes place in the *Magistrates' Court*. The prospective parents apply to the court for custody of the child. An adoption order is given provided the *consent* of the natural parents is received and legal responsibility for the child is then transferred to the prospective parents. In a situation where the natural parents are not available to give consent the child's legal representative, such as the appointed *guardian ad litem*, can give consent.

adrenal glands are situated on the top of each *kidney*. These glands are divided into two parts:

- **Cortex** – the outer part of the gland which produces steroid hormones, cortisol and *aldosterone*. Aldosterone helps to regulate the amounts of *sodium* and potassium found in the body. One of the functions of cortisol is to accelerate the conversion of proteins to glucose.
- **Medulla** – the inner part of the gland which produces the hormone *adrenaline*. Adrenaline prepares the body for the 'fight, fright and flight' response. This is the way in which the body responds during times of crisis, fear and danger. (See *endocrine system*.)

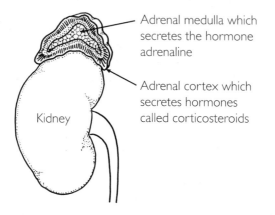

Adrenal medulla which secretes the hormone adrenaline

Adrenal cortex which secretes hormones called corticosteroids

Kidney

adrenaline (epinephrine) is the hormone which is produced in the medulla of the *adrenal* gland. It causes the body to respond physiologically to the effects of stress and sets up the 'fight, fright and flight' response. When adrenaline is produced in large amounts during times of crisis it has the following effects on the body:

- the *skin* becomes pale, because the blood vessels under the surface of the skin constrict and blood is diverted from the surface; this enables more *blood* to be supplied to the *muscles*
- *blood pressure* increases, the *heart* beats faster and more blood is pumped round the body
- the *liver* releases some of its stored *carbohydrate* to supply energy
- the pupils dilate.

adrenocorticotrophic hormone (ACTH) is a *hormone* which controls the secretion of corticosteroid hormones from the *adrenal glands*. It is synthesised and stored in the anterior *pituitary gland*.

adulthood is a stage of life. It is when a person is fully developed and matured and has reached full legal age, i.e. 18 years of age.

advice: *information* which supports *clients, service users* and their *carers*. Advice may be given through advice centres. Such centres can be established by *statutory, private,* and *voluntary* organisations which may also include friends, family or an *informal caring network*. Advice can be offered through libraries, *hospitals,* town halls or other agencies such as the *Citizens Advice Bureau*. Advice centres have major roles in ensuring that information and advice is available to the general public.

Advisory Committee on Resource Allocation: see *NHS Resources*.

Advisory Conciliation and Arbitration Service (ACAS) is an organisation which was set up in 1975 to act as an independent source of expertise in preventing and settling industrial disputes. ACAS offers companies expert, unbiased conciliator or mediator support. Over 70,000 individual cases are handled each year. ACAS has built up a reputation for its unbiased advice and has a policy of not commenting publicly on the cases it manages. Examples of where ACAS offers support may be related to dismissal, redundancy and harassment.

Advisory Group: a group set up by the Department of Education and Employment to advise on personal, social and *health education* in schools. The Advisory Group was an initiative presented in the Green Paper 'Our Healthier Nation' (HMSO 1998)[48].

advocacy: a procedure where a health and social care worker can speak or act on a *client's* or patient's behalf. The role of an advocate will ensure that the client's or patient's rights and interests are supported. Advocates can be either employed or act as volunteers.

The term covers:

- citizen advocacy, which requires the voluntary involvement of a member of the public in the life of a disabled person. Such a person can be recruited as a member of a *support group*, a neighbour or *volunteer*. This is a long-term process involving a one-to-one partnership between the service user and their advocate
- legal advocacy, representation by legally qualified advocates such as solicitors
- self-advocacy, where clients, patients or service users represent themselves and present their own cases for individual *rights and choices*
- formal advocacy, schemes set up by volunteer groups which are not user led. They are usually managed by voluntary service providers such as *SCOPE*
- peer advocacy, where the advocates may be citizen advocates or active users of a service.

aerobic capacity: the capacity of the cardiopulmonary system, i.e. a measure of the way in which the *heart* and *lungs* function to supply *oxygen* to the *tissues*.

aerobic exercises are activities which result in physical exertion. These exercises are aimed at increasing *oxygen* consumption to benefit the *lungs* and *cardiovascular* system. Activities such as running, swimming and skipping are aerobic exercises.

aerobic respiration: respiration in which *oxygen* is used to oxidise food to carbon dioxide and water. There is a high yield of energy. The process is in two stages:

- *Glycolysis* – which does not require oxygen and takes place in the cell cytoplasm. It involves the conversion of glucose into pyruvic acid.
- *Krebs cycle* – which occurs only in aerobic respiration and takes place in the cell *mitochondria*. It is a complex cycle of enzyme-catalysed reactions in which pyruvic acid is oxidised to *carbon dioxide* and water, with the production of large amounts of energy.

aetiology is the science which investigates the causes of *disease*. For example, the aetiology of *typhoid fever* involves studying the causative agent, an organism called Bacillus typhosis, which is found in faulty *water* supplies containing sewage.

affection: the feeling of love, goodwill and kindness which a person shows to another. It is an important aspect of caring for others. For example, children need affection and love to promote their emotional growth and build their *self-esteem*. (See *emotional development*.)

after schools club: see *out of school clubs*.

agar is a jelly-like substance obtained from seaweed. It is used to grow colonies of *bacteria* or fungi. It is a substance with the ability to melt at a low temperature to allow for easy handling and to solidify at room temperature. When bacteria are spread on the surface of agar gel in a petri dish and left for a few days at a blood heat temperature of around 37 degrees centigrade (98.6 degrees Fahrenheit), their numbers will increase and colonies will form. This method of growing bacteria helps *microbiologists* identify which bacteria are responsible for certain *diseases*.

age: stage of development in the life of a human being. This involves a number of processes and changes which take place in the body as it ages. (See also *ageing*.)

age classification: the way in which *health* and *social care services* are classified by the age groups of the clients concerned.

There are different variables reflecting the different age groups. Each age classification is supported by *legislation*, for example, children's services are covered in aspects of the *Children Act 1989*.

Age Concern – the National Council on Ageing: a voluntary organisation which works to improve the *quality of life* for the country's 12 million older people. It provides opportunities for the active and the able, as well as the frail and vulnerable. It is the centre of a network of 1100 local organisations and 180,000 *volunteers* offering a wide range of community-based services, including *day centres*, lunch clubs, home visiting and transport. Nationally, Age Concern supports this work through the provision of *information* and *advice*, policy analysis, publications, and grants towards training for the improvement of the quality of services for older people. It works closely with partner organisations in the UK, Europe and internationally, and is committed to teaching and research through the Age Concern Institute of Gerontology at King's College London. Age Concern is an organisation which campaigns actively on behalf of the elderly. An example of this was a recent *campaign* to fight age *discrimination* in the workplace by giving support to David Winnick's parliamentary bill calling for a ban on *age* limits in job advertisements.

(For further information contact Age Concern England, Astral House, 1268 London Road, London SW16 4ER.)

age of consent: the *age* at which an individual can give their permission for any activity, treatment or therapy. Some examples which are covered by legislation include:

- 16 years of age – age of consent for heterosexual intercourse
- 18 years of age – age of consent for *homosexual* intercourse
- 16 years of age – age of consent for buying cigarettes
- 18 years of age – age of consent for buying *alcohol*
- 17 years of age – age of consent for driving a car
- 16 years of age – age of consent for leaving secondary school (now June/July after becoming 16 years of age)

- 18 years of age – age of consent for voting
- 16 years of age – age of consent for treatment.

Under the *Children Act 1989*, young people have the right to consent or to refuse consent to medical treatment (e.g. *immunisations*) provided such young people are deemed to be of an age or ability to make their own informed choice.

age profile: a method of looking at the structure of the population and predicting future trends. For example, increasing *life expectancy* is likely to lead to more people needing long-term care. This means that each working person will have to provide for more pensioners. In 1953 there were 4.6 people of working age for every pensioner. Today, there are 3.4 and by 2040 the ratio will have dropped to just 2.4, even allowing for the equalisation of the retirement age. (HMSO 1998)[48]

age structure and population: the way in which the ages of individuals are distributed in the national, international or global population. In the United Kingdom the age structure in the population has changed in the last 30 years. These changes include:

- an increase in the proportion of *elderly people*, particularly those over 75 years of age
- a decrease in the proportion of *young people* under 16 years old.

ageing: changes which occur in the body through the different stages of *human growth* and *development*. This process begins at *fertilisation* and continues throughout the life span to the end of a person's life which is *death*. Following conception the *foetus* grows and develops. After *birth* the changes occurring are part of the *ageing* process. The ageing process includes:

- rapid growth and development which take place in the early years of childhood
- physical changes which occur during *puberty*. The secretion of hormones leads to the development of secondary sexual characteristics in boys and girls
- changes in the chemical reactions in the body, e.g. the basal *metabolic rate* which is affected by age. For instance, young people are able to take far more strenuous exercise and cope with a higher metabolic rate than most people in their seventies
- a decline in biological functioning, e.g. in females between the ages of 45 and 55 the reproductive system is affected by a reduction in *hormone* levels. This is called the *menopause*. For men at this age there are also some changes in the *reproductive system*. Other changes include loss of muscle elasticity, stiffness in bones and joints, slowing down of different functions such as those relating to the gastro-intestinal system, e.g. constipation.

There is a range of other factors which may be affected by the ageing process such as *education, employment, leisure*, recreation, *social class* and *status*.

ageism is *discrimination* against or unfair treatment of individuals on the basis of their age. For instance when a person applies for a job they may not be considered as suitable for that post because they are over 50 years of age. Any language which is used to discriminate against people on the basis of age can be viewed as ageist, for example language which characterises the elderly as being inactive, sick and dependent.

agency: the term 'agency' has been used as a general name for any organisation large or small, which is responsible for the delivery of services to individuals and for whom workers may work or act as *volunteers*. (Care Sector Consortium 1998)[12]

agnosia: a disorder occurring when the *information* from the sensory nerves is not properly interpreted in the sensory cortex of the *brain*. Auditory agnosia affects the *ears* and tactile agnosia affects the *skin*.

agranulocytosis: the reduction of *white blood cells* or granulocytes due to *disease*, an adverse reaction to medication, or as a result of *radiotherapy*. This condition may be evident during *chemotherapy* for cancer. Chemotherapy kills off the cancer cells but also destroys white cells in the process.

aids and adaptations are used by individuals to enable them to increase, regain or retrain their ability to carry out the necessary tasks to support their daily lives, improve their *independence* and enable them to care for themselves. An example is special equipment used to help a person with severe rheumatoid *arthritis* to cook, clean, dress and undress. Stairs can be adapted to fit a chair lift. (See *activities for living, occupational therapists, Zimmer frame.*)

(For further information contact the Disabled Living Foundation, 380–384 Harrow Road, London W9 2HU.)

air is the mixture of gases which makes up the atmosphere. It consists of approximately:

- 78 per cent nitrogen
- 21 per cent oxygen
- 1 per cent carbon dioxide and the five rare gases, argon, xenon, neon, krypton and helium.

air passages: the passages found in the *nose* and nasal cavities, the mouth, trachea, the bronchi and bronchioles. The bronchioles end in the *alveoli* of the *lungs*. These passages carry *air* which is breathed into the lungs and carry air, which is breathed out, back to the atmosphere. The trachea has a lining of ciliated *epithelial* cells. Mucus secreting cells trap any particles of dust or dirt and the cilia sweep the mucus with the trapped dust to the back of the throat where it is swallowed, thus preventing dust entering the *lungs* (see opposite).

air pollution is contamination of the air by potentially harmful substances; for example, the fumes from oil and petrol given off by motor vehicles can be harmful to humans. Air pollution is now controlled by the following legislation:

- *Health and Safety at Work 1974* – imposes restrictions on harmful chemicals.
- *Environmental Protection Act 1990* – controls air pollution in the atmosphere.
- *Clean Air Act 1993* – controls all air *pollution.*

alcohol (ethanol) is a depressant drug that is taken as a drink. It may be viewed by individuals in society as a means whereby they can:

- enjoy a 'better social life'; after a few drinks they feel more confident as alcohol depresses the nervous system and produces a sense of relaxation and calm

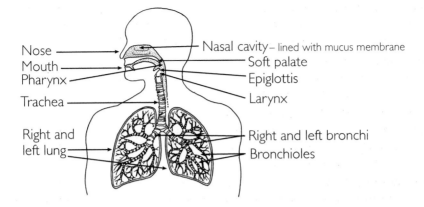

Nose — Nasal cavity – lined with mucus membrane
Mouth — Soft palate
Pharynx — Epiglottis
Trachea — Larynx
Right and left lung — Right and left bronchi
Bronchioles

Air passages

- enjoy a 'better sex life'; it is believed to be an aphrodisiac, however, it has been proved to have the opposite effect, increasing the desire but dulling sexual performance.

There are widely publicised safe drinking limits for men and women. These advise no more than 14 units of alcohol per week for women and up to 21 units per week for men, where one unit represents a half pint of beer or one measure of sherry or whisky. Drinking above such limits could seriously affect a person's health. It can cause:

- psychological and physical *dependence* – people become 'problem drinkers'
- increase in violence – there are links between violence and alcohol
- dangerous driving – people who drink and drive are more likely to have accidents
- serious effects to a person's health – it can cause damage to the heart, brain, liver, kidneys and digestive system.

Alcoholics Anonymous was set up in 1935 in New York. It is a voluntary fellow-ship of men and women who are/were alcoholic who help each other to achieve and maintain sobriety by sharing experiences and giving mutual *support*.

(For further information contact: Alcohol Concern, Waterbridge House, 32–36 Loman Street, London SE1 OEE.)

aldosterone: a hormone secreted by the *adrenal glands* which functions in the *kidney* and is responsible for maintaining sodium and potassium levels in the blood. It aids water balance in the body.

Alexander technique: a *complementary* therapy which enables the individual to become more aware of *balance, posture* and movement. Individuals are taught to use their muscles more efficiently. It is based on the theory that *ill health*, injury and pain can be due to the physical aspects of the body being out of balance. (See *complementary medicine.*)

alimentary canal: a long passage which runs from the *mouth* at one end of the body to the *anus* at the other. The alimentary canal has a number of different functions. These are:

- ingestion – taking *food* into the *mouth*
- *digestion* – breaking large insoluble molecules like starch and *protein* into smaller soluble ones like *glucose* and *amino acids*
- *absorption* – the process by which the soluble molecules resulting from digestion pass through the wall of the alimentary canal into the body
- assimilation – the process whereby simple soluble food materials are incorporated into the *cells* and are either built up into complex materials or broken down for *energy* release
- egestion – the removal of waste material from the gut in the form of *faeces.*

The main regions of the alimentary canal are the oesophagus, stomach, duodenum, ileum, colon and rectum.

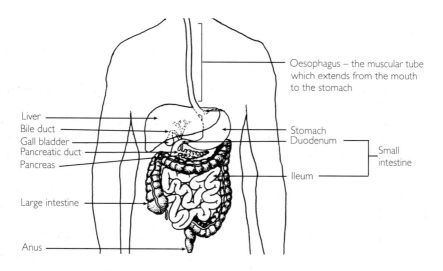

alternative medicine consists of forms of therapy or treatment which are given instead of the standard treatment; an example is *osteopathy.* (See *complementary medicine.*)

alveolus (plural alveoli): one of the many air sacs in the lungs where *gaseous exchange* takes place. The alveoli are lined with very thin, flat cells known as squamous epithelial cells. A number of adaptations make the alveoli efficient gas exchange surfaces:

- the walls of the alveoli are very thin so that there is minimum resistance to the diffusion of gases from one side to the other
- there is a very large number of alveoli and these provide considerable surface area over which *diffusion* can take place
- the alveoli are in close association with an extensive system of blood capillaries; there is a difference in the concentration of respiratory gases either side of the alveolar wall. This difference is kept as high as possible so oxygen is continually being removed by combining with haemoglobin in the blood in the capillaries to form oxyhaemoglobin. (See *gaseous exchange.*)

The air in the alveoli is regularly replaced by the ventilation mechanisms of breathing.

Alzheimer's disease: a neurological disorder which has serious *degenerative* effects on an individual. These effects include:

- difficulty in remembering recent events – leading to confusion and forgetfulness
- developing disorientation – leading to increasing confusion, an inability to recognise people or places
- episodes of hallucinations – leading to the seeing of objects or individual people that are not there
- paranoia, leading to feelings of anger, or feelings that people are watching
- violent mood swings.

Alzheimer's disease results in patients losing the ability to care for themselves and to carry out daily activities such as *washing*, dressing, eating meals, reading and writing. Possible causes include *genetic* inheritance, abnormal deposits of *protein* in the *brain* or the inhalation of environmental toxins. (See also *dementia*.)

(For further information contact the Alzheimer's Disease Society, 2nd Floor, Gordon House, 10 Greencoat Place, London SW1P 1PH.)

ambulance service: a service which deals with emergency (999) calls to road traffic accidents, general accidents, major disasters and to people who become suddenly ill or injured. The service also deals with non-urgent cases such as taking *patients* and *clients* to and from *hospitals* and *day centres*. There are approximately 67 ambulance services in the United Kingdom. There are four main types of personnel employed in the ambulance service:

- Ambulance care assistants or day transport personnel – staff who transport the disabled, elderly, mentally ill and those recovering from treatment to and from hospital or local day centres.
- Ambulance technicians – staff who deal with the full range of calls for accident and emergency care. They respond to 999 calls and are trained to administer emergency treatment on route to hospital.
- Ambulance paramedics – technicians who have undertaken further training so that they can use more advanced forms of life support equipment, such as administering intravenous infusion (setting up a drip to introduce substances into a patient's bloodstream).
- Control room assistants – staff who work in ambulance stations or in ambulance control, answering emergency and urgent calls from *GPs* and the general public. They maintain radio contact with ambulance crews by operating switchboards, receiving and passing on messages. They may use other means of *communication* such as computer terminals, fax machines, e-mail and telex.

The different areas of the ambulance service require varying types and length of training. The minimum age of entry is usually 18 years but there is a cadet scheme run by some ambulance services. (Careers Occupational Information Centre 1998)[49]

amino acids are the basic components of *protein* molecules. Hundreds of amino acids are linked together by peptide bonds to form long chains of peptides, polypeptides and proteins. Of the hundred amino acids that occur in nature twenty three are the building blocks of human proteins. The arrangement of amino acids determines the type of protein molecule. Proteins are broken down into amino acids as part of the process of *digestion*. Amino acids then enter cells where they are built back up into the types of protein which the body requires, for example muscle fibres or plasma proteins. Any excess amino acids are broken down by a process of deamination in the *liver*. During deamination the amino groups are broken off, one at a time and ammonia is formed. Ammonia enters the ornithine cycle, in which it reacts with carbon dioxide to form urea. This urea is taken to the *kidneys* and excreted.

Amnesty International: an organisation which investigates reports of *abuse* and torture suffered by individuals in different parts of the world. It is a *pressure group* which works on behalf of global *human rights* including the rights of political prisoners. It is also a charity which depends on voluntary contributions to maintain its activities.

(For further information contact Amnesty International, Freepost, London EC1 8HE.)

amniocentesis: a technique carried out on a pregnant woman, it is a means of genetic *screening* of a *foetus* inside the womb. *Ultrasound* is used to determine the precise position of the foetus and the *placenta* within the *uterus*. A fine needle is then inserted through the abdominal wall into the amniotic cavity. A sample of amniotic fluid is removed. This will contain some foetal cells which can be examined for any defect in the chromosomes. Amniocentesis is used to detect a range of diseases, disorders or dysfunctions which may be affecting the foetus (e.g. *Down's syndrome*).

amnion: one of the membranes that surrounds a developing *foetus* in the *uterus* of its mother. The cells making up the amnion secrete amniotic fluid which fills the space between the membrane and the foetus. This fluid provides protection and support for the delicate foetal tissues. (See *foetal growth and development*.)

amphetamines (street names pep pills, speed) are *drugs* which act as stimulants to the *central nervous system*. These drugs are used to treat different medical conditions and sometimes to reduce weight as part of a slimming programme. Tolerance to amphetamines can develop rapidly, leading to dependence. In recent years amphetamines have been misused and feature in a growing number of drug abuse cases. Short term effects are:

- sleeplessness and excitability resulting from stimulation of the nervous system
- increased breathing and *heart* rate
- dilated pupils
- generation of a sense of *well-being* when the individual feels alert, energetic, happy and in control
- reduction of tiredness and fatigue
- reduction of appetite.

Amphetamines create short-term effects which can lead to long-term dependence. This means that individuals may only feel happy and in control if they continue to take the drug. Dependence can have harmful effects on general health. Long-term effects include:

- disruption of sleep patterns, so sleep and getting to sleep is difficult
- lowered resistance to disease

- overactivity and excitability leading to damaged blood vessels and possible heart failure
- erratic eating patterns leading to the lack of a healthy diet
- depression and suicidal tendencies as a result of mood swings.

amputation: the surgical removal of limbs or parts of the body, i.e. legs, arms, toes. A *patient* or *client* who has had an amputation is called an amputee.

amylase is an *enzyme* which digests starch. Amylase breaks down starch into soluble sugars by means of *hydrolysis* (a chemical process which involves the addition of water). Salivary amylase is found in saliva and pancreatic amylase is found in pancreatic juices. (See also *digestion*.)

anaemia: a condition in which there is a reduced amount of *haemoglobin* in the *blood*. People suffering from anaemia tire easily. They have pale skin and get out of breath if they exert themselves. Causes of anaemia include:

- a shortage of *iron* in the diet – iron is an important part of haemoglobin molecules
- conditions which lead to a loss of blood – these may be due to accidents or the development of disorders such as ulcers which bleed over a period of time
- conditions which result in the destruction of *red blood* cells – an example is *sickle-cell disorder*, an inherited disease in which the affected person has a type of haemoglobin which is less efficient at transporting oxygen than normal haemoglobin; the red blood cells of someone with this condition also have a shorter lifespan than normal red blood cells.

anaerobic respiration is a form of respiration which takes place in the absence of oxygen.

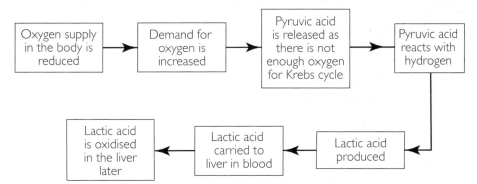

anaesthesia: a loss of sensation. Certain *diseases* such as *multiple sclerosis* can lead to numbness or loss of sensation in the limbs. General anaesthesia uses drugs to induce a loss of sensation which affects the whole body. This method may be used in *hospitals* as part of the preparation for major surgical operations. The anaesthetic is administered by a trained *doctor* who is known as an anaesthetist. In minor operations a local anaesthetic is used. This involves injecting a drug into a local area to induce numbness. The removal of an ingrowing toenail and most dental work require the use of local anaesthetics.

anatomy: the study of different parts of the body and the structural relationships between them. This is linked to *physiology*.

aneurysm: a weakening of the wall of an *artery* which produces a balloon-like swelling at the point where the blood vessel is weakened. The consequences for a person can be very serious if the swelling bursts; it can lead to bleeding into the *brain* causing paralysis in parts of the body.

angiogram: an *X-ray* examination of *blood* vessels using a dye that is opaque to X-rays. An example is cardiac catheterisation which is an examination of the blood vessels surrounding the *heart*.

anorexia nervosa: an *eating disorder* which is characterised by severe weight loss. It is particularly common in young adolescent girls who have a fear of becoming fat. Signs and symptoms include:

- obsession with *food* and eating, not eating large amounts, feeling very uncomfortable about eating anything which might be fattening (fussy eaters)
- overactivity and an obsession for *exercise*
- continuing weight loss to a dramatic and life threatening degree
- excessive tiredness and weakness
- cessation of *menstruation* due to *hormone* imbalance
- fine hair covering the body (called lanugo); the hair on the head thins.

About 50% of all patients need hospital treatment, and 5–10% die from starvation. (See also *bulimia nervosa, eating disorders*.)

anosmia is the loss of the sense of smell. It can happen after a heavy cold when the lining of the air passages becomes temporarily damaged.

antagonistic muscles are *muscles* which produce opposing effects to enable movement to take place. An example of antagonistic muscle action is that of the biceps and triceps muscles of the arm. When the biceps contracts to bend the arm the triceps muscle relaxes. When the triceps muscle contracts to straighten the arm the biceps muscle relaxes.

Muscles are called either flexor or extensor muscles depending on their function.

- Flexor muscles pull two parts of a limb towards each other, e.g. contraction of the biceps muscles causes the arm to bend.

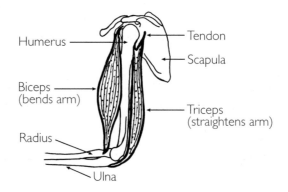

- Extensor muscles pull two parts of a limb away from each other, e.g. contraction of the triceps muscle straightens the arm.

antenatal: the period of time when the *foetus* is growing in the *womb* of the mother. Developments are closely monitored by a medical team which includes the *GP*, the *obstetrician*, the *midwife* and the *health visitor*.

antibody: a *blood* protein produced in lymphoid *tissue*. Antibody production is a response to the presence of foreign substances, for example *bacteria*, viruses or other antigenic substances. Antibodies circulate in the *plasma* and attack the *antigen* making it harmless to the body. Every antibody produced is specific to a particular *antigen*. (See *immunity*.)

anti-discrimination policies are policies which are put together as part of a framework for good practice in organisations. They serve as a deterrent to *discrimination* against individuals on the basis of *age, class, culture, gender, health status, HIV* status, marital status, *cognitive ability, mental health*, offending background, *physical ability*, place of origin, political beliefs, *race, religion*, sensory ability and sexuality. Gender, race and disability policies are supported by legislation. (See also *Sex Discrimination Act, Race Relations Act, Disability Discrimination Act*.)

anti-discriminatory practice: action which is taken to prevent discrimination against people on the grounds of *race, class, gender, disability* etc. It promotes equality as a result of the introduction of *anti-discrimination policies* in the workplace (i.e. the *care settings*.)

anti-diuretic hormone (ADH): a hormone which is produced in the posterior lobe of the *pituitary* gland. It increases the reabsorption of *water* in the renal tubules of the *kidneys* leading to less water being lost in the *urine*.

antigen: a foreign substance, chemical, *bacteria* or *virus* which enters the body and provokes an immune response. (See *antibody*.)

antitoxin: a type of *antibody* produced by the body to counteract a toxin or poison formed by a bacterium or *virus* which has entered the body.

anus: this is the opening at the end of the *alimentary canal* through which waste products (i.e. faeces) are discharged to the outside of the body. The process is called *defaecation*. The opening of the anus is controlled by the anal sphincter.

anxiety: a normal reaction to *stress* or to a situation which poses a threat or uncertainty. Anxiety can also occur in discrete panic attacks when the person is feeling nervous and helpless. However, anxiety can become a focus of a person's life when they worry and feel fearful about everyday situations. The anxiety in these cases can lead to a psychological disorder called neurosis. Anxiety also produces physical symptoms such as dizziness, headaches, tremors, lack of concentration, diarrhoea and breathlessness.

aorta: the main *artery* in the body. Other arteries branch off from it to supply *blood* to all the organs in the body. The walls of the aorta contain baroreceptors which monitor the *blood pressure* and chemoreceptors which monitor the amount of chemical compounds in the blood.

aortography: an *X-ray* examination of the aorta. This procedure involves the injection of a radio-opaque dye into the aorta. X-rays are taken and any *defect, disease* or *degeneration* is shown up.

apgar score: a scoring system which is used to assess the general health of a baby immediately after birth. A maximum of two points is given for each of the following signs measured at one minute and five minutes after delivery. The features recorded are:

- breathing and type of breathing
- *heart rate*
- colour, the healthy appearance of the baby's skin
- *muscle* tone
- response to stimuli such as light.

aphagia: the inability to swallow. This can be life threatening in situations such as choking. However, the loss of the ability to swallow can also be a symptom of severe anxiety.

aphasia: the loss of the power of speech due to a defect or disorder affecting the speech centre which is situated in the cerebrum of the *brain.*

aphonia: the loss of the power of speech due to a localised problem of the throat or mouth. Such problems can include any *disease* of the *nerves* and *muscles* which affects the production or articulation of speech.

appendix: a small tubular organ which is attached to the end of the caecum. It is composed of lymphoid tissue and does not have any known function. It can become infected and inflamed (appendicitis). The treatment for appendicitis is the surgical removal of the appendix under general anaesthetic. Appendicitis requires immediate treatment as it can cause an abscess or generalised peritonitis (inflammation of the lining of the *abdomen.*)

appropriate: a term used in NVQs in Care which indicates that something is suitable for a particular situation or person concerned. The terms 'appropriate' or 'appropriately' are used in performance criteria where there is no set response or 'right' way of doing things – it highlights that the response is dependent on the setting, context and the individual concerned. (See also *National Occupational Standards.*)

approved social worker: a social worker who has been specially trained in the area of *mental health.* An approved social worker is one of the professionals who is required to carry out an *assessment* and make a recommendation on a client who is to be admitted to a psychiatric hospital under the *Mental Health Act 1983.*

Area Child Protection Committee: a multi-agency committee which is set up to provide a forum for *child protection.* The ACPC develops, monitors and reviews local child protection policies and promotes effective and harmonious co-operation between the various agencies involved. Although there is some variation from area to area, each committee is made up of representatives of key agencies such as health and social services, and the police. The committee has the authority to speak and act on behalf of the agency. ACPCs issue guidelines on procedures, tackle significant issues as they arise, offer advice about the conduct of cases in general, make policy and review progress on prevention. They also oversee inter-agency training established in each local authority to manage and monitor the procedures of the different agencies that are involved in the protection of children. (HMSO 1989)[67] (See *Working together under the Children Act 1989.*)

aromatherapy is the use of essential oils and hydrosols (the *water* soluble part of a plant or flower) to promote personal health. Essential oils are concentrated essences extracted from plants and flowers. The healing and therapeutic uses of such oils are achieved either by inhalation or by direct application on to the body using *massage*. Examples of essential oils used in aromatherapy are:

- rosemary – a decongestant oil
- rose – a calming oil
- peppermint – an oil to relieve nausea
- lavender – an oil to relieve insomnia.

arrhythmia: a deviation from the normal rhythm of the *heart*. The normal rhythm is called sinus rhythm. Arrhythmia can include extra or ectopic beats and rapid heart rate (tachycardia). However, it is important to remember that there is a normal variation to the heart beat which speeds up slightly on breathing in (inspiration) and slows down on breathing out (expiration).

art therapy: the use of art as a means whereby individuals learn to express themselves through drawing, painting and modelling. It helps people to release their tensions and stress and promotes positive *self-esteem*.

arteries: blood vessels which carry *blood* away from the *heart*. Arteries have a lining composed of *epithelial cells* (endothelial layer). The walls of the arteries are very thick and contain a large amount of elastic *tissue* and *muscle*. When the ventricles of the heart contract, blood at high pressure is forced into the arteries. This causes the walls to stretch. When *ventricular* contraction stops, the pressure of the blood falls and the elastic tissue contracts. This stretching and contraction of the elastic tissue in the artery walls helps to even out blood flow throughout the body. (See *cardiac cycle*.)

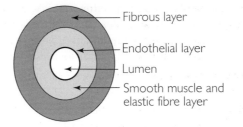

Fibrous layer
Endothelial layer
Lumen
Smooth muscle and elastic fibre layer

arteriole: a vessel which takes *blood* from the smaller *arteries* to the *capillaries*. Arterioles are very small in diameter and, like all blood vessels, have a lining of epithelial cells. Their walls contain large numbers of *muscle* fibres. Many arterioles also have rings of muscle called sphincter muscles where they join with the capillaries. By contraction of the muscle fibres in the walls and the sphincter muscles, the blood supply to particular capillary networks can be regulated to meet the needs of each part of the body.

arthritis is a *disease* which attacks the *joints* of the body causing damage and discomfort. It is closely associated with rheumatism which is a general term used to cover aches and pains in the body. There are two main types of arthritis:

- **Rheumatoid arthritis** is a condition characterised by inflammation of the joints especially of the hands and feet. It can also affect the knees, elbows, hips and other joints in the body. The patient or client complains of pain and lack of movement in the joints. As the disease progresses the joints become more enlarged and disfigured due to the formation of granulation tissue which limits movement and attacks the *cartilage* at the end of the bones. This causes deterioration of the muscles.

- **Osteoarthritis** is a degenerative disease affecting the cartilage in the joints causing deterioration. As the cartilage is destroyed new bone grows in its place leading to increasing pain and stiffness. The hips, knees, and spine are mostly affected causing lack of mobility.

(For further information contact the Arthritis and Rheumatism Council for Research, PO Box 177, Chesterfield, S41 7TQ.)

arthrography: a procedure using *X-rays* to examine the *joints*. This involves injecting a radio-opaque dye into the joint space. It shows up the outline and contents of the joint and any *disease* or *dysfunction* which may be affecting this part of the body.

artificial insemination: a method used to introduce male semen (containing sperm) into the *vagina* of a woman so that she can conceive. The method is applied when the male has difficulty in maintaining an erection of his penis (impotence), or when he has a low sperm count or is sterile. The use of semen provided by the husband or partner is called artificial insemination. When a donor is anonymous the process is called donor insemination.

artificial respiration: an emergency procedure which maintains a flow of *oxygen* into and out of a person's lungs when the normal and natural breathing reflexes are insufficient. The best known method of artificial respiration is mouth to mouth ventilation or resuscitation. (See *ABC of resuscitation*.)

artificial resuscitation: procedures which are used to revive a person from an unconscious state or possible death. In *hospitals*, artificial *resuscitation* may take the form of cardiac massage, manually giving *heart* resuscitation and or the use of electric shock treatment or defibrillation to restore the heart beat. The heart muscle must be revived within three to five minutes or permanent brain damage can occur. (See *ABC of resuscitation*.)

asbestos: a *mineral* substance which does not burn and is slow to conduct heat. Because of its heat resistance it is used in fabrics, boards, brake pads, and the clutch linings of heavy duty vehicles. In recent years the use of asbestos has been reduced because the inhalation of asbestos fibres may cause damage to the *lungs*. Such inhalation causes a lung disease called asbestosis. It can also cause *lung cancer* and mesothelioma which is *cancer* of the pleura (lining of the lung).

Asperger syndrome: a disorder which shares many of the same characteristics as *autism*. Certain traits such as clumsiness are typical in those suffering with Asperger syndrome. The key characteristics are:

- Difficulty with social relationships – unlike those affected by autism, some who suffer with Asperger syndrome try hard to be sociable; however, they find it difficult to understand non-verbal signals, including facial expressions.
- Clumsiness – difficulty with co-ordination skills.

- Difficulty with *communication* – those with Asperger syndrome may speak very fluently but may not take much notice of the listener's reaction; they may talk on regardless of the listener's interest and may appear insensitive to their feelings.

Despite having competent *language* skills, sufferers may sound over-precise and take words too literally. They can learn facts and figures but find it difficult to think in abstract ways. They may develop obsessive interests in hobbies or collections. Sufferers may feel secure with their *routines* and prefer to order their day in a set pattern.

asphyxia or suffocation: a life threatening condition in which *oxygen* is prevented from reaching *tissues* in the body due to obstruction or damage to parts of the *respiratory system.*

assessment: a method used to determine the different needs of a *client, patient* or *service user.* It is an important part of setting up a *care plan.* The various ways of defining assessment are highlighted in the *Working together under the Children Act 1989.* These can be applied in different client groups and care settings as follows:

- Initial assessment – an agreed *multi-disciplinary* composite report on the health and welfare of the client, e.g. in the case of a child, a case conference is set up to discuss and plan the child's immediate future.
- Medical assessment – a specific examination by a *doctor* for a definite purpose e.g. a court request or as part of a *child's health surveillance programme.* Medical assessment of a client may include recommendations for a client's ongoing care.
- Development assessment – an objective assessment of a client, often to some agreed *protocol,* carried out by a doctor, *health visitor* or *psychologist,* for the purpose of determining the client's developmental progress, or a client's daily living skills.
- Special educational needs assessment – a compilation of records from various professionals to assist the local education authority to place a child in an educational setting compatible with his or her abilities. This assessment may, for example, enable a child with special needs to attend mainstream school. The assessment is carried out under the Education Reform Act 1981 which followed the *Warnock Report.*
- Health assessment – an examination undertaken by a health visitor or school nurse to ascertain a child's health status. The health assessment will include information on height and weight, *immunisation,* vision and hearing.
- Comprehensive assessment – a structured time-limited exercise to collect and evaluate *information* about *clients* and their *families* on which to base long-term decisions, for example assessment of an *elderly person* with regard to their long-term care.
- Family assessment – a report prepared over a period of time to assess the functioning of a particular family in relation to the needs of a child. The assessment is usually undertaken by a social worker but may be undertaken by a psychologist or family centre worker. (HMSO 1989)[67] (See *risk assessment.*)

assist describes the role of carers when they support clients or someone else in a particular activity.

association area: a part or area of the cerebral cortex in the *brain*, it is responsible for receiving sensory impulses and for starting the motor impulses. The *neurones* which link these impulses are called association fibres.

Association for Residential Care: an organisation which exists to promote the *quality of life*, maintenance of standards and diversity of residential and day care provision for people with *learning disabilities*. It is a *pressure group* which provides support including:

- a national voice for all members
- a code of good practice to promote professional standards
- access to expertise and support on a local and national level.

(For further information contact the Association for Residential Care, ARC House, Marsden Street, Chesterfield, S40 1JY.)

Association of Community Health Councils for England and Wales: an organisation which was set up in 1977 under provisions in the *National Health Service* (Reorganisation) Act 1977. Its role is to provide a forum for member *community health councils*, to provide information and advisory services to community health councils and to represent the users of health services at a national level. The statutory duties of the Association of Community Health Councils are to:

- advise community health councils with regard to their functions
- assist community health councils in the performance of their duties
- represent those interests in the health service for which community health councils are responsible.

Association of Workers for Children with Emotional and Behavioural Difficulties: a voluntary group which was set up to support children with *behaviour* difficulties and their families. The aims of the group are to:

- voice their concern on behalf of children and young people with emotional and behavioural difficulties and those who work with them
- offer *support* to the parents and workers involved with children suffering from attention deficit hyperactiviy disorder
- promote publicly the belief that the needs of children and *adolescents* with emotional and behavioural difficulties should be identified and supported.

(See also *attention deficit hyperactivity disorder*.)

For further information contact ASWEBD, Charlton Court, East Sutton, Maidstone, Kent. ME17 3DQ.

assumption: a pre-judgement about a person or situation. It relates to *attitude* formation. In health and social care, it should be part of *anti-discriminatory practice* not to make pre-judgements or assumptions about *service users, clients, patients* and colleagues. (See also *stereotyping*.)

asthma: an obstructive disease of the bronchial airways which is caused by a trigger response in the airways leading to constriction of the *muscles, inflammation* and oedema (collection of fluid) in the bronchioles and an increased production of mucus. The asthmatic person begins to cough, starts wheezing and complains of a tight chest and breathlessness. There are a number of triggers or irritants which can cause asthma:

- allergies, e.g. dust, animals, *food*
- *environment*, e.g. changing weather condition/smoky atmosphere
- *infections*, e.g. colds, sore throats
- *stress*, e.g. *anxiety* about exams
- *hormones*, e.g. during the pre-menstrual period
- air *temperature, e.g.* weather, either cold or hot and dry
- *medicines*, e.g. aspirin.

Asthma is closely related to *eczema* and hayfever. It often runs in families. Recent research is being carried out to investigate the links, if any, between pollution and asthma.

(For further information contact the National Asthma Campaign, Providence House, Providence Place, London N1 ONT.)

astigmatism is a defect in the function of the *eye*. An abnormal curvature of the cornea and lens causes astigmatism. As a result the visual image is distorted because not all the light rays can focus on the retina. Astigmatism can be corrected by using cylindrical lenses in spectacles. These lenses effectively refract the light in one plane only.

ataxia: abnormal or unsteady movements in the limbs of the body. This is the result of damage or injury to the cerebellum, the part of the brain responsible for balance. There are different causes of ataxia such as alcoholism, brain tumours, *multiple sclerosis* and *thyroid* disease. (See also *Friedreich's ataxia.*)

atheroma is the formation of fatty deposits or plaques on the inner lining of the *arteries*. This causes *degeneration* and thickening of the artery. When the atheroma is extensive the inner lining of the artery may become rough and the blood flow in the artery turbulent. A clot or thrombosis may form and the whole vessel then becomes blocked so that blood flow is cut off. Atheroma occurring in the heart or brain is likely to result in death. Factors which contribute to atheroma and atherosclerosis include smoking, high *blood pressure* and high *cholesterol* levels.

atomic bonding: the bonding between atoms. There are two different types of chemical bonding, they are:

- ionic bonding – occurs when atoms exchange electrons with each other to form ions
- covalent bonding – occurs when a pair of electrons is shared between two atoms.

atomic structure is the structure of atoms. An atom is made up of a nucleus which contains positively charged particles (called protons) and neutrons, which are particles with no charge. Orbiting the nucleus are negatively charged particles called electrons. In an atom the number of protons equals the number of electrons which is equal to the atomic number.

An atomic structure can be described by its atomic number and mass number.

- Atomic number – the number of protons in the nucleus of an atom. Each element is defined by its atomic number. For example any atom with six protons is carbon regardless of the number of neutrons and electrons it has.
- Mass number – the total number of protons and neutrons in one atom of an element. The mass number of an element can vary because the number

of neutrons can change. The mass number is usually about twice the atomic number.

Isotopes are different forms of an element, with the same number of protons, but different numbers of neutrons. So isotopes of an element have the same atomic number but different mass numbers. Isotopes are distinguished by writing the mass number by the name or symbol of the element, thus: sodium–24 or ^{24}Na. (Stockley, Oxlade and Wertheim 1988)[58]

atrio-ventricular bundle (bundle of His): a collection of modified cardiac *muscle* fibres called Purkinje tissue situated in the septum of the heart between the right and left ventricle. It maintains the rhythm of the heart and the contraction of the heart or cardiac muscle.

atrio-ventricular node: a small area of specialised muscle in the wall of the *heart* between the atria and the *ventricles*. The atrio-ventricular node co-ordinates the heart beat. At the start of each beat, a wave of electrical activity spreads from the sino-atrial node or pacemaker over the walls of the atria. This brings about contraction of the atria. The muscle fibres in the atria are completely separate from those in the ventricle, except in one small area, the atrio-ventricular node. Through this node electrical activity can pass from the atria to the ventricles. There is then a short delay before the electrical activity spreads to the base of the ventricles. This delay allows emptying of the atria to be completed before the ventricles start to contract.

atrio-ventricular valve: this is situated between the atrium and the ventricle. There is one valve on either side of the *heart*. These valves are made of fibrous tissue and are opened and closed by *blood pressure*. During the *cardiac cycle*, when the pressure in the atrium is higher than that in the ventricle, the valve is open and blood is able to flow through into the ventricle. During ventricular systole, the muscle in the wall of the ventricle starts to contract and the pressure of the blood in the ventricle rises. As a result, the valve shuts so that blood is pumped out leaving the heart through the arteries, preventing any backflow of blood into the atria. Heart sounds can be heard when a stethoscope is placed against the chest wall. The first of these in each cycle is due to the atrioventricular valves closing. The valve on the left side of the heart has two flaps of fibrous tissue and is known as the bicuspid valve; that on the right side has three flaps and is called the tricuspid valve.

atrium: one of the two upper chambers of the *heart*. The right and left atria are relatively thin walled and receive blood from the veins. The right atrium receives deoxygenated blood from the body, while the left atrium receives oxygenated blood from the lungs. The deoxygenated blood from the body enters the right atrium from the venae cavae; oxygenated blood from the lungs enters the left atrium via the pulmonary veins.

attachment: the early relationship which develops between an *infant* and his or her mother or primary care giver. Another term for attachment is *bonding*. (See *Bowlby*.)

attachment within the NHS is the operational arrangement between nurses and health visitors, working in association with specific *GPs* caring for registered patients. (See *primary health care*.)

attention deficit hyperactivity disorder: a behavioural disorder in children. The child's behaviour may be characterised in different ways such as:

- hyper- or over-activity leading to disruptive *behaviour*, such as fidgeting and restlessness
- an inability to concentrate
- easy distraction in *play* and learning tasks
- forgetful and disorganised behaviour
- short memory span
- low self-esteem leading to negative behaviour patterns.

Children with this disorder and their parents may need multidisciplinary support. Agencies may work together to produce a co-ordinated procedure so that the individual needs of the child are considered and met. (See *Association of Workers for Children with Emotional and Behavioural Difficulties.*)

attitudes: the way in which an individual organises their thoughts, *beliefs*, feelings and reactions towards themselves and others in society. Attitudes are developed through the process of *socialisation*. Fixed and inflexible attitudes can lead to categorising people and events so that individuality is not recognised. (See *stereotyping.*)

audiogram: a method of measuring an individual's hearing. Hearing is measured at different sound frequencies and results are recorded on a graph. This shows up any defects such as 'glue ear' in children. The machine used for hearing tests is called an audiometer.

Audit Commission: a public spending watchdog, i.e. a central government agency which audits the activities of local authorities and the *National Health Service.* The Audit Commission is based on the policies of *economy, efficiency and effectiveness.* Each organisation is required to conduct an annual audit and examination of their accounts. This annual audit is open to scrutiny. Such precautions are extremely important where public sector organisations are using public money. The reports by the Audit commission relate to many issues in health and social care. Examples include:

- 'Coming of Age: the improving of care services for older people', a 1997 report which made recommendations relating to the care of the elderly.
- 'Children First: A study of Hospital Services' 1993, a report which explored the issues relating to hospital care for children.

(Audit Commission Reports are available through Her Majesty's Stationery Office Bookshop, 49 High Holborn, London WC1V 6HB.)

auditory nerve: the nerve leading from the inner *ear* to the brain.

auriscope: an instrument which is used by *doctors* or *nurses* to examine the eardrum and the *ear* canal. An auriscope enables any inflammation or infection of the eardrum to be detected and treated.

autism: a disorder which disrupts the development of social and *communication* skills. There is no known cause for autism. Up to 75 per cent of those with autism have accompanying learning difficulties, but whatever their general level of ability, they share a common problem in trying to make sense of the world. The degree to which autism sufferers are affected varies but there are common characteristics:

- Difficulty with social relationships – autistic children and adults often seem indifferent to other people, even their parents. The ability to develop friendships is impaired, as is the capacity to understand other people's feelings.
- Difficulty with communication – autistic individuals lack the ability and understanding necessary to engage in meaningful *communication*. *Language* is slow to develop and speech patterns are affected.
- Those with autism find it hard to recognise or interpret messages and signals that others take for granted.
- Difficulty in the development of *play* and imagination – children with autism do not develop creative 'let's pretend' play in the way that other children do.
- Difficulty with change – individuals with autism often become obsessed with particular objects or behaviour, focusing on them to the exclusion of everything else. In marked contrast to these are the 'islets of ability', which some autistic individuals display; for example, some autism sufferers who may be severely disabled in most ways will display a special talent for music, art, mathematics or mechanics.

Early intervention and specialist education are vital if children with autism are to develop to their full potential. The National Autistic Society was established by parents in 1962 to encourage a better understanding of autism and to pioneer a range of appropriate services for those with autism and for those who care for them. (See also *Asperger syndrome*).

For further information contact the National Autistic Society, 276 Willesden Lane, London NW2 5RB.)

Displays indifference   Joins in only if adult insists and assists   One-sided interaction

Indicates need by using an adult's hand   Does not play with other children   Talks incessantly about only one topic

Inappropriate laughing or giggling   Echolalic – copies words like parrot   Bizarre behaviour   Handles or spins objects

No eye contact   Variety is not the spice of life   Lack of creative, pretend play   But some can do some things very well, very quickly but *not* tasks involving social understanding

The aspects of autism

autoimmune diseases are caused by the body when it produces antibodies which destroy normal body cells. An example of an autoimmune disease is *rheumatoid arthritis*. Autoimmune diseases are more common in older people.

autonomic nervous system: the part of the nervous system which controls *muscles* and *glands* but is not under conscious control. It co-ordinates mainly involuntary body activities such as *digestion, blood pressure*, heartbeat and *peristalsis*. (See *autonomic response*.)

autonomic response: a response evoked by the *autonomic nervous system*. The effects produced by the sympathetic nervous system oppose those produced by the parasympathetic nervous system.

The **parasympathetic** nervous system:

- slows the *heart*
- dilates *arterioles*
- constricts bronchioles
- constricts the iris
- stimulates the tear glands
- speeds up gut movement
- relaxes the *bladder* and anal sphincters
- inhibits sweat secretion.

The **sympathetic** nervous system:

- accelerates the heart
- constricts the arterioles
- dilates bronchioles
- dilates the iris
- slows gut movements
- contracts bladder and anal sphincters
- causes contraction of the bladder
- increases sweat secretion.

autonomy: personal freedom. Individual *clients* should have their different *rights* and *choices* respected. This is a major factor in *caring*. *Carers* should encourage clients to be independent and to be involved in all decisions related to their care.

autopsy: examination and dissection of the human body after *death* has occurred in order to ascertain the cause of death. It is also a way of determining whether there was any *disease* or *dysfunction* of the different processes which occurred in the body.

AVPU code: a method used by first aiders to check the response of a casualty. There are different degrees of impaired awareness. The casualty can be assessed quickly by using the AVPU code:

- A – Alert
- V – responds to voice
- P – responds to pain
- U – Unresponsive.

Other checkpoints should be considered:

- Eyes – do they remain closed?

- Speech – does the casualty respond to the questions the first aider asks?
- Movement – does the casualty obey commands? Does he respond to a painful stimulus such as pinching? (St. John Ambulance 1997)

axilla: the area under the arm or armpit. During *adolescence* hairs grow in the axilla in response to hormonal changes. The axillary hair absorbs sweat which accumulates under the arm. When caring for *clients* needing complete physical care, it is important to wash and dry the axilla so that the client does not get sore. A method of measuring the body *temperature* involves putting a *clinical thermometer* in the axilla. This is a *safety* precaution, because young children may be tempted to bite a thermometer if it is put into their *mouths*.

axon: one of the components of a *nerve cell*. The axon conducts impulses away from the nerve cell body. It is enclosed within a fatty, myelin sheath which protects the nerve fibre and speeds up the transmission of impulses.

baby: see *infant.*

bacillus: a rod-shaped bacterial cell. Examples of bacilli include *Lactobacillus bulgaricus* which is found in yoghurt and *Salmonella* , many species of which cause *food poisoning.*

bacteria: an important group of micro-organisms. Bacteria are small and do not have nuclei or other organelles. Some bacteria can be harmful and cause diseases such as cholera. There are different types of bacteria and they can be classified according to their different shapes. These are:

- **bacilli** or rod-shaped bacteria, e.g. *Salmonella typhi* which cause typhoid fever
- **cocci** or circular shaped bacteria, e.g. *Staphylococcus aureus* which causes boils
- **spirilla** or spiral shaped bacteria, e.g. *Treponema pallidum* which causes syphilis
- **vibrio** or curved shaped bacteria, e.g. *Vibrio cholerae* which cause cholera.

Bacilli – rod-shaped   Cocci – spherical   Spirilla – corkscrew-shaped   Vibrio – curved

Types of bacteria

Another approach to classification which helps to identify bacteria is a technique called *Gram's staining.*

balance and the ear: see *ear.*

balanced diet: a diet which contains all the essential *nutrients* in the appropriate quantities for the body to grow and function efficiently. There are seven components to a healthy diet.

Food component	Function	Examples of sources
Carbohydrate	Provides energy	Bread, sugar
Fat	Provides energy and insulation	Dairy products milk, meat
Fibre	Healthy functioning of the digestive system	Vegetables potatoes, cereals
Minerals	Maintain body metabolism	Vegetables milk
Protein	Used for body growth and repair	Chicken, cheese, nuts, eggs

cont.

| Vitamins | Maintain body metabolism | Green vegetables, fruit |
| Water | Supports chemical reactions in the body | Water supply |

(See also *feeding, weaning.*)

banning or time out: a procedure which is a form of *behaviour management* involving the exclusion of a child or young person from a play or care setting for reasons of unacceptable *behaviour*. A child should always be warned of banning in advance and the banning should always be for a fixed period of time.

bar chart: a chart or graph which shows a comparison between variables. It is a method used to present *information* and is widely used in health and social care research. An example of a bar *chart* used in such a research project would be one showing the number of children who attend nursey school over a period of three years. (See *histogram.*)

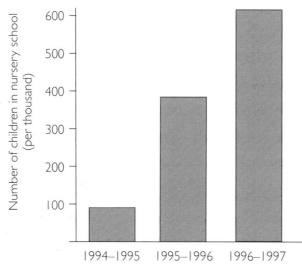

A sample of a bar chart

barbiturates: a group of *drugs* which depress the activity of the *central nervous system*, e.g. phenobarbitone. Barbiturates are used in the treatment of insomnia (the inability to sleep). They are drugs which produce adverse side effects on the body such as slurring of speech, loss of balance and sleepiness. Their effects are exaggerated when taken with *alcohol.* They are known as class B prescription only drugs, and are included under the Misuse of Drugs Act 1971 because they can cause physical and psychological dependence. Unauthorised production, possession or supply of the drug is an offence. (See *drugs legislation.*)

Barclay report 1982 (entitled 'Social workers: their roles and tasks'): a government sponsored report published in 1982 which reviewed and examined the role of social work. The main points raised in the report included:

- *care planning*
- *continuum of care* options – *clients* needing *care* being given choices of community-based or residential care
- *decision making*
- development of community-based social work to reinforce and strengthen the client's own networks. (HMSO 1982)[8]

Barnardos is a charity set up in 1866 by Dr Thomas Barnardo in response to the growing needs of young children mistreated, abused or exploited in the workplace. For many years Barnardos was associated with children's homes and orphanages, but over the last 25 years the long stay homes have closed down. Most of the children in Barnardos were not orphans, but were placed with Barnardos either because their families were too poor to care for them, or because social attitudes at the time did not approve of mixed race, disabled and illegitimate children. Modern day Barnardos is an organisation which tackles issues such as:

- *unemployment* and *poverty* – offering support with welfare and advice, community shops and credit unions, providing holidays for poor families
- *disability* – offering support in the form of *advice* and *counselling, advocacy,* short term breaks, residential care, befriending clubs and supporting families with disabled children
- *fostering* and *adoption* – Barnardos is one of the UK's leading fostering and adoption agencies
- families – providing parent support, *child protection, counselling* and advice, *parent and toddler groups, toy* and book *libraries* and after-school and holiday activities
- *homelessness* – providing emergency accommodation, *support* and advice, *drop in centres* which offer a service to refugees and travelling families
- advising and helping young people to develop the skills to be independent
- HIV/*AIDS* – supporting families and young people affected with HIV and AIDS through counselling, education and advice
- *sexual abuse* – offering support and counselling for abused parents, children and young abusers, helping them cope with their difficulties
- lobbying – working towards influencing public policy to highlight disadvantage and inequality.

(For further information contact Barnardos, Tanners Lane, Barkingside, Ilford, Essex 1G6 1QG.)

barrier contraceptives: used as a form of birth control. They provide a barrier between the head of the male penis and the inside of the female *vagina*. Use of this method should prevent the sperm which has been ejaculated into the vagina from travelling into the *womb*.

barriers of access to health and social care services: difficulties which are experienced by *clients* and *service users* in terms of access to the health and social care services which they need. These can be due to a number of factors:

- physical access, e.g. stairs with no lift, narrow doorways limiting access for wheel chairs
- financial access, e.g. services are expensive and the client is unable to pay

- location, e.g. the service is in a geographical area which clients without transport will have difficulty in reaching
- psychological factors, e.g. clients may lack confidence and may be anxious about visiting a service
- *culture*, e.g. a client may be self-conscious because they cannot speak English very well and there is no provision in the service to accommodate this
- non-provision of services, e.g. the client may live in a rural area, where the services may be limited
- lack of knowledge/*information* – client may be unaware of the existence of the service.

(See also *access to services.*)

barriers to communication: difficulties which can occur when a careworker is working with *clients*. Barriers are put up when misunderstandings occur and individuals feel that their *rights* and abilities are not respected. Factors may include *attitudes* with regard to *culture, learning disabilities* and *physical disabilities*. There are common problems which arise within care practice, such as:

- Lack of awareness of the needs of the client – this includes not listening to the client, not giving the client time to express themselves, no eye contact with the client, no rapport or other evidence of the carer trying to make conversation with the client.
- Lack of sensitivity during the practical care of the client – this could include carers rushing the client during *bathing*, not cutting their fingernails, not washing their hair, or not attending to their personal needs with gentleness. These tasks are reinforced by the carer working in silence.
- The carer may use their position to control the client. An example of this is when the carer makes all the decisions for the client, decides what they should wear, where they should sit, who they should see and talks to them without waiting for a reply.
- Negative verbal communication towards the client – this is where the carer shouts at the client, calls them names such as stupid, silly or dirty or any term which makes the client feel embarrassed. Such abuse may cause the client to become silent and withdrawn.
- Negative body language – this may involve the carer using non-verbal signals to communicate. This might include *gestures* such as rolling the eyes, not engaging in eye contact, shrugging the shoulders or wearing a worried and anxious expression.
- Lack of resources – which include the various communication systems for those who have hearing and visual impairments, those who are unable to speak, those with learning disabilities, and clients where English is a second language.

The relationship between client and carer is a very important one and is a focus for all the aspects of care given to clients. Barriers to communication which are apparent and affect the health and well-being of a client should be recognised and handled by the appropriate manager. (See also *caring relationship, team and care management, confidence building.*)

barristers are qualified lawyers who are allowed to conduct cases and appear in court. When a *solicitor* has a case they will 'brief ' a barrister to appear in the Crown Court or the High Court. A barrister cannot be approached directly by a client. The client must instead go through a solicitor. There are approximately 6000 barristers in England and Wales and they are allowed to appear in all courts. Barristers are paid a fee to appear on a case. When a client is being given legal aid, the barrister's fee is included. Barristers must have a law degree and, following this, must complete an appropriate vocational stage of training in order to develop relevant skills for court work.

basal metabolic rate (BMR) is the measurement of the energy given off by the body while it is at rest. It is an indication of the way in which oxygen is taken up by the body. Before the BMR is measured, the person concerned undergoes a standardised rest period of 12–18 hours of physical and mental relaxation. No meal is eaten during this time. This ensures that the *alimentary canal* is empty before measurements are taken. 'Basal' refers to the energy required to maintain the continuing activities of the body (i.e. *heart* beat, respiration, *kidney* function). The *oxygen* consumed by the individual is measured for at least ten minutes and this value is converted into oxygen consumption per hour. The BMR is measured either in calories per second or joules per second.

A number of factors affect BMR, such as:

- *Age* – the basal metabolic rate has a maximum value at about one year old. It then falls more or less continuously for the rest of a person's life.
- *Sex* – at all ages, females have a slightly lower basal metabolic rate than males
- State of *nutrition* – people who are undernourished tend to have a lower basal metabolic rate
- *Health* – a fever raises the BMR
- Environment – a cold environment raises the BMR
- Thyroid activity – a high metabolic rate can indicate an excess of *thyroid* hormone; a low metabolic rate can indicate too little thyroid hormone.

baseline: the frequency at which an individual carries out an activity or a particular form of *behaviour.* It is determined before giving a *client* a programme of help and *support.* In the treatment of a person who has a drinking problem, for example, it would first be necessary to record when the person drinks the most *alcohol* and the reasons for this. From these *records* a pattern is developed and a programme of support drawn up to help at difficult times.

baseline assessments: an approach used to assess young children. These assessments cover the basics of *language, literacy,* mathematics, personal and social development. They are based on teacher observations and specially designed activities. All schools are required by law to assess their pupils from September 1998. (See *excellence in schools.*)

baseline observations: the recording of certain measurements such as *temperature, pulse,* respiration rate and *blood pressure.* These measurements are taken by a GP, nurse or carer and recorded on a chart. They are the patient's own 'norms', against which any subsequent changes can be compared.

bases and alkalis: bases are the chemical opposite to *acids*. They are used to neutralise acids. Where bases are soluble in water they are called alkalis. Examples are zinc hydroxide and sodium hydroxide. Alkalis are ionised in solution.

bathing: a method used to meet the *hygiene* needs of a *client*. If a client is confined to bed then they will require daily washing or bathing. There are different ways in which this can be carried out:

- If the client has some *mobility* they may be able to sit or stand at the edge of the bed close to a wash bowl or wash basin. They may need assistance from the carer with washing their back and their feet.
- If the client is able to walk with support to the bathroom they can be assisted in and out of the bath using equipment such as hoists. (See *aids and adaptation.*)
- If the client is confined to bed for a short period but is able to move around the bed, they may be able to wash themselves with little or no assistance.
- If the client if too ill to wash themselves, they are given a bed bath or blanket bath. This enables the carer to wash the client's body while the client remains in bed.

It is important to remember that supporting a client with their personal hygiene can be embarrassing for the client. They may feel self-conscious about being washed in their genital and anal areas. It is essential for the carer to maintain the client's *dignity* by keeping parts of their bodies covered with a towel or blanket until they are ready to be washed. To maintain *privacy* the carer should make sure that no other person comes into the cubicle or bathroom during that time. It is a time when a carer can maintain conversation by giving a clear explanation of the tasks being carried out. It is also an opportunity to observe the client's body for any abnormalities such as rashes, swelling, redness, bruising and insect or flea bites.

behaviour: the way in which people are observed to act and conduct themselves. Behaviour often reflects *attitudes* towards certain issues. For example a person who is interested in politics may listen to the news on radio and television, read the newspaper, listen to parliamentary speeches, support a political party, attend party conferences and have friends who are equally interested in politics so that they can debate certain issues.

behaviour management: methods and strategies used by health and social care providers to control undesirable and *challenging behaviour*. Guidelines in *behaviour* are often designed to meet the needs of clients in different health and social care provisions. They may involve *discipline* codes for clients; for example, clients learn to cope with their own negative behaviour and begin to appreciate what is acceptable. (See *behaviour modification, banning.*)

behaviour modification is a method used to teach individuals to change their negative *behaviour* by using reinforcers to produce positive behaviour. It is a way of removing the unwanted behaviour and increasing that which is socially appropriate. For instance, a child who is constantly misbehaving and distracting others in class may be given a star for the first ten minutes that they are able to work on their own without causing a distraction. This is a method of positive reinforcement to encourage acceptable behaviour in the classroom. Behaviour modification is based on *learning theories*.

behaviour therapy: any technique of *behaviour* change that is based on the procedures of *classical conditioning*. Other methods of behaviour therapy include modelling, token economics and shaping.

beliefs: thoughts, feelings, *attitudes* and *values* which enable a person to identify with the world in which they live. Beliefs may or not have religious significance, but they are an expression of a person's *identity* and how they live their lives. In health and social care the personal beliefs of the *client* should always be respected even if they conflict with the beliefs of the carer. Ethical dilemmas may be experienced when religious beliefs prohibit necessary medical intervention e.g. a *blood transfusion*.

benefit enquiry line: a source of advice on benefits. This was set up by the *Benefits Agency* for disabled customers who wish to contact them by telephone. They give advice on benefit entitlement and offer help to those who are completing claim forms.

benefit trap: a situation that arises from the *welfare* state concentrating on directly supporting people rather than helping people to support themselves. (See *New ambitions for our country, a new contract for welfare*.)

benefits are the statutory amounts of money which are issued and distributed via the Benefits Agency to those members of society who need this form of support.

Benefits Agency: the agency within the Department of Social Security which is responsible for the assessment and payment of social security benefits.

benign: a condition or illness which is not malignant, for example, if a tumour or growth is benign then it is not cancerous.

bereavement is the loss of a loved one through death. Bereavement affects individuals in different ways and they suffer from *grief*. In the United Kingdom every year over 600,000 people die, leaving at least 1.5 million friends and family members who suffer a major bereavement. CRUSE Bereavement Care is an organisation which was set up in 1959 to offer personal and confidential help to bereaved people and to those who care for them through counselling, information and social support groups.

(For further information contact CRUSE Bereavement Care, Cruse House, 126 Sheen Road, Richmond, Surrey TW9 1UR.)

Beveridge Report 1942: a government report which led to the creation of the *welfare state*. The Beveridge Report identified five major problems which were affecting life in Britain. These were poverty, ignorance, disease, squalor and idleness. The report made recommendations which included the introduction of:

- a social insurance scheme to which employees paid a small sum out of their wages; they could then claim benefits through periods of unemployment, sickness and retirement (this is known as *National Insurance*)
- *benefits* paid at a flat rate regardless of any other forms of income and to be funded by a flat rate national insurance scheme
- maternity grants and benefits for widows
- a 'safety net' which was a means whereby those people not covered by an insurance scheme could have their needs met through unemployment benefit ('the dole')

- an information system to provide individuals with a knowledge of employment opportunities.

bias is the tendency to treat one group or individual in a different way to others. Bias can be either positive or negative. In positive bias, favourable treatment is shown to a group or individual. In negative bias, unfavourable behaviour is shown. Bias can reflect attitudes and prejudices towards a group or individual and in some cases leads to *discrimination*. Within health and social care, bias is actively discouraged as it does not meet the requirements of the *care value base* underpinning care practice.

biased sampling: the over-representation of one category of participants in a survey. For instance the proportion of males, females, students or people of a certain age in a sample may fail to adequately represent the population from which it is taken. There are many ways in which a researcher may unwittingly introduce *sampling* bias. These include:

- giving insufficient thought to the sampling technique being used (e.g. only choosing people who happen to be in the college canteen during a psychology or sociology or GNVQ unit 8 lesson)
- only using people who volunteer – people who volunteer to take part in a research project may not be typical
- only using students – the sample will not represent the population as a whole.

bibliography: a list of books or articles that have been used in researching a subject for assignments, essays, reports or projects. It is usually included at the end of a report, essay or project.

bile: a solution produced by the *liver* and stored in the *gall bladder*. It is a mixture of substances not all of which are involved in *digestion*. It aids the digestion of fats by bringing about their emulsification. Bile neutralises the *acid* from the stomach to help the pancreatic enzymes to work. It also contains two bile pigments, bilirubin and biliverdin, breakdown products of *haemoglobin*.

bile pigments: chemicals formed by the breakdown of *haemoglobin*. *Red blood cells* die after about 120 days in circulation. When this happens the haemoglobin which is contained in the cells is broken down and the waste products of this process are converted into bile pigment and excreted in *bile*.

bile salts: are components of *bile* which are involved in the *digestion* and absorption of fat. Although bile does not contain any digestive *enzymes*, it does contain bile salts which aid the breakdown of fats in *food*. Without the presence of bile, the digestion of fats would be less efficient and there would be an increased amount of undigested fat passed out of the body in the *faeces*. Most of the bile salts are reabsorbed in the small intestine and transported back to the *liver* for re-use.

bilingualism: the fluent use of two languages. (See *English as a second language*.)

biochemistry: the study of the chemical processes which occur in living things.

biodynamic massage: a complementary therapy which is a form of *massage*. It is a technique which mobilises the body by helping to release blocked energy flow and chronic muscular tension, so reducing stress.

biofeedback is a process which has been developed to control physiological responses such as *heart* rate, *blood pressure* and *muscle* tension. In certain situations, these responses can have negative effects on the body. For instance when a person is under *stress*, the heart beats faster, the blood pressure increases and there are generalised aches and pains. In biofeedback, the person looks at ways in which these responses can be controlled by using relaxation techniques, deep breathing exercises and massage. This technique has been used on individuals who suffer from anxiety attacks. Such attacks cause the heart to beat faster, the breathing to be more rapid and shallow, the *skin* to break out in a cold sweat and the mouth to become dry. When clients feel these symptoms approaching, they are encouraged to undertake deep breathing exercises to alleviate the *anxiety*.

biographical and health data: *information* which is collected at the initial *assessment* of a patient or client. This is the first part of the admission procedure when they enter hospital or community care. The details collected include:

- name, address, telephone number, family members, next of kin, date of birth, and religion
- health history – any diseases or inherited conditions, previous treatments which include operations, drug treatment or any other therapy/previous admissions
- allergies to certain foods, materials or drugs
- different terms for daily items or tasks. With children it is important to find out their likes, dislikes, their favourite toy, if they have a special name for anyone or anything which is important to them. For example, some children have a special name for going to the toilet
- disabilities – the patient's daily living skills, how they cope with everyday activities, what is the level of their dependence/independence (see *activities of daily living*).

biological determinism: a psychological theory by which it is believed that an individual's growth and development is determined by their inherited characteristics. The opposite view is social determinism where an individual's growth and development is said to be affected by social influences on their lives such as their social status and the social class to which they belong.

biology: the science of life which examines the structure, function and organisation of living things.

biopsy: the removal of a sample of tissue for examination, often by microscopy. It is done to observe any evidence of *disease* or degeneration so assisting diagnosis and treatment. (See *pathology*.)

birth: contraction of the muscles of the mother's *womb* in order to expel the *foetus*. When the baby is ready to be born and the birth is about to start the mother will have some of the following signs:

- 'a show'; a plug of blood-stained mucous discharged through her *vagina*
- her waters will break; the membranes which contain water and surround the baby rupture
- contractions of the muscles in the wall of the *uterus*; these become regular and strong and the intervals between contractions shorten (labour pains).

There are three stages involved in birth:

- Stage 1 – the cervix widens or dilates so that the baby's head can pass through. The length of time for this stage can be anything from two to twenty four hours. Most babies are born head first but in some cases the baby may come feet first in what is called a *breech presentation.*
- Stage 2 – the baby is pushed out by the mother. At this stage every time the uterus contracts the mother pushes very hard so that the baby can be born.
- Stage 3 – the placenta and membranes are pushed out. These are examined and checked. Pieces of placenta left in the womb can cause further blood loss.

Stage 1

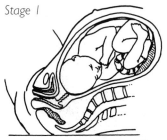

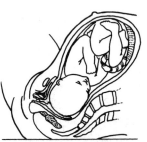

Baby turns in uterus and is in a position for birth

The baby's head pushes the cervix; a plug of mucous is released and 'waters break'

Stage 2

Stage 3

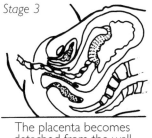

The uterus contracts and the baby is pushed out through the vagina

The placenta becomes detached from the wall of the uterus

Stages of labour

birth injuries or trauma are injuries to a baby during delivery and at the end of labour. These may result in damage to *bones, nerves* or *skin* and can cause infection or brain damage:

- Bones – during difficult births, breech deliveries and the birth of big babies, bones may *fracture.* Fracture to the legs and arms are recognised immediately as the baby may not be able to move the damaged limb. Fractures of the skull are usually associated with the use of forceps during a difficult delivery.
- Nerves – nerves to the neck may be stretched during delivery and the nerve known as the brachial nerve may be damaged. This will affect the nerve supply to the upper arm muscles and the arm will hang down at the baby's side and turn inwards. Nerves supplying the face may be damaged by a forceps delivery.

- Skin – minor scratches and abrasions may appear on a baby's face after a forceps delivery. When a baby has been born as a result of *a breech delivery* the baby's bottom and genital area may be bruised.
- *Infection* may be contracted during birth.
- Brain damage can be caused by a lack of *oxygen* in the baby's bloodstream.

birth statistics/birth rate: the number of children who are born each year. This is recorded as children born per 1000 people within the population.

Black Report 1980: a government report 'Inequalities in health' produced by Sir Douglas Black in 1980. The report was based on research carried out in the late 1970s. The report highlighted different aspects of material deprivation, *poverty* and *social class*. There were clearly-defined areas of *inequalities in health* and status between the different *social* and *economic groups*. In the Green Paper (a Government document for discussion) *'Our healthier nation' 1998*, the social case indicated that income, class and health are connected.

bladder: a muscular sac situated in the lower abdomen. The bladder acts as a container for *urine*. Urine is passed into it from the *kidneys* for temporary storage. Urine is held in the bladder by a small muscle called a sphincter muscle which closes the exit from the bladder. When the bladder is full the pressure on the nerves in the bladder causes a message to be sent to the *brain* and the person feels the need to pass urine. Understanding this process is an important part of working with clients. Children are trained to use their bladders through toilet training. In the elderly, the sphincter muscles of the bladder often lose their elasticity and the *elderly person* may dribble urine frequently. In both cases regular toileting is an essential part of the caring process.

blind and partially sighted: see *visual impairments*.

Bliss system: an electronic board which shows up different words and phrases. It is used specifically for people with a speech impairment. A person touches the words or phrases that they want to use to convey a message.

blood: a vital body fluid which consists of *plasma, platelets, red blood cells* and *white blood cells*. An adult has about 5.5 litres (9.5 pints) of blood circulating in their body. Blood is a type of *connective tissue*.

The functions of blood are:

- to carry different substances such as oxygen, carbon dioxide, dissolved food materials, hormones and urea around the body
- to produce *antibodies*, to engulf *bacteria* and to produce histamine
- to aid the *clotting process* using *platelets*.

blood cells: cells which are found in blood. There are two main types of cells:

- *Red blood cells* or erythrocytes. Their main function is to carry oxygen from the respiratory organs to the tissues.
- *White cells* or leucocytes. Their main function is to provide the body with a defence against disease.

blood clotting: the way in which blood forms a solid mass where there has been damage to the *tissues* and bleeding. When the body is wounded, soluble fibrinogen which is present in *blood plasma* is converted to insoluble fibrin. This forms a mesh over the surface of the wound where red blood cells are trapped and form a clot. Clots stop further blood from escaping and also help to prevent the entry of pathogenic bacteria. A complex mechanism controls the process of blood clotting. Fibrinogen can only be converted into fibrin in the presence of prothrombin which is converted into thrombin by the enzyme thrombokinase.

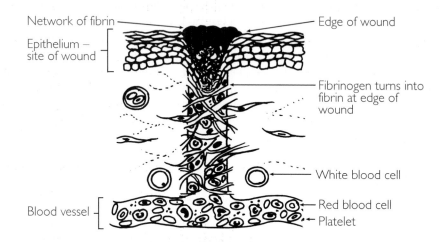

Network of fibrin — | — Edge of wound
Epithelium – site of wound
Fibrinogen turns into fibrin at edge of wound
White blood cell
Blood vessel — | — Red blood cell
Platelet

blood count: a term used to describe the number of each of the types of blood cells in a given volume of *blood* (e.g. per cubic millimetre of blood).

blood culture: a method of testing for micro-organisms in *blood*. A sample is taken from an individual and is tested for evidence of *bacteria*. The sample is also examined under a microscope. Blood cultures are taken if septicaemia (infection of the blood) is suspected.

blood groups: a system used to categorise blood types. *Red blood cells* have protein molecules on their cell surface membranes. Some of these proteins act as *antigens* and it is the presence or absence of specific types of these antigens which determines blood group. There are many different systems of grouping blood but the ABO system is probably the best known. There are four blood groups in this system; A, B, AB and O. These are determined by the presence of the *antigens* A and B. Individuals with blood group A have antigen A in their red blood cell membranes; those who are group B have antigen B; group AB individuals have both antigen A and antigen B while group O have neither A nor B. It is the presence of these and other antigens which determines whether or not one person's blood may be safely given to another during blood transfusion.

blood plasma: the liquid part of blood. A pale straw coloured liquid composed mainly of water containing a variety of dissolved substances; it is transported from one part of the body to another. Plasma carries *food* substances from the small intestine to the *liver, hormones* from the ductless glands to their target organs, urea from the liver to the *kidneys*, and *carbon dioxide* from the cells to the *lungs*. Plasma is the medium through which continual exchange takes place. Plasma also contains proteins including albumin, globulin, fibrinogen and the *antibodies*. Other important constituents of plasma are the ions of sodium, potassium, calcium, chloride, phosphate and hydrogencarbonate. Blood plasma from which the fibrinogen has been removed is called serum.

blood pressure: the pressure of *blood* against the walls of the main arteries. Blood pressure is highest during systole, when the ventricles are contracting (systolic pressure) and lowest during diastole when the ventricles are relaxing and refilling (diastolic pressure). Blood pressure is measured in millimetres of mercury using an instrument called a sphygmomanometer placed on the brachial artery of the arm. To measure blood pressure, an inflatable cuff is placed around a person's upper arm and the pressure in the cuff is increased until it is above the pressure in the artery. As the pressure is released, the blood begins to flow in the artery and can be felt at the pulse or heard with a stethoscope. The procedure is not painful but creates a sensation of pressure. It is important to explain the procedure to the client since distress or even mild anxiety can raise the blood pressure. Blood pressure should be taken with the person in a lying or sitting position in order to obtain an accurate reading. The expected systolic pressure should be approximately 120 mm and the diastolic pressure 80 mm. High blood pressure is called hypertension and low blood pressure is called hypotension.

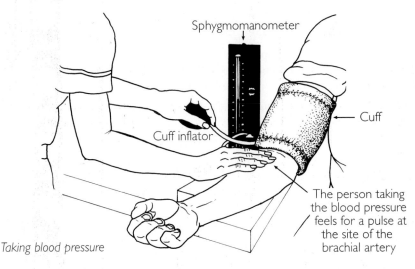

Sphygmomanometer

Cuff inflator

Cuff

The person taking the blood pressure feels for a pulse at the site of the brachial artery

Taking blood pressure

blood sugar level is the amount of *sugar* or glucose which is contained in the blood. The blood *glucose* level is controlled by the secretion of insulin from the *pancreas*. The normal blood glucose level is 4–6 mmol per dm^3 of blood.

blood system: the human body's transport system. Its functions include:

- the transport of nutrients, blood gases, hormones and waste products from one part of the body to another
- the distribution of heat from respiring tissues (e.g. the liver and muscles) to other parts of the body.

blood transfusion: the transfer of *blood* from one person to another. The ability to do this safely depends on the *blood groups* of the individuals concerned. *Red blood cells* have *protein* molecules in their cell surface membranes. Some of these proteins act as *antigens* and it is the presence of these which determines blood group. For example, the red blood cells belonging to group A individuals have antigen A on their surface while those belonging to people with group B blood have antigen B. In addition to this, these individuals also have antibodies present in their plasma. Someone with group A will have a specific antibody against antigen B. It is convenient to call this antibody b. Similarly, a person with group B blood will have antibody a.

Because of this, group A blood can be safely given to someone else with blood group A. Both have antigen a but neither has antibody b.

bloodflow: the way in which blood is pumped around the body via the *heart*. The flow of blood through the body is measured by recording the *pulse*. This indicates the frequency at which blood pulsates through the body. The flow of blood is maintained by the pumping action of the heart, by muscle contraction and by the breathing mechanism. (See *cardiac cycle*.)

body temperature: the amount of heat produced in the body is balanced by the amount of heat which is lost. This is the way in which a healthy body maintains a stable temperature of 37 degrees Celsius (98.4 degrees Fahrenheit). Body temperature is regulated by the heat regulating centre in the hypothalamus of the *brain*. Body temperature may be measured using a *clinical thermometer*.

boiling: the process which results in changing a liquid into a gas or vapour at a temperature called its boiling point. For water this is about 100 degrees Celsius at normal atmospheric pressures. Boiling appears as the formation of bubbles throughout the liquid. All pure samples of the same liquid at the same pressure have the same boiling point. An increase in pressure increases the boiling point.

bolus: the mass formed as a result of chewing food in the mouth through movement of the jaw and the muscles of the mouth. The tongue rolls the food into a ball or bolus which is then pushed to the back of the throat for swallowing.

bonding: the development of a close relationship between two individuals. This is the first relationship in the life of a *newborn baby* when an *attachment* is formed between the baby and its mother or primary care giver. The bonding process is reinforced by:

- eye contact with the baby
- holding the baby closely and securely
- skin contact – holding hands, *breast* feeding
- talking – cooing at the baby and making sounds.

In the early months of a baby's life these actions from their carer help to promote a sense of love, security and *well-being*. This gives the baby a positive view of itself and the world it lives in. As the baby grows into a child this sense of security will help the development of relationships with others. (See also *Bowlby*.)

bone: a *connective* tissue which is impregnated with large deposits of *calcium* salts, mainly calcium phosphate. The salts make the bone extremely hard. Bone is formed by the process of ossification which is the formation of bone tissue from cartilage or membrane. This involves the laying down of bone by bone cells or osteoblasts. The osteoblasts arrange themselves in rings around *nerves* and blood vessels. Eventually the osteoblasts surround themselves with bone and at this stage they are called osteocytes. This type of bone is called compact Haversian bone. Spongy bone is less compact and not as hard as compact bone. Compact bone is found in the shafts of the limb bones, while spongy bone is found at the ends of these bones. Covering the bone is a dense layer of connective tissue called the periosteum.

Bones have a variety of functions including:

- movement and stability – bones form a supporting body framework and provide attachments for muscles, ligaments and tendons which reinforce the support and movement of the body
- protection – bones form a framework which protects the organs of the body
- storage – bones store minerals such as calcium, phosphorous and magnesium
- *cell* production – *red blood cells* are manufactured in the *bone marrow.*

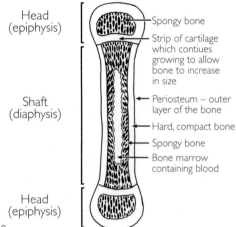

The structure of the long bone

bone marrow: a substance which fills the cavity in certain bones. There are two types of bone marrow. They are:

- red bone marrow – where all the *red blood cells* and some white cells are made
- yellow bone marrow – which stores fat.

Bowlby, John: famous for his views on the importance of *attachment* or *bonding*. He investigated the bond that forms between the primary care giver and the infant or young child. Deprivation of this bond may have consequences for the infant or young child, on both their short and long term development. Bowlby believed that an infant should experience a warm, intimate and continuous relationship with his or her mother. Drawing upon evidence gathered from a variety of sources, including studies of hospitalised children, institutionalised children and evacuees, as well as experimental work with motherless monkeys, Bowlby suggested that prolonged separation from the primary care giver (usually the mother) or the failure to form an attachment bond (privation) leads to adverse effects in later life. This may include the development of difficulties in forming intimate relationships with others. Bowlby claimed that children who were deprived of maternal love would always be disadvantaged in some way, either physically, socially or emotionally.

Braille: a type of writing and printing using raised dots to represent letters, which allows blind and *visually impaired* people to read and communicate by touch.

brain: the most highly developed part of the *nervous system*. It is contained in the cranial cavity of the skull and is surrounded by three membranes called meninges. The brain is made up of the:

- cerebrum – this is the most highly developed part of the brain consisting of two cerebral hemispheres. It is the site of functions such as vision, smell, hearing, touch, speech and memory.
- midbrain – which is an area which joins the diencephalon to the pons. It carries impulses in towards the *thalamus* and out from the cerebrum towards the spinal cord.
- medulla or medulla oblongata – the area of the brain which is responsible for many involuntary actions such as breathing. (See *hypothalamus.*)

Brain stem is a term used to describe the area comprising the midbrain, pons and medulla.

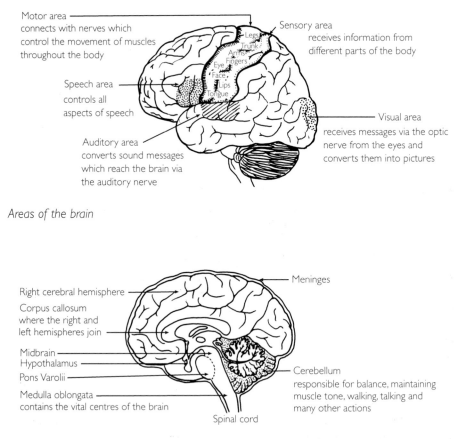

Areas of the brain

A section through the brain

breast self-examination: a method which women use to examine their *breasts* to check for abnormalities. It is recommended that in the first part of the examination of her breasts a woman should sit in front of a mirror and look carefully at each breast. She should note the normal size, shape and position of the nipple, checking that there has not been any change in size, texture of skin, swellings, discolouration, rash or very prominent veins. In addition to this she should check the nipple to see if it has become retracted or turned in. Self-examination and palpation of the breasts should never be rushed. The woman should give herself sufficient time for this process. Having completed the self-examination she should decide whether her breasts have undergone any changes or if any unusual swellings or other features have appeared. If she is worried she should contact her doctor or visit her family planning clinic who can offer help and advice. It may be that she should have a test or special *X-ray*, of her breasts (called a mammogram, see *mammography*). These procedures can be viewed as a method of breast screening. (See *screening programmes*.)

breasts: mammary glands which are situated in the upper part of the chest. They are important parts of a woman's anatomy because:

- they are stimulated by hormones to produce milk following the *birth* of a *baby*
- they are significant in terms of sexuality; they contain sensory areas which are sensitive to touching and stroking, they are erogenous and the nipple responds when the woman becomes sexually excited
- they are an essential part of early contact between the mother and baby; this includes breast feeding and skin to skin contact between mother and child.

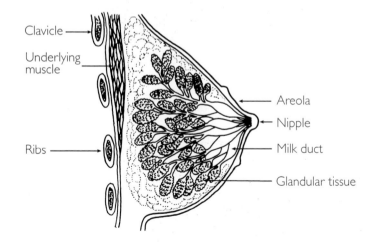

breathing mechanism: the way in which the body:

- takes in air by inspiration; this enables *oxygen* to be taken to all parts of the body via the *lungs* and the *heart*
- lets out air through expiration which enables *carbon dioxide* to be excreted from the body via the heart and the lungs. (See *respiratory system*.)

breech presentation: the position of the *baby* in the *uterus* before *birth* which suggests that the bottom or buttocks of the baby will be born first. The normal position is head first.

British Agencies for Adoption and Fostering: organisations which promote the interests of children who have been separated from their families. They provide *advice, information* and training for *social workers*, lawyers, *doctors*, adoptive parents, foster carers and those with an interest in *adoption* and *fostering*. These agencies also contact families with children who have special needs through newspaper and newsletter links. The agency publishes books, leaflets about fostering, adoption and related child care issues. (See *foster care*.)

(For further information contact British Agencies for Adoption and Fostering, Skyline House, 200 Union Street, London SE1 OLX.)

British crime survey: a *survey* which involves *interviewing* a *sample* of 10,000 adults about their experiences as victims of crime. These surveys are carried out by Home Office researchers. Surveys were carried out in 1982, 1984, 1988 and 1992.

(For further information contact Victim Support, Cranmer House, 39 Brixton Road, London SW9 6DZ.)

British Heart Foundation: a voluntary organisation which aims to highlight the issues relating to *heart* disease. *Heart surgeons, hospital doctors, nurses* and *GPs* rely on funding from the British Heart Foundation to support their research, education and training. The Foundation is a charity which receives no government funding.

(For further information contact the British Heart Foundation, 14 Fitzharinge Street, London W1H 4DH.)

British Red Cross is an international organisation which helps to meet the needs of vulnerable people in times of emergency, both in the UK and in countries across the world. The British Red Cross espouses a policy that they:

- are neutral in conflict – impartial to race and creed. Because of their neutrality they can work in a battle zone, bringing *food* and medical supplies.
- care for people in the local community – there are over 90,000 volunteer workers offering a range of services in the community, including *first aid* training.
- have staff that are trained and skilled to respond to emergencies.

The principles of the Red Cross stand for humanity, impartiality, neutrality, independence, voluntary service, unity and universality.

(For further information contact the British Red Cross, National Headquarters, 9 Grosvenor Crescent, London SW1X 7EJ.)

British Sign Language is one of the languages used by those with a hearing *impairment*. Language users make *gestures* involving movements of hands, arms, eyes, face, head and body, to conduct a *conversation*. The development of British *sign language* has been an amazing breakthrough and it is much used by those with severe hearing loss. (See *sign language*.)

(For further information contact the British Deaf Association, 1–3 Worships Street, Carlisle, Cumbria, CA1 1HU.)

bronchitis: inflammation of the *air passages*, that is the bronchii/bronchioles of the lungs. This causes coughing, shortness of breath and a general feeling of being unwell (malaise). Treatment involves rest and the taking of fluids. In some cases, when bacterial infection is evident, antibiotics are given.

bruise: a discolouration of the *skin* due to any impact or injury. A bruise is formed when the tiny *blood* vessels in the skin bleed and there is swelling and discolouration under the surface of the skin.

Bruner, J: a cognitive psychologist. He believed that *intellectual* development in a child depends very much on the way in which the mind uses the information that it receives. Bruner believed that children develop different ways of representing the environment around them. These ways of using information include:

- enactive – children represent the world through their sensor-motor actions for example, trying to describe a spiral staircase without using physical actions is a means of making an individual aware of the nature of this type of representation
- iconic – thinking based on the use of mental images
- semantic – the representation of the environment through language; this enables the child to access much of the knowledge available in their surroundings and to go beyond the information given.

Bruner believed that *language* is the vital component which opens up new horizons of *intellectual development* for the young child.

buddies: those individuals who become friends, partners or counsellors. They usually help a person through a particular health condition and treatment, psychological problem, period of study or any life stage where support is valuable. Examples include buddies who are recruited by the Terrence Higgins Trust to support victims with *AIDS*, study buddies, where two students will support each other through a course or programme of study, birth buddies when a friend will support a woman through the ante-natal phase and through the labour and *birth* of her *baby*.

budgets: see *funding*.

bulimia nervosa: a compulsive *eating disorder*, characterised by episodes of compulsive overeating, usually followed by self-induced *vomiting*. The disorder appears mainly to affect girls and women. In recent years, however, there has also been a rise in the number of men suffering from this disorder. There is no single cause for the condition but sufferers are said to have a fear of being fat. Bingeing and vomiting are often in secret. The individual has to be able to recognise that they have a problem before treatment can begin. Treatment involves supervised eating sessions and psychotherapy. The Eating Disorders Association offers help and support for families, friends and sufferers of *anorexia nervosa* and bulimia.

(For further information contact the Eating Disorders Association, Sackville Place, 44 Magdalen Street, Norwich, Norfolk NR3 1JU. Telephone: 01603 621 414.)

bullying is the way in which a person may intimidate, threaten or harass another person. Bullying is closely linked to *abuse* as it often involves name calling, aggression and in some cases acts of violence. In schools, a group of children may single out one child because they think he or she is different. For example a child may wear glasses and the group will constantly threaten this child. The child becomes frightened and often does not want to go to school. The victim will be threatened to keep silent and will often find this a major stress in their life. In some cases bullying has led to the victimised child committing *suicide*. *Schools* have developed anti-bullying policies where children are encouraged to talk about bullying and the perpetrators are disciplined within the framework of a *code of practice*.

Caesarean section or delivery: a surgical procedure which removes the unborn *baby* from the *womb* of its mother. Caesarean section may become necessary when:

- a problem affecting either the mother or the *foetus* has been identified during *pregnancy*
- there has been severe bleeding during labour and the life of foetus is at risk
- the baby has grown to a large size and it is difficult for the mother to deliver the baby through the vaginal canal
- induction of labour has failed and the life of the foetus is at risk
- the mother is weak and cannot sustain the labour
- the *foetus* has become distressed and instant delivery is essential
- the *placenta* is covering the cervix and is in danger of being delivered before the baby (placenta praevia).

caffeine: a stimulant found in coffee, tea, chocolate and cola drinks. A high daily dose of caffeine can induce agitation, tremors, insomnia and irregularities in heart rate and rhythm.

calling the emergency services: calling the *emergency services* by telephone requires the caller to state their name clearly and to mention the fact if they are acting in the capacity of a *first aider.* It is essential to give the following details:

- the telephone number
- the exact location of the incident, the road name or number if possible, and any junctions or other landmarks
- the type and gravity of the incident, for example, 'traffic accident, two cars, road blocked, three people are trapped'
- the number, sex and approximate ages of the casualties, and anything known about their condition, for example 'man, early fifties, suspected *heart attack,* cardiac arrest'
- details of any hazards such as gas, hazardous substances, power-line damage, or relevant weather, for example fog or ice.

(St. John Ambulance 1997)[57]

calliper: a metal frame which gives support to a weak limb (leg, ankle or *foot*). It provides an individual with the support needed for increased *mobility* or walking. Callipers can be full limb length or half limb length.

campaign: an organised course of action which is carried out by a group in order to increase awareness of a particular issue in society. For example, the *Child Poverty Action Group* draws attention to the issues of *poverty* and the needs of children.

cancer is a disease of which there are over 200 types. Each cancer starts in the same way. It is linked to changes in the normal make-up of a *cell,* leading to the uncontrolled growth of abnormal cells. There are differing views as to why this occurs. For instance, *stress,* excessive *smoking* or intake of *alcohol* are viewed as predisposing factors. There are different methods of treating cancer which include *chemotherapy, radiotherapy* or *surgery*. The Calman-Hine Cancer Report 1997 (a policy framework for commissioning cancer services) was set up in response to concerns about variations in treatment across the country. It recommended that cancer services should be organised at three levels:

- *primary care*
- cancer units in local hospitals with *multi-disciplinary* teams able to treat the more common cancers
- cancer centres situated in larger hospitals to treat the less common cancers and support cancer units by providing services such as radiotherapy, which are not available in smaller hospitals.

(See *The New NHS – Modern, Dependable 1997.*)

Cancer Relief Macmillan Fund: an organisation which provides *care* and support for *cancer* patients in *hospitals, hospices* and patients' homes. It was founded in 1911 by Douglas Macmillan. Macmillan *nurses* and *doctors* are skilled in the treatment and nursing care of cancer patients and are financed through the Macmillan Fund. The fund also provides financial support for patients and their families and for the development of *day care* and *information* centres.

(For further information contact Cancer Relief Macmillan Fund, Anchor House, 15/19 Britten Street, London SW3 3TZ.)

cannabis: an illegal *drug* derived from the plant *Cannabis sativa*. Cannabis may be used to relax the person and give them a sense of *well-being*. Cannabis is classified as a Class B drug and is controlled by the Misuse of Drugs Act 1971. It is illegal to grow, produce, possess or supply cannabis. It is also an offence to allow any building or place to be used for growing, preparing, supplying or smoking cannabis. Cannabis can produce psychological dependency, making the person dependent upon *smoking* it in order to cope with life. Cannabis smoked regularly can have harmful effects on the body. Some of the organs affected are:

- *brain* and *central nervous system* – cannabis causes short-term memory loss, poor concentration, anxiety and panic attacks
- *heart* – cannabis speeds up the heart beat and therefore increases blood pressure
- reproductive system – cannabis causes a decrease in the sperm count, causes egg damage and alters hormone levels; *newborn* babies of habitual cannabis users may have a lower birth weight
- *lungs* – cannabis causes damage to lungs; this is increased when cannabis is smoked together with tobacco
- *immune system* – cannabis affects the way in which the body protects itself against infection.

The use of cannabis for therapeutic purposes is on the increase. There is a growing debate with regard to the possible medicinal benefits of cannabis, e.g. in the treatment of multiple sclerosis or for individuals who suffer from disorders which cause acute pain. (See *drugs – legislation*.)

capillaries: small *blood* vessels which connect *arteries* and *veins* and form a network in the *tissues*. The walls of capillaries are one *cell* thick. Arteries and veins carry blood but the important exchange between the blood and the tissues takes place in the capillaries. High pressure in the arterial end of the capillaries forces water and small soluble molecules out through the walls forming the tissue fluid which surrounds the cells of the body. Much of this water flows back into the capillary at its venous end since the water potential of the tissue fluid is higher than that of the blood plasma at this point. There is, therefore, a continuous circulation of fluid out of the capillaries and back into them. This takes useful substances to the cells and returns waste products to the *blood* and then to the *kidneys* and the *respiratory system*. Blood flows into capillaries from arterioles. Arteriole walls contain muscle fibres which can contract to reduce the diameter of the vessel. In this way the blood supply to the capillary system in a particular organ is always being adjusted to meet its needs.

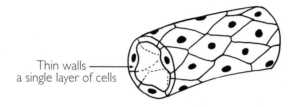

Thin walls — a single layer of cells

capital expenditure is spending on the acquisition of land, premises and equipment. This includes the provision, adaptation, renewal, replacement or demolition of buildings, items or groups of equipment and vehicles, where the expenditure exceeds £5000. (See *NHS: The New NHS – Modern, Dependable 1997.*)

carbohydrates are made up of carbon, hydrogen and oxygen. The simplest carbohydrates are monosaccharides. These can be built up into disaccharides and polysaccharides through the process of *condensation* involving the removal of water. The function of carbohydrates in the body is the production and storage of *energy*. They are a main energy source for the different chemical reactions in the body and an integral part of a healthy *diet*. (See *balanced diet, sugar.*)

carbon is a non-metallic *element* which occurs in all living matter. It combines with other elements as a result of chemical reactions. Examples of the compounds formed include:

- *carbon dioxide* – a waste product of metabolism in the body
- *carbon monoxide* – a poisonous gas which is released through *smoking* or pollution
- *carbohydrates* which are composed of carbon, hydrogen and *oxygen*.

carbon dioxide (CO_2): a colourless gas produced as a result of chemical processes in the body. It is a *waste product* which is carried in the *blood* from the different parts of the body via the *veins*, through the venae cavae to the right atrium of the *heart* and to the pulmonary arteries from the right ventricle, where it is pumped to the *lungs* and breathed out into the general atmosphere.

carbon monoxide (CO): a poisonous gas found in smoke. It is either drawn into the body or released into the atmosphere through tobacco *smoking* and exhaust fumes from motorised vehicles. Carbon monoxide once in the system combines with *haemoglobin* in the *blood* to form carboxyhaemoglobin. This reduces the blood's ability to carry oxygen to all parts of the body. *Oxygen* is vital to the different chemical reactions and functions in the body. A lack of oxygen and an increase in carbon monoxide can lead to:

- increased risk of blood clots or thrombosis
- the formation of *atheroma* – which leads to atherosclerosis, fatty deposits which occur in artery walls; this in turn can lead to the narrowing of the arteries

cardiac cycle: the events which take place to produce a *heart* beat. It is a continuous cycle which is controlled by the sino-atrial node (the pacemaker) situated in the wall of the right *atrium*.

The cardiac cycle:

- The walls of the atria contract and blood is forced into the ventricles. This is called the atrial systole.
- The walls of the ventricles contract and blood is forced out of the heart into the pulmonary artery and the aorta. This is called the ventricular systole.
- The walls of the atria relax and blood flows into the atria from the venae cavae and pulmonary veins.
- The walls of the ventricles relax and blood flows into the atria. This is called the ventricular diastole.

cardiac muscle tissue: *muscle* tissue which is found only in the *heart* walls. It consists of many branching fibres which contain nuclei and striations. The cardiac muscle contracts and relaxes causing the heart to beat and pump *blood* around the body. It works under involuntary control and produces its own electrical impulses. These nervous impulses increase or decrease the heartbeat.

cardiograph: an instrument used to record the force and form of the heartbeat. The results are recorded graphically. (See *electrocardiograph*.)

cardiology is the study of the structure and function of the *heart*. This includes any heart *disease*, degeneration or functional disorders. A cardiologist is a fully trained *doctor* who specialises in the diagnosis and treatment of heart disease.

cardiorespiratory system includes the *heart* and *lungs* and the blood vessels associated with them. The cardiorespiratory system can be monitored by a carer by measuring and recording *pulse*, *blood pressure*, and efficiency of breathing (i.e. respiration rate and *lung* volume) which relate to the supply of oxygen and the removal of *carbon dioxide*.

care: an umbrella term for the different types of *caring* which take place under the auspices of health and social care.

care assistants provide practical help, support and care. They give *direct care* to a range of client groups in different settings which may be residential, day care or in the client's own home. A *residential care* assistant helps residents with their daily *routine*, including getting up, *bathing*, dressing and any toileting which may be necessary. The care assistant also serves food and helps with feeding residents as necessary. *National Vocational Qualifications* are a means whereby care assistants can be trained in the workplace. (See *care awards*.)

care awards: nine qualifications make up the *National Vocational Qualifications* in health and social care. These qualifications have been revised and updated through the combined efforts of all health and social care employment interests across the United Kingdom and the full scale *collaboration* of the care sector awarding bodies. The new awards are accredited from 1998 to 2003. The *National Vocational Qualifications* and the Scottish National Vocational Qualifications (NVQs in Scotland Levels 2 and 3) cover those who are involved in the direct delivery of care. The different care awards involve working:

- under the supervision, direction or guidance of qualified professional staff such as *nurses, midwives, health visitors, chiropodists, occupational therapists, physiotherapists, speech* and language *therapists* and *social workers*
- under the supervision, direction or guidance of a designated line manager
- under the auspices of a workplace which may be in the *public, private* or *voluntary* sector across the full spectrum of *residential, hospital, day care, foster care* and *domiciliary* settings. (Care Sector Consortium 1998)[12]

(See also *Care Sector Consortium, Care – principles of good practice* and *National Occupational Standards.*)

care component: see *disability living allowance.*

care context and care environment: the setting, time and surroundings in which *caring* takes place. Health and social care workers are expected to be able to optimise or make as effective as possible the caring process which takes place within a care context. This includes:

- making a client comfortable by ensuring that they are warm, happy and secure and have sufficient personal space
- when working with a number of clients at the same time – prioritising the individual needs of each client and supporting non-discriminatory care practice
- communicating with colleagues – sharing experience and knowledge through discussion, reflection and feedback
- providing a safe environment – ensuring premises and equipment are made safe for clients, monitoring that there are adequate numbers of staff on duty to care for the clients
- providing stimulating activities to build up positive personal relationships.

(See also *safety, care value base, codes of practice, optimised interaction.*)

care management: co-ordination by a named care manager appointed to supervise the assessment and purchasing of appropriate care for clients. Under the *NHS and Community Care Act 1990*, the local authority's general duties concerning care management include:

- defining need – looking at the needs or requirements which a client may have to enable them to maintain their independence
- devising forms of assessment – reviewing the type of assessment necessary for the client, such as home assessment, assessment of *mobility*, daily living skills
- *care planning* – including the *service requirements*, the priorities for client care
- reviewing the existing service – looking at any other options and agreeing the care with the service user, their *informal carers* and the team involved

- securing appropriate resources – including the cost of the *care package*, reviewing budgets
- monitoring the care – ensuring the care being given is consistent with the care plan and that the *carer* is meeting the ongoing needs of the *client*
- controlling the delivery of the *care plan*
- reviewing the care plan in order to reassess the client's needs.

The government White Paper *The New NHS: Modern, Dependable* outlines proposals for integrated care with all care planners and providers working collaboratively. (HMSO 1997). (See *activities of daily living*.)

care order: an order made by the court under the Children Act 1989. It relates to placing a child in the care of a designated *local authority*.

care organisations are *statutory, voluntary, private, independent, self-help* and support agencies which provide care for different client groups in a number of different ways. These include:

- *day care* – setting up luncheon clubs for the elderly, *parent and toddler groups* for parents with young children and playgroups
- *health centres* – GP surgeries
- *residential care* – for those clients who will benefit from full-time caring
- information centres – offering information and advice in a number of areas
- voluntary groups
- *counselling* and *support* – offering opportunities for people to talk about the different issues affecting them
- *respite care* – offering carers a break from the heavy responsibility and the often exhausting burden that long-term caring for a family member can bring
- *hospitals*
- transport – Dial-a-Ride provides transport for the disabled and elderly to go shopping or to the theatre
- *support groups*
- *pressure groups* – to highlight the needs of clients and their carers, environmental issues with regard to the disabled etc.

These are just a few of the ways in which care organisations can support the caring process.

care plan: a procedure set up to outline a course of care, treatment, or therapy between professional carers and their *clients, service users* or *patients*. Setting up care plans is an important aspect of a professional carer's work. There are stages of development in the care plan:

- assessing the client's needs
- identifying their current provision
- deciding the type of care needed and how the services will be provided
- setting aims and goals for the client and writing these into the care plan
- implementing the care plan
- monitoring the care plan

- reviewing the care plan
- evaluating the care plan.

Care plans may be:

- developed by one professional, for example a *care manager, nurse* or *social worker.*
- jointly devised by a multi-professional or *multi-disciplinary* team, i.e. a team of people who may be responsible for developing a care plan for a client with *physical disabilities.*
- developed by the client themselves, working with the appropriate health and social care professionals. This is an important aspect of setting up a care plan as it enables the client to take control of their own care. The role of clients in their care planning is recognised in current legislation such as *Children Act 1989, NHS & Community Care Act 1990, The Carer (Recognition) Act 1995.*

care – principles of good practice: agreed principles which underpin the most recent *National Occupational Standards* for workers in health and social care. These are:

- balancing people's rights with their responsibilities to others and to wider society and challenging those who affect the rights of others
- promoting the values of equality and diversity, acknowledging the personal *beliefs* and preferences of others and promoting *anti-discriminatory* practice
- maintaining the *confidentiality* of *information* provided that this does not place others at *risk*
- recognising the effect of the wider social, political and economic context on health and social well-being and on people's development
- enabling people to develop to their full potential, to be as autonomous and self-managing as possible and to have a voice and be heard
- recognising and promoting health and social *well-being* as a positive concept
- balancing the needs of *clients* who use services with the resources available and exercising financial probity
- developing and maintaining effective relationships with people and maintaining the integrity of these relationships through setting appropriate role boundaries
- developing oneself and one's own practice to improve the quality of services offered
- working within *statutory* and organisational frameworks.

(Care Sector Consortium 1998)[12]

Care Sector Consortium: a national government committee. The committee co-ordinates the development and review of *National Occupational Standards* and National and Scottish Vocational Standards for the care sector workforce in England, Northern Ireland, Scotland and Wales. National Occupational Standards are designed to support continuous improvement in the delivery of Care Services.

care settings are places where health and social care practice is carried out. These are *residential, hospital, domiciliary,* and *day care.* Each of these settings is regarded as important in supporting client care. They include:

- residential care – carried out in different *nursing* and residential homes, hostels, sheltered housing and warden-controlled accommodation
- *hospitals*
- *domiciliary services* – carried out in the client's home
- *day care* provision – carried out to offer *direct care* and provide assistance whenever necessary including support with *daily living skills* development
- social services carried out by social workers working with different client groups
- education provision carried out by nurseries, schools, colleges and universities.

care team: those who have the formal or informal responsibility for care, whether they are paid or unpaid and regardless of their position in the system. The care team includes the *client* or *patient*. (Care Sector Consortium)[12]

care value base: a theoretical framework which promotes good practice within health and social care. Originating in the *National Vocational Qualifications* (*NVQs* in care) the care value base was devised by the *Care Sector Consortium* in 1992. It provides for carers a common set of values and principles within which to work. The care value base addresses five areas of practice:

- Promoting anti-discriminatory practice – policies and practice to ensure that clients and patients are not treated to a lower standard of service because of *age, race, gender, class, culture*, sexual orientation or religious belief.
- Maintaining *confidentiality* of *information* – to ensure that a *client's* or *patient's* personal information is restricted to those who have need of such access, with the client's or patient's *consent*.
- Promoting and supporting individual rights and choice within service delivery – maintaining the *dignity,* uniqueness and the individuality of each client/patient. Clients should be encouraged to make decisions with regard to their daily living.
- Acknowledging an individual's personal beliefs and choices – this supports the first national standard in the *Patient's Charter* which states that there should be '*respect* for privacy, *dignity,* religious and cultural *beliefs*'. This should include how a client or patient is treated with regard to personal and practical requirements such as *diet, privacy* and opportunities for worship.
- Supporting individuals through effective communication – verbal and non-verbal communication should be used in a positive way in order to build a client's or a patient's self-esteem. (See *confidence building.*) This principle was updated in 1998. (See also *National Vocational Qualifications, care – principles of good practice.*)

care workers: see *care assistants.*

carer: the individual who takes responsibility for the care and support of a person who cannot care for themselves, such as a child, a disabled person or an *elderly person.* Carers can either be formal or *informal carers.* (See also *caring, Carers National Association.*)

Carers National Association: an organisation set up to represent the interests of all *carers.* The Carers National Association has four aims which are to:

- encourage *carers* to recognise their own needs
- develop appropriate advice for carers
- provide information and advice for carers
- bring the needs of carers to the attention of government and those responsible for making care policies.

In 1998 the Carers National Association worked alongside the government to produce the National Carers' Strategy. This strategy is designed to improve support for informal carers and will be published in 1999. The Carers National Association is a membership organisation and individual carers can join as can others who wish to support the organisation. It is managed by a national committee consisting of 16 elected carers and one co-opted member.

(For further information contact the Carers National Association, 20/25 Glasshouse Yard, London EC1 4JS.)

Carers (Recognition and Services) Act 1995: an Act of Parliament which sought to provide an assessment of the ability of *carers* to provide care. It includes:

- The assessment of carers who provide care in England and Wales. It will take into account the service which the carer provides or intends to provide on a regular basis. This includes provision for a disabled child under Part III of the *Children Act 1989* or person under Section 2 of the *Chronically Sick and Disabled Persons Act 1970*.
- The assessment of carers who provide care in *Scotland*. This includes Section 12A of the Social Work (Scotland) Act 1968 which was amended with regard to the local authority's duty to assess the needs of a person and their carer. It addresses similar issues as for England and Wales.

The Act does not apply to *Northern Ireland*. (HMSO 1995)[14] (See *caring for the carer*.)

caring is supporting and looking after another person. This can be formal or informal caring:

- Formal care is provided on an organised and paid basis through health and social services.
- *Informal care* is provided on an unpaid basis, usually because the person being cared for is a family member, close friend or partner.

People who work in health, social care and the *early years* service may be involved in direct care or indirect care.

- Direct care is caring and working with *clients, patients* and *service users* providing the appropriate health or social care support (e.g. *nurses, nursery nurses, physiotherapists*).
- Indirect care is providing the support services which are necessary for care (e.g. *hospital* laboratory staff, catering or security staff).

caring for the carer: a term indicating an awareness of the needs of *carers* who care for others in a variety of settings. In the last ten years there has been a growing awareness of the needs of those who care for relatives long term. Such issues have been at the centre of the *Carers Recognition and Services Act 1995* and the philosophy of the *Carers National Association*.

Caring for People 1989: a government White Paper produced in 1989 as a response to the *Community Care Agenda for Action 1988*, more commonly known as the *Griffith's Report*. 'Caring for People' sets out proposals for care in the community. The proposals include:

- Delivery of a better community care service – with key objectives, which include promoting the development of *domiciliary* day and *respite* services to enable people to remain in their own homes, and of practical support for *carers*, assessment of care needs, promotion of the *independent sector*, key responsibilities of the various agencies involved and better value for tax-payers' money.
- Prioritising *community care* – which promotes teams of professional health and social care workers working together in the community to care for the elderly, mentally ill and the disabled.
- Reviewing the roles and responsibilities of social service authorities.
- Reviewing roles and responsibilities in the health service-producing community care plans, looking at the role of the *GP* and the idea of continuous health care.
- Achieving high standards of care – each *service provider* to become responsible for the care, and the planning of care, through centralised monitoring arrangements.
- *Collaboration* between the different services with a distinction between health and social care in terms of funding.
- Recognition of services for people with *mental illness*.
- Resourcing in *community care* – looking at the growth and expenditure in both health and community care services. Consideration was given to how funds would be managed and distributed within health and social care.

The report also considers aspects of community care in Scotland and in Wales. (HMSO 1989)[13]. The principles outlined in this report are now enshrined in the *NHS and Community Act 1990*.

caring relationship: the rapport, *respect* and the professional relationship which is developed between *clients* and their *carers*. This involves:

- assessing and monitoring the client's individual needs
- *communicating* effectively with the client, creating the right balance between talking, *questioning* and *listening*
- maintaining the *confidentiality* of the client; carers must not discuss client details without their permission
- maintaining *rights and choices*, creating *autonomy* and *independence*, enabling the client to feel that they are in control of decisions affecting their lives
- *respecting* the client's sense of *dignity* with regard to personal and cultural *lifestyle* and *beliefs*
- retaining professionalism within the caring relationship; this is based on both the client and carer setting boundaries for the relationship which involves partnership and working together.

(See also *codes of practice, care – principle of good practice, care value base, equal opportunities policies*.)

cartilage: a hard, flexible supporting tissue important to the skeletal system. Cartilage has various functions. It is more compressible than bone so cartilage is found at the ends of *bones* and between the *vertebrae*. It enables the body to withstand the shocks and jarring which accompany movement. Its flexibility is ideally suited to supporting such structures as the *nose*, the larynx and the *trachea*.

case conference: a formal meeting. It consists of different professional representatives who get together to exchange *information* and to decide on a course of action in relation to a particular *client* (or family) with whom they have been working. (See *child protection*.)

case control study is a method used to combat epidemic disease; it involves finding the cause of the disease and the means of control for future prevention.

case history: an historical account of a person and their family. This may include any significant events which might explain any of the problems that the person or family may be experiencing. These events are recorded in chronological order and are kept up to date by the relevant health or social care professional. Some agencies may use the term 'social history' and in the health service the term 'medical case records' is used. (See *Working together under the Children Act 1989*.)

case or judicial law: the way in which laws are interpreted and applied by judges in a court of law. Judgements are recorded and are sometimes used as examples or precedents when similar cases are heard at a later date.

case study: a *research method* which explores the in-depth *behaviour* and experiences of an individual, small group, organisation, community, nation or of an event. Case studies enable researchers to explore wider issues surrounding their chosen subject. GNVQ students may find this method useful if they wish to study a particular area of health and social care, such as the roles and responsibilities of social workers.

cash limit: the amount of money the government proposes to spend or authorise on certain services or blocks of services during one financial year. (See *NHS: The New NHS – Modern, Dependable 1997*.)

cell: a living structure, millions of which make up the human body. Cells vary in size and shape. In all cases, they are bound by a plasma membrane which encloses the cytoplasm. The cytoplasm contains the following cell organelles:

- **Nucleus** – containing nucleoplasm bounded by a nuclear membrane. The nucleoplasm contains *chromosomes* made mostly of *deoxyribonucleic acid* (DNA). DNA provides the information which determines the characteristics of the organism and transmits hereditary characteristics to the next generation.
- **Centrioles** – found outside the nucleus and are necessary for cell division.
- **Ribosomes** – responsible for protein synthesis.
- **Endoplasmic reticulum** – canals in the cytoplasm which form a connecting network and are responsible for transporting nutrients and substances around the cell.
- **Mitochondria** – oval shaped structures in the cytoplasm which produce energy and are sometimes called the 'powerhouses' of the cell. The more energy a cell requires, the greater the number of mitochondria it contains.

These are the sites for the *Krebs cycle*.

- **Lysosomes** – are membrane-bound organelles which contain enzymes. These enzymes digest bacteria and any damaged or worn out part of a cell. Lysosomes may be thought of as disposal units.

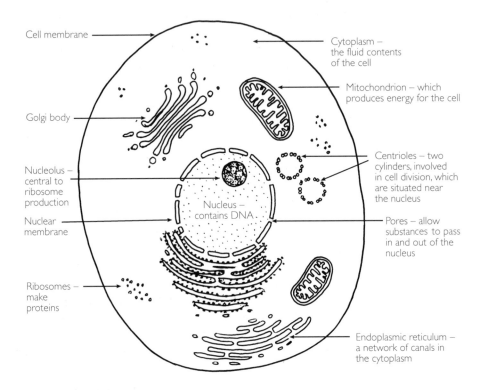

cell cycle: the sequence of events between one *cell* division and the next. The cell cycle consists of three main stages:

- **Stage 1** interphase – the cell grows and increases in size and prepares for the next division. New proteins are synthesised and new cell organelles are made.
- **Stage 2** *mitosis* – the genetic material (DNA) divides.
- **Stage 3** cytokinesis – the cytoplasm of the cell and its organelles divide more or less equally between two daughter cells.

The length of an individual cell cycle, even in the same organism, is very variable. Many factors combine to determine its precise length. It depends, for example, on temperature and the supply of nutrients.

The cells of many higher organisms are generally only able to go through a limited number of cell cycles. Once they have become specialised, they are unable to divide any more. *Cancer* cells, however, can carry on dividing indefinitely. Greater understanding of the mechanism which controls the cell cycle may lead to the discovery of ways in which tumour growth may be limited.

Celsius is a scale of *temperature*. The scale is divided into small divisions called degrees Celsius (°C), with the freezing point for water being 0°C and the boiling point for water at 100°C. Temperatures in degrees Celsius are for practical purposes the same as those in degrees centigrade, which may still be encountered.

census: a national social survey. It has been instigated by the government every 10 years since 1801(except 1941). The most recent census was in 1991. Every household in the United Kingdom is required to take part. The information gathered is used to provide statistics which relate to all aspects of national life (e.g. *family structures*).

centile charts are charts which are used to record a child's body measurements such as height and weight. The measurements can be taken in the following ways:

- Standing height measurements are taken from age two years onwards. The measurement is taken without shoes, standing with heels, buttocks and shoulders in contact with an upright wall. The child is encouraged to look straight ahead.
- Supine height measurements are taken with the child lying down on his or her back.
- Weight measurements are taken with the baby or young child lying, sitting or standing on the scales. Children under one year should be weighed without clothes or nappy for an accurate reading.

The child's measurements are carefully recorded at each age and stage. The distribution of the measurements is expressed in *percentiles*. A percentile refers to the position which a measurement would hold in a recording series of 100 children. The 50th percentile represents the middle measurement or median. Such a percentile chart shows the normal growth curve. A number of measurements are taken over a period of time so that the growth curve can be plotted.

central nervous system (CNS): consists of the *brain* and *spinal cord*. It is composed of:

- Types of matter – consisting of grey matter, which contains *blood* vessels and *nerve cells*, and white matter, which contains nerve fibres and a few blood vessels.
- Meninges – consisting of three membranes with a tough outer layer and a middle layer with spaces filled with cerebrospinal fluid which acts as a shock absorber. A lining membrane containing blood vessels supplies the nervous tissue. *Meningitis* is inflammation of the meninges due to infection.

The central nervous system is the body's control centre. It co-ordinates both mechanical and chemical actions. The millions of nerves in the body carry 'messages' or nervous impulses to and from the following central areas:

- **Brain** – the organ which controls most of the body's activities. It is made up of millions of *neurones* (nerve cells) arranged into sensory, association and motor areas. The sensory areas receive information via nerve impulses from various parts of the body. Association areas in the brain analyse the impulses and make decisions. The motor areas send impulses or information back to muscles or glands. The impulses are carried by the fibres of 43 pairs of nerves – 12 pairs of cranial nerves serving the head and 31 pairs of spinal nerves. (See *cerebrum*.)

- **Spinal cord** – a long string of nervous tissue running down from the brain inside the vertebral column. Nervous impulses from all parts of the body pass through it to the brain and back again. Some are carried into or away from the brain, some are dealt with in the cord (i.e. *involuntary actions*). Thirty-one pairs of spinal nerves branch out from the cord through the gaps between the vertebrae. Each spinal nerve is made up of two groups of fibres called the dorsal root and the sensory root. They comprise fibres of sensory neurones (bringing impulses in) and a ventral or motor root, made up of the fibres of motor neurones (taking impulses out).
- **Neuroglia** – special cells which support and protect the nerve cells (neurones) of the central nervous system.

Centre for Policy on Ageing is an independent organisation. It was established in 1947 following the publication of the Rowntree Report, 'Old People'. It aims to raise issues of public importance on matters connected with *ageing* and old age. It raises awareness, promotes debate and influences policies which further the interests of older people. The Centre for Policy on Ageing provides:

- a policy and research department
- a library and information service
- the publication of policy and research papers highlighting issues associated with ageing and the ageing process.

(For further information contact the Centre For Policy on Ageing, 25–31 Ironmonger Row, London EC1V 3QP.)

cerebral palsy: a medical condition caused by damage or injury to the developing brain. This may occur during *pregnancy, birth* or in the early *post natal* stages. There may be minor disabilities such as late walking and clumsiness or more severe disorders of *posture*, movement and co-ordination. There are different types of cerebral palsy depending on the part of the body affected. Children with cerebral palsy may suffer from movement which is jerky and uncontrolled. Often one movement will start off a series of other movements, which can be distressing to the child. Children with cerebral palsy may need continuous medical treatment and social support throughout their lives.

(For further information contact SCOPE, 12, Park Crescent, London W1N 4EQ.)

cerebrospinal fluid: a colourless fluid which is found in the *ventricles* of the *brain* and the central canal of the *spinal cord.*

cerebrovascular accident or stroke: the effect of a serious interruption of the *blood* supply to the *brain*. It may be caused by a blood clot or by the rupture of an *artery* wall. The actual effects vary according to the part of the brain involved. Damage to the right side of the cerebellum, for example, may produce loss of feeling or *paralysis* of the left side of the body.

cerebrum: part of the forebrain, made up of the two cerebral hemispheres. These hemispheres are responsible for the control of voluntary behaviour. This part of the *brain* is very large and covers most of the midbrain and hindbrain. Different parts of the cerebrum have different functions.

- Sensory areas – these receive sensory information. They include areas such as vision and hearing, as well as those concerned with sensory information from the general body surface. The size of the area is related to the number of receptors involved.

- Association areas – those parts responsible for interpreting sensory information in the light of experience. They are principally associated with memory and learning.
- Motor areas – the areas from which originate the impulses which go to voluntary *muscles.*

cervical smear: a test which involves removing some *cells* from the neck of the cervix as part of an investigation for degenerative disease. It is integrated into the cervical *screening programme* which was set up in 1987. This offers cervical smears to women over the age of 20 years and under the age 64 years, at least every five years. Some *GPs* recommend a smear every three years. Cervical smears are an important procedure in detecting early signs of cervical *cancer.*

challenging behaviour: displays of difficult or problem *behaviour* which affect the safety of the person, their carer and others. Challenging behaviour may be displayed by people with learning difficulties, children or any individual client, care manager or carer who is under stress. It may take the form of:

- shouting, screaming, biting and kicking (e.g. child's *tantrum*)
- uncontrolled outbursts of temper leading to violence, which can be dangerous to the instigator and to others (e.g. a schizophrenic client who is suffering from delusions and may be hearing voices)
- periods of disorientation and confusion (e.g. a client with learning difficulties who may suffer from *epilepsy*)
- excessive mood swings and periods of frustration if a person's routine is interrupted (e.g. an elderly client who finds moving into residential care a difficult transition).

Working with clients with negative or challenging behaviour may involve *behaviour therapy* to help the clients manage their *behaviour.* Carers under stress can develop difficulties in their behaviour which may take the form of shouting and bullying clients and colleagues or physically hitting out at helpless clients. Carers should be supported with strategies on *stress management* such as *relaxation techniques. (See behaviour management.)*

change: experiences which occur during the life stages can be predictable or unpredictable, negative or positive. Predicted change is that which may be controlled or managed by an individual. For instance, if a person feels that their life has become routine and that they are in a rut, then change could be a relief and could present them with a fresh challenge and cause for excitement, for example falling in love, changing jobs, planning a foreign holiday. However, unpredicted change could be another matter, for instance, those incidents which happen 'out of the blue' (e.g. an unexpected and distressing phone call with news that the return of a daughter from abroad has been delayed due to a road traffic accident). Other situations may include redundancy, sudden illness or a breakdown in a long-term relationship. It is inevitable that many changes do occur in a person's lifetime. However, it is the methods of *coping* with these *changes* that are the most relevant to health and social care workers.

Predictable events	Unpredictable events
Giving *birth*	*Miscarriage, stillborn birth*
Starting *school*	Child death/ *terminal illness*
Leaving school	Lack of education opportunities due to family illness or family problems
Further *education/ employment*	*Unemployment/*redundancy
Partnership/marriage	*Divorce/*separation
Permanent *housing*	*Homelessness*
Financial security	Sudden loss of income

charities are non-profit-making organisations. Charities were first set up during the eighteenth and nineteenth centuries as a response to the nation's *poverty*, failing education and poor health and living standards. They were organised by wealthy people who believed in 'doing good'. In recent years some charities have developed into large *voluntary organisations* which play an important part in community life. There are now approximately 175,000 charities registered under the Charities Act 1993. Information about different charities can be found in the Charity Commissioners Central Register. In order to qualify as a charity, an organisation must be set up with the aim of developing initiatives which will benefit the community. They are funded from various sources including:

- central government grants to finance specific projects
- local authority grants – usually to provide non-statutory services
- grants from organisations and business
- contracts with health authorities and social services departments, who employ the voluntary organisations to provide statutory or non-statutory services
- fundraising
- individual donations
- benefit from charitable status, related to taxation (i.e. covenant schemes).

(See also *Barnados, National Society for Prevention of Cruelty to Children, funding.*)

Charter Mark: a mark of quality service or excellence in public sector organisations. The Charter Mark is issued to organisations who have been assessed with regard to the service they offer. The views of the service users are taken into account during this process. The Charter Mark is seen as a recognised achievement for achieving quality standards.

charter standards were introduced by the government in 1992. Charters are a means whereby all *health authorities* are expected to publicise their local standards. *Clients, patients* and *service users* can then be assured of a level of care which meets their needs. National Charter Standards are the appropriate benchmarks which apply to:

- *respect* for a client's need for *privacy* and *dignity*, including their religious and cultural beliefs
- *access to services* – arrangements to ensure that everyone can use services
- *information* – to relatives and friends with regard to treatment
- *waiting times* – e.g. for the ambulance service, 14 minutes in an urban area, 19 minutes in a rural area; for initial assessment in *accident and emergency*

services, waiting at out patients clinics

- dates for operations – information with regard to the arrangement or cancellation of operations and a review of procedure
- a named qualified nurse, midwife or health visitor – responsible for individual patients
- discharge from hospital – aftercare should be co-ordinated.

(See also *community care charters*.)

charts: a way of documenting relevant information. Charts are used by health and social care workers to:

- record the results of *research* (e.g. used by GNVQ students in the production of their assignments)
- record the readings of *temperature, pulse, respiration* and *blood pressure,* and fluid balance, for example in *hospital* by *doctors* and *nurses*
- record the administration of *drugs* in the form of medication charts
- record the observation of growth in the form of *centile* charts.

chemical poisoning is one of the harmful effects of chemicals. Chemical substances can be dangerous to work with as they can be corrosive, explosive, toxic or highly inflammable. Any chemical which can be hazardous should carry a symbol enabling it to be identified. All chemical experiments require a risk assessment before they are undertaken. Factors such as the chemicals, techniques and apparatus used are considered and recorded. The *Health and Safety At Work Act 1974* reviews safe practice and is reinforced by the *Control of Substances Hazardous to Health 1988* (COSHH) regulations.

Chemical poisoning can occur due to:

- uncontrolled experiments in the laboratory
- overdosage of *chemotherapy* in the treatment of *cancer*
- explosions where poisonous gases are released into the atmosphere
- high toxic levels in the atmosphere as a result of *pollution*.

chemicals are used to:

- conduct experiments to produce substances used in many areas such as industry, manufacturing, the treatment of sewerage, the manufacture of fuels and disinfectants and in agriculture.
- combat *disease* in the treatment of *cancer*.

(See also *chemotherapy*.)

chemistry: the study of the *elements* which form all substances. It examines their structure, how they can combine to form other substances and how they can react in certain conditions. Chemistry covers:

- physical chemistry – the study of the structures, properties and behaviour of substances
- inorganic chemistry – the study of all the elements in the periodic table except carbon chain compounds
- organic chemistry – the study of the structures and the various groups of carbon chain compounds
- environmental chemistry – the study of the effects of *pollution* and the interaction of naturally occurring chemicals (Stockley, Oxlade and Wertheim 1988)[58].

chemotherapy is the use of specific *drugs* and *chemicals* to treat *cancer*. *Cytotoxic drugs* are used to either kill or prevent cancer cells from reproducing. However, in the act of working on the cancer cells, these drugs can also kill the body's healthy *cells*, such as the *white blood cells*. Other side effects of this treatment can include hair loss and baldness, nausea, sickness and *vomiting*.

child abuse is deliberate ill treatment of a child. It can take the form of:

- abandonment – the child is left alone with no adult care
- educational neglect – the child does not attend school and has no parental guidance
- emotional abuse – the child may be subject to name calling, negative reinforcement, lack of love or building of self-esteem
- emotional neglect – the child is ignored and isolated
- medical neglect – the general health of the child is not considered, no medical supervision is encouraged, or there are no *immunisation* or *child health surveillance* checks
- physical abuse – the child may be hit or hurt in some way, such as smacking or suffering cigarette burns
- physical neglect – the child is not given an adequate diet or physical care
- sexual abuse – the child is subjected to sexual acts
- multiple maltreatment – a combination of the other different forms of *abuse*.

In November 1998, government changes have redesigned child abuse procedures to incude:

- criminal record agency – keeping track of people with criminal records who work with children
- duty of care by local authority being extended from 16 to 18 years

Child Accident Prevention Trust: a voluntary organisation which works closely with health, social and childcare professionals to draw attention to issues relating to child safety.

(For further information contact Child Accident Prevention Trust, 4th Floor, Clerks Court, 18–20 Farringdon Lane, London EC1R 3AU.)

Child Care (NI): a charity which promotes the rights of the child in Northern Ireland. The aims of Child Care (NI) are:

- to promote in Northern Ireland the preservation and protection of health and personal development of children without distinction of sex, race or political, religious or other opinions
- to advance public education in child care by associating the appropriate voluntary *agencies* with the object of improving life for children.

The charity offers training and information services. It provides an overview of the child care issues in Northern Ireland. (See also *Children in Wales, Children in Scotland, National Children's Bureau.*)

(For further information contact Child Care (NI), 216 Belmont Road, Belfast, BT4 2AT.)

child-centred: policy and practice that starts with a child's needs which act as the principal consideration in the health and *well-being* of the child. (See *Children Act 1989.*)

child development: see *growth and development.*

child health clinics are run by *health visitors* and *doctors* as part of a community service for families. Health visitors and *GPs* offer *routine child health surveillance*, programmes of *immunisation* as well as general *information* and *advice.*

child health surveillance programme: designed to ensure that the developmental progress of a child is reviewed at certain times during their first eight years of life.

Child Poverty Action Group is a *pressure group.* The CPAG is committed to raising awareness and working towards eliminating poverty for children and their families. It offers an information service with publications available which provide advice on benefits, etc.

(For further information contact Child Poverty Action Group, 94 White Lion Street, London N19 PF)

child protection involves a series of guidelines which promote and safeguard the welfare of children. Child protection is supported by the *Children Act 1989.* This Act seeks to protect children from harm arising from failures within the family and as a result of unwarranted intervention in family life (HMSO 1997)[16]. It enables social workers to investigate children's circumstances and to make decisions about them. *Working Together under the Children Act 1989* provides guidance with regard to *child* protection. The following guidelines are included:

- Child protection conference – in a child care context this is defined as a formal meeting attended by representatives from all the agencies concerned with a child's welfare. Increasingly this includes the child's parents and the *Children Act* promotes this practice. Its purpose is to gather together and evaluate all the relevant information about a child and to plan any immediate action which may be necessary to protect the child (e.g. seeking a Court Order). Where the meeting decides that the child and its family need support, a *key worker* will be appointed to co-ordinate an inter-agency plan for use with the child and the family. The child's name plus those of any other children living in the same household may be entered on the Child Protection Register.
- Child Assessment Order – a court order which requires any person who can do so, to produce the child for assessment and to comply with the terms of the order.
- Child Protection Register – a central record of all children in a given area for whom support is being provided by inter-agency planning. Generally, these are children who are considered to be at risk of *abuse* or neglect. The Register is usually maintained and run by the *social service departments* under the supervision of a custodian (an experienced social worker able to provide advice to any professional who may make enquiries about the child).
- Children in need – a child is 'in need' if:
  a) he or she is unlikely to achieve or maintain or have the opportunity of achieving or maintaining a reasonable standard of health or development without the provision of services by a *local authority*

b) his or her health or development is likely to be significantly impaired, or further impaired without the provision of such services

c) he or she is disabled.

- Children living away from home – children who are not being looked after by the local authority but are nevertheless living away from home (e.g. children in independent schools). The local authority has a number of duties towards such children, to take reasonable steps to ensure that their welfare is being adequately safeguarded and promoted.

(See *Working Together under the Children Act 1989, child abuse.*)

Child Support Act 1991: an Act of Parliament passed in 1991 and implemented in April 1993. It created a new child benefit system designed to replace existing procedures. Child maintenance was assessed using a formula with set rules and amounts, instead of being left to a negotiable formula followed by the Department of Social Security, by reliable relatives, or at the discretion of the courts. Maintenance henceforth would be assessed, collected and enforced by the *Child Support Agency*. The Child Support Act was amended in 1995 to make provision for child support maintenance and other maintenance and to provide for a child maintenance bonus i.e. provision for payment by the Secretary of State in certain circumstances. *Under the New Ambitions For Our Country – A New Contract For Welfare,* the Child Support Act is expected to face further fundamental reform which includes changes to the role of the *Child Support Agency*.

Child Support Agency: a government agency set up in 1993 following the implementation of the *Child Support Act 1991*. It has responsibility for the assessment, review, collection and enforcement of child maintenance payments from estranged parents. The law also requires that absent parents should make regular payments for child maintenance.

childcare: the care of children in a variety of settings which include their family homes, *day nursery,* homes of *childminders, playgroups and family centres.* Childcare involves caring for the different physical, intellectual, emotional, cultural and social needs of children and young people. In May 1998 the government introduced a consultation paper '*Meeting the childcare challenge*'. Many of the issues raised in the consultation paper are relevant across the UK although this Green Paper covered proposals specific for England. The Secretaries of State for *Scotland, Wales* and *Northern Ireland* are responsible for policy relating to the development of childcare in those parts of the UK and each of the Secretaries of State plan to issue their own documents on childcare. The Green Paper included:

- the need for a national childcare strategy
- raising the quality of care
- making childcare more accessible
- delivering the national childcare strategy through partnerships of national and local government, other statutory agencies, employers, parents, private, public and voluntary childcare providers
- a programme of implementation (HMSO 1998)[42].

Childline: a free, confidential, 24 hour helpline for children and young people in trouble or danger. Childline was set up in Spring 1986 after the BBC consumer programme 'That's Life' (presented by Esther Rantzen) appealed to viewers for their help in conducting a survey on child abuse. The response was overwhelming and, following the programme, a special childwatch team was set up. The childwatch team met with *childcare* professionals from both the voluntary and statutory sectors and it was decided to establish a permanent free telephone helpline, which would provide a way of comforting and advising those who could not be reached in any other way. Children phone about many problems, including sexual and physical abuse, bullying, problems with families, friends and worries about schoolwork. Each of the phone calls is followed up by the Childline team at the request of the child.

(For further information contact Childline, 2nd floor, Royal Mail Building, Studd Street, London N1 OQW.)

childminders offer day care for young children in their own homes. Childminders are registered by the *local authority* and the home is inspected according to criteria which include the number and size of rooms, toilets and washing facilities. There are standard ratios for minders/children: one minder to one baby under one year, one minder to three children under five years of age, one minder to five children between five and seven years of age, one minder to six children under eight years of whom no more than three should be under five years of age. The childminder's own children are taken into account when the number of places are allocated to a childminder by a local authority. Monitoring of childminders is the ongoing responsibility of the local authority which sends representatives to make regular inspection visits. Under the *Children Act 1989*, 'Local Authorities have the power to cancel an individual caregiver's registration on the grounds of 'inadequate care', and to have regard to the child's religious persuasion, racial origin and cultural and linguistic background'. All services to children need to be planned and delivered to meet their racial, cultural and religious needs. The Children Act 1989 (Volume 2) and the Child Minding and Day Care Registration and Inspection Fees Regulations 1991, contain regulations which set the fees to be charged for the registration of child minders and the providers of day care under Section 71 CA 1989. They also specify the fee for annual inspection and for issuing a copy certificate. In addition to this, a panel of reporting officers is set up.

(For further information contact the National Childminding Association, 8 Masons Hill, Bromley, Kent BR2 9EY.)

Children Act 1989: an Act of Parliament which was introduced to bring about radical changes and improvements in the law with regard to children. The Children Act was a means of updating previous childcare law. The main sections deal with:

- children and their families
- *parental responsibility*
- court proceedings including the *welfare principle*, that the welfare of the child is viewed as 'paramount'
- local authority services for children and families
- children in the care of *local authorities*
- *child protection*
- welfare of children away from home, such as those in childminding, day care and residential care

- *adoption*
- juvenile offenders (HMSO 1989)[15].

children's homes: 24 hour *residential care* for children and young people. There are four different types of residential care:

- community homes maintained, staffed and controlled by *local authorities*
- homes maintained, staffed and controlled by the voluntary sector
- registered children's homes run by private companies
- independent homes accommodating between 4 to 50 pupils.

Children in Scotland is the national agency for organisations and individuals working with children and their families in Scotland. It exists to identify and promote the interests of children and their families and to ensure that relevant policies, services and other provisions are of the highest possible quality and are able to meet the needs of a diverse society. The framework for Scotland's children, young people and families includes:

- supporting families
- recognising diversity and promoting equal opportunities
- supporting children and families in the early years
- preparing young people for adult life.

Children in Scotland works in partnership with the *National Children's Bureau* and *Children in Wales*. (See also *Child Care (NI)*.

(For further information contact Children in Scotland, Princes House, 5 Shandwick Place, Edinburgh EH2 4RG.)

Children in Wales is an organisation which offers *advice* and support with regard to children and their families in Wales. It was established as a charity in 1993. Its purpose is to identify and promote the interests of young people in Wales and to improve their status in a diverse society. It publicises good practice in children's services through research, policy development, publications, seminars, conferences and training and through links with influential opinion and the media. The service includes:

- the early childhood unit – offering support and advice to staff involved with young children in early years groups
- library and information service – providing a reference library of books, journals, reports, statistics, newscuttings, booklists and lists of organisations; there is access to the *National Children's Bureau* library database, which is the largest in the country concerned with children
- membership – providing regular updates of information relevant to children, young people and their families.

(For further information contact Children in Wales, 7 Cleeve House, Lambourne Crescent, Cardiff CF4 5GJ.)

children with disabilities: a framework for children with disabilities which was identified in the *Children Act 1989*. This framework was set up to integrate children with disabilities into mainstream service provision. Children with disabilities are automatically included in the 'in need' category of the Act and are therefore recommended for quality service provision. Integrating children with disabilities is a way of working towards meeting their social, intellectual, cognitive, emotional, cultural as well as their physical needs. In the Act local authorities are encouraged to liaise with other organisations such as the *health authority* and relevant voluntary bodies in making arrangements for integrating such children. In these cases careful consideration has to be given to the health and *safety* of the physical environment, staff:child ratios and relevant staff training (e.g. *portage, sign language, Braille*). Some children's disabilities may be so severe that they require separate services. In such cases, where possible, this provision is attached to a service used by other children so that joint activities can be arranged from time to time (HMSO 1989)[15]. (See *special needs.*)

children's rights are protected by the *Children Act 1989* in terms of their treatment and welfare. Children's rights require that the wishes and feelings of the child should be taken into account at all times. (See also *UN Rights of the Child Charter, Children Act 1989, child protection.*)

chiropody is the theory and practice relating to the maintenance of healthy feet. It involves the treatment of feet and their associated disabilities and diseases. Individuals qualifying in chiropody are known as chiropodists or podiatrists. They have an essential role within a community health team, holding surgeries in hospitals, health centres, clinics and residential homes. Some chiropodists run private practices but there are also community chiropodists who visit people in their own homes. *Patients, clients* and *service users* can be referred to a chiropodist through their *GPs* or they can arrange a private appointment. Training as a chiropodist involves a three year, full-time degree course, although some centres offer the course on a part-time basis.

chiropractic: an alternative treatment which uses a technique involving the manipulation of the spine. It is based on the belief that *disorders* of the body are due to the incorrect alignment of *bones* causing abnormal functioning of *nerves* and *muscles*. Chiropractic treatment is performed by trained chiropractors. Training as a chiropractor involves four years study at the British College of Chiropractic.

cholesterol: a lipid (fatty substance) which plays an important part in living organisms. Some of the cholesterol required by the body is taken in the *diet* and some is formed in the *liver*. Cholesterol is an important component of *cell* membranes and is a precursor of *bile* salts and steroid hormones such as testosterone and progesterone. High levels of cholesterol in the blood are associated with *atheroma*. Its level is often monitored in older people or people with high cholesterol levels in the blood. *Drugs* may be given to reduce blood cholesterol.

Christmas disease: a disease which is due to a defective gene in the *X chromosome*. It is a sex linked recessive disease which means it affects males. It is similar to *haemophilia* and inhibits the blood clotting process. This is due to a deficiency in factor IX in the *plasma*.

chromosomal defects are the abnormal structure of *chromosomes*. These can cause medical conditions and *disabilities* of varying severity. Examples of conditions caused by chromosomal defects are *Down's syndrome*, and Turner's syndrome.

chromosome: one of the thread-like structures found in the nucleus, in which the genetic material of the *cell* is organised. Chromosomes consist of DNA and protein. There are 23 pairs (46) of chromosomes in all human body cells. The gametes (eggs and sperm) have 23 unpaired chromosomes.

chronic conditions and illness: diseases or disorders which are long-term and lead to slow and progressive deterioration despite treatment. An example of such a disease is chronic myeloid leukaemia which occurs mainly in men and may be present for many years with few symptoms.

Chronically Sick and Disabled Persons Act 1970: an Act of Parliament which identified the need for provision for people with chronic disease or disabilities. This Act gave *local authorities* a range of duties which include providing services and amenities to give support to the disabled.

cilia: microscopic hair-like projections, drawn out from the cell membrane. Mucus-secreting cells are usually associated with ciliated cells. The cilia exhibit a continual flicking movement, keeping up a constant stream of mucus in the cells lining the *air passages* of the respiratory tract; *smoking* has a harmful affect on these cilia.

circulation: the passage of fluids around parts of the body. Examples of circulation in the body include:

- the passage of *blood* from the *heart* to the *arteries* to the *capillaries* and from the capillaries to the *veins* and back to the heart
- the passage of *bile* from the *liver* cells, where it is made, to the small intestine via the *gall bladder* and bile ducts (some constituents are reabsorbed into the bloodstream in the small intestine and returned to the liver).

(See *circulatory system*.)

circulatory system: a network of *blood* filled tubes (blood vessels) which circulate fluid to different parts of the body. There are three main types of blood vessels known as *arteries, veins* and *capillaries*. A thin *tissue* layer (endothelium) lines arteries and veins and is the only layer in capillary walls. Blood is kept flowing one way by the pumping of the heart, and by the muscular tissue in the walls of arteries and veins. In different parts of the body muscles contract and relax and these actions encourage bloodflow.

circumcision: a surgical procedure which involves the removal of the foreskin of the male penis. The procedure is often part of religious or ethnic tradition although, sometimes, the foreskin may become unnaturally tight and needs to be removed. In certain cultures, women can be circumcised. This involves the surgical removal of the clitoris and the inner and outer lips of the vagina. Female circumcision can often be carried out non-surgically and without *consent*. The Prohibition of Female Circumcision Act 1985 makes female circumcision, excision and infibulation (female genital mutilation) an offence except on physical and mental health grounds.

cirrhosis of the liver: a disorder of the *liver* in which liver tissue becomes damaged and the healthy tissue is replaced by fibrous tissue. This scarred or fibrous tissue affects the normal working of the liver. The main cause of cirrhosis is 'heavy drinking' or excessive intake of *alcohol*. The best treatment is for the person concerned to stop drinking alcohol. This usually helps the liver to recover.

Citizens Advice Bureaux (CAB): a service which provides valuable *information* to members of the public. The Citizen's Advice Bureaux are situated in all parts of the United Kingdom. They offer general *advice* on a number of issues including *housing* and *benefits*. If more specialised or detailed advice is needed then the CAB will be able to tell a client where to go to receive further help. Some of the Bureaux provide a free appointment with a *solicitor*. At present, there are 700 Citizens Advice Bureaux with 1000 service outlets in England, *Wales* and *Northern Ireland*. Approximately 5.5 million people seek help from the Bureaux each year.

(For further information contact National Association of Citizens Advice Bureaux, Myddelton House, 115–123 Pentonville Road, London N1 9LZ.)

civil law: laws which involve the rights and duties individuals have in society towards each other (in contrast to criminal law; see *criminal justice system*).

civil proceedings: court cases which do not involve criminal acts but deal with certain issues including those affecting children and other legalities related to the *Children Act 1989*.

class: see *social class*.

classical conditioning: see *learning theories*.

classification of care services is a method of dividing and grouping health and social care services with regard to *care settings*, client *age* and individual client need.

client: an individual receiving support, *treatment* or *therapy* from a health or social care service. The individual is the focus of the health or social care activity.

client classification is the way in which clients can be grouped together. Clients may be grouped according to:

- *age* – child, adult or *elderly person*
- needs – *mental health, learning disability* or *physical disability*, for example
- *type of care* – *acute, chronic, social* care or *priority* care
- *level of care* – primary, secondary or tertiary
- *care setting* – *domiciliary*, day care, clinics, residential or hospital care
- service being supplied – *physiotherapy, chiropody, probation, hostels, psychiatric care* etc.

client rights and choices: the freedom which individual people in society have to choose their own preferences, beliefs and *lifestyles*. Within the context of health and social care provision, *clients* or *service users* have the same individual rights and choices. This means that every client or service user should have their views acknowledged and supported.

clinic a department in a *hospital*, or at an established service provider, which specialises in a particular *disease, disorder* or *dysfunction* and its treatment. This includes:

- a follow-up appointment in the out patient department of a hospital
- a meeting of medical professionals and students at a hospital ward specialising in a particular disease, providing examination and treatment of patients
- an established service in the community which advertises a specialist diagnosis and treatment of specific diseases or conditions
- a system for monitoring and maintaining health, such as child health, Well Man or Well Women clinics.

clinical governance: a new initiative in a government White Paper to assure and improve clinical standards at local level, throughout the NHS. This includes action to ensure that risks are avoided, adverse events are rapidly detected, openly investigated and lessons learned, good practice is rapidly disseminated and that systems are in place to ensure continuous improvements in clinical care. (See *NHS: The New NHS – Modern, Dependable 1997, hospitals.*)

clinical medicine: the study of *disease* by diagnosis and treatment through direct contact with the patients/individuals suffering from the disease. This is different to diagnosis of a disease through the study of body or *blood* cells. Direct contact with the *patient* is an important part of this branch of medicine.

clinical nurse specialist: a qualified *nurse* who has developed skills and experience in treating a group of *patients* suffering from a certain condition or *disease.* Examples include nurses who work with *cancer* patients, nurses who work with patients who suffer from *diabetes,* or from head injuries following a car *accident.*

clinical procedures: any clinical activity, treatment or care in which *health care workers* may be involved.

clinical thermometer: an instrument used to measure the body *temperature* of a human being. Body temperature can be taken:

- in the *axilla* – placing the thermometer under the arm
- in the rectum – putting the thermometer into the anus
- in the *mouth* – placing the thermometer in the mouth and under the *tongue.*

The clinical thermometer is a small glass tube with a mercury indicator, the level of which rises and falls with body temperature. Normal temperature is 36.8 degrees *Celsius* or 98.4 degrees Fahrenheit.

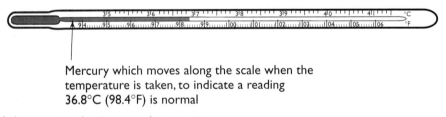

Mercury which moves along the scale when the temperature is taken, to indicate a reading 36.8°C (98.4°F) is normal

A thermometer showing normal temperature

clinical work areas: any work area or environment in which *clinical procedures* take place. This term is used generally, and would cover areas such as operating departments/theatres. However clinical procedures might take place in a range of different settings.

clinician: any health professional who is directly involved in the care and treatment of patients, for example a *nurse, doctor,* therapist or *midwife.* (See *New NHS Modern and Dependable 1997.*)

Clostridium botulinum: a common type of bacterium frequently found in the faeces of humans, in animals, soil, dirt, flies, raw meats, poultry and dehydrated *food.* *Clostridium* spores can survive cooking and grow without *oxygen.* Infected meat or poultry left out on warm and unwashed surfaces or stored before it has fully cooled down can activate the organism. The toxins are released when infected food is eaten and cause abdominal pain and diarrhoea within 8–22 days. The disease lasts for 1–2 days and can be fatal in sick and elderly people.

cluster sampling: a *sampling* method, used in research, which looks at the *survey* population and divides this into smaller groups or clusters. It is used when the survey population is unusually large. For example, a London Borough will have a large population, so it may be appropriate to break the sample down into groups by *race, class, gender, age.*

cocaine: a stimulant derived from the leaves of the coca shrub. It produces temporary euphoria and makes the user feel more alert. In its purified form it is taken intra-nasally ('snorted'). It is classed as an illegal *drug* because of the danger of *addiction.*

code of professional conduct for nurses, midwives and health visitors: a *code of practice* drawn up by a professional body for registered *nurses, midwives* or *health visitors* who are personally accountable for the way in which they carry out their duties. Each qualified nurse, midwife or health visitor is required to act in a way that demonstrates:

- promoting the interests and *well-being* of the patient; no behaviour should put the patient at risk as their safety is of utmost importance
- updating professional knowledge and *competence*
- co-operating with patients, clients and their *families,* fostering their independence and recognising and respecting their involvement in the planning and delivery of care
- collaborating and working with other health care professionals including others involved in providing care, and recognising and respecting their particular contributions within the care team
- recognising and respecting the uniqueness and dignity of each patient and client and responding to their need for care, irrespective of their ethnic origin, religious beliefs, personal attributes, the nature of their health problems or any other factor
- reporting to an appropriate person or authority, at the earliest possible time, any conscientious objection which may be relevant to their professional practice
- avoiding any abuse of their privileged relationship with patients and clients and of the privileged access allowed to their person, property, residence or workplace
- protecting all confidential *information* concerning patients and clients obtained in the course of professional practice and making disclosures only with *consent,* where required by the order of a court or where one can justify disclosure in the wider public interest
- reporting to an appropriate person or authority, with regard to the physical, psychological and social effects on patients and clients of any circumstances in the care environment which could jeopardise standards of practice
- reporting to an appropriate person or authority any circumstances in which safe and appropriate care for patients and clients cannot be provided
- reporting to an appropriate person where it appears that the health or safety of colleagues is at risk, as such circumstances may compromise standards of practice and care

- assisting professional colleagues, in the context of their own knowledge, experience and sphere of responsibility, to develop their professional competence, and assisting others in the care team, including informal carers, to contribute safely and to a degree appropriate to their roles
- refusing any gift, favour or hospitality from patients or clients currently in their care, which might be interpreted as seeking to exert influence to obtain preferential consideration
- ensuring that their registration status is not used in the promotion of commercial products or services, declaring any financial or other interest in relevant organisations providing such goods or services and ensuring that their professional judgement is not influenced by any commercial considerations. (UKCC 1983)[19]

The code of professional standards for nurses, midwives and health visitors requires that the members of these professions should practice and conduct themselves within the standards and framework provided by the United Kingdom Central Council for Nursing, Midwifery and Health Visiting. This council is the regulatory body responsible for standards and it requires its members (registered nurses, midwives or health visitors) to be personally accountable for their professional practice.

code of professional practice for social workers: each qualified social worker is required to act in a way that demonstrates:

- positively using knowledge, skills and experience for the benefit of all sections of the community and individuals
- respecting clients as individuals and safeguarding their dignity and rights
- ensuring that there is no prejudice which is evident to others, on the grounds of origin, *race*, status, sex, sexual orientation, *age, disability, beliefs* or contribution to society
- *empowering* clients through their participation in decisions and defining services
- sustaining concern for clients even when they are unable to help them or where self-protection is necessary
- making sure that professional responsibility takes precedence over personal interest
- being responsible for standards of service and for continuing education and training
- collaborating with others in the interests of clients
- ensuring clarity in public as to whether acting in a personal or organisational capacity
- promoting appropriate ethnic and cultural diversity of services
- ensuring *confidentiality* of information and divulging only by consent or exceptionally in the event of serious danger
- pursuing conditions of employment which enable these obligations to be respected.

(British Association of Social Work 1992)[11]

codes of practice: a theoretical framework which shapes how practitioners behave in a professional setting. (See also *code of professional conduct for nurses, code of professional practice for social workers, care – principles of good practice.*)

cognitive development: the development of an individual's thinking systems linked to problem solving and reasoning. This is particularly important to children as part of their learning, *intellectual development* and *language development.*

collaboration: different health and social care agencies working together to provide help and support for individual *clients.* (See *care planning, joint commissioning.*)

colon: the part of the *alimentary canal* between the small intestine and the rectum. Its main function is the absorption of *water.* The colon contains many bacteria. Some of these are mutualistic (both human and bacteria gain a nutritional advantage). These *bacteria* receive a continuous supply of nutrients from the material in the intestine, in turn they synthesise a number of *vitamins* which may be absorbed by the body. The *food* passes from the colon to the rectum and is then evacuated from the body through the *anus.*

coma: a state of unconsciousness which can last for hours, days or longer. It is a state which indicates that the functioning of the *brain* has been affected. A person in a coma cannot be woken up or roused. There are different degrees of coma. In some *patients* there may be a pupil reaction to light, some restlessness, or some movement when touched. Other patients can be deeply unconscious and make no response to any stimulus such as light and touch. Causes of coma include severe injuries suffered due to a car *accident,* barbiturate poisoning or inflammation in the brain or encephalitis. (See *consciousness.*)

combination order: a sentence which has been introduced under the *Criminal Justice Act 1991,* where the courts may combine a period of community service of between 40 and 100 hours with a period of supervision of between 12 months and three years.

Commission for Health Improvement: a national body which was set up under the White Paper *The New NHS – Modern, Dependable 1997.* The function of the commission is to support and oversee the quality of *clinical governance* and of clinical services.

Commission for Racial Equality: an organisation set up following the *Race Relations Act 1976.* The Act sets out the duties of the Commission. These are:

- to work towards the elimination of discrimination
- to promote equality of opportunity and good relations between persons of different racial groups
- to keep under review the working of the Act, and when required by the Secretary of State or when it thinks necessary, to draw up and submit to the Secretary of State proposals for amending the Act

As part of its function the Commission for Racial Equality supplies information about its working within the context of the Race Relations Act. In addition to this, the CRE has powers to carry out investigations into any circumstances covered by the Act.

(For further information contact the Commission for Racial Equality, 10–12 Allington Street, London SW1E 5EH.)

Committee on Medical Aspects of Food Policy (COMA): a committee of the Department of Health which produces important reports relating to nutrition and food. (See *National Advisory Committee on Nutrition Education.*)

Committee on Toxicology (COT): a committee of the Department of Health which advises the government on the safety of food additives. (See *E numbers*.)

common health emergencies are those which occur most frequently in care settings. These are identified in GNVQ units and they include:

- *asthma* – supporting a *client* with breathing difficulties
- broken *bones* or *fractures* – supporting clients who have broken bones as the result of a fall, a heavy blow to a bone, or twisting and wrenching a bone; elderly people tend to be more vulnerable to broken bones because *age* and *disease* can weaken bones
- burns or scalds – supporting a client with a burn or scald which has damaged the skin; burns are caused by fire, dry heat, chemicals, friction, the sun's rays, or radiation while scalds are caused by the wet heat from boiling liquids and vapours
- choking – supporting a client with an obstruction in their *throat* which can block the passage of air and therefore requires quick action to remove it
- concussion – supporting a client who has had a blow to the head causing loss of *consciousness*
- cuts – supporting clients who have cut or scratched themselves on a sharp object
- electric shock – supporting a client who has suffered an electric current running through their bodies (in these circumstances it is crucial that the carer **does not touch the body of the client**, the source of electricity should be first identified and turned off using a broom handle or other non-conducting object)
- *heart attack* – supporting clients with chest pain.

Dealing with these health emergencies is an important aspect of a carer's work. Whenever an emergency arises a carer should:

- think 'danger' (check their own safety)
- determine the response of the casualty (levels of *consciousness*)
- check the casualty's airway, breathing and circulation and if necessary carry out the *ABC of resuscitation*
- place the casualty in the *recovery position* if this is appropriate
- get help – using the telephone, knowing what to say and giving the relevant information to the paramedics or *ambulance* crew. (St John Ambulance 1997)

Whenever possible carers should be trained as *first aiders* by appropriate agencies such as St. John Ambulance. (See *calling the emergency services*.)

communication: the exchange of *information* between individuals, groups and organisations. There are different methods of communicating such as:

- verbal/oral communication – which involves using voice including variation of the voice's tone and pitch. Use of *language* is also an important part of oral communication. Verbal communication is used in conversations, speaking on the telephone, in team and group meetings, conference speaking or giving a 'talk'. Interacting with *clients* using conversation enables the carer to offer encouragement and support and show interest. Asking questions and finding out how the client is feeling is an important aspect of care. There are some clients with disabilities which may make oral communication difficult. For example clients who are unable to speak may use a system called a *Bliss board*. Clients with visual impairments can use *Braille*. Clients with hearing difficulties can use *sign language* or special hearing aids. In others cases where clients do not speak English then information can be translated into their first language or an oral interpreter can be provided.

- non-verbal communication – body language includes the use of the eyes and eye contact, facial expressions, body movement, posture which relates to how people sit or stand, proximity to others, touching and gestures and physical body movements such as the use of arms and legs. Non-verbal communication is a way in which messages can be conveyed to others. Positive non-verbal communication can involve maintaining eye contact, or leaning towards a person. Facial expressions, smiling, looking interested, with *gestures* such a putting a hand on the arm of another person, can convey support. However, sometimes these messages can be misunderstood; for instance in some cultures, maintaining eye contact can be viewed as being too confident, while looking away is seen as being 'sly'. Learning the different aspects of body language from a transcultural perspective is an important aspect of working in the caring profession.
- visual communication includes writing, typing and illustrating information which is sent and received by individuals, groups and organisations. Every day millions of letters, memos, reports or lists are written and used to convey a message to others.
- multi-media communication includes the use of television, video, computer, CD ROM, telephone, fax, e-mail, and the Internet. These methods support global, national and local communication networks.
- using advocates when necessary to support a client, *patient* or *service user.*

Communication is viewed as an integral part of the caring process and developing such interpersonal skills can enhance this process. (See *interpersonal skills, barriers to communication, confidence building, care value base.*)

community: a group in society which may be determined by factors such as geographical boundaries, common values, *culture* and *religion.* The idea of 'community' implies shared *lifestyles,* relationships and individuals being in regular contact with each other.

community action is the process whereby locally based groups organise themselves to achieve objectives. They are usually associated with disadvantaged groups who seek redress for their grievances through *self-help* organisations. They organise themselves as *pressure groups* to draw attention to the different needs of their groups. In addition to this, they tend to look for funding from national and local government to help them achieve their objectives.

community care: a service which provides care in a person's home (*domiciliary care*). This can include a house which provides living accommodation for three or four people. *Sheltered housing,* offered to mentally ill people coming from long stay institutions, is another example. Community care may enable a person to carry on their daily routine within the comfort of their own home. It can involve a number of the following services:

- Family support services support family members who provide the vast bulk of caring. Probably over 80 per cent of those being cared for receive little or no help from formal agencies, and are instead looked after by a wife, daughter or husband. (See *informal care*.)
- Home helps support clients in a wide range of domestic tasks including cleaning, shopping, making beds. The extent of services offered depends on assessment by a home help organiser. In some areas, charges may be made through the process called *means testing*.
- *Community psychiatric nurses* support *clients* with *mental illness* and there is a specialised branch for people with learning difficulties.
- *District/community nurses* support *patients* across the entire range of physical illnesses and disabilities.
- *Health visitors* support specific client groups such as young children and their parents, and elderly clients.
- *Social workers* support and visit clients and assess their social needs. They then arrange appropriate services whenever possible.
- *General practitioners* (GPs) support and treat patients in surgeries or *health centres* or at home, and will liaise with social and health services (particularly through district/community nurses) to address the needs of the client.
- *Day care* support takes place within a centre run by Social Services or by a health authority. The services vary, but usually there are meals, activities and other facilities such as bathing available. The *health authority* centres provide a range of medical services. Transport can also be arranged to these centres if necessary.
- Meals on Wheels provides cooked meals for the elderly and disabled in their homes. All clients pay a standard charge which may differ from area to area.
- *Macmillan nurses* support those who are suffering from *cancer* and wish to remain in their own homes. They are specially trained in cancer care.
- *Respite care* is offered in the form of a centre that takes elderly or ill people for a week or for a few days, so that the carer can have a break from his/her task.
- *Occupational therapists* provide support which includes assessment of the limitations of physical abilities, and organise appropriate aids, such as chair lifts, etc. They are also trained to help people work with their disabilities so that clients are able to become more independent. (See *aids and adaptations*.)

Community care – agenda for action: see *Griffiths Report*.

community care charters are documents which apply to key health, *housing* and social services. They form an essential part of effective *community care* which includes the *assessment* process. Such charters are developed locally to make sure services work well together to meet the needs of clients identified under community care *legislation*. Individual service providers have developed standards which are worked towards to ensure quality care. Working together is a means whereby the arrangements in caring for people can be linked to provide a co-ordinated service. (See *charter standards, Charter Mark.*)

Community Care (Direct Payments) Act 1996: an Act of Parliament which gives *local authorities* the power to give disabled people the relevant finance they need in order to buy their own health and social care services. The Act applies to England and Wales and there are corresponding procedures in Scotland and Northern Ireland. Local authorities have set up procedures under the Act which provide *advice* and *information* to clients with regard to their needs, requirements and appropriate care which they must have to support their daily living (HMSO 1996)[20].

Community Care (Residential Accommodation) Act 1998: an Act of Parliament which allows elderly people the right to savings of £16,000. Local Authorities must start paying residential costs when savings begin to fall below that amount. (HMSO 1998)[21]

community care plan: produced annually by *social services departments* stating how community care is implemented in their areas over a three year period. The need for such a plan was a recommendation of the *NHS and Community Care Act 1990.* These plans show how community care services are developed, co-ordinated and provided within a particular geographical/local authority area. Since 1992 (following the NHS and Community Care Act) all *local authorities* are required to publish community care plans annually. A community care plan may include:

- the aims and objective of the plan
- community care needs and requirements
- resourcing of the different agencies involved
- the identified care i.e. care which is necessary, for different client groups such as *elderly* people, clients with physical and *learning disabilities, mental health, drug* and *alcohol* misuse, *domestic violence* and clients with *HIV/AIDS.*

There is a separate community care plan for children.

community drug team: a team of professionals who work in a local area giving advice and information regarding the dangers of drug misuse as well as visiting schools and youth clubs, running workshops and giving talks.

Community Health Council: an independent body which monitors the services commissioned by the *health authorities.* It represents the views of Health Service *clients, patients* and *service users.* (See *Association for Community Health Councils.*)

community health services are provided for people wherever they are, in homes, *schools, clinics* and on the streets. Examples are *health visiting,* school nursing, *chiropody,* speech and *language* therapy. Services such as community nursing, psychiatric nursing and *physiotherapy* can enable people with short- or long-term illness or disability to be cared for in their own homes.

community midwife: a qualified professional whose main role is to care for women through *pregnancy* and up to 28 days after the *birth.* They work closely with *GPs* and *health visitors* in providing *health promotion* advice to expectant mothers. (See *midwifery.*)

community service order: a legal requirement under the Criminal Justice Act 1991. It requires that an offender over the age of 16 years carries out unpaid supervised work for any period between 40 and 240 hours. The service is usually completed within 12 months of the order being imposed.

community nurse: see *district nurse.*

community work involves the tasks and activities which explore and review the needs of a local community. It includes:

- encouraging members of the community to act together to confront and deal with problems or difficulties as they arise
- stimulating neighbourhoods to form groups and provide self-help
- co-ordination and liaison between groups which can be *voluntary groups, support groups* for *informal carers.*

In addition to this, community work looks at improving the *quality of life* of those individuals who live in the local *community* or neighbourhood. (See *community action, pressure groups.*)

companion: a term used in NVQs in Care to signify a relative, partner, friend, carer or individual who accompanies an individual during an activity. This activity may be an assessment or may involve accompanying a client who is attending an appointment for a course of treatment. (See *escort.*) (Care Sector Consortium 1998)[12]

complaints and complaints procedures: a complaints procedure is a formal way in which a *service user* can make a complaint, i.e. to voice a grievance or concern about medical treatment or social service. Within the procedure there are usually requirements for each health or social care provision to respond to that complaint. A complaint procedure requires the following:

- the complaint should be made in writing and each of the issues must be addressed
- a named member of staff is designated to deal with complaints
- a clear timescale is laid down for any complaint to be carefully examined
- a complaints committee is set up to hear the complaint; an independent member should be present at the hearing
- a method of responding to the complaint is formulated.

complementary medicine: treatments or therapies which work alongside conventional medical care. Appropriate techniques may be selected which relate to the patient's physical, mental, spiritual and emotional needs. Complementary medicine adds another dimension to the healing and treatment of *disease* (see *holistic care*). In using complementary medicine individuals recognise that they have a crucial part to play in their treatment. There are different types of complementary medicine such as:

- eastern therapies – *acupuncture, acupressure*
- massage and touch – *massage, aromatherapy, reflexology*
- mobility and posture – *chiropractic, osteopathy*
- natural healing – *homeopathy*
- *nutrition* and diet – *diet* therapies, *naturopathy.*

(For further information contact the Institute for Complementary Medicine, 21 Portland Place, London W1N 3AF.)

compounds: two or more different *elements* chemically bonded together. Examples of compounds within the human body are *water, carbohydrates, lipids, proteins* and *vitamins.*

compulsory admission to hospital: legal procedures employed under the *Mental Health Act 1983* to admit a person to *hospital.* The person may be suffering from a *mental disorder* and can be detained in hospital for up to 28 days for their own health and *safety* and/or the safety of others.

compulsory competitive tendering: a statutory requirement that *local authorities* should put specified services out to tender. This means that services are offered on the *contract* market so that private organisations can compete for the business. This is a way of opening up local authority services to the private sector. In 1989 the Local Government Act extended the services which were subject to competitive tendering to include cleaning, catering and the management of leisure facilities.

computer axial tomography (CAT scanning): a method of diagnosing *disease* using radiology to examine the soft tissues of the body. *X-rays* scan the body and view the differences in tissue density. The computer then constructs on a screen cross-sectional images of what is being examined. *Tumours*, abscesses and other types of disease can be seen, diagnosed and treated with the aid of such visualisation. (See *magnetic resonance imaging.*)

conception is the biological process which involves an egg being fertilised by a sperm so that it then becomes implanted in the wall of the *womb* or *uterus.* (See *fertilisation.*)

conciliation: a service which is offered to couples who are considering separation or *divorce.* The *Court Welfare Service* gives assistance and support to this as a means whereby couples can discuss their problems either for the purpose of reconciliation or to form a working relationship which should prove a positive aspect of post divorce care for their children.

confidence building is a method in which the *carer* can help a *client* to feel more positive about themselves. This can take the form of:

- attention – the client feels that a carer is taking time to be with them
- praise – when a carer says 'well done' for a task achieved
- *listening* – the client feels a sense of self-worth when a carer takes time to listen
- seeking client opinions – the client feels that their opinion is valued
- *decision making* – the client gains a sense of independence when they are able to make decisions
- creating a positive environment, enabling the client to feel at home, safe, happy and positive about themselves.

(See *care value base, care – principles of good practice.*)

confidentiality: respect for the privacy of any *information* about a *client.* It is one of the principles which underpins all health and social care practice. It is supported by legislation such as the *Access to Medical Records Act 1988, Access to Personal Files Act 1987, Data Protection Act 1984.* (See *care value base, care – principles of good practice, codes of practice.*)

congenital disorders: *disorders* which are present at *birth*, e.g. congenital dislocation of the hip.

connective tissues are *tissues* which connect tissues and *organs,* protect and support organs and allow movement between the different organs. Connective tissue consists of *cells* supported in a fluid or semi-fluid substance called matrix which is produced by the tissue cells. There are different types of connective tissue:

- Areolar connective tissue – found all over the body: beneath the skin, connecting organs together and filling the spaces between organs. This tissue consists of a transparent semi-fluid matrix containing fibres and cells. There are two types of fibre: unbranched flexible, strong, non-stretchable white collagen fibres which occur in bundles and a loose network of yellow elastin stretchable fibres. The cells include the fibroblasts which produce fibres, mast cells which secrete an anti-coagulant, fat-filled cells and phagocytic histocytes which are important in defending the body against disease.
- *Fibrous* connective tissue – There are two types of fibrous tissue. White fibrous tissue consists almost entirely of closely packed, white collagen fibres. The bundles of white fibres are bound together by areolar tissue. Such tissue is found where strength with limited flexibility is required (e.g. tendons which attach muscles to bone). Yellow elastic tissue consists mainly of yellow elastic fibres. It is found where strength with great elasticity is required (e.g. *ligaments,* which join bones). This tissue is also found in the walls of *arteries* and in the bronchioles.
- Adipose tissue – areolar tissue with a matrix of closely-packed fat-filled cells. It is important for storage. It is found in the dermis of the skin where it prevents heat loss, above the kidneys and in older people around the heart.
- Skeletal *cartilage* tissue – tissue which contains cartilage cells called chrondroblasts. Cartilage is found at the end of bones, in the spine and in the walls of the windpipe. Skeletal tissue has more solid matrix.
- Bone – tissue which consists of cells supported in a solid matrix containing calcium, phosphate, carbonate and *fluoride* minerals.

consciousness: a state of being fully awake, alert and aware of the surrounding environment. Consciousness is controlled by the nervous system which co-ordinates the functions of all the body systems. When a person is involved in an *accident* or is injured in some way, he or she may lose consciousness and become *unconscious.* (See *AVPU Code, coma.*)

consent: the agreement of a client to treatment or therapy. There are different ways of obtaining consent:

- oral consent – the client gives their spoken agreement.
- written consent – the client gives consent in writing
- informed consent – information given to the client enables them to come to a decision
- capacity to give consent – when a person has the ability to give consent and no-one else is allowed to withdraw that consent
- consent for minors – consent for children under the age of 16 years is given by a parent or guardian.

consent form: a method of recording the agreement to, or the giving of, *consent.*

Consumers' Association: an independent, non-party-political, non-profit-making, information-distributing organisation. It was set up in 1957 and its income comes from magazine subscriptions, from the sale of publications and from research carried out for non-trading organisations. The Consumers' Association is a research organisation which tests and investigates goods and services and reports on them in its magazines *Which?*, *Holiday Which?*, *Gardening from Which?* and in books or through the media. The Consumers' Association also campaigns on a wide range of public interest issues which affect consumers, including *safety*, fair trading and professional standards, and works to ensure that the provision of goods and services is in the consumer's interest.

Contact a Family: a national *charity* which offers support to any parent or professional who is caring for a child with *special needs.* This support is offered through a *network* of local, national and *self-help groups* which offer *advice.* (See *children with disabilities.*)

(For further information Contact a Family, 170 Tottenham Court Road, London W1P 0HA.)

contact order: a term used under the *Children Act 1989* which sets out the contact between the child and another person. It covers visits, stays, outings and *communication* by letter and telephone. Under section 34 of the Act, a *local authority* is under a duty to require a child in care, reasonable contact with a number of persons, including the child's parents. (See *Working together under the Children Act 1989.*)

contact tracing: methods used to find out the number of people with whom a person has had contact. This occurs when a person has contracted an infectious *disease.* To avoid the disease spreading to others, the *doctor* or health worker may ask the person concerned who their contacts were. Contact tracing is used in cases of *HIV*, *sexually transmitted diseases* and other potentially fatal infections.

contagious diseases: those *diseases* which are transmitted from one person to another. Examples include influenza and impetigo, a *skin* infection which is contracted by others when the infectious part of the body is touched.

content analysis is a research method. Researchers define a set of categories and then classify various materials in terms of the frequency with which they appear in the different categories. Content analysis involves a systematic study of different sources of material such as government reports, photographs and biographies relating to the issues which form the common themes or categories relevant to the *research.* For example, research into *child abuse* using content analysis may consider categories such as *race, class,* and *gender.* In this way the researcher would be able to determine the different type of perpetrator or child abuser and details of the child and their background.

continuum of care: a *care* service which is continuous, each part blending smoothly with others (a seamless service). *Clients* experiencing a continuum of care should feel that each service works together to meet their different health and social care needs. This can involve:

- care at home such as *domiciliary care*
- care in a *residential home*

- care from home, such as visiting a *day centre* or *hospital* clinic
- transport may also be provided.

(See *multi disciplinary teams*.)

contraceptives are methods used to prevent *conception* (see table on facing page). They are an important aspect of a sexual relationship where an unwanted *pregnancy* may cause *stress* and other problems. The use of a condom is also an effective means of preventing sexually transmitted diseases such as gonorrhoea and HIV. (See Table opposite.)

contrast media techniques are methods used to give more detailed information on *X-ray* examination. They involve injecting a radio-opaque dye into the appropriate part of the body. This outlines any space or soft tissue. There are different techniques used on different parts of the body. Examples of contrast media techniques are *angiograms*, which investigate *blood* vessels and barium meals which help visualise the digestive tract.

contribute to: a term in the care *occupational standards* used when the care worker is acting as part of a team. The team has a collective responsibility for the achievement of an outcome. When 'contribute to' is used in the *occupational standard* this means that the worker can influence the achievement of an outcome but cannot take full responsibility for it. This is clearly defined in the NVQs in Care. (Care Sector Consortium 1998)[12]

control of substances hazardous to health (COSHH) 1993: regulations set up by the Health and Safety Commission which require all employers to carry out a *risk assessment* with regard to hazard and risk. A hazard can be any item, piece of equipment, chemical or biological agent which has the potential to cause harm. Risk is any harm which is likely to be caused by a hazard. For example, an unlocked cupboard containing cleaning materials in a day nursery could be assessed as a risk, because children could open the cupboard and interfere with the *chemicals*. The risk assessment procedures need to meet certain requirements:

- identifying any hazardous substance or equipment which is to be used or is being used in the workplace
- identifying those who use the substance or equipment
- evaluating any risk to the person or persons who use the substance/equipment and assessing any likely damage to health
- deciding on a procedure which will introduce systems of control when using the substance/equipment
- recording the risk assessment
- reviewing the risk assessment.

The *Health and Safety Commission* is responsible to the Health and Safety Inspectorate. Health and safety inspectors visit a workplace to check that the COSHH requirements are adhered to. (See *environmental health*.)

control systems of the body: the way in which different parts of the body are co-ordinated to perform different functions. *Communication* between the different parts is via the nervous system and/or chemical reactions brought about by the *hormones* of the *endocrine system*.

Examples of contraception

Method	Function	Advantages	Disadvantages
Combined pill (progesterone and oestrogen)	Prevents ovulation. Prevents womb lining build up. Increases mucus in cervix so prevents the sperm from entering the womb.	Reliable form of contraception. Reduces blood loss. Relieves period pain. Does not interrupt sexual intercourse.	Possible thrombosis. High blood pressure.
Male condom (There is a female condom)	Covers the penis and collects the semen, so it prevents sperm from entering the vagina.	Suitable for any person. Can protect the individual from contracting sexually trans- mitted disease including HIV.	Interrupts sexual intercourse.
Intrauterine device	A copper wire is inserted in the womb to make it unsuitable for embryo implantation.	Does not interfere with sexual intercourse.	Can cause heavy periods. Can lead to fertilisation of egg in Fallopian tube.
Spermicide	Cream, jelly or foaming tablet inserted high up in the vagina	Kills sperm.	Not reliable – should only be used with a condom.

controlled drugs: drugs which are included in the Misuse of Drugs Act 1971. (See *drugs and legislation*.)

convenience sampling or non-representative sampling: a *sampling* method where the researcher uses the subjects or number of people who are available and the most convenient. For example, a student studying Health and Social Care issues may choose a subject such as *drug misuse* and their sample group may be a number of students in their college or school.

conversational skills are ways in which individuals can use *language* to communicate with each other. They are a means by which a *carer* can:

- introduce themselves to a *client* or patient and get to know the client. Talking is a way of gaining relevant *information* such as address and health history.
- build rapport with clients by finding out their hobbies, interests and their favourite subjects, such as television 'soaps'.

- sustain a relationship, asking a client how they feel, or remembering previous conversations can be a way of introducing security and trust as the client feels that the carer has listened to them; reminding a client of positive and familiar topics can provide positive reinforcement and can build *self-esteem*.

It is important to remember that the art of conversation has to be learned and developed. *Questioning* should be structured in such a way that the client/patient does not feel intimidated or threatened.

The development of language and conversation is the way in which babies and young children learn to relate to the world in which they live. When language is delayed, or there is a speech impairment, other methods of making conversation are used such as *sign language, body language* and *gestures*. (See *communication, confidence building*.)

co-ordination: the way in which different parts of an organisation or the body work together in an efficient and organised manner. For example, the different changes in the *National Health Service* have led to the co-ordination of care through the *health authority*.

coping is the way in which individuals learn to live with *changes* occurring in their everyday lives. These changes can be predictable or unpredictable. *Change* can bring happiness or heartache to an individual's life. In order to cope with change people develop different strategies. These help them to understand themselves as they experience difficult and painful situations. *Coping* strategies can include:

- identifying the reactions, thoughts and feelings that the change is bringing to the surface
- being aware that change has happened and that there is something that can be done to support that change
- coming to terms with life after the change.

It is important to remember that different people cope with change in different ways. Some people may react with anger, frustration, depression and helplessness. Whatever the reaction, people going through change may need *support* and help.

There are different support methods available to help individuals cope. These include:

- family and friends and a *network* of support
- *counselling* using a professional agency
- support or *self-help* groups provide empathy and advice
- information services such as *Citizens Advice Bureaux*.

cornea: the transparent area at the front of the *eye*. The function of the cornea is to focus light onto the retina. When light rays pass from one medium to another with a different density they are bent. This process is called refraction. Refraction occurs in the eye when light rays pass from the air into the cornea and through the lens. The angle through which rays of light are bent by the cornea is always the same. This creates a potential problem because light rays from objects which are close to the eye need to be bent more if they are to be focused. Therefore the lens is able to change shape. It is the lens, therefore, which alters the amount of refraction, allowing both close and distant objects to be brought into focus on the retina. This process is called *accommodation*. The cornea consists of living cells which are supplied with nutrients (such as glucose) from the aqueous humour – a liquid which lies directly behind it.

There are medical conditions which can affect the cornea and so affect an individual's sight. Sight can be clouded or sometimes lost completely. Such problems can be treated by a corneal transplant where a small piece of cornea is transplanted from a donor.

coronary arteries are *blood* vessels which carry *oxygen* to the muscles of the *heart*.

coronary heart disease: disease affecting the *coronary arteries* which supply the muscle of the *heart*. When one of these arteries becomes blocked, the area of heart *muscle* that it supplies is deprived of *oxygen*. The muscle therefore dies and gives rise to what is known as a heart attack or a myocardial infarction. There are three main reasons why blockages occur in the coronary arteries:

- Atherosclerosis – this is due to the build-up of fatty material or *atheroma* in the lining of the artery wall. Eventually this material, along with fibrous tissue and calcium salts, forms hard plaques which lead to the narrowing of the lumen of the artery.
- Thrombosis – the presence of a *blood* clot in one of the coronary arteries. This is often associated with atheroma. It is thought that the blood clot forms when the surface of one of the plaques breaks away. The clot blocks the lumen of the artery.
- Spasm – the *muscle* in the wall of the coronary artery contracts and goes into a spasm. The reasons for this are not really understood but it again produces a narrowing of the lumen.

coroner: a medical practitioner or lawyer who has practised for at least five years. A coroner is the government official presiding at an inquest. An inquest is an official judicial enquiry set up to determine the cause of a person's death. It takes place when the death has been sudden or occurred under suspicious circumstances.

cost effectiveness: procedures which monitor and review how organisations work in terms of financial prudence and resourcing. Such procedures have been introduced into most public sector organisations over the last few years. Health and social care providers have to work within a framework of short- and long-term costings for different care packages. Professional *carers* work constantly against a backcloth of financial cuts in services and a reduction in staff, while having to implement changes in *legislation*.

cost improvement programmes: procedures in place which review spending. Health and social care organisations are encouraged to review their spending every year to assess how money has been spent and the quality of the service being offered. The programme is based on government plans for more efficiency and obtaining greater value for money. These cost improvement programmes are viewed as cost–benefit methods which will generate savings for new services. (See *cost effectiveness, funding*.)

cot death: see *Sudden Infant Death Syndrome*.

Council for Voluntary Services (CVS): the main bodies and charities which support the voluntary sector within a geographical area. These councils were set up in 1974, following a government report. The function of the CVS is to:

- develop the *voluntary* sector in a district or area
- recruit *volunteers*

- provide information about *voluntary organisations*
- provide *informal care* support
- train volunteers
- work with other voluntary organisations.

counselling: the process or interaction by which one person helps another person to help themselves. It is a way of relating and responding to another person so that they are helped to explore their thoughts, feelings and *behaviour*, in order to reach a clearer self-understanding. This enables the person to find and use their strengths and draw on their resources so that they can cope more effectively with their lives. Counselling has basic principles which are applied when a counsellor works with a client. These principles include providing:

- an opportunity for a *client* to work towards behaving in a more satisfying and resourceful way in dealing with a problem or difficult situation
- a voluntary service for the client
- an opportunity for the counsellor to clarify with the client the basis on which counselling is to be given
- the client with reassurance that their *rights* and decisions are respected
- the means whereby a counsellor may continue to monitor and develop their own skills, experience, resources and practice
- a service which ensures that counsellors are properly trained for their roles and are committed to maintaining their *competence*
- relevant support to counsellors so that they have regular and appropriate supervision/consultative support
- a *confidential* service so that all information which passes between counsellor and *client* is treated with discretion.

The British Association for Counselling is a national voice for counselling.

(For further information contact the British Association for Counselling, 1 Regent Place, Rugby, Warwickshire CV21 2PJ.)

court of appeal: part of the judicial system in England and Wales which reviews verdicts passed in the Courts. The person accused can appeal against their conviction or sentence if they feel it to be unfair. In the court of appeal other aspects of the case or any additional evidence may be put forward so that the conviction/sentence might be considered for withdrawal or reduction.

court or common law is the way in which the law is structured to take account of custom or practice or the accepted way of doing things within a particular country. The law relating to the 'duty of care' is based on the common law. Duty of care is the responsibility which people in society in general have to care for each other. However, in health and social care, carers have a statutory duty to care for their *clients/patients.*

court system of England and Wales: a judicial system set up to enforce law and order. The system includes tribunals, magistrates' courts, *juvenile courts, coroners courts,* county courts, Crown courts, *courts of appeal* and the High Court. In addition to this, the House of Lords and the *European Court of Human Rights* work within the court system to review appeals.

court welfare officer: a person appointed to provide a report for the court about a child and the child's family situation and background. The court welfare officer will usually be a *probation officer*. The court may request either the local authority or the court welfare officer to prepare a report. (See *Working Together under The Children Act 1989*.)

court welfare system: a structure set up within the *probation service* to manage family court work. *Court welfare officers* are probation officers, some with specific training in this field; they are involved in *family* work in three different types of court:

- family proceedings courts which involve work on cases closely related to family matters
- local court with magistrates dealing with family matters
- county and high court where judges decide the outcome of the cases.

Court welfare officers are frequently required to prepare welfare reports to assist judges and magistrates in their deliberations over the care of children when there are unresolved disputes between parents.

'crack' is a stimulant which is a form of *cocaine* usually smoked or mixed with *heroin* and injected.

creative play: a way in which children learn about the world around them. This involves exploring, experimenting and imagining. Creative *play* makes a major contribution to the way in which children develop. It reinforces the enjoyment and satisfaction that children achieve through making objects and through discovery. It is creative play that enables children to explore the function of materials and to find out how things work. This develops their senses and also encourages their fine motor skills and *hand/eye co-ordination*. Examples of creative play are painting, collage, sand play, water play and imaginative play or make believe.

crèche is a form of childcare provision which offers informal, short-term, group care for children while their parents attend courses or classes, or go shopping. If creches are provided for more than two hours a day or for more than six days a year, they must be registered with the *social services department* (*SSD*).

Creutzfeldt–Jakob Disease (CJD) or Bovine Spongiform Encephalopathy (BSE) are diseases which affect the brain. Spongiform lesions similar to those found in the brains of cattle with BSE (or 'mad cow disease') are found in human beings suffering from CJD. This has led to increased debate about the connection between eating beef and the onset of CJD. It has been discovered that CJD can be carried in the blood and, therefore, strict precautions must be taken with regard to *blood transfusions*. The government's Spongiform Encephalopathy Advisory Committee monitors any developments with regard to CJD and BSE.

crime involves breaking the legal codes set up in society and supported by the judicial system. This can include burglary, theft, violence and other acts against a person or their property. The criminal is the person who has carried out the crime. The victim is the person on the receiving end of the crime. People are often asked to declare any past criminal offences when they apply for employment within the health and social care sector (see *victim support*). Criminology is the study of crime and reviews its extent, and the nature of offenders within society.

Crime and Disorder Bill 1997: an Act of Parliament which makes provision for preventing crime and disorder. It created a framework to:

- deal with racially-aggravated offences
- abolish the rebuttable presumption that a child is '*doli incapax*', that is incapable of committing an offence
- make other changes to the *criminal justice system*
- make further provision for dealing with offenders
- make further provision with respect to remands and committals for trial and the release and recall of prisoners
- amend Chapter 1 of Part II of the Crime (Sentences) Act 1997 and to repeal Chapter 1 of Part III of the Crime and Punishment (Scotland) Act 1997. (HMSO 1997)[22]

crime prevention: procedures or methods used to educate the general public about ways of avoiding becoming victims of crime. For example, local *police* education officers work with *schools* and colleges and talk to pupils about crime. Local neighbourhoods may join together with the police to set up *neighbourhood watch schemes*. In this way local groups can take part in crime prevention by watching for any suspicious behaviour in the area.

Criminal Courts are courts which deal with people who break the criminal law. Criminal activity is harmful to society.

criminal justice system: a range of professional groups whose roles and responsibilities are to enforce law and order in society. Professionals involved in law and order include *police forces*, the *Probation Service*, *youth justice workers*, *Crown Prosecution Service* and *victim support*.

Criminal Justice and Public Order Act 1994: an Act of Parliament introduced to reinforce issues relating to Law and Order. These issues include:

- *Young offenders* – reviews *legislation* with regard to secure training orders, custodial sentences, secure accommodation, arrest and *police* detention of young persons.
- Bail – reviews the Bail Act 1976 with amendments to bail for those who are charged or convicted of murder or offend while on bail, and the police powers to grant conditional bail.
- *Court of Justice* (i.e. evidence and court procedure) reviews the way in which evidence is looked at with regard to imputations on character or corroboration, inferences from an accused's silence, juries, powers of magistrates' courts, sentencing, publication of reports, child testimony, intimidation and criminal appeals.
- Police powers – reviews the Police and Criminal Evidence Act 1984 and the powers of the police to take body samples and 'to stop and search'.
- Public Order – reviews the legislation with regard to trespassing by large groups such as those involved in raves, squatting and camping.
- Prevention of terrorism – extends the way in which the Courts and the police deal with matters related to terrorism.
- Obscenity, *pornography* and video recordings – reviews and updates the law with regard to obscene publications and indecent photographs of children,

video recording, obscene, offensive and annoying phone calls.

- Prison services.
- Sexual offences – reviews the acts of *rape*, buggery, *homosexuality* and revised penalties for such offences.

Certain aspects of this Act also apply to Scotland and Northern Ireland such as prisons and prisoner escorts. In Scotland, this amends the Prisoners and Criminal Proceedings (Scotland) Act 1993 (HMSO 1994)[23].

criminal proceedings: the way in which a person who is suspected of having committed a criminal offence is dealt with by the *Criminal Justice System*. This is a process which includes:

- arrest and charge by the police
- the different outcomes, either a police caution or prosecution
- if prosecution is imminent, the person may be placed on remand
- all criminal proceedings which start in the magistrates' court.

crisis: an episode in an individual's life which may be difficult to cope with. Examples include an *accident*, sudden *death*, redundancy, *unemployment*, diagnosis of illness or *abuse*. When the episode is found to be difficult or impossible to handle, then *voluntary* or *statutory* workers can support or organise a *routine* to help the individual involved. If a child or older person is seen to be vulnerable then *court orders* may have to be obtained.

Crown Prosecution Service: a government agency of lawyers who make the decision as to whether a case will be formally heard in court.

culture relates to a way of life. All societies have a culture or common way of life. A society's culture includes the following:

- *language* – the spoken word and verbal communication
- customs – *rights*, rituals, *religion* and *lifestyle*
- shared system of values – *beliefs* and morals
- social *norms* – patterns of behaviour which are accepted as normal and right (can include dress and diet).

The different cultures evident in society reflect the richness of cultural diversity, where they live and work together but retain their individual identity.

curfew order: a procedure introduced under the *Criminal Justice Act 1991*. It is a means whereby the Courts may require a young offender under the age of 16 years to remain in the same place for 2–12 hours a day for a defined period of time. The procedure is presently being reviewed by the government as a statutory requirement for children under 16 years.

curriculum vitae (cv): a summary of the main aspects of a person's previous experiences. A curriculum vitae may be used by individuals when they are applying for employment or voluntary work. There are usually four main areas covered in a cv:

- Personal data – name, address, telephone number, date of birth. This can also include place of birth, marital and family status and whether or not the applicant has a driving licence.
- Education and training – the level of education, including the names of schools and colleges attended with dates and a list of qualifications gained.

Any further training courses attended should be included, with details of certificates or diplomas achieved, written in chronological order putting the most recent qualifications first.

- Work experience – name and details of previous employers with dates of employment. There should be a list of each job held with details of the skills and abilities required to carry them out, and wherever appropriate the level of responsibility attained and a description of any specialist achievements and skills.

- Leisure activities – general interests and positions held (e.g. club secretary, youth club leader, membership of any groups). Any particular skills that have been acquired through leisure activities can also be mentioned here.

cystic fibrosis: a *genetic disorder* affecting children. It leads to the *exocrine glands* becoming defective. The production of thick mucus obstructs the intestinal glands including the pancreas and the bronchi. *Signs and symptoms* of the disease include *failure to thrive*, weight loss, coughing and a gradual deterioration of the *respiratory system*. Some children display the symptoms at birth, while others may not develop symptoms for weeks or even years. Cystic fibrosis is progressive and incurable. It can be detected through the 'sweat test' when a sample of the child's sweat is analysed.

(For further information contact the Cystic Fibrosis Trust, Alexandra House, 5 Blyth Road, Bromley, Kent BR1 3RS.)

cytotoxic drugs are used to combat and treat malignant disease such as *cancer*. Such drugs inhibit cancer cells by slowing down cancer cell division. However, they can also have harmful side effects such as damaging and destroying white blood cell growth. Some patients may also suffer from hair loss, baldness, vomiting and sickness as a result of the treatment. Use of such drugs should be carefully monitored. (See *chemotherapy*.)

D

data: facts and information collected by a researcher during a course of study. Data can be *qualitative* or *quantitative*. Qualitative data is descriptive and is often about attitudes, beliefs or feelings. Quantitative data is measurable and is expressed in numerical form.

data analysis: the methods used to examine *data* which has been collected by a researcher. The results are sometimes compared with other *research*.

data collection is the way in which researchers gather the *information* necessary to support their *research*. The researcher decides whether the data will be *quantitative* or *qualitative* or a combination of both. To collect the data a representative sample of the population is usually selected. Careful *sampling* is crucial to the research findings, particularly if they are to be applied to the population as a whole.

Data Protection Act 1984: an Act of Parliament giving people the right to access *information* regarding their personal records, which is being stored on a computer. (See *access to information*.) The main points of the Act include:

- data users must register the fact that they have information about living individuals, or from which individuals can be identified, with the Register of Data Protection
- data must be collected, stored, processed and disclosed only in accordance with specified data protection principles
- *data* subjects (i.e. living individuals) have the right to view the Register, and apply to view the data of any user who may have personal data about them held on computer. Such information must be revealed within 40 days of the request, in a form easily understandable to a layman
- under certain circumstances the data subject will have the right to correct inaccurate information, request erasure, and receive compensation for any loss suffered due to incorrect data
- the creation of the Registrar of Data Protection, and a new Data Protection Tribunal (similar to an industrial tribunal) for the resolution of disputes. (HMSO 1984)[25].

(See also *information technology*.)

day care is the provision which is available to young children, *elderly people* and the disabled during the day. In day-care, the physical, emotional, social, intellectual and cultural needs of the *client* are supported. *Carers* are available to supervise and support the clients as their individual needs arise. Examples of day care are *day nurseries*, *playgroups* and *day centres*.

day centre: a care setting which people can attend between one and five days a week. The centre provides:

- meals and snacks
- *leisure* and recreation
- supervised care activities

- *respite care* for carers
- opportunities to meet and socialise with others.

Day centres are a valuable means of support for clients with physical, mental and *learning disabilities*, for *elderly people* and for *families* in need of support and care. Day centres can be *statutory, voluntary* or *private* provision.

day nurseries provide full- or part-time day-care for children up to five years of age. Only a few nurseries take children under six months. Day nurseries are staffed by trained *nursery nurses*, some of whom have additional *social work* qualifications. Private and council day nurseries must conform to national and *local authority* standards, and be registered and inspected by the *social services department* every year.

day surgery is the provision offered by a *hospital* or health centre which involves treating a *patient* within a single day. Patients are admitted for an operation and return home the same day. Day surgery is a cheaper form of treatment than longer term admission to hospital.

deafness or hearing impairment is the temporary or permanent loss of hearing which can occur in one or both *ears*. The updated term for deafness is hearing impairment. Temporary deafness can be caused by an ear infection or a build-up of wax in the external canal. Permanent deafness is usually caused by damage to the ear, the *auditory nerve* or the hearing centre in the *brain*. Deafness can be:

- total – which means that no sounds can be heard
- partial – which means some sounds can be heard but not others; it is often difficult for sufferers to understand what others are saying.

The nature of deafness may vary as follows:

- Outer ear deafness – usually caused by a build up of wax which blocks the ear canal or when a bead or small object has been pushed into the ear blocking out sound waves.
- Middle ear deafness – repeated infection damages the middle ear. The minute ear bones or ossicles become stuck together. This is termed 'glue ear'. The sound waves no longer cause the ear ossicles to vibrate and sound impulses are not transmitted to the brain.
- Inner ear deafness – is due to damage to the cells in the cochlea. This inhibits the conversion of vibration into sound impulses.

Damage to the auditory nerve can also cause deafness.

death is the result of the total shutdown in the systems of the body. The number of deaths per year is measured and compared locally, nationally and globally. These are called *mortality rates*. Mortality rates are usually recorded in an HMSO publication 'The Social Trend', or are provided by the *World Health Organisation. Local authorities* keep their own local mortality rate records. *Infant mortality rates* are the number of deaths of babies under one year old in a given year as a proportion of the number of babies born that year × 1000. A death certificate is issued after death, following a medical examination of the body.

death rate is the number of deaths per year per 1000 people in the population. Age-specific death rate is the number of deaths of people within a specified *age* range per year per 1000 people in that age range. This is termed the crude death rate.

decision making: a process which involves the *client* or *patient* discussing their treatment and *care* with their professional *carers*. This relates closely to *consent*. It should be acknowledged that the *client, patient* or *service user* has the individual right to make a decision with regard to their care. (See *care value base, autonomy*.)

defaecation: the expulsion through the *anus* of human waste matter or *faeces* which have been stored in the rectum.

defence mechanisms: unconscious strategies that protect the conscious mind from *anxiety*. According to Freudian theory, defence mechanisms invoke a distortion of reality in some way so that we are better able to cope with a situation. There are different mechanisms including displacement, projection, identification and repression. (See also *Freud*.)

Defence mechanism	Behaviour
Identification	Person unconsciously copies the behaviour, or lifestyle of a person she/he secretly envies.
Repression	A person may repress a negative feeling from their consciousness, if this causes anxiety then they will choose to ignore the situation. They may forget to go for a cervical smear check up because they do not want to think about the implications of the smear results if they are not negative.
Projection	A person blames everybody else, the place where they work or management system. This is a way of covering over their own inadequacies.
Displacement	When a person is annoyed or frustrated by a situation they will often take this out on someone else. The actual feelings are displaced into an inappropriate situation.

deficiency diseases are the result of a person not eating a healthy and varied *diet*. Deficiency diseases cannot be transmitted to other individuals and can usually be cured by adding the missing substance to the diet. A *vitamin* deficiency disease is one which develops as a result of a shortage of vitamins. A person who lacks vitamin C may develop scurvy; scurvy can be cured by eating oranges which contain vitamin C.

degenerative disease: a *disease* or illness which affects the body in such a way that it causes physical or psychological deterioration which cannot be rectified. An example of a degenerative disease is *Parkinson's disease*.

dehydration: the loss of fluid or *water* from the body. This can have serious side effects. Dehydration occurs when an individual has lost more water than he/she has taken in through *food* and drink. This may happen if they have:

- a severe *infectious disease* which causes sweating and vomiting
- drunk a large amount of *alcohol*
- taken vigorous exercise
- spent time in a hot and dry environment without drinking.

When dehydration occurs the fluid must be replaced as soon as possible. This can be done by giving the person a mixture of 1 teaspoon of salt and 8 teaspoons of sugar to 1 litre of water. This replaces the water and mineral loss through sweating, vomiting or diarrhoea. *Medicines* such as Dioralyte can be bought over the chemist's counter to produce the same effect. In severe cases, a person may be admitted to hospital and given extra fluids by intravenous infusion or drip.

dementia: a range of illnesses involving the *degeneration* of the *brain*. This can lead to a serious decline in mental faculties including loss of *memory*. There are a number of different types of dementia, but the most common are:

- cortical dementia – memory impairment, personality changes, loss of speech (e.g. *Alzheimer's disease*)
- sub-cortical dementia – memory impairment, personality deterioration which can result in degeneration of cognition, emotion and movement. (e.g. *Huntington's chorea.*)

There are different methods of treatment for dementia, and the process of diagnosis forms an important part of how the *patient/client* will be treated. If the dementia is due to some underlying disease such as *HIV/AIDS*, or a *brain* tumour, then these conditions will be treated. However, if there is no apparent cause for the dementia then the level of the dementia itself will be assessed. *Drugs* such as neurotransmitters are the main type of treatment for dementias. It is important to remember that dementia is not part of normal ageing. Most elderly people show no signs of dementia.

(For further information contact The Dementia Relief Trust, Pegasus House, 37–43 Sackville Street, London W1X 2DL.) (See *Admiral Nurse Service.*)

demographic trends: information about the way in which society is changing. Government bodies review statistics so that they can construct social policies relevant to the needs of the population. For instance, the rising number of *elderly people* in the population is an indicator of the increasing need for health and social care provision for the elderly. Examples of different types of demographic trends are:

- *age* profiles – *birth* and *death* rates, numbers of children, elderly people etc.
- the geographical distribution of the population, for example the numbers of people who live in towns, cities or in rural areas
- patterns of *health* and *disease*, for example the numbers of people who suffer from different diseases, children who suffer from different types of *infectious disease*, the number of cases of *meningitis* which are reported in geographical areas
- *ethnicity* – the different ethnic groups which make up society such as Chinese, Welsh, Afro-Caribbean
- *social and economic groups*, for example, the unemployed, persons on *benefit*, *lone parents.*

Demographic trends are based on local, regional, national and global statistics.

demography: the study of population, especially with reference to distribution and size. The *information* or *data* on which the study of demography is based is obtained by *census*. The registration of *births*, marriages and *deaths* also provides a continuous flow of information. Demography is a useful tool for those delivering and administering services, both at national and local level as it enables them to predict and plan for future needs in society. For example, the white paper *The New NHS – Modern, Dependable 1997* states that 'over the next decade the NHS expects to provide services for an extra 100,000 people over the age of 85 years: but this is just one-third of the increase that it has coped with over the last decade'. (HMSO 1997)[61]

denial is a common type of *coping* mechanism. It is a way in which people manage different events, circumstances and situations in their lives. Denial is a mechanism often used in the following circumstances:

- *death* of a family member or friend
- news of *terminal illness*
- *redundancy*
- sudden incident or *accident.*

In order to cope with a situation the person tries to ignore or refuse to believe what is happening. To deny the occurrence of an event can make the situation unreal. It is part of the process of *grief* and the person needs support to accept what is happening and to work through the different dimensions of the incident and its impact on their relationship with others.

dentists: professionals who treat the *teeth* and gums. They also promote dental health and oral hygiene. Dentists work in their own practices or in *hospitals*

- as orthodonists giving specialist advice on straightening teeth
- on oral and maxillafacial surgery, correcting facial defects as well as damaged features, resulting from accidents and disease to jaw and face
- for the community dental service – providing a service to young children, expectant mothers and people with special needs.

Dentists either work in the National Health Service or in private practice. Dentists qualify as Bachelors of Dental Surgery after training which takes five years.

There are other careers within dental health, including technicians who make dental appliances, therapists and hygienists who advise people on how to look after their teeth and gums and dental *nurses* who work with dentists in hospitals and private practice. Such nurses prepare fillings and dressings, pass instruments to the dentist and generally attend to patients.

deoxyribonucleic acid (DNA): a nucleic acid mainly found in the *chromosome* of cells. It is the hereditary material of all organisms except some viruses. DNA can be extracted from small samples of tissue and examined (DNA 'fingerprinting'). Such testing is used in situations such as:

- solving crime, through forensic science investigations – fingerprints or body fluids are often left at the scene of a crime, and are unique to a given individual
- detecting inherited diseases, where signs and symptoms have not appeared – DNA profiles can sometimes identify those members of the family who have inherited a given disease (this method may be used in forecasting the occurrence of the disease in a family)
- monitoring bone-marrow transplants – DNA fingerprinting can predict whether new bone-marrow is likely to be accepted or rejected
- revealing family links – DNA can indicate whether claimants are part of a given family.

Department of Health: the central government body responsible for the administration of health and social care. It is presided over by the Secretary of State for Health. Under the White Paper *The New NHS – Modern, Dependable 1997,* the

Department of Health and, within it, the NHS Executive, shoulders responsibility for action needed at a national level. It integrates health and social services policy to give a national lead. It also works with the clinical professions to develop *national service frameworks*, linked to action to be implemented across the NHS. For the first time, there will be an annual survey to allow systematic comparisons of the experience of patients and their carers over time, and between different parts of the country. A new *NHS Charter* sets out rights and responsibilities for patients. The *Secretary of State* has reserve powers to intervene where *health authorities, primary care groups* and *NHS trusts* are failing.

Department of Health and Social Services Northern Ireland: the department responsible for health, social services and social security in Northern Ireland. The department co-ordinates the different services in association with four boards. A junior minister is responsible for this department and he or she reports to the Secretary of State for Northern Ireland.

Department of Social Security (DSS): the central government department responsible for policies with regard to welfare benefits and how they are distributed to clients. All DSS areas have customer services managers who supervise the provision of advice to either claimants (or someone acting on their behalf) on *benefits* and on how to make claims. (See *benefits agency*.)

dependency ratio: the proportion within a population of those under 15 years and over 65 years to those between 16 and 65 years (i.e. of working age). Those under 15 make up the 'young dependants', and those over 65 the 'elderly dependants'. Together they are referred to as the 'dependent population'. (See *demography*.)

dependant: a person who relies on another person for physical, social, emotional, intellectual or economic support. For example, a child or young person under the age of 16 years is dependent upon his or her parents or primary care giver.

depression is a nervous disorder. Depression may be indicated by the loss of social and emotional functioning which can either be biologically based (endogenous depression) or related to life events (reactive depression). Those with depression experience a feeling of sadness, worthlessness and guilt. They find the challenge of living overwhelming. Depression is probably the most widespread of mental disorders affecting 1 in 20 people. (See *mental health disorder*.)

designated senior professionals: qualified persons such as senior *doctors* and *nurses* who co-ordinate *child protection* policy procedures within the *health authority*, *schools* and other health and social care organisations. (See *Working together under the Children Act 1989*.)

desirable learning outcomes have been developed by the School Curriculum and Assessment Authority. They set out important areas of learning for young children which early years providers should be aiming to achieve. The outcomes provide national standards for early years education. They emphasise personal, social, physical and creative development, langage and literacy, knowledge and understanding of the world. They are designed to provide a robust first step towards the *National Curriculum* (HMSO 1997)[31]. (See *Qualifications and Curriculum Authority*.)

devaluing: having a fixed attitude which *stereotypes* views and *beliefs* held by others as being of no importance, for example, disregarding a person because of their *culture*, their religious belief or their personal *lifestyle*.

developmental norms: the average or typical skills and *behaviours* that might be present in a child of a particular *age*. These are established by studying large numbers of children of the same age.

developmental tests: see *child health surveillance programmes*.

deviance: a person's *behaviour* which breaks the rules of normal conduct and norms of behaviour within a particular social group. Deviance very much relies on the concept of majority rule, i.e. the way that most people behave in a group. For example, most *nurses* wear a uniform when working on a hospital ward. If one nurse chooses to work on the ward in shorts and T-shirt this would be viewed as deviant behaviour. However, deviance is a relative term which can change from time to time and from place to place.

diabetes mellitus is a condition in which the amount of glucose in the body cannot be properly controlled. Glucose comes from the *digestion* of starchy foods such as bread or potatoes and sugary foods, and from the *liver*. Glucose levels are controlled by insulin, a hormone produced in the *pancreas* which lowers such levels by converting glucose into glycogen which is then stored in the liver. The main symptoms of untreated diabetes are thirst, the passage of large amounts of *urine*, extreme tiredness, weight loss, genital itching and blurred vision. The main aim of treatment is to restore near normal *blood* glucose levels. Together with a healthy *lifestyle* this will help improve well-being and protect against long-term damage to the *eyes, kidneys, nerves, heart* and major *arteries*. There are two different types of diabetes mellitus:

- Type 1 is insulin-dependent diabetes. This develops when there has been a severe lack of insulin in the body because most of the pancreatic cells which manufacture insulin have been destroyed. This type of diabetes usually appears before the age of 40 years. The cause is not known but viruses may play a part. It is treated with insulin replacement and diet.
- Type 2 develops when the body can still make some insulin, though not enough for its needs, or when the insulin that the body does make is not used properly. This type of diabetes usually appears in people over the age of 40 years. It is most common among the elderly and overweight. The tendency to develop this form of diabetes may be passed from one generation to the next. It is usually treated by diet alone. It is estimated that between 75 per cent and 90 per cent of people with diabetes are Type 2 dependent. Between 1,035,000 and 1,242,000 (around 3 per cent) of the UK's population have diabetes.

(For further information contact the British Diabetic Association, 10 Queen Anne Street, London W1M OBD.)

diaphragm: a thin, tough sheet of *muscle* and fibrous *tissue* which separates the trunk of the body into two parts. The upper part is called the thorax (chest) and contains the *heart* and *lungs*, while the lower part is called the abdomen and contains the main organs of *digestion, excretion* and *reproduction*.

diarrhoea: loose and watery stools forming part of the *faeces*. When a person suffers from diarrhoea they pass frequent watery stools. *Babies* with diarrhoea may quickly suffer *dehydration* because the fluid lost is greater than the amount of fluid which they are taking in.

diet: the amount and type of *food* and drink which is regularly consumed. A person's diet will often depend on:

- the different types of food available
- cultural and religious influences
- personal preference
- how physically active a person is
- the amount of money available to spend on food.

A *balanced diet* is one which contains the appropriate amount of all the essential nutrients, i.e. *carbohydrates, fats, protein, vitamins, minerals* and fibre.

dietary reference value (DRV): dietary standards which refer to different *foods* and *nutrients*. This also includes the estimated average requirements (EAR) in the diet. (See *Committee on Medical Aspects of Food Policy*.)

dieticians are trained professionals who advise others with regard to *food* and *nutrition*. Their special skill is to translate scientific and medical knowledge relating to food and health into terms which everyone can understand. Dieticians, as part of a team, care for people in *hospital* or in the community. They also work to promote good health by teaching the public and other health professionals about *diet* and nutrition. Qualified dieticians join the British Dietetic Association following a recognised degree or two year post graduate diploma. Degree courses in dietetics, which include state registration, last four years.

(For further information contact the British Dietetic Association, 7th Floor, Elizabeth House, 22 Suffolk Street, Queensway, Birmingham B1 1LS.)

differential growth rate: this measures how different parts of the body grow and develop at different times and rates. For example, the *nervous system* grows rapidly in the first few years of life, the reproductive organs hardly grow until *puberty*, while general bodily growth occurs steadily throughout childhood. (See *centile charts*.)

diffusion: the movement of substances, molecules or ions from where they are high in concentration to where they are in lower concentration. It is an important means of transport of substances through *cell* surface membranes. The rate at which substances move in and out of cells can be affected by a number of factors such as:

- *temperature*
- surface area of the membrane
- difference in concentration on either side of the membrane
- thickness of the membrane.

An example of diffusion can be seen in the way that *oxygen* is passed from the alveoli to the blood in the capillaries of the *lungs*.

Food and *oxygen* move by diffusion from the *blood* or *tissue* fluid into the cells. *Carbon dioxide* and other waste materials diffuse in the opposite direction from the cells into the blood. Therefore an exchange of materials takes place.

digestion: a process which breaks down *food* from a solid form. Large molecules of food are broken down into soluble matter so that they can be absorbed into the bloodstream for transport to different parts of the body. The *digestive system* is responsible for the process which begins as soon as food enters the mouth. Food then proceeds through the *oesophagus* to the stomach, into the *duodenum,* the rest of the small intestine, the large intestine, the rectum and out through the anus. During digestion, food is broken down by both physical (including mechanical) and chemical means.

digestive system: a tube which extends from the *mouth* through the body to the anal canal. It is responsible for passing *food* from one end of the body to the other. The main parts of the digestive system include:

- *Mouth* – food is introduced into the mouth and chewed by the teeth which break it down and mix it with saliva. *Enzymes* in the saliva start breaking down starch. The taste buds on the *tongue* ensure that food is enjoyed but they can also give the person warning of anything which is unpleasant or harmful to the body. The tongue rolls the food into a bolus and pushes it to the back of the throat where it is swallowed and enters the *oesophagus.*
- Oesophagus – this is a long muscular tube which links the back of the throat to the *stomach.* The movement of food through the oesophagus is by *peristalsis* which enables the food to be pushed down into the stomach.
- Stomach – the stomach is a muscular pouch which acts as a reservoir for food collection. Food is stored in the stomach and after a period of time the muscular activity of the stomach churns up the food and mixes it with gastric secretions. These consist of mucus, hydrochloric acid and the enzyme precursor pepsinogen. The pepsinogen is converted into pepsin which then begins to break down the proteins. Hydrochloric acid is responsible for activating pepsinogen and also kills any harmful bacteria which may have been swallowed with the food. The mucus which is mixed with the food lubricates it. The food passes from the stomach to the duodenum, through the pyloric sphincter, in a liquid form called chyme.
- Duodenum – this is the first part of the small intestine which is C shaped and is approximately 20 cm long. The chyme goes into the duodenum where digestive juices from the *pancreas* are secreted on to the partly digested food. *Bile* is sent from the *liver* to break down (emulsify) fat into smaller droplets.
- Ileum – the food passes on into the ileum where further enzymes are secreted from the intestine wall to complete the conversion of all *carbohydrates* to sugar, all *proteins* to *amino acids* and all fats to *fatty acids* and glycerol. Absorption of food takes place in the small intestine, although a small amount of water, glucose, alcohol and other substances which do not need to be broken down further may be absorbed in the stomach. The wall of the small intestine provides a large surface area through which *absorption* takes place. From the small intestine the food is passed into the colon.
- Colon – the colon (large intestine) is the final part of the muscular tube which carries semi-liquid digested food or chyme. Here 90 per cent of the remaining water is absorbed from the chyme and the semi-solid faeces remain. When the lower part of the colon (the rectum) is full of faeces

pressure is put on the walls of the rectum which contain nerve endings. These send messages to the brain which inform the person that they need to open their bowels. The food is passed out through the anus, an opening at the end of the rectum which is controlled by a ring of muscle called the anal sphincter.

It is necessary for health and social care workers to have a basic understanding of how the digestive system works. For example, when helping elderly clients or children with toileting it is important to observe the *faeces* for colour, formation and amount. Such *observation* can lead to early recognition of disease or disorder. For example, stools which are pale, putty coloured and fatty can indicate a malabsorption disorder of the intestines, for example gall stones. The appearance of fresh *blood* in stools, or of *diarrhoea*, can also indicate some *disease* or *disorder* of the *alimentary system*.

dignity: a *carer* should ensure that their *clients* are given the type of care which enables them to feel that they are worthy of *respect* and should have pride in themselves and positive *self-esteem*.

direct care: see *care*.

direct payment: payment which is taken out of a person's *benefit* (i.e. income support) for different reasons such as mortgage payments, water charges, council tax, or rent arrears.

directly managed units are *hospitals* or health care organisations which are directly managed or controlled by *health authorities*.

disability: a substantial and long-term mental or physical impairment of a person's ability to carry out normal everyday *activities for living*. Disability affects the lives of a large proportion of our society. There are over 6.5 million people with disabilities living in the UK – together with millions more involved as family carers. According to the latest national estimates, two-thirds of those with disabilities are living in or on the edge of *poverty*. Unemployment is much higher amongst the disabled, with three out of four relying on state *benefits* as their main source of income. (See *benefits, informal carers, Disability Alliance Educational and Research Association, Royal Association for Disability and Rehabilitation, National Disability Council*.)

Disability Action is a development agency working to ensure that people with disabilities attain their full rights as citizens. Disability Action has over 180 member groups covering every aspect of disability from learning to physical, sensory and hidden, i.e those disabilities which are not obvious to others.

(For further information contact Disability Action, 2, Annadale Avenue, Belfast BT7 3JH.)

Disability Alliance Educational and Research Association (DAERA) is a national, registered charity which has the principal aim of relieving *poverty* and improving the living standards of disabled people. Founded in 1974, DAERA brings together over 300 member groups, from national organisations covering all aspects of disability, to local, *self-help* groups. Such a wide membership base plays an active role in shaping policies, in developing services and in influencing a highly effective campaign strategy. Only voluntary organisations can act as full voting members of DAERA but *local authorities, health authorities* and departments of local authorities can become affiliated members. The aims of the alliance include informing the disabled and their carers about their rights to state *benefits* and services. The alliance also undertakes research into their needs – with particular emphasis on income and, through its campaigning, promotes a wider understanding of the views and circumstances of all those with disabilities, looking to end the link between disability and poverty. (See *pressure groups.*)

(For further information contact DAERA, Universal House, 89–94 Wentworth Street, London E1 7SA.)

Disability Discrimination Act 1995 is an Act of Parliament which makes it unlawful to discriminate against disabled persons with respect to employment or the provision of goods, facilities and services. The Act established the *National Disability Council* (HMSO 1995)[26].The Act incorporated the Disabled Persons Employment Act 1944 and 1958 and the Disabled Persons Act 1981 and 1986. The 1944 Act implemented recommendations following the Tomlinson Report 1943 which aimed at ensuring that those with a disability were given a fair chance of employment. Three key features were:

- the Register of Disabled Persons
- a duty placed on employers to recruit a percentage of people with a disability (quota scheme) into their workforce
- the provision that certain jobs were to be reserved for those with disabilities.

The Disabled Persons Act 1981 placed a duty on the providers of buildings and premises to comply with standards of access for those with a disability, and also placed a duty on highway authorities to 'have regard for the needs of blind and disabled persons'.

Disability Living Allowance: a tax-free benefit for those under the age of 65 years with care and *mobility* needs, or for those who are terminally ill and need help with personal care. It is:

- not dependent on *national insurance* contributions
- not affected by any savings or (usually) by any income that the person or their partner may have
- usually ignored as income for those on income support or on jobseekers' allowance.

There are two qualifying components:

- Care component – where an individual needs help with personal care because they are ill and disabled, for example with activities such as *bathing*, dressing, or using the toilet. If the individual is 16 years and over, they can get DLA even if no one is actually caring for them but they are still receiving the care they need.
- Mobility component – where person between the ages of 5 and 65 years needs help in getting around, for example if they cannot work or have difficulty in walking because they are ill or disabled. If they can work but need help with walking then they can also apply for financial support. (See *benefits.*)

Disability Rights Commission: an organisation set up in 1999 to protect, enforce and promote the rights of disabled people.

Disability Scotland is the national umbrella organisation on disability issues in Scotland. Through campaigning and information programmes it works to promote equality of opportunity for those with disabilities throughout Scotland. The main areas of activity are:

- *access* and *mobility*
- *campaigning*
- *community care*
- *information* provision
- leisure and arts.

In addition to this it offers *research* and information services which provide a national resource for Scotland by collecting and disseminating data on all non-medical aspects of disability. Users of this service include disabled people, carers, professionals and mainstream organisations.

(For further information contact Disability Scotland, Princes House, 5 Shandwick Place, Edinburgh EH2 4RG.)

Disability Wales is an independent charity working to promote the rights, recognition and support of all disabled people in Wales. Disability Wales operates a central unit which can provide general information on a wide range of subjects such as:

- access
- *aids and equipment benefits*
- *education*
- *employment*
- holidays
- *housing*
- leisure activities
- transport and *mobility*.

The organisation actively *campaigns* for greater awareness and understanding of the disabled people in Wales and, in particular, Disability Wales works to establish a disabled person's right to be treated as an individual.

(For further information contact Disability Wales, Llys Ifor, Crescent Road, Caerphilly, Mid Glamorgan, CF8 1XL.)

Disabled Living Foundation: a national *charity* providing practical, up-to-date advice and information on many aspects of living with *disability*. It offers support for disabled and *elderly people* and their carers in the following ways:

- The Hamilton Index – a comprehensive directory of daily living equipment with different *aids* and *adaptations*.
- Courses and training – which focus on practical issues surrounding *disability*.
- An equipment centre – this houses a display of over 1000 items of disability equipment with experienced therapists available to provide supporting information and advice for anyone who would like to learn, update or expand their knowledge of equipment.

- A database which is the most comprehensive in Europe on disability equipment containing details of over 14,000 items, including currently available and discontinued products, with suppliers names and addresses and self-help groups.
- A consultancy service which can be tailored to meet the needs of a wide range of organisations involved in the design, building, management and operation of facilities for the disabled.

(For further information contact the Disabled Living Foundation, 380–384 Harrow Road, London W9 2HU.)

discipline: the setting of boundaries for positive behaviour. This addresses codes of behaviour in a variety of health, social care and educational settings. *Codes of practice* are written procedures which outline how professionals should address discipline issues. They are an integral part of professional care and education practice. A code of practice in a care provision should include procedures for:

- clients and their behaviour in different settings
- carers and how they relate to the clients
- teams with appropriate reporting and communication mechanisms.

disclosure is the revelation of information to another person It takes place when a *client* informs another person that *abuse* has taken place. For instance, in an *interview* with a childcare professional, a child may say that they have been abused. Disclosure can be particularly distressing when the abuse has involved a father or a familiar family friend or relative.

discrimination is unfair treatment based on prejudice. In health and social care settings, it may relate to a conscious decision to treat a person or group differently and to deny them access to relevant treatment and care. There is anti-discriminatory legislation in place to cover areas such as *race, disability, gender* and some aspects of employment legislation relating to health status.

Discrimination can take three forms:

- internal – a person develops negative stereotypical and fixed ideas and attitudes about individuals or groups in society
- individual – a person develops negative and discriminatory attitudes towards a person because that person is, for instance, black or homosexual, religious or old
- institutional – a group, organisation or company can reinforce discriminatory practice by the way in which they treat their staff; an example of this would be the attitude towards women and their prospects of promotion to management.

Discrimination can be:

- direct (overt) – as in the behaviour of an individual who openly discriminates against another by making racist jokes or name calling
- indirect (covert) – as in the behaviour of an individual which is less obvious but whose actions can show a subtle form of discrimination; this may happen in employment where there are clear *equal opportunities* policies but a disabled person may still be continually bypassed for promotion.

disease: a state of ill-health when a part or parts of the body are not functioning properly for a number of reasons, for example, *accident* or injury, infection or inflammation, inadequate *diet*, allergic reactions or congenital disorders. Many diseases can be prevented by:

- adequate *health* and *safety* precautions at home and in the surrounding environment
- a healthy and *balanced diet*
- a healthy *lifestyle*, moderate *alcohol* intake, no *smoking* and the taking of *exercise*
- *immunisation*
- a pollution-free environment, clean *water* and *food* supplies including safe sewage disposal.

disempowerment: the denial of the *rights and choices* which *clients* are entitled to make. This includes withholding relevant *information* from the client and not involving them in any form of *decision making* with regard to emotional, physical, intellectual, social and cultural aspects of their lives. (See *empowerment.*)

disinfection: the process of eliminating *infections* or *bacteria* and *viruses*. Infection can be picked up from equipment, instruments, clothes and the surrounding environment. Liquids, sprays and solutions, which are made from chemicals (disinfectants) are used to treat contaminated areas.

district nurse/community nurse: qualified *nurses* who work specifically with patients or clients in their homes, in the community in which they live. They form part of the *primary health care* team. They work closely with *GP*s and are usually based in a health *clinic* or *health centre*.

divorce: the legal dissolution of a marriage. Over the last 50 years there has been a major change in social attitudes towards marriage and family life. This has been reinforced by legislation (i.e. Divorce Act 1969). Following the White Paper 'Looking to the Future, Mediation and the Grounds for Divorce 1995' and the Family Law Bill 1995, there are proposed changes with regard to divorce petitions. For example, it will be possible to present petitions within the first year of marriage. *Social Trends* (1996) records the fall in the number of couples getting married and the rise in divorce rates. Divorce can have a stressful effect on families, especially young children, who find the breakdown in the relationship between parents distressing.

divorce rate: a statistical measure of the number of divorces, usually expressed as the number of divorces in any one year per thousand married couples in the population.

doctor: a health professional who gains a qualification through medical school which is recognised by the General Medical Council.

Doctors:

- detect and diagnose *disease, disorders* and *dysfunctions* with regard to the human body
- treat disease, disorder and dysfunction and monitor recovery
- prevent disease, disorder and dysfunction through *health promotion, child development* and *immunisation programmes.*

Once qualified a doctor has many choices. He/she may decide to:

- work in an NHS *hospital* in specialist areas such as medicine, surgery, pathology or psychiatry
- work in the independent sector, i.e. private hospital, voluntary organisations
- complete further training to become a *GP.*

To qualify as a doctor, an individual completes clinical training which enables them to register with the General Medical Council; training takes five or six years.

domestic roles: the roles which are played by the man and the woman within a home environment. A stereotypical role of a woman is that she cooks, cleans and brings up the children, while a man goes out to work and does not wash up or clean. However, the domestic division of labour has changed in recent years with the emergence of 'new man', that is the man who helps with housework, childcare and other domestic tasks.

domestic violence is physical *abuse* within a relationship. One partner in the relationship might use physical, emotional, economic, sexual or psychological means to exercise control over the other. It is a criminal offence. Domestic violence takes place in partnerships irrespective of *age, race, class, culture* or *religion.* In a majority of cases the violence is committed by a man against a woman. The Domestic Violence and Matrimonial Proceedings Act 1976 has been reinforced by new initiatives which were introduced by the Government in 1997. This should mean:

- much stronger protection for child victims of domestic violence
- that there will be a recognition of the different relationships in which domestic violence can arise (this is viewed by many as a major improvement in the law).

(See *women's aid.*)

domiciliary services are health and social care services which are available in the home. One example of these is the home help service. These services may be *means tested* and some clients may be required to pay a contribution towards the service provided. Such services may be provided by *local authorities,* private or *voluntary organisations.* (See *community care, home care service.*)

Down's syndrome: a genetic condition caused by the presence of an extra chromosome; those with Down's syndrome have 47 chromosomes instead of the usual 46. About one baby in every 1000 has Down's syndrome and they are usually born below average weight and length and have distinguishing features such as a face which appears flattened. They often have large, sometimes protruding tongues in small mouths, their eyes slant and they have broad hands with short fingers. An increasing number of children with Down's syndrome are now attending mainstream schools and are going on to gain employment and lead semi-independent lives as full members of the community. The Down's Syndrome Association is the only national *charity* working exclusively for children with Down's syndrome and their families.

(For further information contact Down's Syndrome Association, 155 Mitcham Road, London SW17 9PG.)

drop-in centres are usually part of a larger scheme or service. They offer an informal facility for clients to 'drop in' for a chat and a cup of tea; elderly clients, for example, may drop in to a church hall for coffee. Parents with young children may drop in to a *health centre* or *family centre*. Another term used for drop in centres is 'pop in' centres. They provide short-term sessions which offer *support* and the opportunity to meet others.

droplet infection: a way in which infection is spread. It involves tiny droplets containing *pathogens* (*disease*-causing organisms) being sneezed, coughed, talked or breathed out and sprayed on to people nearby. Droplets can stay in the air and be breathed in later. The 'common cold' is spread in this way.

drug dependence is addiction which can cause:

- uncontrolled craving for the particular drug
- harmful side effects causing deterioration of physical, emotional, social and intellectual *well-being*
- withdrawal or severe physical reactions when the person stops taking the drug.

There are different types of dependence which include:

- physical dependence – the continual use of drugs leads to physical reactions as the body craves a particular drug
- psychological dependence – the continual use of a drug in order to 'feel good' and to support a sense of *well-being* a feeling that is short-term, disappearing as the effect of the drug wears off. Therefore more of the drug must be taken to promote the effect for more of the time.

(See *drug misuse.*)

drug misuse and drug abuse are terms to describe the use of *drugs* which are taken for non-medical reasons. Taking drugs in this way is harmful to the body and is generally considered to be socially unacceptable. An example of the misuse or abuse of drugs is taking *amphetamines* or 'speed' to produce feelings of pleasure and excitement.

drugs are chemicals taken to alter the way in which the mind or body works. They can be used in the treatment of *infections* and *diseases*. Drugs can be divided into three types. These are:

- Medicines – used to treat and prevent diseases. They can be either bought over the counter at a chemist shop or obtained by prescription from the *GP* or *dentist.*
- Social or recreational drugs – those drugs which are considered to be socially acceptable because they are being taken by a large part of the population. These drugs include *caffeine* which is found in tea and coffee, *alcohol,* and nicotine which is found in cigarettes and tobacco.
- Illegal drugs – these are controlled by *legislation* and are taken to produce feelings of pleasure and excitement but possessing and using them is against the law. (See *drugs and legislation.*)

drugs and legislation: certain drugs are controlled by *legislation*. Controlled drugs are classified into three categories which are differentiated according to the penalties that can be imposed:

- Class A. These drugs are the 'hard' drugs of addiction such as *heroin, cocaine, morphine, pethidine, methadone, opium* and *LSD.*

- Class B. Those most likely to be encountered are *cannabis,* cannabis resin, amphetamine, dexamphetamine and methedrine.
- Class C. These drugs are also considered to be addictive but not as dangerous as Class A or B. The drugs referred to are, as far as the *police* are concerned, relatively uncommon.

There is legislation covering the storage, prescription and illegal misuse of drugs:

- Dangerous Drugs Act 1920
- Dangerous Drugs Act 1925
- Misuse of Drugs Act 1971
- Misuse of Drugs Regulations 1985
- Drug Trafficking Offences Act 1986
- Misuse of Drugs (Amendment) Regulations 1996.

In the Government White Paper 'Tackling Drugs Together' (May 1995), it was recommended that drug action teams comprising chief executives from planning, education, social services, and public health, would join together with police officers and probation officers to form Drug Action Teams. In April 1998 the Government introduced a 10 year strategy for tackling drugs. The White Paper 'Tackling drugs to build a better Britain' is based on a partnership approach between different agencies and is supervised by a UK anti drugs co-ordinator. The strategy for tackling drugs has four target areas:

- young people – to help young people resist drug misuse in order to achieve their full potential in society
- communities – to protect communities from drug-related anti-social and criminal behaviour
- treatment – to enable those with drug problems to overcome them and to live healthy and crime-free lives
- availability – to stifle the availability of illegal drugs on the streets. (HMSO 1998)[60]

(See *pharmacists.*)

drugs – Scotland, Wales and Northern Ireland: strategies which are in place to combat *drug misuse* in these parts of the UK. According to 'Tackling Drugs to Build a Better Britain' significant progress is being made in Scotland, Wales and Northern Ireland:

- Scotland – the 1994 strategy 'Drugs in Scotland: meeting the challenge' was implemented, along with the development of the Scotland Against Drugs campaign and a Scottish Drugs Challenge Fund. The emphasis has been on an integrated approach to service provision, the development of a national information base and strong partnership links with the private and voluntary sectors.
- Wales – a drug and alcohol strategy 'Forward Together' was launched in 1996. The Welsh Drug and Alcohol Unit oversees the strategy and is committed to developing a national prevention campaign, action on treatment and *rehabilitation,* and guidance for those involved in combating drug and alcohol misuse.
- Northern Ireland – the Central Co-ordinating Group for Action Against Drugs was established in 1995 to oversee coherent efforts against drug

misuse within a clearly defined policy statement. The key action areas are education and prevention, treatment and rehabilitation, law enforcement, *information* and *research* – including a major publicity *campaign* – and monitoring and evaluation. (HMSO 1998) [60]

drugs – the scale of the problem: an outline of the extent of *drug misuse* . This is described in the White Paper 'Tackling Drugs to Build a Better Britain' 1998. It includes the fact that, despite progress, the drugs problem remains formidable, for example:

- record levels of drug seizures reveal the increasing threat of a widening range of trafficking routes to the UK, against a background of expanding global production
- offenders dealt with under the Misuse of Drug Act 1971 are up from 86,000 in 1994 to 95,000 in 1996
- the number of drug misusers attending support services was 24,879 in the six month period ending September 1996, 48 per cent higher than the equivalent period three years earlier
- the number of deaths in the UK attributable to the misuse of drugs has risen from 1,399 in 1993 to 1,805 in 1995. (HMSO 1998) [60]

In addition, more localised trends – particularly the increasing availability and use of cheap, smokeable *heroin* – suggest growing exposure and consumption by younger people. (See *drugs and legislation*.)

dying: the process that a person goes through when all the systems in the body begin to slow down in the approach to *death.*

dysarthria is a speech disorder. It occurs when the mechanisms which are involved in speech are limited due to sensory malfunction or tumours, damage or injury to the *muscles* and *nerves* surrounding the *throat* (e.g. in Parkinson's disease).

dysentery: an infection of the intestines. The organism causing it may either be a particular type of protozoan or a bacterium. The infection usually occurs as a result of living in overcrowded and poor living conditions. The disease can spread and can reach *epidemic* proportions. It also causes severe *diarrhoea* and can lead to *dehydration* and weight loss.

dysfunction: impairment, abnormality or disorder affecting a person's physical, emotional, intellectual, cognitive or mental functioning. Such breakdown can affect any body system and/or organ.

dyslexia: a specific learning difficulty caused by a defect in the part of the *brain* which processes *language* and affects the skills that are needed for learning in either or both of the following areas:

- literacy – reading, writing and spelling
- numeracy – arithmetic, problem solving and calculation.

This does not mean that individuals with dyslexia cannot become fully literate or numerate. With suitable help they can succeed and often have different and valuable problem-solving abilities.

(For further information contact the British Dyslexia Association, 98 London Road, Reading, RG1 5AU.)

dyspraxia: a neurological disorder which affects children. Messages are not transmitted to the *brain* in the normal way. The cause is not known. However, there are signs and symptoms which can include the child being:

- slow to reach milestones, for example, speaking
- inhibited by movements which are uncoordinated, e.g. they cannot run, hop or jump; throwing and catching a ball is difficult; they can be clumsy and accident prone
- unable to hold a pencil properly and drawing is difficult; later on they find maths, reading and writing difficult
- excitable, with temper tantrums and a poor concentration span
- affected by poor memory and difficulty grasping concepts.

(For further information contact The Dyspraxia Foundation, PO Box 30, Hitchin, Herts SG5 1UV.)

E

E coli (Escherichia coli) are bacteria which live in the large intestine, colon or bowel of humans. They are found in large numbers in human *faeces*. E coli is a harmless bacterium when it lives in the large intestine but when it contaminates water (or food) through sewage or poor hygiene it can cause diseases such as dysentery and *gastro-enteritis*.

E numbers are *food additives* which have been identified and given a serial number. Foods which contain only additives with E numbers can be supplied in countries within the European Community. Such additives were originally tested and recognised by the EC as being safe for human consumption.

early education: services which support the *care* and learning of pre-school children, for example, *day nurseries, play groups* and *childminders*.

early excellence centres offer integrated childcare and education provision. This includes provision for children with special educational needs, *parent and toddler groups* or similar sessions for parents, and other education and training programmes to develop parenting, employment, and other skills.

ears are the organs of hearing and balance. The position of the ears at the side of the head is important as this enables a person to know the direction from which sounds come. Sound waves reach the ears and produce *nerve* impulses which are transmitted to the *brain* via the *auditory* nerve. (See page 119.) The structure of the ear includes:

- The outer ear is a visible flap of *cartilage* called the pinna. This collects sound waves and passes them through the ear canal to the eardrum (tympanic membrane). The eardrum is a thin sheet of tissue which covers the entrance to the middle ear.
- The middle ear contains the three small *bones* (ossicles) called the malleus (hammer), incus (anvil) and stapes (stirrup). When sound waves reach the eardrum or tympanic membrane they cause it to vibrate and the vibrations are transmitted through the ossicles to the inner ear.
- The inner ear contains fluid-filled tubes called the cochlea and semi-circular canals. The cochlea contains sensory cells which convert vibrations of sound into nerve impulses. The semi circular canals are concerned with balance. The cells in the semi-circular canals are very sensitive to movement of fluid. When a person moves their head, impulses are sent to the brain so that the brain is aware of the person's position. If they make a sudden movement and lose their balance then impulses are again sent to the brain which in turn sends an impulse to the appropriate muscles to bring about a correcting movement.

eating disorder: a disruption in the eating habits or appetite of an individual. This may relate to the amount and the type of *food* that an individual eats or chooses not to eat. These disorders are closely associated with the emotional, psychological or physical *well-being* of a person. Examples include a teenage girl who may overeat, binge and make herself sick. Weight loss can also be caused by physical illness,

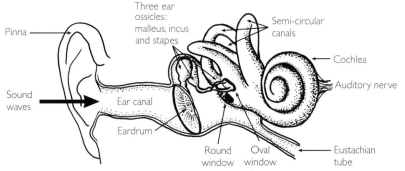

The ear

however; for instance, a young child may lose weight due to poor absorption of nutrients in the small intestine. This is called malabsorption syndrome. (See *anorexia nervosa, bulimia nervosa*.)

echocardiography: a procedure using *ultrasound* as a means of studying the structure and movement of the *heart* in order to diagnose any *disease, disorder* or *dysfunction*.

economy, efficiency and effectiveness are the three major aspects alongside social, demographic, technological and political reform which have determined change in the *National Health Service* in the last 20 years. These aspects of change are defined as follows:

- economy: relates to the different methods and strategies used in *funding* and in the management of resources within the health service i.e. the cost of NHS staff, buying necessary equipment and maintaining NHS buildings
- efficiency: explores how the health service is working in terms of results and competence, i.e. are there positive results in terms of the number of patients being treated?
- effectiveness: looks at the ways in which the needs of service users are being met i.e. are hospital waiting lists being reduced?

Enshrined in these major aspects are *equity* and accessibility, which review the quality of fair and equal treatment of service users.

(See *trends in health and social care*.)

ecstasy: a Class A *drug* in the same category as *heroin* and *cocaine*. It is an illegal drug and other names include 'Disco burgers', 'Dennis the Menace', 'Fantasy' and 'E'. It is taken as white, brown, yellow or pink tablets and acts as a stimulant, producing its effect after 20 minutes. It gives a sense of prolonged *well-being* with a heightened perception of colours and sounds. It has potentially harmful side effects including *anxiety*, panic attacks and insomnia (inability to sleep). It is usually taken at clubs and 'raves' and in this atmosphere may cause severe *dehydration* which can lead to heat stroke.

ectopic pregnancy is the implantation of the fertilised egg outside the uterus. Instead of being implanted in the uterus the egg is implanted in the Fallopian tube. As the embryo grows it puts pressure on the walls of the Fallopian tube. At approximately six weeks into the *pregnancy* the growing embryo can rupture the wall of the Fallopian tube. This is a surgical emergency and the woman needs immediate hospital treatment. (See *fertilisation*.)

eczema is one of the commonest reasons for dry and sensitive *skin*. There are different types of eczema:

- Atopic eczema – is found in babies and young children. It is thought to be hereditary as it runs in families. There are links with conditions such as *asthma* and hay fever. Common symptoms include an overall dryness of the skin usually accompanied by extreme itchiness. The skin may become inflamed, cracked and split and may be prone to infection.
- Seborrhoeic eczema – there are two types of this condition, one which is most commonly seen in babies and the second type seen in young adults. Areas affected tend to be the oily parts of the body such as the scalp, face, groin and chest. Seborrhoeic eczema is not normally itchy.
- Discoid eczema – this condition is usually confined to the arms and legs and consists of scaly, itchy, coin-shaped patches that can blister and weep.
- Varicose eczema – this condition is confined to the legs, commonly found in *elderly people* and in those with varicose veins.
- Contact eczema – there are two types, irritant and allergic. Irritant is caused by exposure to substances such as soaps, detergents, engine oils, hair dyes and bleaches. Allergic is caused by specific sensitivity to a material such as nickel, chrome or rubber.

(For further information contact the National Eczema Society, 163 Eversholt Street, London NW1 1BU.)

education: the process of learning, it involves acquiring and developing knowledge and skills in formal settings such as *schools* and informal settings such as sports and leisure clubs. The government has set up a comprehensive programme to improve schools in England. In the White Paper 'Excellence in schools', a programme of school reforms is based on a series of strategies to improve standards. These include:

- expanding *pre-school education*
- campaigning to improve *literacy* and *numeracy* in primary education to ensure that children have the tools for learning
- reducing class sizes in infant schools
- introducing *education action zones,* which will provide support and development in those geographic areas where they are most needed
- promoting settings, so that the comprehensive system is updated for today's world
- ensuring *autonomy* for all schools and how they are managed
- establishing after school clubs, to enhance children's opportunities to learn, particularly those children at greatest risk of underachieving.

There is a similar initiative in *Scotland.* Learning does not stop at school or even at the university gates. The learning society is one in which everyone has the opportunity to improve their knowledge and skills. *Community, adult* and *family* learning have vital parts to play in the lifelong learning process. (HMSO 1997)[31]

Education Act 1944: an Act of Parliament which introduced a *statutory* requirement for secondary *education*. Three types of secondary school were designed to cater for the needs of pupils from the age of 11 years according to their age, aptitude and ability. The *schools* were meant to provide an appropriate education for what was seen as three different groups of children. The types of school were:

- Secondary grammar schools – designed for the top 20 per cent of children who were thought to benefit from an 'academic' education (single sex or mixed).
- Secondary technical schools – designed for children with largely practical abilities thought capable of becoming technicians and skilled workers. In practice relatively few of these schools were built, largely because of the cost of equipping them.
- Secondary modern schools – a completely new type of school designed for children with practical abilities who were destined to become semi-skilled and unskilled manual workers (single sex or mixed).

Under the terms of the Act, children were selected to the most appropriate type of school according to their ability, which was measured by their performance in an examination taken at the age of 11-plus.

Education Act 1997: an Act of Parliament which amended the law relating to schools and further education in England and Wales. It involved making provision for supervising the award of external academic and vocational qualifications in England, Wales and Northern Ireland. Areas of education that were reformed included the following:

- the assisted places scheme – extending the scheme to include primary and secondary schools
- school *discipline* – the responsibility for discipline in schools, powers to restrain pupils, detention and exclusion of pupils from schools
- *baseline assessments* and pupil's performance – the adoption of a scheme and the assessment of pupils in accordance with that scheme
- the establishment and role of the Qualifications and Curriculum Authority in England and Wales
- school inspections
- careers education and guidance. (HMSO 1997)[27]

education action zones: these have been established under an initiative which involves active partnership between groups of schools. A typical zone is likely to have two or three secondary schools with supporting primaries and associated special educational needs provision. (See *excellence in schools*.)

Education Reform Act 1981: an Act of Parliament which introduced reforms. These included a review of children with special needs following the *Warnock Report*. (See *special needs, statementing*.)

Education Reform Act 1988: an Act of Parliament which introduced educational reforms. These included:

- a *national curriculum* for children of compulsory school age in the maintained sector, accompanied by standardised tests (SATs)
- local management of schools (LMS), under which head teachers and governors were given greater control over their school's budget
- permission for schools to have open enrolment

- a scheme under which schools would be allowed to opt out of *local authority* control and receive grant-maintained status
- the abolition of the Inner London Education Authority (ILEA). (HMSO 1988)[28]

Education Supervision Order: a court order which is supported by the *Children Act 1989*. The *local authority* can apply to the *Family Proceedings Court* if there is evidence that a child is not attending school regularly.

Education Welfare Service is set up to provide social work support to state schools. Education *social workers* are allocated to schools which they visit on a regular basis. Education social workers also carry out home visits where irregular school attendance is becoming a problem and, where necessary, enforce school attendance through the courts. (See *truancy*.)

educational psychologist: a trained professional who is responsible for assessing and supporting children with special educational needs. Educational psychologists are members of a team or panel of professionals who review and monitor a child's education needs and play a responsible role in the statement process. They monitor ongoing special needs children who are integrated into mainstream schools. They may also explore issues such as *intelligence*, management of children in a classroom setting, dealing with children's *behaviour*, psychometric testing, teacher training and any other agency working in direct contact with the education process. (See *special needs and statementing*.)

educational standards: the way in which the quality of educational achievement is assessed. Measurement is usually by the numbers of pupils and students achieving pass grades in external examinations and assessments. (See *National Curriculum*.)

ejaculation: the sudden emission of semen containing sperm through the urethra and out through the end of the penis. During *sexual intercourse* the sperm are deposited in the *vagina* of the female through the process of ejaculation.

elderly people form one group of *service users* or *clients* and *patients* who use the health and social care services. There are other terms for elderly people such as senior citizens, old age pensioners and old people. Elderly people form a high proportion of the population in the United Kingdom. In recent years there has been an increasing number of elderly people and, therefore, this has put pressure on the demand for health and social care services.

elderly people – abuse: a deliberate act to hurt or harm an elderly *client, patient* or *service user*. This can take the form of:
- verbal *abuse*, such as calling a client names, or shouting at them when they need help or they cannot move fast enough
- physical abuse, such as hitting them with a hand or piece of equipment such as a hairbrush or coat hanger; often, the abuser will injure a client in a place which is covered with clothing so that it cannot be seen
- neglect: for example the client might be left alone without being washed, dressed or bathed. Toileting might be carried out infrequently and the client might wet or soil themselves. This may make a client more vulnerable to other forms of abuse (see *washing, bathing*)

- emotional abuse, for example where the elderly client is put on the toilet and the door is left open or they are strip washed in front of others. They are not given any involvement in decisions about their care. There is no sense of kindness and compassion in the caring that they receive and they can easily feel unloved, unwanted, isolated and alone.

Caring for elderly people can be demanding as they may need a great deal of attention, concern and *holistic* care. Every aspect of their different and individual needs should be considered and met.

electrocardiogram (ECG): a test which traces the electrical activity of the *heart*. The tracings form a pattern which is shown on an electrocardiograph. When the heart beats, electrical activity forms a wave which moves from the top to the bottom of the heart. Electrodes are placed on the *skin* and these register the electrical activity as a tracing onto a screen or sheet of paper. This method of testing is a way of detecting whether the heart is working properly and efficiently. For example, after a heart attack the tracing of the waves will indicate damage to the heart muscle.

A healthy ECG trace – a small section is shown

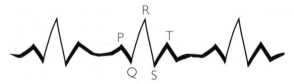

P wave is due to atrial contraction
Q, R, S and T waves are due to ventricular activity

electroencephalogram (EEG): the tracing of the electrical activity of the *brain* forms a pattern, *measured* on an electroencephalograph. When messages are taken to and from the brain they are transmitted by electrical charges called impulses. Electrodes are placed on the head and these register the electrical activities in the brain as a tracing onto a screen or sheet of paper. This method of testing the brain is a way of detecting electrical activity defects such as *epilepsy*.

elements, compounds and mixtures are chemical substances. They are defined as follows:

- Element – a substance which cannot be broken down into simpler substances. There are 105 natural elements. The main ones found in the human body are carbon, hydrogen, oxygen, nitrogen, sulphur, phosphorous and calcium.
- Compound – a combination of two or more elements, bonded together in some way. A compound has different physical and chemical properties from the elements which make it up. The proportion of each element in a compound is constant (e.g. *water* is always formed from two parts hydrogen and one part *oxygen* and so is denoted by its chemical formula H_2O). Compounds are often difficult to split into their elements and can only be separated by specific chemical reactions.

- Mixture – a blend of two or more elements or compounds which are not chemically combined. The proportions of each element or compound are not fixed and each keeps its own properties. A mixture can usually be separated into its elements or compounds fairly easily by physical means. (Stockley, Oxlade and Wertheim 1988)[58]

embolism: a *blood* clot which breaks away from the place where it has formed and is transported in the blood stream until it becomes trapped in an *artery* and is unable to move any further. An embolism is often responsible for:

- *cerebral vascular accident* or *stroke* – a clot in the cerebral artery in the *brain*
- pulmonary embolism – a clot in the pulmonary *artery* in the *lung*
- myocardial infarction or *heart attack* – a clot in the *coronary artery*.

embryo: the product of *fertilisation*; a sperm has penetrated an egg and the embryo is formed, usually in the Fallopian tube. It then moves into the *uterus* where it becomes implanted. The embryo develops all its main organs in the first eight weeks. After this, the embryo becomes known as the *foetus*.

emergency protection order: a court order which gives a *social worker* or a professional from the *National Society of Prevention of Cruelty to Children* or NSPCC the authority to remove a child from their parents or primary care givers and keep him/her in a safe place for up to eight days. This procedure is reinforced under Section 44 of the *Children Act 1989*. It is important to remember that children are not removed from their parents unless their safety is immediately threatened, i.e. they are likely to suffer significant harm. The order gives the applicant *parental responsibility* for the child.

emergency services (999): services such as *police*, fire brigade and ambulance services, mine, mountain, cave and fell rescue, and HM Coastguard. (See *calling emergency services*.)

emotional maturity: the development of a stable *self-concept* or *identity*, which enables an individual to become *independent* and take responsibility for his or her own actions.

emotions are feelings that individuals experience in the relationships that they have with themselves, others and the world they live in. Emotional growth is an important aspect of a young child's development. Emotional needs include love, affection, consistent care, security, praise and encouragement. Meeting these needs in a loving way enables a child to develop a positive *self-esteem*. As a carer, developing a client's *self-esteem* and positive view of themselves is an important aspect of making them feel that they can achieve certain tasks which support their *activities of daily living*.

empathy: a person's awareness of the emotional state of another person and their ability to share an experience with them. It might take the form of a common feeling of sadness and pain in an unhappy situation. It is a reason why *support groups* are successful: they are set up by people who have been through similar situations in their lives. An example is CRUSE, where those who have been through the *bereavement* process can share feelings and relate with others who have themselves been recently bereaved.

employment: working in an occupation in exchange for wages or a salary. (See *work*.)

employment zone: an area where there is a government initiative involving local business partnerships. Partnerships may draw up plans to give unemployed people in their locality opportunities to improve their employability and to move back into employment.

empowerment: the way in which a *carer* encourages an individual *client* to make decisions and take control of her/his own life. A carer should involve a client in conversations which relate to their *care* and *lifestyles*, giving them the opportunity to reply and respond. Empowerment is a process which builds a client's *self-esteem* and confidence in their ability to make decisions. Sharing information enables a client to make informed choices. *(See confidence building.)*

enablement: methods used by health and social care workers to support their *clients* and encourage them to be as *independent* as possible in their daily lives. Methods include:

- teaching life skills or social skills to help them to care for themselves; an example is *activities of daily living*
- helping clients to live as independently as possible, i.e. moving clients into their own accommodation
- helping clients to make decisions about their care and different aspects of their daily lives
- helping clients to take up suitable employment
- encouraging clients to attend support or user groups
- providing relevant *information* and *advice.*

endemic disease: a *disease* which is present only in a certain part of the world (such as malaria in the tropics).

endocrine system: a system made up of a number of ductless *glands* found in different parts of the body. The glands secrete hormones which travel in the blood to target organs where they have a chemical effect on the body. Examples of the main endocrine glands are the *pituitary, thyroid, parathyroid, adrenal, pancreas* and the *gonads* (ovaries and testes).

endocrinology is the study of the *endocrine system.* The endocrine system produces *hormones.*

energy is the capacity to carry out different activities to live, *work* and *play.* There are thousands of chemical reactions which take place in the body cells in order to release or acquire energy. Energy cannot be destroyed.

English as a second language: when a child or person's first language is not English. (See *bilingualism.*)

enquiry methods: methods used as part of the *research* process. They involve using primary sources of *data* which are collected through experimentation and *observation.*

enteritis is the inflammation of the intestine due to a disease or food poisoning. (See *gastroenteritis.*)

environment is the totality of surrounding conditions which affect and support an individual. The living environment should be safe, secure and promote health. Factors which promote the health and well-being of individuals are enshrined in the Green Paper *Our Healthier Nation – a Contract for Health.* These factors include:

- air quality – monitoring and controlling *pollution* (i.e. poisonous gases emitted into the air) through legislation such as the Clean Air Act 1993 and through informal measures, such as no *smoking* policies in organisations such as department stores, offices, public transport and *hospitals*
- *housing* – monitoring *legislation* and policies to improve quality housing and housing management
- *water* quality – monitoring pollution of rivers and streams according to relevant legislation; ensuring that *public health measures* are in place to protect drinking water
- social environment – the people who may influence an individual's *quality of life*, for example family, friends, colleagues, medical and educational services, neighbours, etc.

In addition to this, there are procedures which should be in place to support *the health and safety* of staff and *service users,* such as routines for:

- *food hygiene* and the application of relevant *legislation*
- protection from fire with fire safety regulations such as *fire drills*
- controlling working environments including legislation relating to *health* and safety at work
- *health and safety* regulations including control of hazardous and poisonous substances (such as *control of substances hazardous to health* regulations)
- regulations concerning *disease*
- health, such as immunisation and *health screening*.

Issues concerned with the environment are also covered in the Environmental Protection Act 1990. (See also *care environment*.)

environmental health officers are employed by the *local authority* and have received specialised training. Their role is to protect public health by monitoring the environment with regard to *food, fire*, working environment and *pollution*.

enzymes are chemicals which speed up chemical changes within the body without any change occurring to the enzymes themselves. They are a type of catalyst.

epidemic: episodes of *disease* which spread rapidly and affect large numbers of people. Epidemics occur when:

- there is a lack of *immunity* in a population and people are in a poor state of *health*
- there are conditions in which germs can spread easily
- a particularly virulent strain of disease arises, e.g. the flu *virus*.

epidemiology: the study of the nature, prevalence and spread of *disease*. It explores the causes of particular diseases in order to develop an appropriate approach to prevention and cure. For example, the discovery of the link between cholera and infected drinking *water* was an important advance in controlling the incidence of cholera.

epilepsy: a *disorder* or *dysfunction* affecting the electrical activities in the *brain* which results in recurrent epileptic seizures or fits. Epilepsy is an abnormal electrical discharge in the brain. Epilepsy may be caused by *brain* tumours, *drugs, cerebral* disease such as *dementia*, systemic illness which affects brain function (e.g. *kidney* failure) head injuries and it may be hereditary. There are different types of epilepsy. The most common forms are:

- Grand mal epilepsy, where fits cause the individual to lose consciousness, and fall to the ground with twitching and jerking of the limbs. There may be frothing at the mouth and, in some cases, the individual will pass urine.
- Petit mal epilepsy, which causes the individual to lose consciousness for a few seconds. They may suddenly lose concentration, stop talking and appear blank. As soon as this phase passes the sufferer returns to what they were doing. The individual does not fall to the floor or seem any different except for a blank expression and an inability to respond during the attack.

Epilepsy is diagnosed by a number of tests such as an *electroencephalogram* and brain scans which examine the electrical activity of the brain. Treatment of epilepsy is by anti-epileptic drugs. Those who suffer from epilepsy have to make appropriate career choices as some occupations would be deemed unsuitable, for example, working in the fire or police service. People with epilepsy are not allowed to drive a car. *Cognitive* and *intellectual development* is not impaired, neither is the ability to learn. However, some sufferers feel self-conscious of their medical condition because of the fits, particularly as they do not always know when these will happen. However, some epileptics have an 'aura', a feeling or sense that they are going to have a 'fit'. Babies and young children sometimes suffer from 'fits' when they have a high temperature; these are called convulsions and are not an indication that the individual will later suffer from epilepsy.

(For further information contact the British Epilepsy Association, Anstey House, 40 Hanover Square, Leeds LS3 1BE.)

epithelial tissues: groups of specialised *cells* forming layers which cover or line the surfaces of organs. There are different types of epithelial tissue:

1 Ciliated epithelium – found in nasal passages

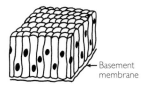

Fine cilia
Intracellular matrix
Basement membrane

2 Stratified epithelium – found in skin

Dead, flattened cells
Compound epithelium composed of more than one layer of cells
Germinal layer (live, dividing cells)
Basement membrane

3 Columnar epithelium – found in lining of stomach

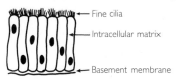

Basement membrane

4 Cuboidal epithelium – forms the duct of a gland

Basement membrane
Intracellular matrix

5 Glandular epithelium

Cells which secrete substances
Basement membrane

6 Squamous epithelium

Base membrane

equal opportunities are principles which reinforce policies contained in legislation. They are the result of anti-discriminatory practices and ensure that every individual has:

- a right to employment and *access to services*
- rights to non-discriminatory medical treatment, independent of *race, gender, class, religion, culture, age* and sexual orientation.

Equal Opportunities Commission (EOC): an organisation which was set up following the *Sex Discrimination Act* 1975. Its main functions are to:

- enforce laws created by Parliament to eliminate unlawful sex *discrimination*
- promote equality of opportunity generally for women and men
- review and propose amendments to the existing legislation such as the *Equal Pay Act 1980* and *Sex Discrimination Act 1975*.

The Commission also supports issues such as:

- improving the individual's access to justice
- establishing a safe and harassment-free working environment
- the equalisation of pension rights, without detriment to the rights of women
- non-discriminatory payment and job evaluation systems
- successful combination of working life with family commitments
- rights for part-time workers
- an independent tax structure for husbands and wives.

(For further information contact the Equal Opportunities Commission, Overseas House, Quay Street, Manchester M3 3HN. Offices also in Glasgow and Cardiff.)

Equal Pay Act 1970 and Equal Pay (Amendment) Act 1983: acts of Parliament which are aimed at eliminating *discrimination* between men and women in terms of payment for work of equal value and contractual conditions. The 1983 legislation brought Britain into line with the European Directive on equal pay for equal work.

equity: the quality of being fair and reasonable in a way that gives equal treatment to everyone.

Erikson, EH: an American psychoanalyst. He believed that a stronger emphasis should be placed on the lifelong relationship between the individual and the social system in which they develop. Erikson suggested that there are eight stages in a person's life, with each stage presenting challenges that are characteristic of that particular period. For example, in mid-life, 'generativity versus stagnation', those without children or without jobs or *lifestyles* that have significant meaning to them may experience a feeling of stagnation. Psychologically healthy individuals meet the challenges of each stage while psychologically unhealthy individuals may fail to meet such challenges and must therefore deal with the conflicts that emerge in the stages that follow.

Erikson's stages of development

Stage	Relationships	Age
1 Basic trust versus basic mistrust	Mother or primary care giver	0–1 years

2	Autonomy versus shame and doubt	Parents or primary care giver	1–3 years
3	Initiative versus guilt	Family units including extended family	3–6 years
4	Industry versus inferiority	School and out of school	7–12 years
5	Identity versus role confusion	Different groups such as peer groups	12–18 years
6	Intimacy versus isolation	Partnerships in different relationships, friendships, family	20s
7	Generativity versus stagnation	Building interest in society or 'Just the home front'	Late 20s–50s
8	Ego integrity versus despair	'Human kind' or my kind	50s and over

erythrocytes or red blood cells are cells in the *blood* whose main function is to carry *oxygen* from the *lungs* to the *tissues*. They do not have a nucleus and only exist for approximately 100–120 days. They are manufactured in the *bone marrow*. They are disc shaped and are able to fold and bend as they pass through blood vessels. Red cells contain *haemoglobin* which carries oxygen. The haemoglobin readings in blood relate closely to an individual's iron count.

ethics: moral codes of practice which are concerned with:

- behaviour (moral conduct) e.g. unprofessional behaviour such as direct *discrimination*
- issues such as legal, religious, social and personal concerns (moral issues) e.g. *abortion*
- debates within society about different codes of practice e.g. the issue of prolonging life in a terminally ill person versus euthanasia

(See *care value base.*)

ethnic groups: groups of people who share and belong to the same cultural tradition, racial origin, sometimes with distinguishing physical features, common language or religion.

ethnic minorities are groups of people from different cultural or religious or racial backgrounds who make up only a small proportion of a country's population. Examples of ethnic minorities in the UK are the Vietnamese, Irish, Turkish, Pakistani and Bengali communities.

ethnocentrism: an individual's assumption that their society's *lifestyle* and culture is the norm and the right way of living with any other *culture* or lifestyle being regarded as inferior or misguided.

Eurocentrism a belief held by those individuals who view the world from the attitudes of white European *culture* and *society*. This way of thinking or value base does not acknowledge issues of diversity of culture or *race*, believing that the holder's views are superior.

European Convention on Human Rights: an international treaty signed by 12 member countries of the Council of Europe on 4 November 1950. It ensures that fundamental human rights are supported. The Court of Human Rights can change laws. For example, its intervention led to the abolition of corporal punishment in state schools.

European Union (EU): a group of 15 countries in Western Europe and Scandinavia representing some 370 million citizens. The European Union has developed a number of key institutions responsible for determining policy and legislation such as a Council of Ministers, European Parliament, European Commission, Economic and Social Committee, European Council and the European Court of Justice.

euthanasia: the killing of someone who is enduring extreme suffering, for example from an incurable disease. The individual involved may give clear directions as to what should happen in the event of their own faculties deteriorating, resulting in limited and restricted *quality of life.*

- Passive euthanasia involves a decision which is made on behalf of an individual who has severe limitations and restrictions on their quality of life, such as a patient or client in a permanent vegetative state or state of permanent unconsciousness. It is the act of letting a person die.
- Active euthanasia involves a deliberate act to end a life.

All aspects of euthanasia provide health and social care workers with ethical and moral dilemmas. A person may be suffering from a particularly painful form of cancer and their loved ones have had to watch them endure considerable discomfort. This may lead to discussion and heartache. Euthanasia is a difficult and contentious subject but, in each area of health and social care, professionals have codes of ethics which act as guidelines forming a framework for practice. (See *codes of practice.*)

evaporation: the conversion of a liquid to a vapour by the escape of molecules from the liquid's surface. It takes place at all *temperatures*, the rate increasing with any one or a combination of the following:

- an increase in temperature
- an increase in surface area
- a decrease in pressure
- the removal of the vapour from above the liquid by a flow of *air.*

Excellence in Schools: the first White Paper of the Labour government produced in 1997. It reviewed:

- education policies and set out to tackle problems such as pupil underachievement
- early years education, assessment, recommended smaller primary classes and raising standards in *literacy* and *numeracy*
- the measurement of performance in schools and colleges to raise standards
- modernising the comprehensive principle which includes setting up *education action zones*
- raising the status and standards of teaching
- helping pupils through improvement in areas such as parental support, discipline, attendance and skills for life

- new partnerships with regard to community aid and foundation schools, school governors, the role of local education authorities, school places, school admissions and independent schools. (HMSO 1997)[31]

excretion: the removal of waste products resulting from metabolic processes in the body. Excretion includes loss of urea through the *kidneys* and *carbon dioxide* from the *lungs*. (See *waste disposal*.)

exercise: an activity which is necessary for the body to keep healthy and in good working order. Regular exercise is beneficial to the body in the following ways:

- it keeps the *joints* supple and mobile, preventing stiffness
- it enables the *muscles* to maintain their strength, tone and healthy condition
- it maintains body stamina, which results from greater efficiency in the different organs, such as the heart
- it helps to develop the *bones* and muscle co-ordination
- it maintains good health, improves appetite, induces sound sleep and prevents excessive body weight.

Exercises which still allow a person to breathe in sufficient *oxygen* to oxidise glucose to provide the necessary energy, are called *aerobic exercises*.

exocrine glands: glands which have ducts or channels which secrete fluids 'externally'. For example *sweat glands* secrete sweat and *salivary glands* secrete saliva.

expiration: breathing out air. It involves the following process:

- intercostal muscles relax and the rib cage moves downwards and inwards
- the *diaphragm* muscle relaxes, moving upwards to become more dome-shaped
- the volume of the thorax becomes smaller so increasing the pressure in the thoracic cavity
- the natural elasticity of the *lungs* and increased pressure on them causes the lungs to decrease in volume and air is forced out.

extroversion: an aspect of the *personality* which is characterised by a number of different *traits* such as impulsiveness and sociability. Eynsenck developed the *Eynsenck Personality Inventory*, a method of testing people along the continuum of *Introversion–Extroversion*. The more sociable, impulsive and willing a person is to take risks, the higher they score on extroversion. Extroverts have a lower level of cortical activity, and therefore must seek stimulation to maintain their psychological state.

eye contact: maintaining eye contact is a way of reading messages in the eyes. It can be a means of giving positive support and is an important part of individual and group communication. Many emotions are mirrored in the eyes. Feelings of happiness, joy, sadness, anger and mistrust can be seen. However, it is important to note that in some *cultures* eye contact is viewed as a negative way of behaving. (See *communication, confidence building*.)

eyes are the organs of sight, sending nervous impulses to the *brain* when stimulated by light rays from external objects. The brain interprets the impulses to produce images. Each eye consists of an eyeball made up of several layers and structures. It is set into a socket in the *skull* and is protected by eyelids and eyelashes.

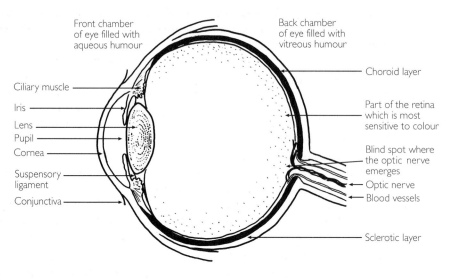

Front chamber of eye filled with aqueous humour

Back chamber of eye filled with vitreous humour

Ciliary muscle

Iris

Lens

Pupil

Cornea

Suspensory ligament

Conjunctiva

Choroid layer

Part of the retina which is most sensitive to colour

Blind spot where the optic nerve emerges

Optic nerve

Blood vessels

Sclerotic layer

The eye consists of the:

- Sclera or sclerotic coat – the 'white' of the eye. This is tough, fibrous and opaque, with blood vessels.
- Choroid or choroid coat – a layer of tissue with blood vessels and dark pigment. Pigment absorbs light to stop reflection within the eye.
- Iris – an opaque disc of tissue, with blood vessels and central hole (pupil). It contains muscle fibres, some of which are in concentric circles, while others radiate out from centre to edge. The former contract to decrease pupil size (in bright light) while the latter contract to increase it (in dim light). The iris has various amounts of pigment producing eye colours.
- Cornea – a transparent continuation of sclera. It protects the front of the eye and 'bends' (refracts) light rays onto the lens.
- Conjunctiva – a thin mucous membrane. This lines the eyelids and covers the cornea.
- Ciliary body – a ring of smooth muscle around the lens. This contracts to make the lens smaller and fatter. It relaxes to make the lens larger and thinner. The ciliary body and the muscles of the iris are known as intrinsic eye muscles.
- Lens – the transparent body whose role is to focus the light rays passing through it (i.e. 'bend' or refract them) so that they come to a point, in this case on the retina. A lens consists of many thin tissue layers and is held in place by the fibres of the suspensory ligament. These join it to the ciliary body, which can alter the lens shape so that light rays are always focused on the retina, whatever the distance to the object being looked at. This is known as *accommodation*. The rays form an upside-down image, but this is compensated for and corrected by the *brain*.
- Retina – the innermost layer of tissue at the back of the eyeball made up of a layer of pigment and a nervous layer consisting of millions of sensory nerve cells or sensory neurons and their fibres. These lie in chains and carry

nervous impulses to the brain. The first cells in the chains are receptors, i.e. their end fibres or dendrons fire off impulses when they are stimulated by light rays. These cells are called rods and cones because of their shape. The receptors are photoreceptors, that is they are stimulated by light.

- Macula lutea or yellow spot – an area of yellowish tissue in the centre of the retina. It has a small central dip, called the fovea or fovea centralis. This has the highest concentration of cones and is the area of acute vision.
- Blind spot or optic disc – the point in the retina where the optic nerve leaves the eye. It has no receptors and so cannot send any impulses.
- *Aqueous humour* – a watery liquid containing sugars, salts and *proteins*. It fills the space called the anterior cavity, protecting the lens and nourishing the front of the eye. It constantly drains away and is replaced.
- Vitreous humour – a fluid similar to aqueous humour, but stiff and jelly-like. It fills the space called the posterior cavity and keeps the shape of eyeball, protects the retina and helps 'bend' or refract the light.

Eysenck Personality Inventory (EPI): a way of measuring personality. It measures the degree of *extroversion–introversion,* and of neuroticism–stability. Participants are asked a series of questions. The responses to these questions provide the relevant information sufficient to construct a score for extroversion and neuroticism. As some may falsify their answers in a way they consider socially desirable the inventory includes a lie scale of questions that can only be answered in one way.

F

facial nerve: the seventh cranial *nerve*. It supplies the muscles of the face responsible for facial expression. It also conveys nerve sensation from the taste buds on the front part of the *tongue*, and supplies the sublingual *salivary glands* and the lacrimal glands (glands which secrete tears).

faeces: waste matter (excrement) which is excreted from the body via the rectum and *anus*. It is composed mainly of indigestible cellulose, water, undigested food and bacteria.

failure to thrive: the description used for a baby who does not grow at the expected rate and develops slowly. (See *centile charts*.) Reasons for failure to thrive include:

- genetic make-up – comparisons with the size of parents and grandparents
- *food* and *feeding* – the baby may be 'a slow feeder' and finds feeding difficult; they may tire easily when sucking
- food absorption – difficulty in digesting milk feeds
- food allergies – they may be allergic to milk
- loss or lack of appetite – the baby turns away from the food provided
- *infection* – the baby may be vulnerable to infections, especially of the ears, nose and throat and these can affect feeding
- home environment – this may affect how the baby grows. For instance the baby may lack attention, may be left alone for long periods or may receive no stimulation from the surroundings.

When babies are not thriving, their growth should be carefully monitored and recorded at regular intervals. Different strategies can be introduced to promote the baby's growth. An example of this is changing milk feeds to soya milk in small amounts for short regular periods. (See *human growth and development*.)

Fair Employment Act 1989: see *Fair Employment Commission*.

Fair Employment Commission: an organisation which was set up following the Fair Employment (Northern Ireland) Act 1989. The Commission was established to eliminate *discrimination* in *Northern Ireland* on the basis of *religion*. The Act determines that employers should fulfil certain procedures with regard to recruitment, training and opportunities for promotion amongst their Catholic and Protestant employees. If discrimination is evident and proved by the commission then a company can be fined or other economic sanctions against the company may be imposed.

Families and Children: a section in the welfare system introduced by the Government Green Paper *New Ambitions for our Country: A New Contract For Welfare*. It supports *families* and children as well as tackling child *poverty*. The aims of this section of the welfare system are to:

- support families with children, especially poorer families, with increases in child benefit; those families on income-related *benefits* are entitled to a further increase in benefit for each child under the age of 11 years
- help *workless* (unemployed) parents into the labour market by lowering the

barriers to work (e.g. the provision of safe, affordable childcare)
- support working parents by improving the quality of childcare
- ensure that financial and emotional support from parents continues even after separation; this involves reviewing the role of the *child support agency* and exploring the policies which enable *local authorities* to provide for the children for whom they have *parental responsibility*
- reduce the rate of conception among girls under 16. This includes implementing the proposals in the White Paper Excellence in Schools to teach pupils about the responsibilities of parenthood. (HMSO 1998)[44]

family: a group of individuals who are related by *blood, adoption* or marriage. (See *family structures.*) The role of the family is influenced by moral issues, because it is a social as well as a biological formation. Some support for selected family groups can be found at:

- Families Anonymous – a self-help fellowship for families and friends of drug abusers. (For further information contact Families Anonymous, 88 Caledonian Road, London N1 9DN.)
- Families Need Fathers – this is primarily concerned with the problems of maintaining a child's relationship with both its parents during, and following, a divorce. (For further information contact Families Need Fathers, 37 Carden Road, London SE15 3UB.)

A government Green Paper 'Supporting Families' was introduced in November 1998 as a result of the rise of lone parent families in modern day Britain. The proposals include the:

- introduction of a new National Family and Parenting Institute, to provide advice and information which meet the needs of the multi-cultural diversity which is present in society
- extension of the role of health visitors to provide programmes of training involving parent and toddler groups and working with teenagers
- review of the role of grandparents – elderly people will be able to volunteer to be surrogate grannies and support young parents
- review of paternity leave with fathers as well as mothers being eligible
- information systems for marrying couples.

family assistance order: an order under the *Children Act 1989*. It provides the time which may be necessary for *families* under stress to work through their difficulties. It is particularly relevant to families where children are involved, e.g. families when there are disputes, and families where the parents are divorced. Families are given support through this period by a court-appointed professional such as a *probation officer* or *social worker*. The order lasts for six months.

family centres: centres which offer a range of services to children, their parents or any other person looking after children. Family centres may provide recreational activities, *counselling, advice* and *self-help* support. These facilities may be purpose-built or attached to a *school* or *day nursery*.

family courts are courts in which all matters with regard to the *family* are dealt with. This includes *fostering* and *adoption* and cases involving unresolved disputes between parents over children. Families are supported by the family court welfare service which is a non-criminal section of the *probation service*, staffed by *probation officers*.

family credit: extra state income benefit to support working families on low incomes. It is *means-tested* and benefits those families with children where wage-earners are in low paid work. It replaced family income supplement following the Social Security Act 1988.

Family Policy Studies Centre: an organisation which researches issues of family trends and public policy. It is particularly concerned with the understanding of contemporary family structures and patterns. This includes changes that are taking place within family structures, and the implications of these changes in terms of policy and practice. The Family Policy Studies Centre acts as a forum which:

- analyses issues with regard to the study of family and related policy using its own research staff
- provides information for dissemination and debate, aiming to serve as a bridge between policy makers, academics and practitioners and to produce a range of material which is available to the public.

(For further information contact the Family Policy Studies Centre, 231 Baker Street, London NW1 6XE.)

family size: the number of children born to a couple. Factors which affect family size may include:

- the availability and reliability of affordable contraception
- social norms governing the 'ideal' family size
- economic decisions by the family regarding the cost of rearing children and its impact on the family's standard of living.

family structure: a group of individuals who live together to form a *family*. There are different family structures:

- a nuclear family is regarded as a man and woman and their dependent children living at the same residence (they co-operate together socially and economically)
- an extended family is one in which the basic nuclear structure has been added to, or extended, either vertically (e.g. grandparents, parents, children) or horizontally (e.g. two or more brothers living together with their respective spouses and children)
- reconstituted or step families – a couple who have divorced and remarried to include the different children from previous relationships
- *lone parent* or one parent families – one adult living with children; this family structure can be due to divorce, partnership break-up or death
- single parent families – one adult who has chosen to maintain single status while rearing dependent children
- *gender* families – couples from the same gender group who have chosen to rear children.

fat soluble vitamins are *vitamins* such as vitamin A, D, E and K which will dissolve in lipids, and only slightly, if at all, in water.

fats (lipids) are made up of *carbon, oxygen* and hydrogen. The proportion of oxygen to hydrogen is less in lipids than in carbohydrates. Lipids/fats are insoluble in water but can dissolve in other organic solvents such as ether and ethanol. Lipids are made up of glycerol and *fatty acids*. Fatty acids can be saturated or unsaturated depending on the presence of double bonds between carbon atoms. The functions of fats are to:

- provide a source of *energy*
- enable the fat soluble *vitamins* A, D, E, and K to be absorbed
- provide layers of protection around the vital organs of the human body
- provide layers of heat insulation around the body.

(See also *adipose tissue*.)

fatty acids are the major components of *fats*. They are made up of a hydrocarbon chain and a terminal carboxyl (acid) group (COOH). If there are no double bonds in the hydrocarbon chain they are saturated. If there is one double bond they are called monounsaturated. If there is more than one double bond present they are called polyunsaturated.

fear: an emotional state which is brought on by a feeling of impending danger. It has a number of characteristics such as increased *heart* rate, sweating, *behaviour* changes, dry *mouth* and occasionally a feeling of numbness or immobility. There are natural fear mechanisms in the body which are activated by the 'fear, fright and flight' functions of the hormone *adrenaline*. However, there are other situations which can cause irrational fears and these may relate to emotional, psychological, mental and physical *disorders, diseases* and *dysfunction*. (See also *anxiety*.)

feedback system: a 'circular' system where the output is used to control the input. A negative feedback system is one in which the rise in the output is used to reduce the input. Control of the level of thyroid hormone in the blood is an example of negative feedback – when the level of thyroid hormone is too high, it suppresses thyroid stimulating hormone production by the anterior *pituitary* gland. (See *homeostasis*.)

feeding: giving food to another person. This is one of the main functions of a *carer*. Feeding a child, *elderly person* or a person with *special needs* requires the following:

- setting aside the time to feed the individual concerned
- checking that the *food* is hot, attractively presented and fulfils the requirements of a balanced and healthy *diet*
- ensuring that the appropriate equipment is set up such as knives, forks, spoons, napkins and tissues to wipe away any excess food which may be on the mouth and face
- concentrating on the task in hand including sitting in a comfortable position for the person being fed and the carer carrying out the feeding, not placing too much food on the spoon or fork
- specially preparing food where there are difficulties in swallowing; mashing or liquidising the food when necessary, remembering to tell the person what the food contains (there is no reason why a 'MacDonalds' may not be liquidised)
- checking the portions; too large a portion may overwhelm a client or patient with feeding and appetite problems

- making sure that the person being fed has eaten sufficient even if it takes a long time to complete the feeding task.

(See also *malnutrition* and *balanced diet*.)

feelings: see *emotions*.

female reproductive system: the part of the female body responsible for reproduction. The female reproductive system consists of the following:

- *Ovaries* – the two female *gonads* which are held in place by *ligaments* in the lower abdomen, below the *kidneys*. The ligaments attach the ovaries to the walls of the pelvis. The female gametes or sex cells (ova, or one ovum) are produced regularly in the ovarian follicles of the ovaries after puberty.
- Ovarian follicles – a fluid-filled ovum and its coating of follicle cells each contains a maturing ovum. The follicles gradually get larger and begin to secrete hormones. Each cycle of follicle production results in only one fully mature follicle which is called a Graafian follicle.
- Fallopian tubes – narrow, muscular tubes linking the ovaries to the uterus. These allow the ovum's passage from the ovary to the uterus through muscular movement known as *peristalsis*.
- *Uterus* or *womb* – the hollow organ inside which a developing baby or foetus is held, or from which the ova are discharged. Once discharged, the ova pass out of the reproductive system. The womb has a lining of mucous membrane (the endometrium) covering a muscular wall with many blood vessels (see *menstruation*.)
- *Vagina* – the muscular canal which leads from the uterus out of the body. During *sexual intercourse* the penis ejaculates semen, containing sperm, into the vagina.
- *Vulva* – the outer part of the female reproductive system containing the labia which are folds of skin surrounding the opening of the vagina and the urethra.

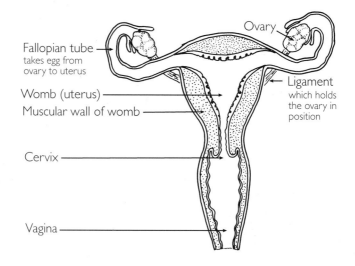

Fallopian tube
takes egg from
ovary to uterus

Ovary

Womb (uterus)
Muscular wall of womb

Ligament
which holds
the ovary in
position

Cervix

Vagina

feminists: those who believe that in society women:

- should have equal rights to men
- are entitled to the same financial rewards in employment as men
- should be viewed by society as equal to men in terms of status, employment and access to opportunities.

Women's groups have campaigned for women's rights in society. (See also *Equal Opportunities Commission, Sex Discrimination Act 1975.*)

fertilisation is the biological process which involves the fusion of a sperm with an egg. This usually takes place in the *Fallopian tube*. Many sperm may reach the egg but only one will penetrate the membrane which surrounds it. Following penetration the membrane changes in structure to form a barrier against any other sperm. The head of the sperm moves through the cytoplasm towards the nucleus of the egg and the nucleus of the sperm and egg fuse together. This produces a fertilised egg (zygote) which now starts to divide, first into two cells, then into four, then into eight and continues to divide as it journeys along the Fallopian tube. By the time it reaches the uterus it is a ball of cells which is called an *embryo.*

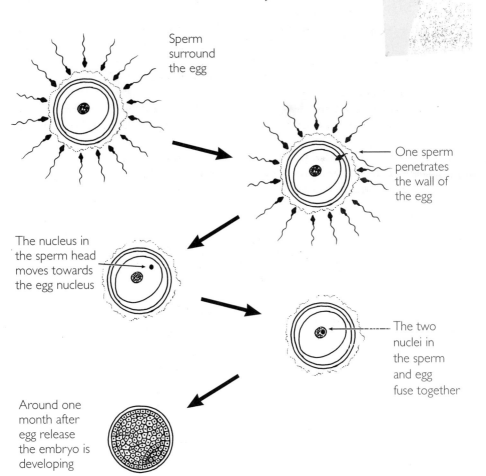

Sperm surround the egg

One sperm penetrates the wall of the egg

The nucleus in the sperm head moves towards the egg nucleus

The two nuclei in the sperm and egg fuse together

Around one month after egg release the embryo is developing

fertility rate: the number of live *births* in a population per 1000 women of child-bearing age, which is usually between 15 and 50 years of age. The figure is often broken down still further into age-specific fertility rates.

fire drill: all institutions are required to implement a procedure which enables people to find the best available exits from a building in the event of fire. Under the Fire Precaution Act 1971 all types of institutions, organisations and settings should review and implement precautions such as:

- providing a means of escape in the event of fire
- providing appropriate equipment to fight a fire
- the methods of giving fire warnings to staff, service users, clients and patients
- training new employees with regard to fire drill.

Every organisation should practice fire drills to simulate the events of a 'real fire'. The local fire brigade will advise any organisation with regard to risk from fire. A fire safety officer will visit organisations and give any advice considered necessary. (See *Health and Safety at Work 1974*.)

first aid is immediate assistance given to a person who has been injured or taken ill. According to St. John Ambulance the aims of first aid are:

- to preserve life
- to limit worsening of the condition
- to promote recovery (St. John Ambulance 1997)[57].

Individuals can be trained to be qualified first aiders. Organisations such as the British Red Cross and St. John Ambulance run programmes of first aid training. The term 'first aider' is used for those who have been trained and have received a first aid certificate.

fluoride: a chemical which is sometimes found in drinking *water*. It is used in *bone* formation, can be effective in protecting *teeth* from tooth decay and is often an ingredient in the manufacture of toothpaste. The Green Paper *Our Healthier Nation 1998* states that there is evidence to show that fluoridation of the water supply to the optimum level of one part in a million can substantially reduce the amount of tooth decay in children. The water supply in Sandwell in the West Midlands was fluoridated in 1986 and by 1995 the amount of tooth decay had more than halved. A comparable unfluoridated area saw little change over the same period. (HMSO 1998)[48]

foetal alcohol syndrome: this is a combination of *signs and symptoms* which occur in a *newborn baby* as a result of the mother's high intake of *alcohol* during pregnancy. These defects can take the form of growth retardation, and *heart* and limb abnormalities. Stimulants other than alcohol can also affect the *foetus* or unborn baby in a similar way. These include:

- *nicotine – smoking* may affect the growth of the foetus in the womb
- *drugs* – when the mother takes heroin for example, the baby can be born with an addiction to heroin
- some therapeutic drugs (see *thalidomide*).

foetal growth and development: stages of growth of the developing *foetus* in the uterus from conception to 40 weeks. The *placenta* provides *oxygen* and the essential *nutrients* which are passed into the bloodstream of the foetus from the mother's bloodstream via the umbilical cord. The foetus grows in a sac of fluid (the *amniotic sac*) which gives it protection from injury and *infection*. Just before the birth the membranes in the amniotic sac rupture. This is known as 'the waters breaking'. The development of the foetus is as follows:

- Age 8–9 weeks: the foetus is approximately 20 mm long. The *eyes* and *mouth* are formed. The hands and feet are forming. The *heart, brain, lungs* and other organs are developing. The heart beats from about 5 to 6 weeks.
- Age 10–14 weeks: the foetus is approximately 60 mm long; it is fully formed. The heart beat is strong. Pregnancy may begin to show.
- Age 23–30 weeks: the foetus is approximately 30–35 cm long. Fat begins to form under the skin. The skin is covered with lanugo (a fine covering of hair), and vernix caseosa (a layer of greasy substance) covers the skin. The foetus is 'viable' from 24 weeks. This is the legal term which means that the baby is capable of surviving outside the womb. Some babies now survive birth at an even earlier age.
- Age 31–40 weeks: by about 32 weeks the baby is usually lying head downwards ready for birth. Some time before birth, the head may move down into the pelvis and is said to be 'engaged', but sometimes the baby's head does not engage until labour has started.

foetus: the developing embryo becomes a foetus after the first eight weeks of development in the *womb*. The foetus develops and grows in the womb until *birth*.

food: substances which are eaten by all humans and other living organisms in order to provide nourishment. Foods contain a number of nutrients such as *carbohydrates, proteins* and *fats, water, minerals* and *vitamins*. Roughage or fibre is also necessary to help to move food through the gut. (See *balanced diet, feeding, malnutrition*.)

food hygiene: the study of the *food* handling methods which are used in the production, preparation and presentation of food. The aim of food hygiene is the production of food which is both clean and safe to eat. There are four main aspects which support food hygiene practice. These are the:

- introduction of hygiene regulations with regard to raw meat, cooked meat and certain other foods before it is delivered to shops, homes, canteens and restaurants
- care and hygiene practice of those handling the food during production and service
- storage arrangements for food
- design and cleanliness of cooking equipment, kitchens and food preparation areas.

See *food hygiene regulations*.

food hygiene regulations: regulations which support legislation on *food* preparation and handling. Food handlers must:

- keep clean, cover cuts with blue waterproof dressings (so they are easily seen if they fall into food), wear suitable protective overclothing, and must not smoke or spit
- report to the person managing the food business if they are suffering from food poisoning or a food-borne disease

- ensure that food preparation areas have a separate basin for washing hands, a good supply of disposable paper towels or an electric hand drier, a clean nail-brush and plenty of soap, hands should be washed before handling food or when changing from handling uncooked to cooked food
- implement building regulations with regard to toilet facilities; these should be provided well away from the main food production or food preparation area, with notices reminding staff to wash their hands. This is to ensure that food is not contaminated with the harmful bacteria which are present in human *faeces*
- be encouraged not to wear heavy make-up which can contaminate food
- ensure that long hair is covered with a hat or tucked into a hairnet so that flakes of skin or hairs do not fall into the food
- not wear strong smelling perfume or aftershave which can taint delicately flavoured food
- not smoke or eat while on duty; they can be permitted to do this when having regular rest breaks and must, of course, wash their hands again before resuming work.

The Food Hygiene regulations, introduced in 1970, were amended in 1991. Under the Food Safety Act 1990 the training of all those involved in food handling was recommended.

food poisoning: an illness caused by eating *food* which has been contaminated with *bacteria* or their toxins. Symptoms include *vomiting, diarrhoea,* nausea or feeling of sickness, or abdominal pain. Some of the organisms responsible for food poisoning are *Salmonella,* Listeria, Staphylococcus and *Clostridium.*

food preservation: methods of food processing which prevent the growth of harmful *bacteria* and fungi and slow down the rate of deterioration (e.g. pickling and freezing).

Food Standards Agency: set up by the government in 1998 to monitor standards of food manufacture and to promote healthy eating. It has taken over some of the responsibilities of the Ministry of Agriculture, Fisheries and Food.

foodborne disease: a disease that can be transmitted via *food* (e.g. *salmonella*).

foot: the part of the body which is an arrangement of interlocking *bones* at the base of the leg. The bones are kept in place by *ligaments* and *muscles* and extend from the heel to the tip of the toe. The functions of the foot are as follows:

- to support the weight of the body in the standing position
- to enable a person to walk with stability on uneven surfaces by having flexible *joints* and interlocking bones
- to act as a lever to produce forward body movement when walking or running.

It is very important that feet are well cared for. This involves hygiene such as washing, changing socks, stockings or tights regularly. Shoes which fit properly and do not rub part of the feet are essential. Feet are growing through the first 18 years of life; it is important to allow young children to walk barefoot whenever possible to allow bones and muscles to grow and develop in a natural way. Children's feet should be measured regularly and shoes fitted which allow for growth. Shoes worn too tight will damage soft and developing young bones. Some common problems caused by ill-fitting shoes include:

- bunion – which is a painful swelling near the joint on the base of the big toe, caused by continuous pressure on the joint
- corn – an area of skin which has thickened due to persistent rubbing or pressure on a part of the foot, causing pain
- hammer toe – the toe is bent up instead of lying flat.

(See *chiropody.*)

foster care is the care of a child or children by a *local authority*. The child is looked after by a qualified foster carer who has been screened by the local authority. The needs of children and the role and responsibilities of the local authority, or recognised voluntary organisation, are set out in the *Children Act 1989* and Foster Placement (Children) Regulations 1990. The foster care of children in Scotland is covered by the *Social Work (Scotland) Act 1969* and Children Act 1975. Children in foster care remain the responsibility of the local authority. Where there is more than one child in a family every effort is made to keep the children together. Children are fostered for a variety of reasons. These include situations where the:

- parents have been deemed unfit to care for their children; this occurs in some cases of *child abuse*
- parents are unable to cope because of illness
- parents are in prison and not in a position to care for their children.

Foster carers have statutory roles and responsibilities which include:

- providing day-to-day care
- helping and supporting a child as they return home to their parents
- allowing access for parents to visit their child or children
- allowing a parent to remove the child if the child has been in care for less than six months, otherwise the parent has to give 28 days notice of removal
- working closely with the child's social worker.

Foster carers apply for the position to the local authority. Following this, they join a recruitment programme which involves a series of interviews, screening, police checks and references. Foster carers work closely with a team of *social workers*. They receive regular ongoing support and training from the local authority. All children from the age of 0–16 years who are in the care of the local authority are entitled to foster care, subject to available spaces. Foster carers receive payment for their service. The amount paid relates to the number of children being fostered.

(For further information contact the National Foster Care Association, Francis House, Francis Street, London SW1 1RQ.)

fracture: the cracking or breaking of a *bone*. The fracture may be caused by a hard blow or fall. Treatment involves supporting the break in the normal position, either with a plaster of Paris splint, fibreglass splint or bandage. There are different types of fracture such as:

Simple fracture – this is a clean break or crack in the bone

Site of fracture

A number of
bone fragments

Comminuted fracture – this produces multiple bone fragments

A split in the cartilaginous
bone of a baby/young child

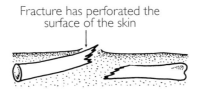

Greenstick fracture – produces a bend in the bone because it is cartilaginous (usually occurs in children)

Fracture has perforated the
surface of the skin

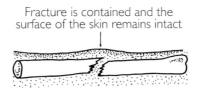

Open fracture – part of the broken bone penetrates the outer surface of the skin and so can cause bleeding

Fracture is contained and the
surface of the skin remains intact

Closed fracture – the bone is broken but it does not penetrate the surrounding skin

fragile X syndrome: a disorder which is caused by an abnormality of the *X chromosome* in human cells. It predominately affects males and may lead to learning disability and retardation.

frail and elderly: elderly people who have been affected by an injury or trauma, *disease, dysfunction*, psychological and psychiatric disorder which makes them more vulnerable. For example, *Alzheimers* disease affects a person's personality and memory. *Arthritis* affects a person's physical *well-being*. An *accident* can have psychological as well as physical effects.

fraud: methods used by individuals to make false claims for money. Examples include claiming state *benefits* by dishonest and illegal means. There is a wide spectrum of fraud from deliberate misrepresentation by individuals filling out forms to organised criminal activity. (See *New Ambitions for our Country: A New Contract For Welfare 1998*.)

free-basing: this is the illegal manufacture of the drug *crack*. It involves the heating of *cocaine* with a chemical which produces hard rocks of various sizes. (See *drugs*.)

free play: the way that children *play* using their initiative and imagination without any guidance from adults. This form of play encourages a child's independence and develops positive *self-esteem*.

Freud, Sigmund invented psychoanalysis which relates both to the body of theory about the unconscious and his therapy based on it. Freud's theories include:

- *personality* theory relating to three aspects of the personality, the id, the ego and the superego, which interact and relate with each other
- *defence mechanisms* which are methods used by the ego to cope with conflict
- the different psychosexual stages of the personality based on the theory that the driving force behind personality is the sex drive or the need to express sexual energy.

Friedreich's ataxia: an *inherited disease* which causes *degeneration* of the *nerve* cells in the *spinal cord*. This leads to muscular weakness and *ataxia* which makes walking and movement difficult. It starts in early childhood and, as the disease progresses, the child's *mobility* is greatly reduced until by adulthood he/she is confined to a wheelchair.

(For further information contact Friedreich's Ataxia Group, The Stable, Wiggin's Yard, Bridge Street, Godalming, Surrey GU7 1HU.)

funding: sources of money which are required to provide health and social care services. Resourcing of health and social care provision is an important influence on the type of provision which is supplied. Funding can come from:

- central government
- local government (*local authorities*)
- *charities*
- business and commercial sources
- public donations
- covenants/bequests.

Under the White Paper '*The New NHS – Modern, Dependable*' 1997 there are revised strategies with regard to funding in the *National Health Service*. Part of the new approach to funding includes the setting of demanding targets on unit cost and productivity throughout the NHS. The Government has developed a programme which requires *NHS trusts* to publish and benchmark their costs on a consistent basis. This provides a national schedule of '*reference costs*' which itemises the cost of individual treatments across the NHS. Costs for major areas of hospital activity will be available in time to be included in long term agreements for 1999–2000. Other initiatives relate to funding quality and efficiency, which promote access to quality care across the country by:

- fairly distributing resources through *health authorities* to inclusive *primary care groups*
- establishing new unified budgets for primary care groups covering *hospital* and community services, *GP* prescribing and general practice *infrastructure*
- allowing clinicians to influence the use of resources by aligning clinical and financial responsibilities. (HMSO 1997)[61]

(See also *cost effectiveness, cost improvement programmes*.)

gall bladder: an organ of the body which stores *bile*. Gallstones develop in the gall bladder as a result of the build up of *cholesterol* which is excreted in the bile.

games are periods of *play* which have instructions or rules enhancing the enjoyment of those taking part. There are different types of play including:

- ball games (e.g. football)
- court games (e.g. tennis)
- board games (e.g. monopoly)
- games involving song and rhyme (e.g. 'ring-a-ring-o'-roses').

Some games such as football are competitive. They may be a satisfying experience for both children and adults alike. Childhood games encourage team spirit and working with others in a positive way. They can develop *cognitive skills* such as problem solving. For example, playing Monopoly can involve counting and the concept of buying and selling property.

gaseous exchange: the process in which *oxygen* is taken into the body and *carbon dioxide* released from the body during respiration. *Air* containing oxygen enters the *lungs*. The oxygen passes through the walls of the lungs into the *blood*. Carbon dioxide passes out of the blood, through the walls of the lungs and into the air contained within the lungs. It is then breathed out. The lungs form a large surface area for air and oxygen to be breathed in and carbon dioxide to be breathed out. The actual gaseous exchange takes place in the air sacs or *alveoli* of the lungs. (See *mechanisms for breathing*.)

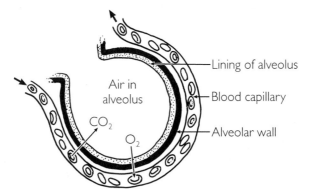

gastric glands are situated in the *stomach*. They are responsible for secreting gastric juices. When *food* enters the *mouth*, gastric juice is produced in the stomach and as the food enters the stomach. Gastric juice contains:

- hydrochloric acid – which acts as an antiseptic, kills off *bacteria* and promotes the action of the *enzymes*, pepsin and rennin
- pepsin – the enzyme responsible for digesting proteins by breaking them down into peptides
- rennin – the enzyme responsible for clotting milk.

(See *digestion*.)

gastroenteritis: inflammation of the lining of the *stomach* and intestine which can be caused by:

- *disease,* such as dysentery, when there has been contamination of the *water* supply with sewage
- *food poisoning* when *food* preparation and hygiene practices have been inefficient; causes include *infections* such as *salmonella,* bacterial toxins such as that of Clostridium, allergy to certain foods such as shellfish or poisoning due to eating toxic chemicals.

gastro-enterology is the study of the *digestive system.*

gays: see lesbians/gays.

gender: the social identity of male and female not restricted to biological differences.

gender role: attitudes, behaviours, personal development and interests that are considered appropriate for one *gender* and inappropriate for the other.

gender stereotypes: fixed beliefs about what it means to be male or female. Examples of gender *stereotyping* are the varying beliefs about which occupations are suitable for men and women.

general practitioner (GP): a *doctor* who is qualified and registered to work within a surgery practice or *health authority* health centre. General practitioners are involved in ongoing changes in the NHS. They will play an active part in *primary care groups* and *local medical committees.*

General Social Services Council: a government organisation set up in 1998. The function of the General Social Services Council is to enforce standards of conduct and practice within the social care workforce. The council ensures that *service users, carers,* practitioners, employers and the general public have confidence in the standards which are set for social care. These include *service standards* and *occupational standards* of *competence.* The Council is accountable to the Secretary of State for Health.

genes: unit of the *chromosome* containing a code or characteristic pattern which is inherited (passed on) through generations. Genes influence hair and eye colour, *blood group,* etc. *Chromosomes* contain thousands of genes. Different chromosomes contain coded instructions which dictate the way in which an individual will grow and develop. (See *deoxyribonucleic acid.*)

genetic counselling: special *counselling* given to people where there is any likelihood that the baby they have conceived or are about to conceive may inherit a *genetic disorder* or *disease.* This is likely if the disease or disorder is one which has:

- affected any other children in the family
- affected other members of the family (i.e. grandparents or close family).

For example, there can be a heart-breaking debate if the mother has conceived and is carrying a child with *Down's syndrome* as to whether she should go ahead with the pregnancy or have an *abortion.* A professional genetic counsellor is available to provide a means of *support,* and the opportunity to discuss options. Furthermore, genetic counselling sometimes takes place after the birth of the baby with a genetic disease or disorder. The questions then are, will future babies be affected and should the parents try for more children?

genetic disorders and diseases: disorders, *disease or dysfunction* which occur when there is a deficiency in a whole *chromosome* or in part of a chromosome. If there is a deficiency in a whole chromosome or more/fewer chromosomes than normal are produced in each cell then the individual being formed will be affected. For example, a child with *Down's syndrome* has 47 chromosomes instead of 46. Genetic disorders are those which are inherited or passed on from one generation to another. Examples include disorders caused by a:

- defective and dominant gene e.g. *Huntington's chorea.*
- defective and recessive gene that a child receives from each parent e.g. *sickle cell disease*
- defective gene which affects a sex chromosome e.g. *haemophilia.* This is where the gene is carried on the X chromosome.

genetics: the study of the factors which relate to inheritance. It involves the study of the effects of *genes* on a child's development and growth. Children inherit genes from their parents. Inherited characteristics influence the development of the different and distinguishing features of each individual (e.g. height, hair colour, shape of the body, appearance) and even types of behaviour. The genetic make-up of a child is called the genotype. The genes influence the appearance (or physical characteristics) of a person and this is called the phenotype. It is important to recognise that genes occur in pairs and that two sets of genes which are inherited occupy the same position within their respective *chromosomes* as they do in the parents.

geriatrician: a qualified *doctor* who is a specialist in the field of *disease,* disorders and *dysfunction* found in the elderly. They are responsible for detection, diagnosis and *treatment* of elderly persons.

gestures are non-verbal messages which are communicated using arms, hands and fingers. It is important to remember that the meanings of gestures differ from one culture to another. (See *communication.*)

glands are special organs (or sometimes groups of *cells* or single cells) which produce and secrete a variety of substances vital to life. There are two types of human gland – exocrine and endocrine*:*

- Exocrine glands are those which secrete substances through tubes, or ducts, onto a surface or into a cavity. Most body glands are exocrine, e.g. the digestive glands. Exocrine glands can secrete fluids, for example digestive juices into the digestive system. Such juices contain enzymes which cause the breakdown of *food.* Other examples of exocrine glands are the *salivary glands,* the *pancreas* and *liver.*
- Endocrine or ductless glands are those which secrete substances called hormones directly into the *blood* (there are blood vessels in the glands). These glands may be separate bodies or cells inside organs such as the *pituitary gland* which is situated at the base of the brain and is directly influenced by the hypothalamus. The pituitary gland is made up of an anterior (front) lobe and a posterior (back) lobe. Many of the *hormones* in the pituitary stimulate other glands to secrete hormones.

glycolysis: a series of reactions in the body which is part of *cell* respiration. It takes place in the cytoplasm or cells. Glycolysis involves a number of stages and links with the *Krebs cycle.*

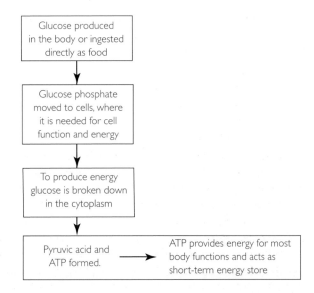

gonads are the male and female reproductive organs in which sex cells (gametes) and hormones are produced. Sex hormones are required for the body to develop normally. In the *male reproductive system,* the reproductive organs are the testes. The main *female reproductive* organs are the ovaries. An important female hormone is *oestrogen* as this promotes the development of the characteristic female physical shape. The hormones oestrogen and progesterone regulate the menstrual cycle. The male hormones are called androgens and include testosterone. *Androgens* are responsible for the physical and muscular development of the male as well as the distribution of body hair and the deepening of the voice. (See *endocrine system.*)

gonorrhoea: see *sexually transmitted diseases.*

GP: see *general practitioner.*

Gram staining is a method of using a blue dye to help identify *bacteria* microscopically. If the bacteria have certain surface features the blue stain is retained and the micro-organism will be gram positive (+). If they are unaffected by the stain they will be gram negative (−).

grant maintained status is the way in which organisations are supported by subsidies of money from the government, charities or from a business investment. Following the *Education Act 1988, schools* can choose to opt out of *local authority* control and receive their grant directly from central government. The grant maintained status was a means whereby schools hoped to be more independent with decisions being made by the governors and parents, not by the local authority.

graphs: a diagrammatic method of presenting *data.* These may take the form of line graphs in which two variables are plotted on a *chart.* The relationship between them can be compared.

grief is a response to loss. This includes loss of a person, relationship, job, pet or any aspect of a person's life which is important to their daily living. Grief is a painful process with the loss of a child, husband, wife or partner particularly difficult to cope with. The process of grief often goes through different stages. These are:

- Shock and disbelief ('it must be someone else, it isn't true'). A person might feel numb, shocked and locked into a state of isolated disbelief.
- Denial, at this stage the bereaved person behaves in an unreal way. They live as though the person has not died; or as if they did not really lose their job. This stage can last for hours or days.
- Despair, as there is a growing awareness of what has happened. In addition to this, the person is filled with longing to know the reasons why? There may be feelings of depression, guilt and anxiety which mingle with despair. A sense of unfulfilled dreams adds to the feelings of despair. During this stage individuals need care and support. This will involve listening and allowing the person to express their anger and their feelings of deep pain.
- Acceptance, the person begins to pick up the aspects of their life and learns to live with the loss they have suffered.

It is important to remember that the timescale between each stage will depend on the loss and the circumstances of that loss. (See *bereavement.*)

Griffith's report – Community Care Agenda for Action 1988 is a government report written by Roy Griffiths. The report was commissioned to determine *community care* policy. This included the discharging of long-term *patients* from large psychiatric *hospitals* into the community and proposals that:

- *social service departments* should have a major role in purchasing community care for their service users
- *local authorities* should draw up *community care plans*
- *service users'* needs should be assessed with regard to the services required
- the supply of services available through the *private* and *voluntary* sectors should be stimulated.

growth hormone is produced in the anterior lobe of the *pituitary gland*. It controls the physical growth of the body and is produced mainly during childhood when physical growth is rapid. A child's growth rate needs to be monitored regularly (see *centile charts*). Deficiency of this hormone can lead to stunted growth. Excess secretion of this hormone can lead to gigantism. Growth hormone can be given to a child who has a growth deficiency due to a malfunctioning pituitary gland. (See *human growth and development.*)

guardian ad litem is appointed by the court to act as guardian to a child. Every *local authority* must establish a guardians' ad litem and reporting officers' panel and appoint persons to be members of it. The administration of the panel must be undertaken by a person appointed by the local authority who is not involved in the day-to-day provision of services for children. Records relating to the functioning of the panel must be kept.

Guthrie test: a test used to detect diseases and disorders such as *phenylketonuria* (PKU) and hypothyroidism. PKU is an inherited condition which affects a baby's ability to metabolise part of *protein foods*. Hypothyroidism is a condition which occurs when the thyroid gland is underactive. The Guthrie test is carried out when the baby is about six days old and has been taking milk feeds for several days. *Blood* is collected from a heel prick to cover four circles on a specially prepared card which is then sent to the laboratory. Early detection and dietary treatment of PKU enables the child to develop in the normal way.

H

haematology is the study of the *blood*. Haematologists study the formation, composition and the functions of the blood. This helps them to detect and diagnose any disorder, *dysfunction* and *disease* which may be present. Blood diseases such as leukaemia and blood deficiency disorders such as anaemia can be detected through the study of a blood sample.

haemocytometer: an instrument which is used under the *microscope* for counting the concentration of cells in the *blood*.

haemoglobin: *iron-containing* pigment in *blood*. It is found in the *red blood cells*. It carries *oxygen* in the form of oxyhaemoglobin. Carboxyhaemoglobin is formed when haemoglobin combines with *carbon monoxide*. It does this readily, which makes carbon monoxide a powerful respiratory poison, as the carbon monoxide combines with haemoglobin at the sites normally occupied by the oxygen molecules.

haemophilia: an inherited 'sex-linked' recessive condition. Generally only males suffer from haemophilia, but it is passed on through female members of the family. The defect causing haemophilia is on the *X chromosome*. The daughter of a man with haemophilia may inherit his X chromosome and so be a carrier. Haemophiliacs suffer from a bleeding disorder because they lack a clotting factor in the plasma. Any cut, knock or injury can therefore be life-threatening. The Haemophilia Society provides support for haemophiliacs, their families and friends.

(For further information contact the Haemophilia Society, 16 Trinity Street, London SE1 1DE.)

hallucinogen: any type of substance which is capable of causing hallucinations. Examples include *LSD* and 'magic mushrooms'. These *drugs* give a person short-term experiences which can be either pleasant or confusing and very frightening. In some cases these drugs can trigger a psychosis or some form of *mental illness*.

Hall Jones classification system: a classification system which is based on more categories than mentioned in the Registrar General's index.

hand–eye co-ordination is what a young child develops while learning to control his/her hands and fingers. The hand–eye movements enable a child to bring an object into their line of vision. When a child holds a spoon and lifts it to the *mouth* this movement is dependent on hand–eye co-ordination. This fine *muscle* control develops gradually throughout childhood.

health: 'a state of complete physical, mental and social well-being' and not merely the absence of disease and infirmity. (WHO 1948)

health action zone: an area in which there is an initiative to form a partnership of health and social care services. These services include primary *care* groups, *local authorities*, community groups, the *voluntary sector* and local business within an area or district. They provide added impetus to the task of tackling ill health and reducing *inequalities in health*. (See also *The New NHS – Modern, Dependable, Our Healthier Nation – A contract for health*.)

Health and Safety at Work Act 1974: an Act of Parliament which regulates health and safety of employees in the workplace. The Act makes recommendations which include:

- all employers and their employees being made aware of health and *safety* issues; personal responsibility is an important requirement
- a comprehensive framework involving legislation and regulations with regard to hazards, potential hazards, *fire regulations* and *codes of practice*
- the setting up of the Health and Safety Commission to ensure implementation of the Act
- regular health and safety inspections to be carried out by inspectors.

The commission may instigate legal proceedings, give help and advice and set up advisory committees to consider employment in areas which involve working with toxic and dangerous substances, i.e. medicine, nuclear safety, industry and dealing with major hazards, dangerous pathogens or germs.

(See also *control of substances hazardous to health.*)

Health and Safety Executive: a major department which was set up within the Health and Safety Commission. The Health and Safety Inspectorate is responsible to the executive as it carries out inspections of premises etc. It ensures that the *reporting of injuries, Diseases and Dangerous Occurrences* regulations, policies and codes of practice within the *Health and Safety Act* are implemented and that *accidents* are investigated.

HSE
Health & Safety
Executive

The HSE logo

health and social care structures: a framework of health and social care provision which is arranged to complement the needs of the different *client* groups. Examples of health and social care services supporting *elderly people* would include *residential care, home care, respite care, occupational therapy, day centres, domicillary* care, *social workers*, parking concessions and voluntary support.

health and social well-being: a term used in NVQs in Care which encompasses all aspects of social, physical, intellectual, emotional and psychological health. This includes the notion of being 'at one with oneself'. (Care Sector Consortium 1998)[12]

health authorities are organisations which manage health care in a particular area. Under *The New NHS – Modern, Dependable 1997*, the functions of the health authorities include:

- assessing the health needs of the local population, drawing on the knowledge of other organisations
- drawing up a strategy for meeting those needs, in the form of a *health improvement programme*, developed in partnership with all the local interests and ensuring delivery of the NHS contribution to it

- deciding on the range and location of health care services for the health authority's residents, which should flow from, and be part of, the health improvement programme
- determining local targets and standards to drive up quality and efficiency in the light of national priorities and providing guidance to ensure their delivery
- supporting the development of *primary care groups* so that they can rapidly assume their responsibilities
- allocating resources to primary care groups
- holding primary care groups to account.

health benefits: *benefits* which are associated with the *National Health Service*. These include free dental treatment, eye tests, prescriptions, milk tokens and *vitamins* for expectant mothers. In addition, those on low income will receive support with spectacles, wigs and travel to *hospital*. Those who qualify for health benefits include *elderly people*, children, disabled people and pregnant mothers.

health care is care which is provided through the *National Health Service*. Health care is available through a combination of statutory, voluntary, private and informal health provisions. Health care provision operates at three levels:

- Primary care – health care offered to individuals through *GPs* and their teams in general practice. Primary care also includes *dentists*.
- Secondary care – health care offered through *hospitals, National Health Trusts* and private hospitals in the *independent sector.*
- Tertiary care – specialist health care offered through special hospitals including *cancer* hospitals such as the Royal Marsden Hospital. The Royal Marsden treats people with cancer from all over the world.

health care assistants provide nursing support in *hospitals* or other health care settings such as nursing homes. They carry out general duties for patients which include:

- recording temperature, pulse, respiration and blood pressure
- assisting with toileting and *bathing*
- encouraging mobility, helping with exercises
- supporting a *patient's* self-esteem, talking, reading, *listening* and sharing *information*
- carrying out 'domestic' duties, such as tidying up, sorting laundry etc.

health centre: a community based organisation which accommodates the *GP* and the *primary health care team*. It may offer other services such as support group sessions for the elderly, back pain clinics, and *screening programmes.*

health education: a programme which informs the general public about issues relating to healthy lifestyles. This allows individuals the benefit of making informed choices. The most recent government initiative '*Our Healthier Nation – A Contract for Health*' has two key aims:

- to improve the health of the population as a whole by increasing the length of people's lives and the number of years people spend free from illness
- to improve the health of the worse off in society and to narrow the health gap.

Health education programmes have three different levels:

- Primary health education aimed at healthy people. For example, giving presentations and targeting people with information on healthy *diets.*
- Secondary health education aimed at those people who already have a health condition. For example, exploring strategies to encourage a heavy smoker with *lung* problems to give up *smoking,* or an overweight person with a *heart* condition to reduce their weight.
- Tertiary health education aimed at those individuals who have a disorder, *dysfunction* or *disease* which could not have been prevented and for which there is no cure. The information issued relates to *rehabilitation* and specialist support programmes.

Health education relates closely to *national health targets.* Health education may explore issues such as:

- reducing the likelihood of disease by promoting *immunisation* programmes, or healthy eating to prevent heart disease
- minimising the risk of potentially harmful lifestyles, e.g. smoking, drinking, taking *drugs, certain* sexual practices, all of which correlate with medical conditions (heart disease, *cancer, HIV*)
- promoting healthy living practices through *diet* and *exercise*
- promoting personal safety and security in relation to the safe use of equipment, safety in the home and at *work.*

Health Education Authority: an organisation which is funded by the government. The functions of the council include:

- providing training for health and social care workers
- researching issues which relate to health
- setting up local and national *health education* campaigns
- providing information on a large number of health issues.

health education campaigns: methods used to communicate health information to the general public. They allow individuals to become aware of the *health* issues which can affect them. Such campaigns cover a number of issues which link closely to *national health targets.* The aim of such campaigns is to provide knowledge by supplying appropriate *information* which enables individuals to make choices about their health. An example might be encouraging people to give up *smoking,* or to look at *fat* content when buying *food* in order to maintain a low fat *diet.* Health education campaigns can encourage individuals to take more control of health issues in their lives. In some cases this can lead to changing *lifestyle* habits, such as taking more *exercise* and learning to manage *stress.*

health improvement programmes: programmes set up in localities to support the *national contracts for health.* The functions of such programmes are to:

- give a clear description of how national aims, priorities, targets and contracts are tackled locally
- set out a range of locally determined priorities and targets to address issues and problems which are judged important with particular emphasis on areas of major *inequalities in health* in local communities

- support specific agreed programmes of action to address national and local health improvement priorities
- show that the action proposed is based on evidence which is known to work from research and best practice reports
- indicate which local organisations have been involved in drawing up a plan, what their contributions will be and how they will be held to account for delivering it
- ensure that the plan is easy to understand and accessible to the public
- be a vehicle for setting strategies in the shaping of local health services.

(See also *Our Healthier Nation – A Contract for Health, national health targets.*)

health inequalities: see *inequalities in health.*

Health of the Nation 1992: a government report presented in the House of Commons in July 1992. It was designed to set out a national strategy for health in England. The key areas selected in the report are coronary heart disease and *strokes, cancers, mental illness, HIV/AIDS,* sexual health and *accidents.* These are all areas identified as major causes of premature death or avoidable ill health. This has been recently updated in *Our Healthier Nation – A Contract for Health 1998.* However, Our Healthier Nation 1998 does not highlight HIV/AIDS and sexual health. See *National health targets.*

health promotion: a method of providing health *information.* Such information is a means whereby individuals may make decisions which will improve their health and give them a healthier *lifestyle.* (See *health education campaigns.*)

health quality service: the quality kite mark for health services was introduced in June 1998. The aim of the new award is to improve patient care. Certain requirements have to be satisfied before the stamp of approval is given. This takes the form of five key indicators. These:

- monitor patients' experiences using methods such as questionnaires
- monitor staff motivation and morale
- develop reliable indicators of clinical outcomes such as infection rates and death rates in *hospitals*
- measure efficiency – looking at staff/patient ratios and bed occupancy rates
- facilitate patients' access to the service.

health targets: see *national targets for health.*

health visitor: a registered *nurse* who qualifies through further training as a health visitor. A health visitor is employed by the *health authority* and is based in a health centre or *GP's* surgery. The health visitor offers support and guidance, monitors the growth and development of babies and young children, and takes part in *child abuse* procedures as well as working with the elderly. Their main concern is *health education* as well as the direct care and welfare of their clients.

healthy settings: this is an area identified by the government as a key focus to improve health and address *health inequalities.* There are three separate initiatives:

- healthy schools – focusing on children
- healthy workplaces – focusing on adults
- healthy neighbourhoods – focusing on older people.

(See *Our Healthier Nation – A Contract for Health*.)

heart: a muscular organ which pumps *blood* round the body. The heart consists of:

- Atria (auricles) – the two upper chambers. The left atrium receives oxygenated blood, i.e. blood with fresh *oxygen* from the *lungs* via the pulmonary veins. The right atrium receives deoxygenated blood from the rest of the body via the superior and inferior vena cavae.
- *Ventricles* – the two lower chambers. The left ventricle receives blood from the left atrium and pumps it into the aorta. The right ventricle receives blood from the right atrium and pumps it via the pulmonary arteries to the lungs.

(See *cardiac cycle*.)

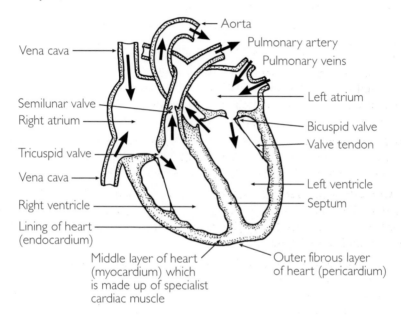

heart attack (myocardial infarction) is the result of a blockage in the *coronary artery*. This can lead to the *death* of a segment of heart *muscle*. The person suddenly experiences severe pain in the centre of the chest. The pain extends to the throat and down the left arm. The person needs calm reassurance and emergency treatment. A person complaining of chest pain should never be left on their own and an *ambulance* should be called as soon as possible.

heart disease and strokes: a priority health target area identified by the government in 1998. *Heart* disease and strokes were selected as a priority area because:

- they are a major cause of early death, accounting for about 18,000 deaths (one-third of all deaths) in men and 7000 deaths (one-fifth of all deaths) in women under 65 years of age
- deaths from *coronary heart disease* alone account for more than a million years of life lost amongst those under 75 years

- heart disease and stroke can often be prevented
- there are marked inequalities of incidence; for example, women born in West Africa and the Caribbean have a higher risk of a stroke than other women. Men of working age in the bottom social class are at least 50 per cent more likely to die from coronary heart disease than men in the overall population.

Although death rates from heart disease and strokes have been decreasing, the health target is to reduce the death rate from heart disease, stroke and related illnesses amongst people under 65 years, by at least a further third by 2010 from a baseline. This is the basic mortality target established in 1996. (HMSO 1998)[48]

heart rate is the rate at which the *heart* beats, usually expressed as beats per minute. At rest an adult heart beats approximately 70 times a minute. It beats faster in a child. Heart rate increases when *exercise* is being taken as the heart supplies the muscles of the body with extra *oxygen* and *food* to maintain the *exercise*. Heart rate increases during times of excitement, fear and *anxiety*. (See *pulse*.)

hepatitis: inflammation of the *liver*, which is caused by *infection*, or damage due to chemicals or *drug* treatment/misuse. The inflammation affects the liver, interfering with *bile* production and yellow pigments of *bile* circulate in the bloodstream causing yellowing of the *skin* and the whites of the eyes and dark yellow *urine*. The most common forms of hepatitis are:

- Hepatitis A – transmitted by *food* and *water* which is contaminated with faeces due to lack of *hygiene* precautions in food preparation. It is also transmitted from person to person or by injecting with unclean hypodermic needles. It can often occur in institutions or amongst large groups of people where food is not adequately prepared. There is *vaccination* available against this disease.
- Hepatitis B – this is transmitted by sexual contact or from a mother to her unborn baby or *foetus*. It can be transmitted through injections, *blood transfusions* using contaminated or unclean needles for either injecting drugs or following *acupuncture* and tattooing. It is caused by a *virus* which can be present in other body fluids such as *saliva*, vaginal fluid and semen. There is vaccination available in the form of gamma globulin containing antibodies to the virus.
- Hepatitis C – this is a non-A and a non-B hepatitis mainly transmitted through infected blood and syringes which have been contaminated with the virus. It is said to be the most common form of hepatitis transmitted through blood transfusion. There is no vaccination available for this.
- Hepatitis E – as with hepatitis A this is transmitted through drinking water contaminated with faeces. It can reach *epidemic* proportions in tropical areas. There is no vaccination available.

heredity: the transmission of *genetic* characteristics from one generation to another, i.e. parent to child.

heroin: a *drug*, a derivative of morphine, which is derived from the opium poppy. The plant is harvested in order to be processed into a painkilling or analgesic drug. The drug is most effective when given by injection to *patients* suffering from severe pain, e.g. those patients suffering from advanced *cancer*. One of its side effects is that individuals can develop tolerance, or physical and psychological dependence. When the medication of heroin is reduced or a patient is taken off the drug, *withdrawal symptoms* can be unpleasant and can last for up to two weeks.

Heroin has addictive properties and individuals can become addicted to the euphoric effects of heroin and become 'mainliners'; mainliners use the injection method to 'rush' or intensify the euphoric experience. Some addicts now choose to smoke heroin and heat it on a strip of tinfoil until it gives off smoke ('chasing the dragon'). Heroin addicts have a mortality rate which is 18 times higher than normal. *Death* is not normally due to the direct effects of heroin use. Death may be due to:

- an overdose
- illness resulting from the use of 'dirty' or unclean needles and injection techniques, including venous thrombosis, *HIV/AIDS, septicaemia* or *hepatitis*
- mixing heroin with other substances
- associated health-related illness due to physical *neglect*.

heterosexuality: an attraction to persons of the opposite sex which may lead to sexual contact.

High Court: part of the law and justice system. There are three different divisions of the judicial court. These are the:

- Queen's bench which reviews disputes involving money, such as the seeking of damages in libel cases
- family division which investigates disputes relating to children and families including *adoption, divorce* and *court orders*
- chancery division which deals with issues relating to wills, taxation and disputes within businesses and companies.

histograms: a method of representing data which has been collected as a result of a research project. The method represents the frequency distribution of the data diagramatically in the form of a *chart*. A histogram consists of a series of blocks or bars with a height proportional to the frequency of an item or event. (See *bar chart*.)

histology is the microscopic study of *tissues*. When, for example, a *tumour* develops in a part of the body a sample of the tissue is sent to the histology department within a pathology laboratory for examination. The method is used to detect many different disorders, *dysfunctions* and *disease*. (See *pathology*.)

HIV (Human Immunodefficiency Virus): a virus which can cause *AIDS*. The *virus* gradually breaks down the *immune system* of an infected person.

holistic care involves caring for the whole person. This means that the physical, intellectual, emotional, social, religious and cultural needs of the *client* are taken into account and *care* for that person is implemented accordingly. It is based on the *belief* that all these aspects are interlinked and should not be considered separately. (See *care value base, complementary medicine, homoeopathy*.)

home care service: the *community care* teams which provide care for elderly and disabled *clients* in their own homes. The care includes shopping, cooking meals, helping clients with washing, dressing and cleaning. The carers are usually employed by the *social services department, voluntary* or private organisations. In some cases, this is a *means-tested* service.

Home Life 1984: a code of practice introduced to improve the standards of care for *clients* in *residential care*. It was conceived by the *Centre for Policy on Ageing* and recommended that:

- special provision be made available for individual client groups
- all *residential homes* for the elderly should be registered with the *local authority*
- all local authorities should be involved in carrying out inspections on private and statutory homes for the elderly under the Registered Homes Act 1984
- all clients have rights and choices which should be respected including those of *confidentiality and privacy*
- client admission procedures should be standardised
- building, room and staffing requirements should be identified.

Home Office: the central government department responsible for the administration of the justice system including the *police*, the *probation* and *prison* services.

Home Start UK: a voluntary organisation set up across the country to help young *families* under stress. It deals with single mothers and broken marriages. Help is given through a *network* of experienced parents who support young families under stress.

(For further information contact Margaret Harrison, 'Home Start UK', 2 Salisbury Road, Leicester LE1 7QR.)

homelessness: the condition suffered by a person who has no home. Under the Housing (Homeless Persons) Act 1997, *local authorities* are required to help homeless people who have priority *housing* needs, i.e. persons who have become homeless when they are pregnant, or have young and dependent children. (See *National Homeless Alliance, housing.*)

homeostasis: processes within the body which maintain its steady state. Conditions outside the body (the external environment) are continuously varying, but the body has mechanisms (homeostatic controls) for adjusting factors within the body so that the internal environment surrounding the *cells* is kept steady. Cells are surrounded by *tissue* fluid. This maintains an environment around the cells which allows them to function well and the body to remain healthy. For the homeostatic mechanism to work there must be:

- receptors capable of detecting changes
- a control mechanism to co-ordinate appropriate corrective mechanisms
- effectors which actually bring about the corrective mechanisms.

Their effectiveness depends on negative *feedback*.

Examples of conditions kept constant within the internal environment of the body by homeostatic mechanisms include:

- *pH* – the body's internal pH has a natural range of 7.33–7.42
- *body temperature*
- respiratory gases
- blood sugar levels.

homoeopathy is an *alternative* system of medicine that regards physical, emotional and mental symptoms as being intimately connected. Minute doses of natural substances are prescribed according to a complex pattern of symptoms in every area of the body. Individual likes and dislikes, and the family history of each individual is also taken into account. People suffering from all kinds of illnesses, from depression to arthritis, migraines to ulcers, and now the 'modern' illnesses, such as *AIDS* and *myalgic encephalomyelitis* (chronic fatigue syndrome), can be helped to regain a better level of health. Homoeopathy treats the individual person rather than the disease. This means that the homoeopath will want to build up a complete picture of a patient and their medical history, as well as all their symptoms, in order to find the remedy that provides the closest match. (See *complementary therapies, holistic care.*) Treatment is carried out by homoeopathic doctors who are qualified doctors with specialist training in homoeopathy, or by homoeopathic consultants who have attended a course in homoeopathy at a college associated with the Society of Homoeopathy.

(For further information contact The Society of Homoeopaths, 2 Artizan Road, Northampton NN1 4HU.)

homosexuality: sexual contact with members of the same sex, or a sexual preference for one's own sex.

hormone replacement therapy (HRT): *oestrogen* administered to women when the natural production of sex hormones has been reduced or stopped for some reason, such as *menopause,* or after a total hysterectomy (surgical removal of the *uterus* and *ovaries*). In some cases the hormone progesterone is given as part of hormone replacement therapy for women who are experiencing the symptoms of *menopause* and who still have a womb.

hormones: chemicals secreted directly into the bloodstream by the *glands* which form the *endocrine* system. They travel in the *blood* to target *organs.* The effects of hormones are slower and more general than *nerve* action. They control long-term changes such as:

- the balance of *water* and salt levels within the body thus maintaining *homeostasis*
- the different stages involved in reproduction
- the rate of *growth and development*
- *sexual maturity*
- the rate of activity.

hospice: an institution set up with the main purpose of *caring* for the dying. The most famous hospice is St Christopher's in London. A hospice may provide the following:

- *holistic care*: explores the social, intellectual, emotional, spiritual and physical needs of the patient
- *palliative care*: supportive and total care to those who are dying
- short- or long-term care: as the need arises
- home care: teams from the hospice support the patient in their own home
- *counselling*: enables the patient and their families to discuss their feelings about the illness.

hospital social workers are also known as medical social workers. They carry out social work services within a *hospital* setting.

hospitals are large institutions which treat people who have health disorders, *dysfunctions* and *disease*. There are approximately 2500 hospitals in England and Wales, 355 hospitals in Scotland and 59 in Northern Ireland. In 1998, new measures for hospitals were introduced based on *clinical governance*. They included:

- success and failure rates after certain types of treatment to be monitored, including *deaths*, complications rates following operations, deaths after *heart* attacks, deaths after a fractured neck or femur
- a national performance framework to be set up focusing on the quality and not just the expense of *NHS* services
- sophisticated measures of clinical quality to be developed on a speciality by speciality and hospital by hospital basis
- details of each hospital's performance in operations to be monitored
- *doctors* to be required to take part in routine inquiries into deaths after surgery, maternal deaths, stillbirths, infant deaths and suicides
- doctors to be required to put their results in an audit of their speciality organised by their Royal College.

hostel: a *residential home* or provision which offers supervision and support to individuals who need somewhere to stay. Examples of people who might need hostel accommodation are:

- those coming out of *prison*
- young people leaving care
- *elderly people*
- those with *learning disabilities*
- those with psychological or *mental health disorders*
- women who need protection following *domestic violence*.

Houses of Parliament: consist of the House of Commons and the House of Lords. Parliament is responsible for determining law and social policy which affect the lives of the general public and the society in which they live. The government is formed from the ruling political party, the leader of which becomes Prime Minister.

housing is a collective term for places of shelter where people live. There are different regulations and legislation to ensure that suitable housing policies are being developed by *local authorities*. Housing and building legislation set standards to promote safe conditions such as:

- an adequate *water* supply with hot water, fixed bath/shower and a water closet (toilet) integrated as part of the internal fittings
- satisfactory facilities for the storage, preparation and cooking of *food*
- proper provision for the storage of fuel and adequate facilities for heating
- sufficient power points for electricity and lighting
- adequate and proper drainage systems and arrangements for the disposal of waste water
- proper lighting and ventilation in each room.
- buildings in good repair and free from damp.

Housing departments within local district councils have the main responsibility for providing council housing. Procedures for local councils are laid down in the Local Government and Housing Act 1989. (See *Housing Act 1985, Housing Associations Act 1985*.)

Housing Act 1985: an Act of Parliament which ensures that certain *housing* and accommodation is provided by a *local authority*. Those people who are *homeless* or live in crowded and unsatisfactory conditions are given preference in the allocation of council homes. Under this Act, local authorities have a responsibility to:

- house homeless people
- prioritise certain categories of need, e.g. a family with a child with a disability
- rehouse people in cases of emergency, e.g. flood or fire
- issue repair notices
- demolish housing unfit for human habitation
- prohibit overcrowding and set down standards to prevent this

Housing Associations Act 1985: an Act of Parliament which relates to the setting up and registration of housing associations. Housing associations are established for the purpose of constructing, providing, improving and managing housing or accommodation. They may be set up by a *charity*, a society, a body of trustees or a company. Once they are registered, a housing association becomes eligible for government housing grants. Their role provides a way in which people can rent housing other than from the *local authority*.

housing benefit: see *benefits*.

human growth and development: the way in which the body changes through the human life cycle. Growth and development includes:

- physical development – for example the development of *bones* and *muscles* which affect body movement and co-ordination
- *social development* – the development of relationships through socialisation and self-management skills
- *intellectual and cognitive development* – the development of learning, problem solving skills and reasoning; this includes *language development*
- emotional development – the development of emotional feelings including the bonding and attachment relationships between the newborn and his or her parents or primary care giver; this evolves later into the development of *self-esteem*
- cultural development – developing the person's cultural *identity* through reinforcing positive *self-esteem*.

In terms of human growth and development, consideration should be given to the individual's cultural and sexual identity. These aspects will develop and mature with the other changes within the lifecycle.

The study of human development is important to health and social care students because it helps them to understand and to clarify the needs of *clients* or *service users*.

Huntington's disease (or chorea) is a hereditary disorder of the *central nervous system*. In the United Kingdom over 20,000 people are affected directly or indirectly by the disease. Huntington's disease or Huntington's chorea is caused by a faulty *gene*. In some way, which is not yet understood, the faulty gene leads to damage of the *nerve cells* in areas of the *brain*. This causes gradual physical, mental and emotional changes. Each person whose parent has Huntington's disease is born with a 50 per cent chance of inheriting the faulty gene. Anyone who inherits the faulty gene will at some stage develop the disease. Its onset occurs in middle age. Recently tests have become available to inform young people whether or not they will develop the disease.

(For further information contact the Huntington's Disease Association, 108 Battersea High Street, London SW11 3HP.)

hydrocephalus is a condition which can be caused by an increase of *cerebrospinal fluid* in the cavities of the *brain*, leading to excessive pressure in the brain. An obvious outward sign that this is happening in infants is an accelerated growth of the head. If the excess pressure is caused by a blockage it can be relieved in order to minimise damage. This is usually done by inserting a valve or shunt which drains off the excess fluid into the abdominal or *heart* cavities. Many babies who are born with *spina bifida* have hydrocephalus but it also occurs independently at *birth* and later in life. Modern advances in treatment and therapy mean that many babies affected with this condition survive into adulthood.

hydrolysis: splitting up chemicals by incorporating water.

hygiene: the procedures involved in maintaining cleanliness which also include *health* and *safety*. Personal hygiene *routines*, such as washing, *bathing* and changing clothes are learnt at an early age. Children learn to wash their hands before meals, after going to the toilet and wash their faces in the mornings. In addition, they learn to clean their teeth, wash their hair and bathe. Learning to dress and change clothes develops as their manipulative skills emerge. Personal hygiene is an important part of caring. Retaining a person's *dignity* is a first priority in helping with washing and toileting. A clean and hygienic environment is essential in maintaining a *service user's health and well- being*. (See *bathing, care environment, food hygiene*.)

hypothalamus: the part of the *brain* situated above the *pituitary gland*. It provides the link between the *endocrine system* and the *nervous system*. Some of the functions of the hypothalamus are as follows:

- it controls the secretion of some *hormones*
- it controls some aspects of *homeostasis*
- it helps regulate the amount of fluid in the body; if the body requires fluids the hypothalamus gives rise to the feeling of thirst.

hypothermia: reduction of body *temperature* below the normal range. It is liable to occur in vulnerable clients such as *elderly people* and *babies*. It is important that babies and elderly people are kept warm and that their body heat is maintained as they can lose body heat very quickly. (See *care environment*.)

hypothesis: a statement or *research* question which is identified at the beginning of an investigation or piece of research. It serves as a prediction or explanation of events. A hypothesis is an important aspect of research because it can be tested against reality (does the result indicate it is true, or not?) and can then be supported or rejected.

I

identity is a person's understanding of his/her self in relation to other people and society. It includes a person's view of themselves and develops in either a positive or negative way from early childhood. (See *self-concept, self-esteem*.)

ill health is a breakdown of general *health* and *well-being*. It can be due to:

- a deficiency of a chemical in the body, e.g. *diabetes*
- a physical disorder or *dysfunction*, e.g. *congenital* dislocation of the hip
- a mental disorder or dysfunction, e.g. *depression*
- an *infection*, e.g. *chicken pox*
- an inherited *disease*, e.g. *haemophilia*
- a degenerative disease, e.g. *arthritis*.

Poor health has complex causes such as *ageing*, inadequate diet, lack of physical activity or the effects of sexual behaviour, *smoking, alcohol* and *drugs*. Social and economic issues also play their part. These include *poverty, unemployment*, and *social exclusion*. Environmental factors such as air and *water* quality and *housing* also contribute to ill health. (See *environment, Our Healthier Nation – A Contract for Health, inequalities in health*.)

image analysis: a *research method* used in *health promotion* which determines the audience or target group's attitudes towards the health topic being discussed. A *questionnaire* is designed to collect evidence which can include:

- awareness of the topic discussed or presented
- *attitudes*
- practice.

imagination: using the creative faculty of the mind to form mental images. Developing imagination can be an effective way of improving a person's *communication skills*. A person can imagine what they might say in a certain situation or how they can be successful in what they do. Children use their imagination when they *play*. They use it in pretend or role play. This can include playing shop with empty cartons and plastic money, dressing up and using face paints. (See *creative play*.)

imitation: copying another person's *behaviour*. Imitation is a powerful means of learning. Children in particular observe and imitate the actions of others. For example, a child might imitate what happens at home in the home corner at *playgroup* where the table is laid for a meal and different scenarios acted out.

immune response is the way in which the body's *immune system* responds when foreign *antigens* are introduced. *Antibodies* are produced which combine with these foreign antigens to inactivate them. This is the basic mechanism of *active immunity*. The main *cells* involved are *white blood cells* called lymphocytes. There are two main types:

- β-lymphocytes – these are manufactured in the *bone marrow* and then transported to the lymph nodes. When an antigen enters the lymph nodes, B-lymphocytes divide rapidly and produce antibodies such as immunoglobulins which travel through the bloodstream. They provide the necessary protection against bacteria and viruses.

- T-lymphocytes – these are again manufactured in the bone marrow but they are matured in the thymus gland. They multiply and circulate around the bloodstream when an antigen enters the body. On contact with the cell containing the antigen they attack and destroy it.

immune system: this controls the way in which the body resists *pathogens*. The system consists of a number of structures and processes including:

- the *skin*, which provides a protective and waterproof covering to the body
- the production of immunoglobulins by bone marrow, spleen and all lymphoid tissue except the thymus
- the layers of mucous membrane which line the *mouth*, respiratory airways, alimentary canal and the *vagina,* can produce antimicrobial *enzymes* as well as mucus which traps any particles
- the *cilia* in the respiratory tract which sweep particles away from the *lungs*
- the clotting of the *blood* which forms a protective barrier over cuts and *wounds*
- the secretion of *acid* in the *stomach* which destroys harmful organisms
- the enzyme lysozyme which is present in tears and destroys *bacteria.*

When foreign organisms enter the bloodstream, the body sets up an active response in order to eliminate those that may cause *disease.* This is called the *immune response.*

immunisation: a procedure which is used to combat many different *diseases.* Immunisation programmes are set up to give *vaccinations* to individuals or groups at appropriate intervals. *Doctors* and *health visitors* advise parents or carers about immunisations and discuss any worries they may have. (See *infectious diseases.*)

Immunisation programmes

Age	Vaccine	Method
2 months	Diphtheria, whooping cough, tetanus + Hib	1 injection
	Polio	by mouth
3 months	Diphtheria, whooping cough, tetanus + Hib	1 injection
	Polio	by mouth
4 months	Diphtheria, whooping cough, tetanus + Hib	1 injection
	Polio	by mouth
12–15 months	Measles/mumps/rubella (MMR)	1 injection
3–5 years	Diphtheria, tetanus	booster injection
(school entry)	Polio	booster by mouth
	MMR	booster injection
Girls 10–14 years	Rubella	1 injection
Girls/boys 10–14 years	Tuberculosis	1 injection (BCG)
School leavers 15–19 years	Tetanus	1 injection
	Polio	booster by mouth

impairment: damage or loss of a physical function in the body. It can involve any part of the body. For instance a visual impairment limits the ability to see clearly as it affects the *eyes.*

in vitro fertilisation is a technique developed to fertilise the human egg using means outside the body. A woman is given *hormones* to increase the number of eggs she produces. Using a fine tube passed through the body wall, a *doctor* collects some of these eggs and places them in a dish containing a *nutrient* solution. Semen containing active sperm is added to the dish. *Fertilisation* of several eggs will occur. They are allowed to develop for three days before they are inserted back into the woman's *uterus*. In most cases at least one of these embryos develops into a baby. The technique is used in cases when a man and woman are unable to conceive naturally for whatever reason. (See *infertility and artificial insemination*.)

(For further information contact National Fertility Association, 114 Lichfield Street, Walsall WS1 1SZ.)

incidence: the number of new cases of an event occurring within a specified time period. This is a method of recording *disease, crime* rates and *mortality* rates from any type of disease.

income is money that an individual or household receives from *employment*, investments and other sources. Income is described in terms of an amount per week, per month, or per year.

income support: a method by which the government provides financial support to members of society who are unemployed or who receive less than a certain amount of money per week for the work they do. (See *benefit*.)

incubation period: the length of time which elapses from initial contact to the outward signs and symptoms of an *infectious disease*. An example of this is rubella which takes 10–14 days for the first signs (rash, raised *temperature* and swollen neck glands) to reveal themselves.

independence: the ability to maintain activities which support an individual's *lifestyle* without the assistance of others. Independence is an important factor in care practice. Encouraging a *child*, teenager, *adult, elderly person* and those who are disabled to make choices, take *decisions* and carry out tasks themselves is an important dimension in *caring. (See activities for living, care value base.)*

independent living: a term which describes the way in which people with disabilities strive or aspire to live so that they have the most control, *choice* or *autonomy* over the manner in which they conduct their daily lives. (See *Disabled Living Foundation, aids and adaptations, activities of daily living*.)

independent sector: provides health and social care services which are independent from the state. These include:

- *Voluntary* organisations – non-profit-making organisations whose management committees provide a service without receiving a salary. However, voluntary organisations do employ and pay administration staff to co-ordinate different programmes and schemes. They operate at national, local and regional levels.
- Private organisations provide a service at a cost. They charge for provision in order to make a profit for owners or shareholders.
- Not-for-profit organisations are set up as a charitable trust, where any surplus income is fed back into the trust. (See *charities*.)

individual differences: a term which recognises that it is important to acknowledge that all people are distinct and vary one from another. These differences may include genetic make-up, *lifestyle, religion, culture, race,* life experiences and *intelligence.*

industrial tribunals are judicial bodies set up to support an individual who has been unfairly treated in their work or *employment* situation. They are made up of a legally qualified chairperson and two other members who are appointed in consultation with employers and employees' organisations. Cases which may be considered by industrial tribunals relate to issues such as:

- aspects of employment law
- *equal pay* for men and women
- women's rights such as issues which relate to *sex discrimination*
- *race* relations
- redundancy
- trade union membership, unfair dismissal and redundancy payments.

inequalities in health: an individual's *well-being* is affected by *social and economic factors* such as *poverty, unemployment* and *social exclusion.* In the Green Paper *Our Healthier Nation – A Contract for Health* social and economic factors are confirmed as a link with ill health. In nearly every case the highest incidence of illness is experienced by the lowest *social classes.* Ill health is not spread evenly across society. Although *death* rates from *lung cancer* have been falling, mortality rates show that more people die from lung cancer in the North of England than in the South. The *National Contract for Health* is viewed as an opportunity to tackle such regional variations in health.

infant: a *newborn baby* completely dependent on the mother. This term is usually for a baby under the age of one year.

infant mortality is a measure of the death of babies under one year old. Infant deaths are measured by the number of babies who die under the age of one year per 1000 babies in the population. This infant mortality rate is used by statisticians as an indicator of child health in different countries.

infection: a condition which occurs as a result of contact with a *disease*-causing organism or *pathogen* leading to *signs and symptoms* indicating that the individual is ill. The degree of infection and its effects will depend on the type of pathogen involved. The most common infections are colds, flu, chest, urinary and *skin* infections.

infection control committee: a *multi-disciplinary* committee set up to formulate procedures to be implemented or carried out in *hospitals* or in the community in order to prevent and control *infection.* The committee consists of an *infection control nurse,* representatives from the different areas of nursing and community care, experts in *food* preparation and a microbiologist.

infection control nurse: a registered *nurse* who has specific responsibilities for the control of infection in *hospital.* He/she is specially trained and their knowledge and skills are used to help other nurses to carry out an *infection* control policy as part of their work. When a specific infection is evident, either in a ward or in an operating theatre, the infection control nurse investigates the source. In recent years the outbreak of *methicillin resistant Staphylococcus aureus* (MRSA) in hospitals has caused much concern; it is a bacterium resistant to certain antibiotics. The nursing care of infected patients should be carefully monitored. The infection control nurse reports to the *infection control committee.*

infertility is the inability of an individual to conceive. Causes include:

- inactive sperm in the semen
- not enough sperm manufactured
- *ovaries* that are not producing eggs
- *Fallopian* tubes that are blocked due to scarring or infection
- mucus lining in the cervix that has thickened to the extent that the sperm cannot enter
- the man being unable to have an erection ensuring full intercourse
- overproduction of prolactin by the *pituitary gland,* which leads to impotence in the male and infertility in the woman
- emotional and psychological pressures on both the man and the woman setting up a cycle of tension.

infestation: evidence of parasites, either on the skin, in the clothes or inside the body. These include scabies, head lice and threadworms.

inflammation is the body's response to any injury which causes damage to the tissue. The *signs and symptoms* of inflammation are:

- heat and redness – due to increased *blood* supply to the area
- swelling – when *tissues* develop oedema, which is the accumulation of excess fluid in the tissues surrounding the area of inflammation
- pain.

Inflammation may be caused by any injury such as a cut or bruise, exposure to ultraviolet light, *radiotherapy* treatment, intense *temperature* such as a burn, scald or frost bite, chemical *burns,* allergic reactions such as nettle rash, viruses and *bacteria.*

informal care is care which is given by family, friends and neighbours. According to the *National Association of Carers*:

- there are approximately six million unpaid and informal carers in Britain
- one in seven adults has a caring responsibility
- 1.4 million carers devote over 20 hours per week to caring
- one in five households contains a carer
- carers tend to be middle-aged women but can be men or even children
- one in five carers cares for someone who is not related to them
- most *carers* look after someone who is elderly
- many carers look after more than one person
- a quarter of carers receive no help from anyone inside or outside the family
- 50 per cent of those caring for a spouse do so unaided.

information: knowledge which is acquired and transmitted from one person or organisation to another. In health and social care the way in which *information* is acquired, given, selected and dealt with is a key requirement within the caring process. There are concerns about *confidentiality* and the *access to information.* Some aspects may be protected by *legislation. Carers* handling information should be aware of the rights and choices of clients. *Clients* should be given as much information as possible. (See *Access to Medical Reports Act, Access to Personal Files Act, Data Protection Act, information technology – supporting quality and efficiency.*)

information technology supporting quality and efficiency: a method of supporting the *National Health Service* with accurate and up-to-date *information* . In 1998, the Government published a new information management and technology strategy for the NHS which was laid down in *The New NHS – Modern, Dependable.* This harnesses the enormous potential benefits of IT to support the drive for quality and efficiency in the NHS by:

- making patient *records* electronically available when they are needed
- using the NHSnet and the Internet to bring patients quicker test results, on-line booking of appointments and up-to-date specialist advice
- enabling accurate *information* about finance and performance to be available promptly
- providing knowledge about *health, ill health* and best treatment practice to the public through the Internet and the emerging public access media, e.g. digital TV
- developing telemedicine to ensure specialist skills are available to all parts of the country.

There need to be robust safeguards to protect patients' *confidentiality* and privacy. The aim is to create a powerful alliance between knowledgeable patients advised by knowledgeable professionals as a means of improving health and healthcare. (HMSO 1998)[61]

infringement of rights: an action or situation that interferes with someone's rights and the freedom to which they are entitled.

inhaler: a device which is used to introduce *drugs* to the *body.* Inhalers are most commonly used in the treatment of lung disorders. The patient breathes in a gas or vapour. The inhaler is designed so that the correct dose of inhalant is given. An inhaler is used particularly in the treatment of *asthma.*

inheritance of sex: the way in which the *chromosomes* determine the sex of an individual. Every *cell* in the human body contains 23 pairs of chromosomes. In 22 pairs of these chromosomes the two chromosomes look alike. The remaining 'pair' are the sex chromosomes. Females have two X chromosomes in the *cell* while males have one X and one Y chromosome. Eggs and sperm contain a single sex chromosome. In the egg the single sex chromosome is always an X. In the sperm the single sex chromosome can be either an X or a Y. When the sperm fertilises the egg there is an equal chance of uniting a sperm containing an X or Y chromosome – to produce XX (a girl) or XY (a boy). Therefore, the numbers of boys and girls born are more or less equal.

inherited disorders: any condition where a defective *gene* has been passed on to a child from either one of the parents. Examples of inherited disorders are *cystic fibrosis* and *haemophilia.*

inherited factors: see *genes.*

injunction: an order made by the court prohibiting an act or requiring it to stop. Under the *Domestic Violence* and Matrimonial Proceedings Act 1996 the County Court has the power to make injunctions. Injunctions can be either interlocutory (temporary) pending the outcome of the full hearing or perpetual (ongoing).

inoculation is the introduction of a substance, usually the injection of vaccine into the body as a means of protecting it against *infectious diseases.* (See *vaccination, immune system.*)

inquiries are procedures set up to investigate the causes of tragic incidents or alleged malpractice. Such inquiries can range from informal, two person panels to formal investigations which are legal proceedings involving a *judge.* The purpose of an inquiry is to ensure that there is justice for the victim and their families.

inspection: procedures which examine practice within an organisation. In health and social care this involves:

- inspection of premises with regard to suitability for client use, e.g. *residential* homes, *day care* provision, *playgroups* and *day nurseries*
- examination of procedures to ensure that legislation is implemented, e.g. *health and safety, equal opportunities*
- checking staff practise quality care, e.g. adequate staff/client ratios, induction and in-service training.

institutionalisation can occur when people have been in *hospital* or residential care for a long time. They become accustomed to the same *routine* and are familiar with the daily tasks which are carried out for them. They find it difficult to carry out any new task for themselves and for this reason may be resistant to any change in their daily routine. *Carers* should ensure that they encourage *clients* to make *decisions* and to take part in personal tasks and activities.

insulin: a hormone produced by the *cells* of the islets of Langerhans in the *pancreas.* The amount of insulin secreted regulates the level of glucose in the bloodstream. When insulin is not produced the glucose level in blood rises reducing the chemical breakdown of *carbohydrate* and increasing the breakdown of *fat* and *protein.* This is a condition called *diabetes* mellitus. (See *homeostasis, feedback systems.*)

integrated care: a system in the *National Health Service* which has replaced the internal market.

Replacing the internal market with integrated care (The New NHS – Modern, Dependable 1997)

Internal market	Integrated care
Fragmented responsibility between 4000 NHS bodies. Little strategic planning. Patients passed from pillar to post.	Health improvement programmes jointly agreed by all who are charged with planning or providing health and social care.
Competition between hospitals. Some GPs get better service for their patients at the expense of others. Hospital clinicians disempowered.	Patients treated according to need, not who their GP is, or where they live. Co-operation replaces competition. Hospital clinicians involved.
Competition prevented sharing of best practice, to protect 'competitive advantage'. Variable quality.	New mechanisms to share best practice. New performance framework to tackle variable standards of quality. *cont.*

Perverse incentives of efficiency index, distorting priorities, and getting in the way of real efficiency, effectiveness and quality. Artificially partitioned budgets.	Efficiency index replaced by new reference costs. Broader set of performance measures. Budgets unified for maximum flexibility and efficiency.
Soaring administrative costs, diverting effort from improving patient services. High numbers of invoices and high transaction costs.	Management costs capped. Number of commissioning bodies cut from 3600 to 500. Transaction costs cut.
Short-term contracts focusing on cost and volume. Incentive for each NHS trust to lever up volume to meet financial targets rather than to work across organisational boundaries.	Longer term service agreements linked to quality improvements. NHS trusts share responsibility for appropriate service usage.
NHS trusts run as secretive commercial businesses. Unrepresentative boards. Principal legal duty on finance.	NHS trusts with representative boards ending secrecy. New legal duties on quality and partnership.

(HMSO 1998)[61]

integrated national transport policy: a government strategy which tackles congestion and *pollution* and their damaging consequences. It will promote cleaner and safer vehicles and the greater use of public transport, cycling and walking. The *health* benefits include better *air* quality, improved levels of fitness, reduced levels of stress and fewer accidents. The strategy works closely with road *safety* initiatives and targets introduced in October 1997.

intellectual development or cognitive development is the development of the parts of the *brain* which are responsible for problem solving, reasoning, remembering and understanding. During childhood the brain grows rapidly. At the age of six years it has already reached 90 per cent of the adult weight. In the first seven years of life a child learns rapidly about the world around them. (See *cognitive development, human growth and development.*)

intelligence: a term which describes a person's mental ability. This is tested to determine an individual's level of intelligence quotient (IQ). Intelligence is influenced by genetic inheritance which is called *nature* and by the opportunities provided in the child's environment which is called *nurture.*

interaction: communicating with others. People working in health and social care need to communicate with clients and with one another. They need to take part in one-to-one interactions with clients and other professionals, and group interactions, such as case conferences, group work or staff meetings.

The purposes of these interactions are to:

- exchange *information*
- explain *procedures*

- promote *relationships* and *client well-being*
- assess client needs
- negotiate and liaise with clients, family members, colleagues and other professionals
- promote learning and support development
- promote group *social development*.

(See *active listening skills, communication, listening skills*.)

inter-agency co-operation is the way in which different agencies within health and social care liaise and work together in the care of *clients*. (See *multi-disciplinary teams, joint commissioning*.)

inter-agency plan: a plan devised jointly by the agencies concerned in a person's welfare to co-ordinate the services they provide. Its aim is to ensure that the support offered meets all the person's needs, so far as this is practicable, and that duplication and rivalry are avoided. The plan should specify goals to be achieved, resources and services to be provided, the allocation of responsibilities, and arrangements for monitoring and review. (See *Working Together under the Children Act 1989*.)

interim care order: an order made by the court. It operates under Section 38 of the *Children Act* placing a child in the care of the designated *local authority*. There are provisions as to its duration, with an initial period of eight weeks. (See *Working Together under the Children Act 1989*.)

International Classification of Diseases: a list of *diseases* which is published by the *World Health Organisation* every ten years.

International Classification of Disorders is a classification system published by the *World Health Organisation* relating to physical and psychological conditions. The WHO provides statistics from different countries on different disorders.

interpersonal skills: the skills that enable individuals to communicate with each other. Interpersonal skills are an integral part of the care process. Examples of such skills include using:

- verbal *communication*, using *language* and *conversation*
- *non-verbal communication*, body language, *gestures*, facial expressions and eye contact
- a safe and suitable environment for interaction to take place
- non-discriminatory policy and practice, respecting differences of *race*, language, *culture, religion, sexuality* and *political persuasion*
- methods to promote the health and *well-being* of those being cared for and promoting a positive *self-esteem*
- non-judgmental attitudes to others and showing *respect*
- policies to maintain *confidentiality* and protect personal information about a client
- routines to encourage clients' *autonomy* and *independence* with regard to their *rights and choices*
- relevant and helpful *information*.

(See *optimised interaction, care value base, confidence building*.)

intervention: a procedure which involves a *carer* taking action to improve the quality of an individual's life. This can include:

- *enabling* which encourages individuals to take control of their lives
- encouraging *coping* which allows individuals to come to terms with the presenting difficulties, disabilities or situations in their lives
- *caring* which gives a person support for their physical, social, intellectual and emotional needs.

intervertebral disc: a pad of fibrocartilage which is found between the bones (*vertebrae*) in the spine. The disc acts as a shock absorber protecting the *brain* and *spinal cord* from sudden impact caused by jumping, running and other body movements. (See *skeleton*.)

interview: a method used by researchers, health and social care professionals and others involving face-to-face contact with an individual. Interviews are a means of gaining detailed and descriptive *information* about a person. For the purpose of research there are different types of interviews, such as:

- Structured interviews – the researcher collects information directly from the interviewee. A number of questions are compiled to ensure that the interview is carried out in exactly the same way with each interviewee. Such questions are called an interview schedule; it is similar to a questionnaire. This is a way of collecting *quantitative* evidence.
- In-depth interviews – the researcher uses this technique to allow the interviewee to talk more freely and in an unstructured way. The researcher can provide guidance as the conversation progresses and the interviewee is encouraged to open up and provide as much detail as possible. In this way the researcher gathers the views and the beliefs of the interviewee. It is a valuable way of collecting *qualitative* evidence.

introversion is an aspect of the personality. It is characterised by a number of different traits such as the individual being passive, quiet and unsociable. In *Eysenck's personality inventory,* introverted people try to avoid stimulation. An introvert may be characterised as a person who is interested in themselves rather than in the outside world. They tend to be self-conscious and find making friends difficult. (See *extroversion*.)

investigation: a term used in NVQs in Care to describe the technical or scientific procedure for measuring and recording physiological variables. (Care Sector Consortium 1998)[12].

involuntary muscle is smooth *muscle* which works without the conscious control of the mind. For example, intestinal muscles work completely independently of conscious thought. Its microscopic structure is different from voluntary or striated muscle.

iodine: a *mineral* which is required in small amounts for healthy bodily growth and development. It is used by the *thyroid gland* in the production of thyroxin or thyroid hormone. A solution of iodine in potassium iodide solution can also be used in liquid form as an antiseptic.

J

jobseekers' allowance: a financial *benefit* which was introduced in April 1996. The benefit is a combination of unemployment benefit and *income support*. It is available for claimants who have been unemployed for six months. During this time they have to prove that they have been actively seeking employment. If after six months they are not in work they receive *means-tested* payments in line with income support levels.

joint commissioning is the process where two or more *agencies* act together to co-ordinate their services and to take joint responsibility for *care* provision. It is often the way in which health and social care agencies work together to achieve:

- joint budgeting between agencies
- a clear assessment of population *health* needs as identified by the relevant agencies
- an agreed strategy of health and social care provision to meet local needs
- procedures for joint service planning, evaluation and monitoring of health and social care provision.

This way of working together is viewed as an efficient structure or framework which enables health and social care professionals to support the different and individual needs of their clients. (See *inter-agency co-operation, multi-disciplinary teams.*)

joint finance: a specific sum of money allocated each year via the Joint consultative committee for innovative projects, e.g. community projects which support clients with *learning disabilities*.

joint planning: the process by which two or more *agencies* act together to plan service provision. It encourages the involvement of providers, users, *carers*, and the voluntary and community sectors.

joints are where the *bones* of the *skeleton* meet. Some are fixed allowing no movement, e.g. the sutures of the *skull*. Most joints, however, are movable and give the body movement and flexibility. The most common types of *synovial joints* are:

- Hinge joints – those which work like any hinge, e.g. the knee joint. The movable part or bone can only move in one plane but in either of two opposing directions.
- Gliding joints, also called sliding joints – those in which flat surfaces glide over each other, e.g. those between the carpals which are the small bones in the hands. They are more flexible than hinge joints.
- Ball and socket joints – the most flexible joints, e.g. the hip joint. The movable bone has a rounded end which fits into a socket in the fixed bone. It can swivel in many directions.

judge: the person appointed to oversee the judicial system in a court of law. They are qualified *solicitors* and experienced *barristers* who are familiar with court proceedings and procedures. They sit in a range of *criminal courts*.

judicial review: an order from the divisional court quashing a *local authority* decision. It relates to a declaration in a particular case as to what the law is, or an order directing the authority to take, or not take, particular steps. The divisional court does not usually substitute its own decision but sends the matter back to the authority for reconsideration. (See *Working Together under the Children Act 1989.*)

justice: the legal right to fairness under the law. Justice is an ethic which is set in a framework of the court system within society.

juvenile offenders are young people under the age of 17 years who commit crime (offend). The number of crimes committed by such young people per year is called the juvenile crime rate. Those who offend usually have their cases heard in a *youth court*, though more serious offences are dealt with in the *Crown court*.

K

keyhole surgery: a surgical procedure involving the use of a special instrument called a laparoscope or endoscope. A small cut is made in the *skin*. The underlying *tissue* and *muscle* is also cut. An instrument is inserted and surgery is carried out, e.g. removal of *gall bladder* or damaged *cartilage* in the knee *joint*. Such surgery is so-called because of the tiny size of the cut or incision. It also known as 'minimally invasive surgery' because of the limited side effects it can have on the *patient*. (See *trends in health care*.)

key worker: usually a named person who co-ordinates the arrangements for a person's care. A key worker is frequently used in caring for children in a *day care* or residential setting. They are usually trained and experienced *carers* in their own particular area within health and social care. (See *named nurse*.)

kidneys: the main organs of the urinary system. They are two bean-shaped *organs* situated one each side of the body in the lower back region. They contain:

- Nephrons – tiny filtering units. There are about one million per kidney. Each consists of a renal corpuscle and a renal tubule.
- Renal corpuscles, or Malpighian corpuscles, which filter fluids out of the *blood*. Each consists of a glomerulus and a Bowman's capsule.
- Glomerulus – a circle of coiled-up *capillaries* at the centre of each renal corpuscle. The capillaries branch from an afferent arteriole entering the corpuscle and re-unite to leave the corpuscle as an efferent arteriole.
- Bowman's capsule – the outer part of each renal corpuscle. It is a thin-walled sac around the glomerulus.
- Renal tubules – long tubes, each one leading from a Bowman's capsule. Each has three main parts – the proximal convoluted tubule, the loop of Henle and the distal convoluted tubule. These tubules have many capillaries wrapped around them. They are branches of the efferent arteriole and re-unite to form larger vessels carrying blood from the kidneys.
- Collecting tubule – a tubule which carries urine into the pelvis of a kidney.

The function of the kidneys is to separate waste products from the large amount of fluid which flows through them daily. Approximately 1.5 litres is excreted as *urine*.

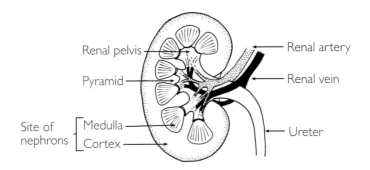

King's Fund: a government 'think tank' which determines policy relating to *health care*. It was founded in 1897 by Edward VII to support London *hospitals* which, at that time, were being run by voluntary organisations. One of its most recent reports relates to transforming health care in London.

Krebs cycle: see *anaerobic respiration*.

L

labelling identifies an individual as being of a certain type, belonging to a particular group whether they are members of that group or not. Labelling is the result of *attitudes* and *values* which becoming fixed and rigid through the process of *stereotyping*, e.g. labels which relate to people who are overweight inferring that they are lazy.

language development: the way in which a *baby* or a young child learns to communicate through noises and repetitive sounds. These gradually develop into words.

The stages of language development

Age	Language development
1–6 months	Cries when hungry or has discomfort. Turns face towards sounds and is startled by sudden noises. Makes cooing noises. Babbles and responds to the sound of voice.
6–9 months	Babbles and starts to imitate sounds. Babbling is now likely to be linked to language of familiar adults, parents or primary care givers. At this age the baby will shout, and make noises in order to be noticed.
9–12 months	Imitating word sounds and begins to string these sounds together. These word sounds have different tones like a conversation. This is called jargon. Understands simple instructions such as 'give it to me' and simple words such as 'cup, duck'. Can point to objects.
12–15 months	Continues to use jargon. Can use 2–6 words but understands many others.
15–18 months	Can say 6–20 words and points to pictures in a book or on the wall. Echoes words which are said by others. This is called 'echolalia'. At this stage they enjoy joining in songs and rhymes.
18 months–2 years	Can say about 50 words but understands many more. Can now put two words together and obey simple instructions.
2–3 years	Saying more words including plurals and pronouns. They can understand what is being said and join in simple conversations. Enjoys song and rhyme and stories.
3–4 years	Words and vocabulary are developing. Sometimes they have difficulty with pronunciation. Asks question 'Why' many times a day. Knows age and name.
4–5 years	More developed use of correct speech.

laser treatment: a treatment method involving a device which produces a very thin beam of light. The energy in the beam of light is very concentrated and therefore can be used to operate on a small body area with an abnormality such as in the treatment of gall stones. This method is also effective in dealing with certain conditions in the *eye*. Lasers can be used to unblock small *arteries* such as *coronary arteries*.

learning disabilities: a range of disabilities of mental capacity. *Clients* with learning disabilities may have a limited mental capacity but will generally be able to function to the full extent of such abilities. The causes of learning disabilities are as follows:

- *genetic disorders, e.g. Down's syndrome*
- intrauterine injury, injury to the growing *foetus* in the *womb* such as an *infection* which causes damage to the *brain* and to parts of the *nervous system, e.g. paralysis* of a limb and loss of mental function
- *birth injuries,* any injury to the *baby* during *birth* affecting the brain and nervous system, e.g. *cerebral palsy*
- anatomical injuries to the brain or *spinal cord* such as *spina bifida* and *hydrocephalus;* there are different degrees of such disabilities which range from mild through moderate to severe or profound learning impairment.

A recent document published by the Department of Health 'Signpost for Success' 1998 reviews strategies which apply to those who provide health services for clients with learning disabilities.

learning theories seek to explain how individuals achieve a permanent change in understanding and behaviour. Change usually occurs as a result of experience and is dependent on cognitive abilities such as *memory* and *perception*. There are two well known levels of learning theory. They are:

- Classical conditioning or learning by association – this is involved in the *socialisation* of young children and also plays a part in the development of phobias. The principles of classical conditioning are seen in the treatment of phobias. For example, it is used in the treatment of alcoholics by creating a phobia. This is called aversion therapy. A special drug can be implanted under the *skin* so that it remains active in the body over a long period of time. If the alcoholic person has a drink during that time they are instantly sick. The taking of *alcohol* becomes linked with nausea and so the patient learns to avoid it.
- Operant conditioning – this relates to responses that bring about satisfaction or pleasure. When this happens such responses are likely to be repeated. This is termed positive reinforcement. Those reactions that bring about discomfort are not likely to be repeated and are termed negative reinforcement. *Behaviour* shaping or modification is associated with achieving the approved behaviour by rewarding the actions which produce the desired response. It is often used deliberately to generate socially acceptable behaviour. The control and management of misbehaving children at school is one example.

The management of behaviour can involve using:

- primary reinforcers – those which satisfy basic needs or drive, e.g. *food, water* or praise
- secondary reinforcers – acquire their reinforcing properties through association with primary reinforcers, e.g. tokens, stars, money.

Carers may reward a client with signs of approval such as smiling. Praise is important in building self-esteem. (See *confidence building, behaviour modification*.)

legal aid: legal support which is available in both criminal and civil cases. It supports a person who demonstrates that they need legal representation but cannot afford to pay for it. This support is set out within the Act of Parliament 'Legal Aid Act' 1988. However, due to a sharp increase in the amount of financial support given through the legal aid system, the Lord Chancellor has announced changes. These involve more rigorous methods of testing to assess whether individuals and their families are eligible for legal aid. Legal teams assess individual cases to decide whether a legal aid contract is possible.

legislation: the making of laws by parliament. Legislation determines the policy framework and reflects the different *statutory rights* of organisations, groups and individuals. For instance, the *NHS and Community Care Act 1990* sets out a policy framework for health and social care organisations, professionals, *carers, clients,* and *patients* or *service users.*

leisure is free time. People will have different ways of using their leisure time, such as watching television and videos, reading or sports activities. Individuals may also have hobbies, e.g. collecting antiques, stamps, DIY, shopping or gardening.

lesbians/gays are those who form physical and sexual relationships with individuals from the same *gender* grouping. Females in a gender partnership are termed lesbians and males in such a partnership are gays or homosexuals. The consenting age of a male homosexual relationship is 18 years of age.

life expectancy is an estimate of lifespan. It enables comparisons between the *ages* and stages of life to be made across the population. It is affected by *mortality rates* including *infant mortality rates.*

life skills training: the techniques used to support those with disabilities to lead more *independent* lives. (See *activities of daily living, aids and adaptations.*)

lifestyle: the way in which a person chooses to live their life. Health educators believe that if a person has a healthy lifestyle then they will live longer. In order to maintain a healthy lifestyle a person is encouraged to:

- eat a healthy *diet*
- have plenty of *exercise*
- learn to manage *stress*
- take time out for *leisure* and recreation
- not to *smoke* cigarettes
- drink *alcohol* in moderation
- use *contraception* and not to have unprotected sex (i.e. use a condom)
- live in adequate *housing.*

However, it is important to add that not every person in society today has a choice in lifestyle. The more affluent the person the more choices they have as to the lifestyle which they adopt.

ligament: a tough band of yellow elastic *connective* tissue which is found linking two *bones* together at a *joint.* Ligaments bind the articular surfaces together giving joints protection and strength. When the ends of one of the bones forming a joint is displaced it may interfere with the proper working movement of the joint. The ligament at the joint may be torn as a result of the displacement and this is the cause of a sprain.

lipids: see *fats*.

listening skills: the ability to listen to others in a way that conveys interest and positive regard. The person speaking then feels that what they are saying matters. Listening is an important aspect of the *caring* process and involves the following:

- sitting or standing in a position that enables the *client* or *patient* to feel that they are being listened to, keeping the 'open position', not folding arms or crossing legs
- making and maintaining *eye* contact demonstrating to the client that they are being listened to
- learning to control facial expressions so that whatever is being said can be seen to be important
- giving the client or patient time to express what they want to say; this is particularly important when the client has a speech impairment, or their use of English is limited.

(See also *active listening skills, communication and interpersonal interaction, English as a second language*.)

literacy is the ability to read and write. In recent years there have been concerns about literacy standards in *schools*. This has been reviewed and a new government scheme is being introduced to include:

- a daily literacy hour where children concentrate on reading and writing
- the appointment of 200 consultants to carry out literacy training and support professional development in schools
- literacy training of head teachers
- school literacy action plans for 1998–2000.

(See *Excellence in schools*.)

liver: the largest internal organ of the body. It is situated beneath the *diaphragm* in the upper right side of the *abdomen*. It is protected by the ribs and weighs approximately 1–1.5 kg. It is dark brown in colour and has a smooth surface. The *blood* supply to the liver is provided by the hepatic *artery*, hepatic *vein* and hepatic portal vein. The hepatic vein takes blood from the liver.

The liver has many functions which include:

- regulation of *glucose*
- regulation of lipids
- regulation of *proteins*
- detoxification
- *bile* production
- breakdown of sex *hormones*
- formation of *red blood cells*
- breakdown of *haemoglobin*
- formation of *plasma* proteins
- storage of *vitamins*
- production of heat.

local authorities have statutory duties and powers with regard to the implementation of health and social care in their geographic area. Since 1992, local authorities publish their services through their *community care plans*. In some cases, they work closely with the *health authority* and with representatives from the voluntary sector to ensure that health and care services meet the needs of local people. They have responsibility for various services such as:

- *Social service departments* – supporting personal social services including care of children, clients with disabilities and elderly people; the registration for these services is also covered.
- *Housing* – council housing, residential and sheltered housing.
- *Community care* – *elderly people, physical disability* and *sensory impairment, learning disabilities, mental health, drugs/alcohol, domestic violence, HIV/AIDS*. This involves *care management, home care, day care services* including *palliative care* and *occupational therapists*.
- *Benefits* and employment opportunities in their localities.

The areas of responsibility are outlined in local government Acts, the *Children Act 1989*, the *NHS* and *Community Care Act 1990, The New NHS – Modern, Dependable, Our Healthier Nation New Ambitions for our country*.

local commissioning groups: groups of *GPs* who work closely with their *health authority* to plan and commission services.

local education consortia: groupings which bring together representatives from *NHS trusts* and *health authorities* to assess the workforce and development requirements of local health care services. They provide a forum to ensure workforce planning reflects local service needs.

local medical committee: the statutory local representative committee for all *GPs* in the area covered by a *health authority*. The health authority has a statutory duty to consult this committee on issues including *GPs* terms of service, *complaints* and the investigation of certain matters of professional conduct.

localised services are those provided within a locality by local government or the *local authority*. They include the health and social care provisions supported by local authorities but funded by the government.

lone-parent families: *families* consisting of a dependent child or children living with only one parent. This is usually the mother but may be the father. Over the last three decades, partly as the result of changing *family structures*, there has been a substantial increase in the number of lone parents. In 1995 the proportion of families with dependent children with only one parent in the home was 22 per cent compared with 8 per cent in 1971. So, one in five families is headed by a lone parent, almost three times the figure 25 years ago. The causes of lone parenthood have altered. Few lone parents are widows. During the 1970s, the main increase was in the number of divorced women with children. During the last decade, the most substantial growth has been in unmarried lone mothers, including a large number of those where cohabiting partnerships have ended. Unmarried lone mothers are typically younger, with younger children, and with lower qualifications and job prospects than lone parents as a whole. (See *New ambitions for our country: a new contract for welfare, 1998*.)

(For further information contact the National Council for One Parent Families, 255 Kentish Town Road, London NW5 2LX.)

LSD (lysergic acid diethylamide) is a hallucinogenic or psychedelic *drug* which causes disturbances in understanding and a changed state of consciousness and awareness. It is taken in small tablets and can make a person behave in an erratic and unpredictable way. For example, a person on an 'LSD trip' may climb to the top of a building and 'try to fly'.

lungs are the main organs of *respiration*. There is a right and a left lung. They fill the thoracic cavity and are situated on either side of the heart. (See *respiratory system*.)

lymph: see *lymphatic system*.

lymphatic system: a system of *lymph* vessels, lymph nodes and small organs of lymphoid tissue which are important in the recycling of those body fluids which help the body in the fight against disease. It produces *lymphocytes* which are disease-fighting *white blood cells*. The vessels of the lymphatic system transport a fluid called lymph around the body and return it into the *veins* and the lymphoid organs as a means of fighting infection. Vessels carry lymph from all body areas towards the left side of the chest. Lymph vessels are lined with endothelium tissue and have valves in order to prevent backflow. The thinnest vessels are called lymph capillaries. The *capillaries* join to form larger vessels called the lymphatics, which eventually unite to form two main branches which empty into the blood via the right subclavian vein via the right lymphatic duct and the left subclavian vein via the thoracic duct. Lymphoid organs connected by the lymphatic system include the *spleen*, tonsils and *thymus* gland.

magnetic resonance imaging (MRI): a technique used to produce images on a monitor of the soft tissues of the body such as the *brain* and *spinal cord*. The MRI scan has all the benefits of a *computer axial tomography* scan but without the exposure to *radiation*. It is a method used to diagnose *diseases* such as *cancer* and *multiple sclerosis*.

mainstream schools are those which offer compulsory education for children from the age of 5 to 16 years. These *schools* follow the *national curriculum* from key stage 1 to key stage 4.

male reproductive system: responsible for the male role in sexual reproduction. It is made up of primary *organs*, or *gonads*, which consist of two testes, and a number of additional organs. *Cells* in the gonads also act as *endocrine glands* secreting many important *hormones*.

- Testes – contain tubelike canals called seminiferous tubules which manufacture sperm. They are situated in the scrotum which hangs below the *abdomen*. The optimum temperature for sperm production is slightly lower than normal body temperature.
- Penis – the organ through which sperm are ejected via the urethra during intercourse. It is made of soft, spongelike erectile tissue, which has many spaces or blood sinuses, blood vessels and nerve endings called receptors. When a man is sexually excited, the sinuses and blood vessels fill with blood and this makes the penis stiff and straight. This is called an erection.

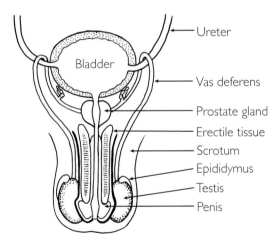

malnutrition: a disorder brought about by an inadequate *diet* or lack of *food*. Children and adults in countries where there is famine and war often suffer from severe malnutrition, sometimes leading to *death*. Once malnutrition occurs a person's physical condition deteriorates. Recent research shows a rise in the number of people in *residential care* or in *hospitals* in the United Kingdom who are also suffering from malnutrition. A report by the *Association of Community Health Councils* in 1997 stated that some patients do not receive adequate food and fluids while in hospital. The report includes anecdotal statements from patients and relatives and suggests several reasons why *patients* do not receive their meals. It made the following observations:

- patients who were incapable of choosing meals were left to fill in their menu order without adequate help
- there was a lack of nursing assistance at mealtimes
- patients were not given the appropriate cutlery/utensils.

The report suggests that 'shortages of staff, combined with pressure on nursing staff to undertake more 'pressing' and glamorous duties, will prevent them from offering assistance to those who need it at mealtimes'. (Association of Community Health Councils 1997)[7] (See also *feeding, balanced diet.*)

mammography: a special screening test of the *breast* employing low dosage *X-rays* which are used to detect the presence of cysts or *tumours.* (See also *breast examination.*)

management of social services takes place through a number of organisations which are under the supervision of the Secretary of State for Health. These organisations include:

- county councils, metropolitan boroughs, London boroughs
- *local authorities*
- *social service committees*
- local *social service departments.*

Marie Curie Cancer Care: the UK's largest *cancer* care charity which provides nursing care for people with cancer through 11 in-patient Marie Curie centres. Over 6000 Marie Curie nurses nationwide are also available to look after patients in their own homes. All services to patients are free of charge. Marie Curie Cancer Care runs its own research institute and education department which provides training courses and conferences for health professionals on cancer and related topics.

(For further information contact Marie Curie Cancer Care, 28 Belgrave Square, London SW1X 8QG.)

marks of safety are labels which are put on potentially hazardous appliances to warn users of the danger. The safety marks should be included in manufacturers' instructions which should also include warnings. The most regularly occurring marks of safety are:

- British Standard kitemark – this symbol means that the product has been examined and is deemed to be safe. The kitemark can be found on:
  - domestic appliances
  - children's equipment such as highchairs, prams and pushchairs
  - oil heaters.

Kitemark

- fire resistant mark – which ensures that the equipment and goods purchased are fire resistant and meet the appropriate regulations.
- British Gas seal of service – which is found on all gas appliances which have been tested for safety.
- British Electrotechnical Approval Board mark of safety – which ensures that all electrical goods and equipment have met the government safety regulations.

massage therapy is the gentle manipulation of the soft tissues of the body. Usually the hands are used as touch is an integral part of massage therapy, but sometimes other parts of the body such as the forearms, elbows and feet can be utilised. Massage can be an important part of a person's health and fitness programme. The functions of massage are to:

- reduce *muscle* tension
- improve *blood* and *lymph* circulation
- increase mobility and the range of movement in the *joints*
- relieve acute and chronic muscular pain
- encourage relaxation and reduce *stress*
- stimulate and soothe the *nervous system*.

maternal deprivation is the way in which a child reacts when separated for extended periods of time from their mother or primary care giver. Some children become anxious and stressed when separated from their mother. (See *separation, attachment bonding*.)

meals on wheels: a home care service which enables *elderly people* to have a meal delivered to them in their homes. There is a standard charge for the service. The delivery of this service varies from one area of the country to another. The meals are provided by *social services department* and are sometimes delivered by the *Women's Royal Voluntary Service*.

means-testing: a system used to determine whether individuals are eligible to receive certain *benefits*. Means testing is a way of delivering benefits to *clients* who are 'in need', i.e. the system allows benefits to be targeted to those with the least financial resources.

mechanism of breathing is made up of inspiration (breathing in) and expiration (breathing out). Both actions are normally automatic, controlled by nerves from the respiratory centre in the medulla of the *brain*. The medulla is particularly sensitive to changes in the concentration of *carbon dioxide* in the *blood*. A slight increase in carbon dioxide causes deeper, faster breathing. Mechanisms of breathing therefore include:

- Inspiration or inhalation; the act of breathing in. The intercostal muscles between the ribs contract, pulling the ribs up and outward and widening the cavity. The *diaphragm* also contracts and flattens, lengthening the chest cavity. The overall expansion lowers air pressure in the *lungs*, and air rushes in to fill them (i.e. to equalise internal and external pressure).
- Expiration or exhalation; the act of breathing out. The intercostal muscles and diaphragm relax, and air is forced out of the lungs as the chest cavity becomes smaller.

(See also *respiratory system*.)

media/mass media: all methods of transmission of *information* to a mass audience within society. They include television, radio and newspapers.

Medic Alert is a registered charity. Medic Alert provides internationally recognised medical identification emblems in the form of bracelets and necklets for people with hidden medical conditions, e.g. *diabetes, asthma, epilepsy* and *heart* conditions. These emblems are engraved with a personal identification number, medical condition and/or prescribed medication, plus a 24-hour emergency telephone service. How does Medic Alert work?

The symbol is engraved with a person's medical condition, personal identification number and Medic Alert's 24 hour emergency number.

When needed, doctors or other medical professionals can immediately get vital information by a telephone call, from anywhere in the world.

The vital medical records help medical personnel provide proper diagnosis and could save life.

The Medic Alert membership also provides its members with updated records whenever they inform the charity of changes to be made to their computer files.

meiosis: *cell* division which takes place in the sex *organs* to produce the gametes. The gametes produced contain half the number of *chromosomes* present in the parent *cell*. Each gamete therefore contains 23 chromosomes rather than 23 pairs of chromosomes, as in other cells. (See Figure on opposite page.)

melanocyte stimulating hormone: a hormone manufactured in the anterior lobe of the *pituitary gland* and responsible for controlling the production of the pigment in the *skin*. The hormone acts on the melanocytes which produce melanin or skin pigment.

memory is the individual's ability to retain *information* about life, events and situations. The information is then stored and retrieved when the individual wishes to remember the incident and when it happened. Long-term and short-term memory may be affected by the *ageing* process. For example *elderly people* often find it easier to remember incidents from the distant past. Events which occurred only a day or week before are harder to remember.

Mencap is a registered *charity* and voluntary organisation which supports clients with *mental illness* and disorders. It provides various services such as *day care, respite care* and *residential care* as well as *campaigning* for the rights of the mentally ill.

(For further information contact Mencap, 123 Golden Lane, London EC1Y 0RT.)

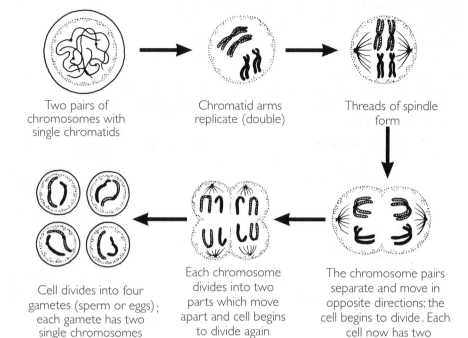

Two pairs of chromosomes with single chromatids	Chromatid arms replicate (double)

Threads of spindle form

Cell divides into four gametes (sperm or eggs); each gamete has two single chromosomes

Each chromosome divides into two parts which move apart and cell begins to divide again

The chromosome pairs separate and move in opposite directions; the cell begins to divide. Each cell now has two single chromosomes

Meiosis

meningitis is the inflammation of the meninges in the lining of the *brain*. There are two main forms of meningitis:

- viral meningitis which is caused by a *virus*
- bacterial meningitis, caused by several different types of *bacteria*; meningococcal and pneumococcal meningitis are the most prevalent.

The bacteria that cause meningitis live in the back of the *throat* or nose of about 10 per cent of the population and in up to 25 per cent of young adults. They rarely give rise to illness but when they do, infection progresses very rapidly and is fatal in one in ten cases.

Most cases of meningitis are seen in young children under five years of age with the greatest risk at around six months. The next highest incidence is among teenagers between 15 and 19 years and recent figures have shown an increase in cases of young people under the age of 25 years.

Antibiotics should be given immediately if bacterial meningitis is suspected. Oral antibiotics are recommended for close household or family contacts to prevent further spread. Early diagnosis is vital and most doctors now carry appropriate medication at all times.

(For further information contact National Meningitis Trust, Fern House, Bath Road, Stroud, Glos. GL5 3TJ.

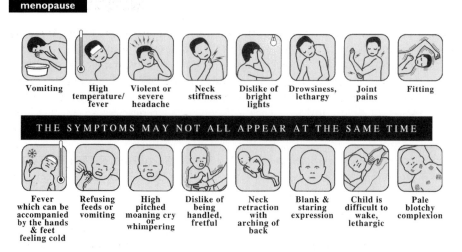

| Vomiting | High temperature/ fever | Violent or severe headache | Neck stiffness | Dislike of bright lights | Drowsiness, lethargy | Joint pains | Fitting |

THE SYMPTOMS MAY NOT ALL APPEAR AT THE SAME TIME

| Fever which can be accompanied by the hands & feet feeling cold | Refusing feeds or vomiting | High pitched moaning cry or whimpering | Dislike of being handled, fretful | Neck retraction with arching of back | Blank & staring expression | Child is difficult to wake, lethargic | Pale blotchy complexion |

Some symptoms of meningitis in adults and young people (above) and babies (below)

menopause: the cessation of *menstruation*, usually occurring naturally in women between 45 and 55 years of age. It marks the end of a woman's capacity for sexual reproduction. The menopause is associated with changes in the balance of *hormones* in the body, particularly a reduction of the level of oestrogen. Women going through the menopause may experience signs and symptoms such as:

- hot flushes – at certain times the woman may feel unbearably hot and become red in the face
- night sweats
- instability, mood swings, *depression*
- loss of elasticity in the *skin*
- reduction in vaginal secretions
- reduced oestrogen weakens the bones which may lead to *osteoporosis*.

Some women going through the menopause may be prescribed *hormone replacement therapy* (HRT).

menstruation: the process in a woman's body which leads to a discharge of *blood* every four weeks. It occurs in women of child bearing age. The period during which blood is discharged may vary from three to seven days. Menstruation starts at about *puberty*. Young girls in their senior years of junior school are encouraged to learn about menstruation. Personal *hygiene* during the times of 'a period' is discussed. Menstruation is a series of changes which form the menstrual cycle. The cycle is controlled by *hormones* secreted by the *hypothalmus*, ovaries and *pituitary*

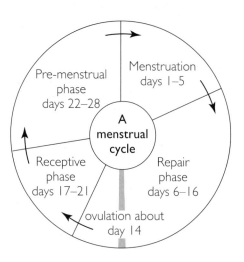

gland. These hormones cause changes in the *uterus* lining or endometrium. After ovulation the empty follicle undergoes changes and becomes the corpus luteum. If the egg is not fertilised the corpus luteum persists, in the ovary, for about 14 days and then degenerates. The unfertilised egg disintegrates and the thickened wall of the uterus breaks down. The discarding of this tissue together with the loss of blood constitutes menstruation. If *fertilisation* does occur the lining gradually develops a new inner layer rich in blood vessels. Each menstrual cycle lasts about 28 days and occurs continuously from *puberty* to *menopause* (usually between the ages of 45 and 55), when ovum production ceases. The events of the menstrual cycle work in conjunction with the ovarian cycle, where the regular maturation of an ovum in Graafian follicles is followed by ovulation i.e. the release of the ovum into a Fallopian tube.

mental health: a person's ability to organise their thoughts in a coherent pattern and to act accordingly. Mental health is closely linked with a person's social and emotional state. It has been identified as a *national health target* within the *Our Healthier Nation – A Contract for Health.* The report identifies the following areas of concern:

- Mental health problems are a major cause of ill health. In 1995, a health survey for England showed that 20 per cent of women and 14 per cent of men may have suffered *mental illness* and that such disorders accounted for an estimated 17 per cent (more than £5 billion) of the total expenditure for health and social services.
- There is evidence of an increase of poor mental health amongst children and young people over the last three decades, particularly in young people who are socially disadvantaged. Early action in a child's life may improve their *health* and mental state in later life.
- There are marked inequalities amongst those who suffer most from mental and health problems, e.g. men of working age who are unskilled are more than twice as likely to commit *suicide* as men in the overall population, and women are more likely than men to suffer from anxiety, *depression*, phobias and panic attacks. Similarly, women born in Sri Lanka, India and the East African Commonwealth are more likely to commit suicide than women in the United Kingdom population as a whole.
- Suicide is still a significant cause of early *death.*

(HMSO 1998)[48]

Mental Health Act 1983: an Act of Parliament which reinforces the rights of people with mental disorders and confirms the necessary procedures required to give them the appropriate care. (See *approved social worker, mental health disorder* and *compulsory order.*)

mental health disorder: a condition which affects the *mental health* of a person. Under Section 12 of the *Mental Health Act* 1983, mental disorder is referred to in four specific forms:

- mental illness, e.g. *schizophrenia*
- arrested or incomplete development of the mind, e.g. *learning disabilities*
- extreme personality disorders, e.g. psychopathic disorder.
- any other disorder or disability of the mind, e.g. *autism, dementia.*

(HMSO 1983)[38]

Mental Health (Patients in the Community) Act 1995: an Act of Parliament which makes provision for *patients* with mental disorders in England and Wales to receive care under supervision after leaving hospital. The Act also includes setting up community *care orders*.

Mental Health (Scotland) Act 1984: an Act of Parliament which reinforces the role of those in Scotland who work with, and manage, clients suffering from *mental health disorders*.

mental illness: *disease* or *ill health* affecting the psychological, emotional, social, physical, cognitive or general *wellbeing* of an individual. Examples include psychotic conditions such as *depression* and *schizophrenia* and neurotic illnesses such as phobias.

Mental Incapacity Bill 1995: Law Commission proposals to reform the law with regard to *clients* 'without capacity'. These are individuals who are:

- unable by reason of mental disability to make a decision on relevant issues
- unable to communicate a decision in that matter because they are unconscious or for any other reason.

(HMSO 1995)[41]

methadone is a manufactured synthetic opiate which is much longer acting than *heroin*. It is addictive and is used in clinics as a prescription for people undergoing withdrawal from heroin addiction. (See *drugs*.)

methicillin-resistant Staphylococcus aureus (MRSA): a bacterium which is resistant to most antibiotics. MRSA is not a risk to healthy people, but to those whose resistance is low and who are vulnerable to *infection*. Examples are those being treated for *cancer* using *chemotherapy*. They can easily become infected with MRSA, because their *white cell* count is low. *Signs and symptoms* usually include high tempera-ture or fever and the patient feels unwell. When MRSA has occurred the *infection control nurse* is informed and methods to prevent the infection being transmitted to others are implemented. The *patient* may be isolated from others and visiting may be restricted. All those in contact with the patient may be required to wear gloves, plas-tic aprons or overclothing as preventative measures.

microbiology is the science and study of micro-organisms. In medicine it is mainly directed at the isolation and identification of organisms which cause *disease*.

micrograph: a photograph of a *tissue* sample taken through a light *microscope*. If an electron microscope is used the photograph is called an electron micrograph.

micro organisms are those organisms which are too small to be seen with the human *eye* but can be identified under a *microscope*, for example, *bacteria* and some algae.

microscope: an instrument used to examine *cells* and *tissue* specimens. Microscopic examination is an essential part of detecting *disease*. There are different types of microscope.

The light microscope functions in the following way. A mirror reflects light through the specimen, the objective lens, the barrel and the eyepiece lens, and into the *eye*. In this type of compound microscope, magnification occurs twice, at the objective lens and at the eyepiece. The magnifying power of a microscope is, however, not its most impor-tant feature. The degree of detail that can be seen, or its resolving power, is more

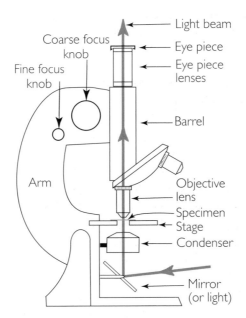

A *light microscope*

relevant when viewing a specimen. If a microscope has high
resolution it allows two points
which are close together to be
seen as two separate points,
whereas a microscope with
lower resolution may be
unable to distinguish the two
points so that they would
appear as a single point. The
resolving power of the microscope is inversely
proportional to the wave-
length of light being used.
Because the wavelength of
light is limited to the visible
spectrum, the resolving power
of a light microscope is con-
strained. It can never
distinguish between points
which are closer together
than 0.3 µm.

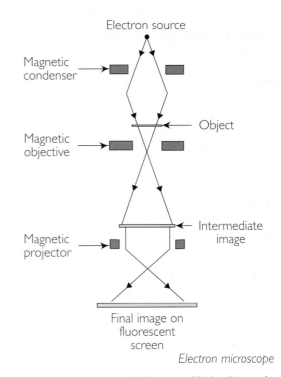

Electron microscope

The electron microscope uses beams of electrons instead of beams of light. Since electrons have a much shorter wavelength than light an electron microscope has a much
higher resolving power than the best light microscope. However, to prevent the electron beam from being deflected by air molecules, the microscope has to be kept

under vacuum which means that only dead specimens can be observed. The electron microscope functions in the following way. It uses electromagnets to focus beams of electrons. These cannot be detected with the eye, so they are projected onto a fluorescent screen. Areas of the specimen then absorb electrons and these appear as dark areas on the image. If the electrons pass through the specimen, these areas appear bright on the image. The process can also be used to give a three dimensional image.

In the scanning electron microscope solid specimens are bombarded with a beam of electrons. This causes secondary electrons to be emitted from the surface of the specimen. Details of the surface of the specimen can be clearly seen.

midwife: a qualified professional who works with women before, during and after they give *birth* to their *babies*. The midwife's role is to:

- give care and advice to women during pregnancy
- work alongside the mother during labour
- deliver the baby
- support and visit the mother following the birth of her baby.

Midwives can either qualify through a three year direct entry midwifery qualification or take an 18 month course following general nurse training.

MIND: a registered *charity* and *voluntary* organisation which supports the needs of the *mentally ill*. It actively *campaigns* for their rights, e.g. on such issues as the care of mentally ill in the community.

(For further information contact MIND, Granta House, 15–19 Broadway, Stratford, London E15 4BQ.)

minerals: are inorganic substances many of which are essential for general *health*. (See Table on opposite page.)

minimum wage: see *national minimum wage*.

miscarriage is the spontaneous loss of a *foetus* from the *uterus* in the early stages of *pregnancy*. This is very distressing for a woman and she will need sensitive support to enable her to grieve for her lost baby.

The Miscarriage Association provides information and support for those who have suffered the loss of a child through miscarriage. (See also *abortion*.)

(For further information contact Miscarriage Association, 4 Ashfield Terrace, Thorpe, Nr. Wakefield, W. Yorks.)

mitochondria: spherical or cylindrical bodies within the *cell* cytoplasm, which are the sites of internal respiration.

mitosis: *cell* division which takes place when new cells are produced for growth and to replace worn out, mature or damaged cells. The cells produced through mitosis contain the same number (46 in humans) of *chromosomes* as the parent cell and are genetically identical. (See Figure on page 196.)

mixed economy of care: the way in which community and social services are provided through different organisations in the statutory, independent and voluntary sectors, e.g. respite care may be offered through a local voluntary group such as *Mencap*.

Minerals

Mineral	Source	Function	Deficiency
Iron	Liver, eggs, chocolate, meat	Forms haemoglobin in red blood cells which carry oxygen around the body.	Anaemia, pallor, breathlessness, lack of energy.

Mineral	Source	Function	Deficiency
Calcium	Milk, cheese butter, bread flour	Builds strong bones and teeth. Aids clotting of blood when injured. Aids normal working of muscles.	Rickets (bones fail to harden), dental cavities, delayed blood clotting, cramp in muscles.
Phosphorous	Milk, cheese, fish, oatmeal	Helps to build strong bones and teeth, needed for the formation of enzymes and all body tissue.	
Iodine	Seafoods, water supply, vegetables, may be added to salt	Used by the thyroid gland to make thyroxine which regulates use of food in body	Adult – goitre (enlarged thyroid gland). Baby – causes cretinism (retarded development)
Sodium chloride (salt)	Added to food kippers, bacon	Needed to maintain salt balance concentration of blood.	Cramp in muscles.
Fluoride	Water supply; may be present naturally or added artifically.	Combines with calcium in teeth, so making enamel more resistant to decay.	Dental cavities.
Zinc	Meat and dairy products, breast milk, infant formula milks	Needed for growth and healing wounds. Helps activity of enzymes	Mild – poor growth; poor healing. Severe – skin rashes, disturbances in the brain, gut and immune system.
Potassium	Cereals, some fruits	Needed for growth and healthy cardiac muscle.	Muscle weakness, tiredness.

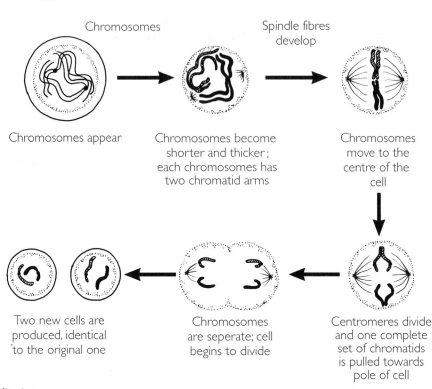

Mitosis

mobility: the ability that a *person* has to walk, run and use the range of movements necessary for daily living. A *client's* mobility is assessed as part of their *care plan.* (See *activities for daily living.*)

Modernising Health and Social Services: National Priorities Guidance: 1999–2000, 2001–2002: government initiatives which are designed to review local authority targets and to develop shared responsibility working to improve health and social care services. The local authority targets relate to children's welfare, interagency working and implementation of the social care White Paper. The shared responsibility enables health and social care professionals to work more closely in the areas of mental health, health inequalities and promoting independence in adult service users and clients. (Department of Health 1998)[43]

Modernising Social Services 1998: a government White Paper introduced by the Secretary of State for Health in December 1998. Some of the proposals outlined include:

- toughening the regulation of care by establishing a network of independent, regional inspectorates. These would take over the existing regulatory functions of the local and health authorities. They would also embrace the unregulated care agencies, establishing a level playing field across the public and private sectors (Commissions for Care Standards)
- the setting up of children's rights officers to act as a safeguard against the abuse of children and of young people in care

- establishing the *General Social Services Council*
- allowing people older than 65 years to become eligible for direct payment of care funding, and to decide for themselves what care to purchase.

molecules are formed when atoms are chemically bonded together. For example, a molecule of *water* is represented as H_2O because it consists of one atom of *oxygen* with two hydrogen atoms bonded to it.

Mongolian blue spot is a disorder which causes a bluish patch on the skin. It looks rather like a *bruise*. It usually affects children of Afro-Caribbean origin.

monosaccharides: contain one simple *sugar* unit. In digestion all *carbohydrates* are broken down to simple sugars. Examples include:

- glucose – found in honey
- fructose – found in sweet fruits
- galactose – forms milk sugar or lactose.

morbidity data is the information which is collected with regard to illness, its type, nature and extent within the population. It is usually measured by the number of *hospital* admissions and *doctor/patient* consultations. Statistics relating to time off work as a result of sickness and self-reported illness data are gathered from health surveys.

morphine is a narcotic derived from opium. It is used as a powerful pain killer or analgesic, administered particularly to those who are suffering from severe pain. It is given to patients with *cancer*, for example. It can be addictive and is therefore registered under the Misuse of *Drugs* Act 1971.

mortality rates: the number of *deaths* per thousand of the population during a year. These rates are often split into the following groups, *age, class, race, gender, children,* and *infants*. (See *infant mortality rate, standard mortality rate, standard mortality ratio*.)

motivation is the way in which a person uses their thought processes to encourage themselves to carry out tasks and activities. It is often related to a person's self-esteem and their belief in their ability to perform.

motor development is the development of the large and fine *muscles* which are found in the body.

motor neurone disease: a progressive *degenerative* disease which affects the motor neurones in the nervous system. It occurs in middle age and leads to increased muscle weakness. The Motor Neurone Disease Association assists sufferers and their families.

(For further information contact the Motor Neurone Disease Association, PO Box 246, Northampton NN1 2PR.)

mouth: composed of the upper and lower lip, *teeth,* hard palate and soft palate (which forms the roof of the mouth), *tongue,* tonsils and uvula, which is a projection from the soft palate. The mouth has important functions. The mouth:

- is the point of entry to the body for *food* and drink
- chews food and mixes it with *saliva* to help with swallowing
- enables food to be tasted
- is an *air passage* to the *lungs*
- makes speech possible.

Care of the mouth is an important part of the physical care of *clients*. Examination of a person's mouth reveals any gum disease or gingivitis. Looking at a person's tongue can also indicate their state of *health*. For instance, when a person is dehydrated the tongue is dry and cracked and the surface is coated and furred. The reason why the tongue is such a clear indicator is because its surface is consistently shed and replaced, with all the debris being washed away by saliva giving the tongue a healthy pink, clean appearance. However, if the amount of saliva being produced in the mouth is reduced, due to a high *temperature* or fever, thirst or a disorder causing loss of appetite, then the mouth feels dry and the surface of the tongue cannot be cleaned effectively. When people are very ill they are unable to clean their mouths and so it can become very sore and uncomfortable. Regular mouth washes and checking of the surface of the tongue is important. When lips become dry and cracked, soft lanolin can be applied to keep them moist.

multi-agency purchasers: different agencies who jointly commission and pay for services. For example, *health authorities* and *social service departments* may jointly purchase an adolescent *mental health* service. It is important in the light of recent changes in the NHS to understand the differences between purchasing and commissioning. Purchasing means buying the appropriate care for a *client,* while commissioning looks at *service requirements* for a geographical area or locality. The relevant organisation is then authorised to provide the various care services identified. (See *joint commissioning.*)

multi-disciplinary teams: health and social care professionals, each with different skills, who work together to meet the individual needs of the *client.*

multifunds: groups of fundholding *GPs* who agree to pool their budgets and work together. (See *NHS: The New NHS – Modern, Dependable.*)

multiple sclerosis: a disease affecting the nervous system which is characterised by the formation of patchy degenerative change in areas of the *brain, spinal cord* and the optic nerves. The signs and symptoms include numbness, weakness and unsteadiness in the legs, and *eye* problems such as double vision. The *disease* goes through cycles of relapse and remission.

(For further information contact the Multiple Sclerosis Society, 286 Munster Road, Fulham, London SW6 6BE.)

Munchausen syndrome: a personality disorder where an individual tries to gain *hospital* treatment or surgery for a non-existent disease. Munchausen syndrome by proxy is a disorder where the individual inflicts harm on others, such as a child or *elderly person*, to gain medical attention.

muscles may be voluntary muscles, i.e. able to be controlled by conscious action or involuntary muscles, i.e. those not under conscious control.

- Voluntary muscles – contractions of voluntary muscles are brought about as a result of nerve impulses reaching the muscle. Voluntary muscles are made up of voluntary muscle tissue. All voluntary muscles, except some of the muscles of the *tongue*, are attached to the *skeleton* by means of *tendons*. They cause movement of the skeleton by contraction of the muscle fibres. Skeletal muscles work in pairs. Flexor muscles cause bending at a joint and extensor muscles cause straightening. Skeletal muscles are usually arranged in antagonistic or opposing pairs. (See *antagonistic muscles.*)

- Involuntary muscles – are present in the wall of the gut, in blood vessels and in the dermis of the *skin*. These muscles are under involuntary control. Involuntary muscles usually open and close tubes or cavities.
- Cardiac muscle is found only in the *heart*.

muscular dystrophy: disorder which affects the *muscles* and the *nerve* supply to the muscles. There are several different types of the condition, which are all progressive, hereditary and result in muscle weakness.

The progressive breakdown of the muscle fibres over several years leads to the destruction of the muscle tissues. During this time the damaged fibres attempt to regenerate but are replaced by fibrous *tissue* and *fat*. The resulting muscle weakness and loss of muscle bulk cause difficulty in walking and affect the use of arms and legs, reducing mobility.

(For further information contact the Muscular Dystrophy Group of Great Britain and Northern Ireland, Prescott House, 7–11 Prescott Place, London SW4 6BS.

muscular tissue is a type of *tissue* which is contractile. There are three different types of muscle tissue.

Striated or striped muscle – voluntary muscle tissue which makes up skeletal muscles. It consists of long cells called muscle fibres grouped together in bundles called fasiculi. Each fibre has a striped or striated appearance and is made of many smaller cylinders, called fibrils or myofibrils. Fibrils contract when a fibre is stimulated by a nerve.

A section of striated muscle to show
actomyosin banding within the fibre

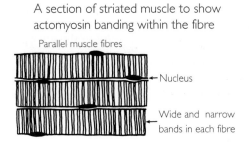

Parallel muscle fibres

Nucleus

Wide and narrow
bands in each fibre

Cardiac muscle – involuntary muscle tissue, which makes up cardiac muscle in the heart. It is a special kind of striated muscle. Its constant rhythmical contractions are caused by stimulation from special areas of the tissue itself, which produce their own electrical impulses.

A surface view of cardiac muscle

Cardiac muscle
cell

Nucleus

Smooth muscle or visceral muscle – involuntary muscle tissue which makes up the visceral muscles supporting the organs of the body. It consists of spindle-shaped cells, much shorter than the complex fibres of striated muscle.

A surface view of smooth muscle

music and singing are activities which help to develop different skills in young children. They can be used to:

- teach different sounds and noises
- develop vocal and singing skills
- give a child the opportunity to learn an instrument
- develop *memory*.

Just as music and singing are satisfying experiences for young children, they can be beneficial in other age groups, particularly the elderly. A regular 'sing song' round the piano helps elderly people to retain their memories. It gives them a creative experience which promotes happiness and satisfaction. *Reminiscence* using songs and music from the past is an excellent way of communicating with the elderly.

music therapy: the use of music to help individuals cope with stress and aggression in their lives. Music can be soothing and relaxing. The ability to make music and create sound can be a satisfying experience.

myalgic encephalomyelitis (ME): a disorder or disease which is characterised by extreme fatigue. Other symptoms include poor circulation, pain in the *joints* and *muscles*, dizziness, general tiredness and a feeling of being unwell or malaise. The cause is unknown, but it often occurs after a *virus* or *infection* and, therefore, can be referred to as post-viral fatigue. Treatment involves rest and medication until the *patient* begins to feel better. In some cases ME can be a prolonged and debilitating disorder.

myocardial infarction: see *heart attack*.

named nurse: the *nurse, midwife* or community nurse who is responsible for a patient's care. Whenever a *client, patient* or *service user* requires treatment or care then they should be told the name of the qualified nurse, community carer or midwife who is looking after them. (See *charters, keyworker.*)

nannies are employed privately by parents to look after children in the family home. Nannies are exempt from registration if they look after the children of only one or two families, but must be registered by the *social services department* if they care for the children of three or more families. Nannies can also work as au pairs which means they are employed for a limited period of time and can work in foreign countries. They may or may not be qualified as *nursery nurses*. Au pairs may be expected to carry out some housework and usually 'live in' with the host family.

National Advisory Committee on Nutrition Education (NACNE): a government committee which issues nutritional guidelines for *health education* in Britain. A report was produced in 1993 which dealt with health-related issues such as body weight, *carbohydrate* and *fat* intake, *coronary heart disease, salt* and *blood pressure* and the effects of *alcohol.* The report concluded that being overweight increased a person's health risk. It made the following recommendations:

- Fats – total fat intake should be reduced and ways of increasing the ratio of *polyunsaturated fatty acids* to saturated fatty acids should be considered. It provided evidence that a diet with a high proportion of polyunsaturated fatty acids could reduce the incidence of cardio-vascular disease.
- Carbohydrates – sucrose (sugar) intake should be reduced and that of complex *carbohydrates* and fibre should be increased. The reduction in sugar is part of a strategy to reduce the overweight proportion of the population. They also identified a link between sugar intake and tooth decay.
- Fibre – to increase intake by 50 per cent. The report suggested that low levels of dietary fibre were associated with large bowel disease, including irritable bowel syndrome, constipation, diverticulosis and colon cancer.
- Salt – to reduce the salt intake. The report indicated that high intakes of sodium chloride led to high blood pressure (hypertension).

The NACNE report looked particularly at the health education aspects of nutrition and how these related to *lifestyle.* Therefore, the targets set were those which would lead to a beneficial change in people's attitudes to nutrition and diet. (See *Committee on Medical Aspects of Food Policy.*)

National Children's Bureau: a registered charity which identifies and promotes the interests of children and young people. It is a *multidisciplinary organisation* and its aim is to promote co-ordination and co-operation amongst all those *agencies* serving children and young people. The Bureau provides a statement of principles and a brief summary of the values that it believes should underpin its work. The Bureau has adopted the *UN Convention on the Rights of the Child.* The various statements are inter-related and should be read as a whole. The term 'children' is taken to include young people up to the age of 18 years, but also beyond 18 in cases where their needs or service implications extend further than this age, for example, in connection with the 1981 Education Act. According to its guiding principles the National Children's Bureau:

- sees children's needs as a whole rather than from the viewpoint of education, health or social services alone
- consults and supports children, parents, families, other carers and professionals
- draws attention to the needs and interests of children and seeks to influence policy and practice
- celebrates the richness and diversity of childhood, including the different strengths deriving from ability, age, colour, culture, ethnicity and gender
- seeks to eradicate prejudice and discrimination against children as a group or because of colour, disability, ethnicity, gender, health, race, religion, sexual orientation or social class
- is committed to hearing and responding to the views of children
- uses research and other ways to identify and promote the best conditions for children whatever their circumstances, whether living with their families or apart
- fosters co-operation, collaboration and effective communication between all those who work with and for children.

(For further information contact National Children's Bureau, 8 Wakley Street, London EC1V 7QE.)

national contracts for health: a government initiative set up to improve health in four priority areas, namely *heart disease and strokes, accidents, cancer* and *mental health* (see the table opposite).

National Council for Voluntary Organisations: the main umbrella body for the *voluntary* sector. It acts as:

- a focal point for formal and informal debate
- an *information* centre
- a focal point for networking
- an influence with regard to policy
- a campaigner for the voluntary sector
- a promoter of voluntary sector interests.

(For further information contact the National Council for Voluntary Organisations, Regent's Wharf, 8 All Saints Street, London N1 9RL.)

National Curriculum: a government reform introduced in 1988 as part of the *Education Reform Act*. Education is compulsory for all children between the ages of five and 16 in state *schools*, including special schools. The National Curriculum is divided into four key stage areas. There are regular and standard assessment tests (SATS) at the end of each key stage. The stages are:

- key stage 1 – children aged 5–7 years
- key stage 2 – children aged 7–11 years
- key stage 3 – children aged 12–14 years
- key stage 4 – children aged 14–16 years.

A contract for health

Government and national players can:	Local and community players can:	People can:
Provide national co-ordination and leadership.	Provide leadership for local health strategies by developing and implementing health improvement programmes.	Take responsibility for their own health and make healthier choices about lifestyle.
Ensure that policy making across the government takes full account of health and is well informed by research and the best expertise available.	Work in partnerships to improve the health of local people and tackle root causes of ill health	Ensure their own actions do not harm the health of others.
Work with other countries for international co-operation to improve health.		
Assess risks and communicate those risks clearly to the public.	Plan and provide high quality services for every one who needs them.	Take opportunities to better their own and their families' lives, through education, training and employment.
Ensure that the public and others have the information they need to improve their health.		
Regulate and legislate where necessary.		
Tackle the root causes of ill health.		
(HMSO 1998)[48]		

National contracts for health

National Health Service: see *NHS.*

National Health Service and Community Care Act 1990: see *NHS and Community Care Act.*

national health targets: set by the government in four priority areas. These are: *heart disease and strokes, accidents, cancer* and *mental health.* (See also *health education, Our Healthier Nation – A Contract For Health.*)

National Homeless Alliance: an organisation set up by the government in 1997. The National Homeless Alliance seeks to:

- link together the different local organisations which are working on homelessness issues
- explore the resourcing of ways of dealing with the growing number of problems related to homelessness
- review other issues which relate to homelessness such as poverty, unemployment and family breakdown
- co-ordinate services to avoid duplication
- be a *pressure group* to keep homelessness on the national agenda
- work in a close relationship with government in determining social policy.

(See also *homeless.*)

National Institute of Clinical Excellence: an organisation set up under the recent government reforms for the *NHS.* The Institute's membership is drawn from individuals in the health professions, NHS academics, health economists and those representing patients' interests. It gives coherence and prominence to *information* about care and clinical treatment and its cost effectiveness.

National Insurance: see *benefits.*

national minimum wage: a wage per hour set at a level decided by the Low Pay Commission. No employee should be paid less than this agreed sum.

National Occupational Standards specify the knowledge, understanding, practical and thinking skills that underpin the outcomes staff are required to achieve in the work place. There are five component parts to a national occupational standard. These are grouped together to form units of competence which can be used as the building blocks for qualification structures. (See *National Vocational Qualifications.*)

The structure of an occupational standard

The standard – what should happen

The outcome (title of the standard)
What should be achieved, the result of successful action, not the action itself.

Performance criteria
How to know that the outcome is of the right quality

Range
Situations and contexts to which the standard applies

Knowledge specification
What the individual needs to know, understand and apply to achieve an outcome

Evidence requirements
The types and sources of evidence required to prove that the outcome has been achieved.

National Schedule of Reference Costs: costs incurred by *NHS trusts,* which will be published on a regular basis. These will include organisational, management and health care costs.

National Society for Prevention of Cruelty to Children (NSPCC): a voluntary organisation with *statutory* powers to act in the care of children and their families. It has the authority to take legal action on behalf of a child and to obtain access to records such as the register of children at risk. To carry out this work it employs qualified *social workers* and operates closely with the *statutory social services* and the *police*. A child may be referred to the NSPCC who investigate the case and work with the family. If there is a need for the child to be taken into care, then the case may be taken to court by the NSPCC or passed over to the *local authority* social services department. The emphasis of the organisation is on protecting children, working with families and seeking to prevent their break-up.

(For further information contact the NSPCC, 42 Curtain Road, London EC2 3NH.)

National Training Council: a training organisation for personal social services set up in June 1998. It is responsible for the development of education and training strategies for all *personal social services* staff across England and Wales.

National Vocational Qualifications (NVQs) are those qualifications which provide proof of competence in the workplace. The holder of the award has met the requirements of the relevant *national occupational standards*. In 1998, the *Care Awards* were updated and revised. There are a variety of awards including community work, care, hospital operating department support, caring for children and young people, *early years* care and education.

nature–nurture: a debate which discusses the factors influencing the way in which children grow and develop, comparing the impact of *home environment* (nurture) and inherited traits (nature). (See *socialisation*.)

needs: the requirements necessary for maintaining life at a certain standard. There are basic needs such as warmth, fresh air and sunlight, healthy *diet*, affection, good health, independence, good *hygiene*, a sense of belonging, social contact, *play* (to be occupied in *work* or involved in a hobby), protection from harm, and *safety*. *Care* involves providing the relevant support to meet all of these, within the context of a client's *physical, intellectual, emotional, cultural* and religious needs.

negative behaviour: the *behaviour* of an individual which may be interpreted as antisocial. This includes *tantrums*, screaming, shouting and swearing. This form of behaviour needs firm but sensitive handling. (See *challenging behaviour*.)

neglect is the failure to provide a child or person with the basic necessities of life such as *food, warmth*, clothing, *housing* and the security of being cared for. Carers who neglect their *clients* may:

- leave them alone for long periods
- not make adequate provision for their clothing and hygiene needs
- not consider their dietary needs and routine of regular feeding
- isolate them by not giving them love and companionship.

(See also *abuse*.)

nerve impulses are messages carried or conducted along the various *nerve* fibres in the body. For example, sound, light, touch and heat stimulate the sense *organs* to send impulses along a nerve *cell* or neuron to the brain and to any part of the body. *Neurones* are linked to each other and form a body network connecting with the *brain* and *spinal cord*. However, the neurones are not joined directly together. There is a small gap or synapse between adjoining neurones. When an impulse is conducted along a nerve, a release of chemicals at the synapse enables the message/impulse to be conducted to another nerve cell. Neurones are nerve cells which carry messages to and from the *brain* via the *spinal cord* and the peripheral nervous system. They vary in size and shape but are classified in groups according to their different functions, which include:

- *sensory neurones* – carry messages or relay impulses from the sensory organs to the central nervous system
- motor neurones – carry messages or relay impulses from the central nervous system to *muscles* and *glands*
- intermediate neurones – relay messages between the different neurones.

nerves are bundles of fibres which are responsible for carrying messages or relaying impulses to and from the *brain* via the *spinal cord* and the peripheral nervous system to all parts of the body. There are 43 pairs of nerves situated in the *central nervous system*. These consist of:

- 12 pairs of cranial nerves which connect the brain to all parts of the body
- 31 pairs of spinal nerves which connect the parts of the body to the brain.

Each nerve contains bundles of fibres which vary in thickness and number. Some nerves consist of one or two fibres and are thin threads while others are thicker with many more fibres. Nerves continually branch off and therefore penetrate all parts of the body. Such fibres may be sensory or motor nerves; which they are determines the type of action they initiate.

nervous system: this provides the fastest method of communication within the body. There are two parts of the nervous system: the *central nervous system* (CNS) and the peripheral nervous system. It is a network of *nerve cells* called neurones which carry messages to and from the *brain* via the *spinal cord* and peripheral nervous system to all parts of the body. The central nervous system consists of the brain and spinal cord. The peripheral nervous system consists of bundles of motor and sensory fibres which take messages to and from different parts of the body.

nervous tissue is composed of *cells* which conduct messages or impulses to and from the *brain* and other parts of the body. The nerve cells are also called neurones.

network: the formation of a number of friends, colleagues or people who group together to offer *support* in the following ways:

- *counselling*
- sharing *information*
- sharing expertise
- fundraising for local self help projects
- publicising a service
- setting up localised training sessions.

(See *support groups*.)

New ambitions for our country: a new contract for welfare: government plans to reform the *welfare state*. The plan includes:

- promoting work through new employment zones and reforming the tax and *benefit* system
- reviewing the state retirement pension system
- improving *health* and *education* opportunities
- improving *housing* and housing management
- working on behalf of the disabled to reduce *discrimination* and to increase the number of the disabled who are able to work
- reviewing systems for *families and children*
- promoting strategies to deal with *social exclusion* such as *homelessness*.

(See also *new welfare state*.)

newborn baby (neonate): the *baby* in the first month of its life. When babies are born they are curled up in the foetal position (arms and legs are bent inwards towards the body). After *birth* the newborn begins to adopt different positions such as:

- Prone – the baby lies on its front with its head turned to one side. The bottom is raised and the knees are curled up under the tummy. The arms are bent at the elbows and tucked under the chest. The fists are clenched.
- Supine – the baby lies on its back. The arms are turned inward and bent towards the body. The knees are also bent towards the body. The baby exhibits jerky kicking movements in the legs.
- Ventral suspension – when held horizontally under the tummy the baby's head and legs fall below the level of their back and the baby's body forms a downwards curve.
- Sitting – when the baby is pulled into the sitting position its head falls back. This is called head lag. As the baby's body comes up its head flops on to its chest.

(See *reflex actions of the newborn*.)

new deal: see *welfare to work*.

new welfare state: reforms with regard to the *welfare state* recommended by the government in the Green Paper '*Our New Ambitions For Our Country –A New Contract For Welfare 1998*'. The government set out key principles which include:

- The new welfare state helping and encouraging people of working age to be in paid employment.
- The private and public sectors working in partnership to ensure that, wherever possible, people are insured against foreseeable risks and able to make provision for their retirement.
- The new welfare state providing public services of high quality to the whole community, as well as cash benefits.
- Those who are disabled getting the support they need to lead a fulfilling life with dignity.
- Specific action attacking social exclusion and helping those in *poverty*.
- A system encouraging openness and honesty with the gateways to *benefit* being clear and enforceable.
- The system of delivering modern welfare should be flexible, efficient and easy for people to use.

(HMSO 1998)[44]

NHS and Community Care Act 1990: an Act of Parliament following the white paper 'Caring for People' 1988 which introduced reforms into *NHS* and social care services. The principal areas covered by the Act included:

- local authority *community care plans*
- assessment and *care management*
- *purchasing, providing, contracting* and the introduction of the *internal market*
- *GP* fundholding
- community care reforms
- NHS reforms.

(HMSO 1990)[45]

The most recent government reforms in the NHS have amended or replaced some of these recommendations.

NHS Charter: a new charter informing people about the standards of treatment and care which they can expect from the *NHS.* It also explains patients' responsibilities.

NHS Direct: a new 24 hour telephone *advice* line staffed by *nurses* to deal with enquiries from the general public.

NHS Executive: the organisation within the *Department of Health* which provides leadership for the *NHS* and a range of central management functions to the NHS.

NHS (National Health Service): a free, comprehensive and state provided health system. The NHS was set up in 1948 following the Act of Parliament, the NHS Act 1946. The shape of the NHS in 1948 consisted of three distinct and separately managed areas. These were *hospitals* – run by management committees, primary care (*GPs, dentists, opticians* and *pharmacists*) – run by executive councils and *community health* (district nursing, ambulances) – run by *local authorities.* The NHS was reformed in 1974 when there were major changes to its structure and to that of local government. A new three tier system of managing the NHS was introduced, i.e. regional *health authorities,* area health authorities and district health authorities. The aim was to separate responsibilities to the different levels, and to improve management and resource allocation. There was further major reform following the *NHS* and *Community Care Act* in 1990. The aim this time was to create a more efficient NHS by making it more business-like through the setting up of an *'internal market'*. It divided the service into *'purchasers'* and *'providers'* of health care. Purchasers – such as district health authorities and GP fundholders would draw up *contracts* with providers such as *NHS trusts* to deliver health care. This introduced an element of competition into the system which was designed to improve efficiency and reduce costs (see *economy, efficiency and effectiveness*). Another reform was to introduce *care in the community.* This was a means whereby mental health and learning disability care was provided in the community.

Social services were to be responsible for assessing the *'package of care'* and then for organising the delivery of that care for the client (see *community care*). Following the White Paper in December 1997 '*The New NHS – Modern, Dependable*', further changes are planned. A new NHS (see page 210) is to be based on partnership and to be driven by performance. It is planned to provide:

- fair access to high standards of care. (See *NHS – The New Framework*)

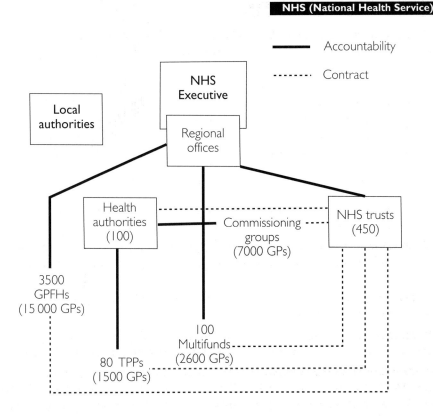

The old NHS before 1997

- national service frameworks – ending two-tier GP fundholding and giving all GPs the same level of influence
- new primary care groups – involving all GPs, other primary care professionals and Social Service input i.e. shape services in line with local needs
- more responsibility inside NHS trusts for their clinical staff
- health authorities to monitor a *health improvement programme* with a new legal duty of partnership which includes stronger links with local authorities
- partnership as the starting point for the new *health action zones*
- new arrangements to improve quality, i.e. the responsibility of every NHS trust Board is monitored through *clinical governance*. Similar arrangements are extended to primary care
- new national bodies – *National Institute for Clinical Excellence* leads on clinical and cost effectiveness – *Commission for Health Improvement* underpins local commitments to *quality assurance*
- a new framework for performance management monitoring cost volume, like outcomes, health gain and patient experience
- a means of breaking down unnecessary barriers between budgets so that primary care group money can go where the need is greatest
- *funding* through quality and efficiency.

(HMSO 1997)[61]

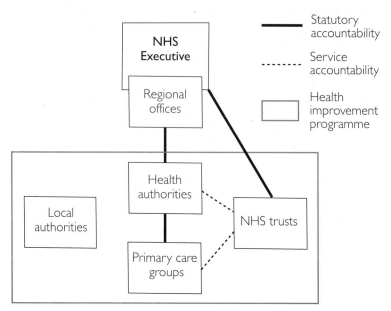

The new NHS Source: The New NHS – Modern, Dependable 1997

NHS – new information technology: see *information technology supporting quality and efficiency*.

NHS performance: a framework for national *NHS* performance intended to measure progress in meeting the goals set by government reforms of 1997. This has six dimensions:

- *health improvement* – improving the general health of the population
- fair access – access to all health services in relation to people's needs, irrespective of geographical area, *class ethnicity, age* or *sex*
- effective delivery of appropriate health care – complying with agreed standards
- efficiency – using NHS resources to achieve value for money
- patient/carer experience – measuring the way in which patients and carers view the quality of the treatment they receive
- health outcomes of NHS care – assessing its direct contribution to improvements in overall health, completing the circle with the goal of improving health.

(HMSO 1997)[61]

NHS resources: *funding* which applies to the *NHS*. The NHS is financed through general taxation. In recent government reforms (being implemented from 1997), the Advisory Committee for Resource Allocation is being set up to improve the arrangements for distributing resources for both primary and secondary care. Alongside this, a Capital Prioritisation Advisory Group will be set up to assess which major capital development projects should proceed. There will be further development of public and private partnerships in non-acute areas such as *information technology* and *community health services*.

NHS – the new framework: see *NHS*.

NHS – the third way: the central policies of government reform to the *NHS*, identified in the White Paper *The New NHS – Modern, Dependable*. It seeks to run the NHS through a system based on partnership with other agencies and driven by performance. (See *NHS trusts*.)

NHS trusts: organisations which provide *patient* services in *hospitals* and in the community. Trusts are responsible for providing health and community care for millions of people in the United Kingdom. They employ the vast majority of NHS staff and their expenditure accounts for 72 per cent of the NHS budget. In partnership with local universities and other research bodies, many NHS Trusts also carry out important education and research responsibilities alongside their commitment to patient care. Under recent reforms, NHS trusts will:

- help to shape the *health improvement programmes*
- set up new standards for quality with local agreements between *health authorities* and *primary care groups* based on new measures of efficiency
- involve *doctors, nurses* and other senior professionals in designing *service agreements*
- support *clinical governance.*

Nolan Committee Report 1997: a government report prepared by Lord Nolan and his committee on standards in public life. It reviewed the relationship between the *voluntary* sector and *local authorities*. The recommendations of the report have become known as the 'Nolan Principles' and include:

- improved rules on *whistleblowing* and wider access to complaint and whistle-blowing procedures
- a clear code of conduct for councillors
- each council to have a standards committee to deal with matters of propriety
- a new local government tribunal to be an independent arbiter of each council's code of conduct
- a new statutory offence of misuse of public office.

(HMSO 1997)[47]

non-accidental injury: the act of deliberately physically hurting a child, causing injury. Physical injuries can take the form of:

- *bruises* – marks which may be caused by beatings with belts, shoes and sticks
- *burns* – such as cigarette burns
- *fractures* – caused by hitting, or dropping on the floor
- head injuries – hitting or shaking a child which may cause *brain* damage
- *poisoning* – feeding a child harmful substances such as *alcohol.*

(See *abuse*.)

non-profit-making organisations: health and social care services which provide care for *clients* on either a voluntary basis or for a minimum cost, e.g. Dial a Ride, a transport service for the disabled and the elderly.

non-verbal communication: ways of communicating with others using body language such as:

- the *eyes* – using eyes to make contact and build rapport can indicate interest. However, in some cultures a sustained eye contact with another would be viewed as showing a lack of *respect*.
- facial expressions – the face can show whether the person is happy, bored, irritated or concerned.
- *gestures* and body posture – how a person uses their bodies to send out strong messages to others.
- physical proximity – how close a person is in proximity to another person is very important. Moving too close can often be viewed as an intrusion of body space. (See *optimised interaction*.)
- tone of voice.

(See also *communication, barriers to communication, confidence building, interpersonal interaction*.)

norms: patterns of *behaviour* that are expected to be followed by members of a particular group. Different groups have their own sets of norms to which members are expected to conform. (See *peer groups*.)

Northern Ireland health provision: health and social care services are managed through health and social care service boards. A Department of Health and Social Services report 'Fit for the Future' proposes to set up local care agencies. These agencies will have a dual role. They will commission and provide services and also work in partnership with professionals involved in *primary care* and *social work*. The role of *GP*'s and *hospital* services in Northern Ireland is similar to that in the rest of the UK (see *Fair Employment Commission*). Following the 'Good Friday Agreement' 1998, there will further changes in the way that Northern Ireland will be governed. (HMSO 1998)[34]

notifiable diseases: a list of *diseases* including *diphtheria*, hepatitis, *food poisoning*, tetanus and *HIV*. When they occur they must be reported to the relevant authority. Notifiable procedures are a means whereby:

- *records* of diseases or infections are maintained as they occur
- adequate provision is made for available *hospital* beds
- research is kept up to date
- local *doctors* are regularly informed of any outbreak of disease in their area.

(See *Reporting of Injuries, Diseases and Dangerous Occurrences Regulations 1985*.)

nurse: a professional qualified to care for people in a variety of settings. Nursing involves training for three years. Half way through this training, nurses specialise in one of the four main branches, adult, *mental health, learning disability* and children's nursing. The professional qualification in nursing can enable a person to develop their skills in other career directions, such as *health visiting*, oncology or caring for *cancer* patients.

nursery nurse: a trained professional person who works with children from newborn babies to rising eight-year-olds in a variety of childcare settings. Nursery nurses promote the *physical, emotional, social, intellectual, cognitive* and cultural development of children. They work in *nurseries*, infant or special *schools*, *hospitals*, family homes, as holiday play representatives and play scheme workers. Nursery nurse training takes two years, culminating in the award of the Diploma in Nursery Nursing. Other qualifications such as *National Vocational Qualifications* may be completed over a shorter period of time. (See also *nannies, human growth and development.*)

nursery education: childcare provision for children from three to five years old. There are different types of *early years* provision with varying specified numbers of staff to the number of children. The provisions include:

- Local education authority nursery *schools* – open ten half-day sessions a week, for 40 weeks each year. The schools may take up to 50 children per session, and *staff* must have teacher or *nursery nurse* training.
- Independent nursery schools – with opening times similar to *local authority* establishments, with up to 30 children per session.
- Nursery classes – childcare provision situated within primary schools with up to 30 children per session.
- *Day nurseries* – provision for children which offer full-time day care for children from three months to five years.
- Independent day nurseries – similar to those operated by the local authority except they are privately owned.
- *Playgroups* – childcare provisions which are supported by the Early Years Alliance, formerly the Pre School Playgroup Association. Children usually attend for morning or afternoon sessions.

nursing home: residential accommodation which provides professional nursing care. Nursing homes are defined by Part II of the Registered Homes Act 1984 as 'Any premises used, or intended to be used, for the reception of, and the provision of nursing for persons suffering from any sickness, injury or infirmity'. This definition also includes *hospices*, maternity homes and acute independent *hospitals*, but excludes NHS hospitals. This part of the Act also extends to nursing homes for the mentally ill. Such homes may be run by registered *charities*, voluntary or private organisations (HMSO 1984)[37]. They are inspected at least once a year by the *local authority*. Some homes may have dual registration to function as a *rest home* and as a nursing home.

nutrients: are the essential components of *food* which provide the individual with the necessary requirements for bodily functions (see *carbohydrates, energy, proteins, fats, water, minerals, vitamins, balanced diet*).

nutrition: the study of the food process in terms of the way that it is received and utilised by the body to promote healthy growth and development. The science of nutrition explores aspects of different diets, and of diseases caused by dietary deficiency. (See *balanced diet, minerals, vitamins.*)

O

obesity: the excessive deposit of fatty *tissue* in the subcutaneous region around the body. Obesity is caused by the consumption of an excessive amount of *calories* taken in the form of food and drink. Obesity is measured by body weight against body height, which calculates the body mass index (BMI).

observation: a procedure in which one person watches or studies another person or a group of people. There are different types of observation:

- Direct observation – the researcher remains detached from the subjects he or she is observing. Subjects can be watched as they go about their daily lives. Both *qualitative* and *quantitative* data can be collected. Observers can count participants in terms of *race, class, gender* and *age* and any other characteristic. They can also record qualitative data such as how individuals behave towards each other. Direct observations are the only way to monitor some groups. Observation of *clients* as a means of *assessment* involves noting the general appearance of the client, their colour, dress, *mobility*, facial expressions, body *posture, gestures,* and the way they speak.
- Participant observation – means that the researcher becomes part of the group being studied. Some researchers have spent years living and working with their subjects, while at the same time recording *data* about them.
- Naturalistic observation – observing people in their natural setting, i.e. watching children interact with their mother or primary care giver.

Recording an observation can be simple, e.g. writing what is being observed in a note book. In some cases a video camera may be used or photographs may be taken, if permission is given beforehand. Permission is sought from the client, *carer* and in some cases the *care manager* if necessary, so that the individual *rights* of the client are protected. Observations may be recorded:

- for a defined period and with a specific aim in mind, e.g. a childcare student may wish to observe an aspect of a child's development, such as their physical co-ordination, as they play
- at regular intervals in order to collect evidence for a project, i.e. a student may observe others in the college refectory every lunch time for a week in order to note the eating habits of students
- on a *chart*, e.g. quantitative readings such as temperature, pulse and respiration.

occupational diseases result from particular types of employment, usually as a result of long-term exposure to a specific substance, environment or a repetitive physical act. Examples are conditions caused by:

- dust, asbestosis is for example caused by breathing in *asbestos* dust which results in damage to the *lungs*
- chemical *poisoning*, such as lead compound poisoning which results in *bone marrow* damage
- working with continuous loud noise which can result in damage to hearing

- being exposed to *radiation* which can result in some *cancers*
- repeated movements of parts of the body which can result in repetitive strain injury
- the constant glare of a computer screen which can result in visual disturbance.

occupational health nurses are registered *nurses* who work with people in their place of employment. They promote physical and *mental health* and carry out *risk assessment* with regard to any physical hazard which may result in employees contracting work-related *diseases*. They are often involved in health *screening, record* keeping, environmental monitoring, accident prevention, health *education, rehabilitation* and any follow-up treatment. They also deal with minor accidents.

occupational health service: the department within an organisation which looks after the health needs of employees.

occupational therapists are trained professionals who treat *patients, clients* and *service users* with temporary or permanent physical or learning disability or mental illness. Following the *NHS and Community Care Act 1990* and the growing emphasis on *care in the community*, occupational therapists work in a number of different settings supporting clients from a variety of backgrounds. These settings can include general and *specialist hospitals*, health centres, local authority social services, *residential homes* and *day centres*, children's and mental health services, in people's own homes and in industry and commerce. An occupational therapist has to combine knowledge and skills when working with people of all ages. They support clients with different problems, such as psychological or physical illness, accident recovery or ageing. Fundamentally their role is to encourage individuals to take action for themselves. They assist clients to improve the quality of their own lives and enable them to remain independent and autonomous for as long as possible. This may involve visiting a client's home and assessing their need for necessary aids and adaptations. Registered occupational therapists qualify after a three year course at university.

(For further information contact the College of Occupational Therapists, 6–8 Marshalsea Road, Southwark, London SE1 1HL.)

Office of Population Censuses and Surveys: an organisation which collects data to be published in national, local and medical population tables. The results recorded include *morbidity rates, mortality rates, employment* statistics, marriage and *divorce* rates.

Office of Standards in Education (OFSTED): an *organisation* which inspects, monitors, and reports on the performance of *schools*. Visits to schools are carried out by teams of inspectors who include lay members (people who do not have a background in education). It is intended that schools should be inspected at least once every five years. Summaries of the reports must be published, and a copy sent to the parents of every child in the school.

opinion poll: a survey method to collect data with regard to public opinion on different issues. *Quota sampling* and street *interviews* are methods often used to test public opinion.

ophthalmic optician: see *optometrists*.

ophthalmologists are qualified *doctors* who have specialised in the treatment of the *eyes* and visual impairments. They also detect, diagnose and treat eye infections. They care for the visually impaired and look at strategies for preventing loss of sight or blindness.

opticians are professionals trained to examine and test the eyesight of *clients* and customers. They can detect *eye* disorders and prescribe the appropriate lenses to be fitted into spectacles or glasses. Opticians usually charge for eye tests. However, there are certain individuals who are exempt from this charge, such as *elderly people* and the disabled. (See *health benefits, optometrists, opthalmologists.*)

optimised interaction is a way of ensuring that the relationship between *client* and *carer* is beneficial. To optimise effective *interpersonal interaction*, contact should be evaluated with regard to:

- amount of eye contact
- facial expressions, e.g. smiling
- *posture* and position, e.g. sitting, standing
- *gestures*, e.g. nodding, moving hands.

The results of this evaluation should suggest ways of improving *communication* practice and developing interpersonal skills. Optimised interaction is a key requirement for students studying Unit 2 on the GNVQ (Advanced) Health and Social Care programme. (See *confidence building, barriers to communication, interpersonal interaction, personal space.*)

optometrists are professionals involved in testing eyesight to detect and measure any visual *disorder* or impairment. They may prescribe lenses to correct such defects. They are also able to detect any *disease* or *dysfunction* of the *eye*. They either work in private practice or within the *National Health Service.*

organ transplant: see *transplants.*

organisations are bodies of people set up to achieve specific aims. They are characterised by a structure and a culture. Organisations are often placed where there are *decision making* processes and *information* exchange. Those in health and social care have been established to meet the health and social care *needs* of society, both at a local and national level. They will usually be managed by a senior group who will direct different *teams* working with various *client* groups (see *hospitals, social service departments)*. However, there are also much smaller organisations such as *playgroups* and *day centres.* In such examples there is usually just one senior leader of a team which works together in the care of their clients.

organ: a structure consisting of different *tissue* types carrying out a particular function or functions; an example is the *heart* which is made up of *muscle tissue* called cardiac muscle, nervous tissue, supported and bound by *connective* and *epithelial* tissue. When different *organs* work together they form an organ system, e.g. the circulatory system which includes the *heart, lungs, arteries, veins* and *capillaries.*

orthopaedic specialist: a qualified *doctor* who specialises in detecting, diagnosing and treating *diseases*, disorders and *dysfunctions* of the *bones* and *joints.*

orthoptists are professionally trained people who work with individuals, usually children, who have any visual defect or disorder, abnormal *eye* movement or any other correctable eye condition. Their role is to prescribe eye exercises and to monitor the patient's progress during the course of treatment. Most orthoptists work in *hospitals* but some operate in the community providing vision screening in *schools*, mobile units and health clinics. (See *optometrists, opticians*.)

osmosis is the process by which solvents pass through a semi-permeable membrane under osmotic pressure. The solvent molecules, e.g. water, pass from an area of lower solute concentration to an area of higher solute concentration until the concentration of solutions on both sides of the semi-permeable membrane is equal.

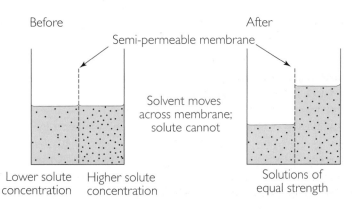

Before   After

Semi-permeable membrane

Solvent moves across membrane; solute cannot

Lower solute concentration   Higher solute concentration   Solutions of equal strength

osteopathy: an *alternative* treatment which focuses on dysfunctions or disorders of the *muscles* and the skeletal system. A method of manipulation is used to help the body to heal itself. The basic principles applied in osteopathy are:

- the body has self-healing mechanisms which can be identified by the osteopath and put to work
- the body is made up of units and parts which inter-relate to each other and can work together to maintain *health* and *well-being*; this indicates the *holistic* nature of the treatment
- the structure and functions of the body link and inter-relate with each other, for example sore and painful muscles may lead to poor circulation so by diagnosing the different causes of pain and releasing the blood flow, the healing process is facilitated.

Qualifying to be an osteopath takes four years. For qualified *doctors* it takes thirteen months.

osteoporosis is a disorder which affects the *bones*, causing thinning or reduction in the mass of bone present in the body. It is frequently to be found in the elderly. Lack of physical activity can promote generalised osteoporosis. *Fractures* and *disability* are linked with this *disease*, because of its effect on the bones. It affects women more than men due to the reduction of oestrogen (female sex hormone) following the *menopause*. *Hormone replacement therapy* is sometimes given to reduce or slow down the process of osteoporosis. Taking sufficient calcium as part of a woman's daily diet may help to prevent osteoporosis in later life.

'Our Healthier Nation – a Contract for Health': a Government Green Paper which sets out ways to improve the health of the population by increasing the length of people's lives and the number of years that people spend free of illness. It also explores strategies which seek to improve the *health* of the worse off in society and to narrow the health gap. The report considers issues such as:

- *health inequalities*
- *the causes of ill health*
- setting up national contracts for health
- setting national targets for health – *heart disease and strokes, accidents, cancer* and *mental health.*

outdoor play: a type of *play* which children enjoy outside, in the open air. Outdoor play, when weather permits, is an integrated part of a child's *school* day. Opportunities to run, skip, hop, play ball, chase, and play *games* are encouraged. *Physical play* gives a child's *muscles* the exercise needed to develop body co-ordination and movement.

out-of-school care or after school clubs is the provision available to children before and after school. *Social service departments* are now required to register all supervised provision for children up to the age of eight. For those children of *school* age this includes provision in out-of-school clubs, playcentres, adventure play-grounds and holiday play schemes. Children are delivered to, and collected from school, during term time by club workers they know and trust. Once at the club, children are registered, given *food* and offered *play* opportunities until collected by a parent at a later time. Some clubs operate all day throughout school holidays. There are different types of provision for children of this age, including facilities run by *local authorities, voluntary* organisations, the *private sector* and those that are employer sponsored. Parents usually make a contribution towards costs. Other clubs may operate only during term time, or for certain parts of the year.

ovulation: the release of an egg or ovum from one of the *ovaries* occurring about every 28 days. The egg is moved along the Fallopian tube towards the *uterus* by muscular movements called *peristalsis.* In addition to this the lining of Fallopian tubes has ciliated epithelium, which helps the movement of the ovum. The journey from the ovary to the uterus usually takes about seven days. (See *menstrual cycle.*)

oxygen: a colourless, odourless gas that makes up 21 per cent of the atmosphere. It is vital for life. It supports combustion, dissolves in *water* to form a neutral solution and is a very reactive oxidising agent (e.g. it oxidises iron to iron oxide). Oxygen is essential for some of the chemical processes in the body, and it is breathed in via the *lungs* and taken to different parts of the body. It is used in *cell respiration.* (See *gaseous exchange mechanisms for breathing.*)

oxytocin is a *hormone* produced in the posterior lobe of the *pituitary gland.* It causes the *uterus* to contract during labour. *Oxytocin* also controls the release of milk during the suckling period.

P

paediatrician: a qualified *doctor* who specialises in treating children. Paediatricians usually work in *hospitals* and have a specialist knowledge of the disorders, *disease* and *dysfunctions* which affect children. Children are referred to a paediatrician by their *GP*.

paedophile: a person who is sexually attracted to children. They may be involved in sexual offences involving children. (See *Sex Offenders Act 1997.*)[56]

palliative care: care which is given to a *patient* who is suffering from *terminal illness*. 'It affirms life and regards *death* as a normal process, neither hastens nor postpones death, provides relief from pain and other distressing symptoms, integrates the psychological and spiritual aspects of patient care and offers a support system to help the family cope during the patient's illness and in their bereavement'. (WHO 1994)

This type of provision involves home and day care, and in-patient hospital care, *bereavement* support and voluntary support. (See *Cancer Relief Macmillan fund, Marie Curie Cancer Care, MENCAP, holistic care.*)

pancreas: a large *gland* situated in the first loop of the *duodenum* at the back of the *abdomen* behind the lower part of the *stomach*. It is a large whitish *organ*. The pancreatic duct links the pancreas to the duodenum. During *digestion* the pancreas secretes digestive juices which are poured onto *food* as it passes into the duodenum. These digestive juices are alkaline, to provide optimum conditions for the pancreatic enzymes to work. The functions of the pancreas are as follows:

- It produces pancreatic juice containing the *enzymes* lipase which digests *fat,* amylase which digests starch, and trypsin which digests *protein.*
- It produces insulin from special pancreatic cells called the islets of Langerhans. Insulin reduces the level of glucose in the *blood* ensuring that the glucose level is kept constant. Excess glucose enters the cells of *muscles* and the *liver* for storage as glycogen.
- It produces glucagon in the islets of Langerhans. This raises the level of glucose in the blood by causing the release of glycogen in the liver.

paralysis: loss of nervous function to part of the body. This may be due to damage to the sensory or motor nerves or to both. There are many different causes of paralysis, which can either be temporary or permanent. It may be due to:

- pressure on *nerves* blocking off any nerve reactions, e.g. tumour
- disease of the *spinal cord*, e.g. *multiple sclerosis*
- *brain* damage. e.g. *cerebral palsy*
- injury to the spinal cord or peripheral nerves. e.g. injury in a car accident.

paramountcy principle: the concept that the welfare of the child is the paramount consideration in proceedings concerning children. (See *Children Act 1989, Working Together Under The Children Act.*)

paraplegia is *paralysis* of a person from the waist down.

parasympathetic nervous system: part of the *autonomic nervous system* which slows the heartbeat rate, lowers *blood pressure* and promotes *digestion*. There are two important nerves which form part of the parasympathetic *nervous system*. They are:

- the vagus *nerve* which extends from the base of the spine networking to all parts of the body
- the pelvic nerve which extends from the lower part of the spine networking to the lower parts of the body.

It works in opposition to the *sympathetic nervous system*.

parathyroid glands: there are four such *glands* embedded in the *thyroid*, two in each lobe. They secrete a *hormone* called the parathyroid hormone. This hormone controls the level of calcium in the *blood*. (See *endocrine system*.)

parent and toddler groups are small informal groups which offer *play* opportunities for children. The children are usually under the age of three years and attend the group with their parents or carers such as *childminders*. These groups may be linked with other forms of provision, such as *schools, playgroups* and *clinics*.

parental responsibility defines the duties of parents or primary care givers under the *Children Act 1989*. 'All the rights, duties, powers, responsibilities and authority which by law a parent of a child has in relation to the child and his property.' (HMSO 1989)[15]. Parental responsibility can be given to a person who is not the biological parent and can be shared amongst a number of people. It may be acquired through an agreement or court order. (See *adoption*.)

Parentline: a national voluntary *organisation* offering telephone support, guidance and counselling services to any parent or carer of children. It provides help for parents under stress and facilitates and maximises a family's capacity to care for its children. It helps to break the cycle of family unhappiness by enabling those who are parenting to share with others the difficulties of bringing up children. Parents can telephone when they are in a crisis or when they just feel the need to talk.

(For further information contact PARENTLINE, Endway House, The Endway, Benfleet, Essex SS7 2AN.)

Parkinson's disease: a slowly progressive, degenerative *disorder* of the *central nervous system*. The cause of Parkinson's disease is not known but it is believed to be associated with one small group of nerve cells in the *brain* (the basal ganglia) failing to function normally. This affects the production of dopamine, a chemical substance involved in the transmission of messages between *nerves* and the *muscles* they supply, causing the muscles to stiffen and respond slowly or not at all. Once established, the symptoms may be mild, but they can increase gradually over the years, although there may be a period of time when they seem to remain static. *Intelligence* is not affected and life expectancy is normal. There are three main symptoms which are usually present to some degree in each case of the disease.

- Tremor is not always present but, if it is, this slight shaking begins in one hand or one arm. It generally decreases when active or asleep.
- Rigidity or stiffness in the muscles is an early sign, and everyday tasks become difficult.

- Slowness of movement plus a difficulty in initiating movement are characteristic. Walking becomes an effort and voluntary movement may be interrupted.

(For further information contact Parkinson's Disease Society, 36 Portland Place, London W1N 3DG.)

participant observation: see *observation*.

passive immunity is the process by which antibodies produced in one individual are passed into the body of another to reduce the risk of specific *disease*. Passive *immunity* can take the form of:

- injection of *antibodies* from another mammal – when these are injected in the form of a serum, they are absorbed into the bloodstream and the individual gains immunity, e.g. treatment of diphtheria and *tetanus*
- immunity transfer between mother and *newborn infant* – antibodies cross the placenta from the mother's blood. Therefore the baby has the same protection against the same diseases as the mother. When the baby is *breast* fed, the baby receives antibodies in the breast milk. These antibodies also provide some immunity for the first few months of a baby's life.

pathogen: any micro-organism which causes a *disease*.

pathologist: the trained professional who is responsible for examining specimens of body *tissue* and detecting any *disease, degeneration* or *dysfunction*. (See *histology*.)

pathology: the study of *disease* and how it progresses. Pathology also explores the causes of disease and its other aspects. Specimens of *tissues* and *cells* and other samples from the body are sent to the pathology laboratory. Here they are examined using a variety of methods such as microscopy. The presence of any disease, disorder, *degeneration* or *dysfunction* is detected and a report written. This is a good example of indirect care as the laboratory technicians have little or no contact with their *patients*.

patient: a person who is receiving medical treatment and nursing care.

Patient's Charter: see *charters*.

peak flow is the maximum speed at which air can be forced out of the *lungs*. A peak flow meter records the maximum speed at which the air is forced out from the lungs. It is used to assess the width of the trachea and bronchi. If the trachea and bronchi are narrowed, the air rushes out more slowly. This happens when a person is suffering from *asthma*.

peer group: a collection of people who share common characteristics or circumstances. Peer groups have an important function in the *socialisation* process. Through peer group membership, individuals learn different roles and identify with the *norms* and *values* of the group. A set of friends of the same age in a class at *school* represents a kind of peer group.

pelvis: the bony structure situated in the lower part of the trunk. The pelvis consists of the ilium, ischium and pubis. These units form the two innominate bones. This framework supports the *bladder*, rectum and *reproductive organs*. (See *skeleton*.)

percentiles are the 100 sections on a *centile* chart which indicate, for example, the range of weight of boys and girls. The 50th percentile is called a median and represents the middle of the range. Children move from one percentile to another if their weight increases or decreases more or less than the 'average' for their peer group. The percentile positions are calculated from a typical sample of 100 children. (See *centile charts*.)

periodic table is an arrangement of the chemical elements in order of their atomic numbers.

peristalsis is the rhythmic contraction and relaxation of the longitudinal and circular layers of smooth *muscles*. This muscular action moves objects in a particular direction. It is the process whereby *food* is passed through the *oesophagus* into the *stomach* and by which it is pushed along the *alimentary canal*.

personal medical services are provided by family *doctors* and their teams. These are currently known as the general medical services.

personal social services provide care for vulnerable people including *client* groups with *special needs* such as the elderly, children and the disabled. *Local authorities* have statutory responsibilities to provide care for these clients. For example, *social workers*, home helps, *residential homes* for the elderly.

personal space: the physical separation between one person and another which is both culturally and individually determined. It is an important aspect of *communication*. When a person stands too close to another while they are in conversation, it may be viewed as intimidating, especially if the conversation is between two people who do not know each other that well. Personal space and positive communication practice rely on:

- the distance between the people; too close is viewed as intimidating, too far can be viewed as the person being disinterested or 'stand-offish'
- the different culture patterns of *behaviour*
- body language and *gestures* used
- how well the people know each other.

Learning what is acceptable in terms of personal space is an important aspect of working with people and is a skill which should be developed. Students should spend time observing communication in different settings. They should also evaluate what they feel is an invasion of their own personal space. (See *observation, optimised interaction*.)

personality: the characteristics or traits of an individual that underline the consistencies in the way that they behave over time and in different situations. (See *introvert, extrovert*.)

pH scale: this indicates the degree of acidity or alkalinity of a solution. It is particularly important for *carers* and *nurses* when they are testing the pH of a *patient's urine* as the results can contribute to a clinical picture of a patient's medical condition. It is a simple test to perform. This involves using a small plastic strip with pH sensitive areas which is dipped into the patient's urine sample and left for the time specified. The resulting colour change gives the pH of the urine and provides an indication of how the *kidneys* are functioning. The kidneys play a vital part in regulating acid levels.

phagocytosis: the process used by white *blood cells* to engulf the micro-organisms which attack the body (see facing page).

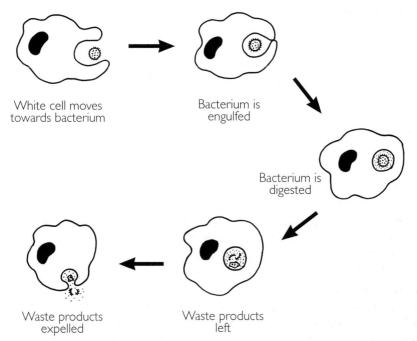

White cell moves towards bacterium

Bacterium is engulfed

Bacterium is digested

Waste products expelled

Waste products left

Phagocytosis

pharmacists are professionals qualified in the field of *drugs* and *medication*. They are trained to dispense *doctors'* prescriptions and may also sell *medicines* for minor ailments. People often ask a pharmacist for advice with regard to mild medical ailments. In order to carry out their roles and responsibilities pharmacists have an indepth knowledge of drugs and their impact on the body, as well as any adverse reactions that drugs may cause. There are three different categories of medicines which the pharmacist will manage:

- prescription-only medicines – as their name implies, these medicines are only available on a prescription written by a doctor and are dispensed by a pharmacist from approved premises
- pharmacy medicines – only available for sale from a pharmacy under the supervision of the pharmacist
- general sales list medicines – these are freely available from pharmacies and other retail outlets, such as supermarkets.

phosphorous: a non-metallic element which can be poisonous (toxic) in its natural state. However, phosphorous is also used to help maintain healthy body tissues. (See *minerals.*)

physical disability: a disorder, *disease* or *dysfunction* which affects or restricts movement and co-ordination of one or more parts of the body. Physical disabilities can be:

- *congenital* – present at *birth*, e.g. congenital dislocation of the hip
- *genetic* – passed through the generations e.g. *Huntington's chorea*
- *acquired* – through *accident,* disease or a disorder which occurs at any time in a person's life, i.e. *multiple sclerosis.*

physical growth and development: the way in which the body increases in size, e.g. height and weight, and its ability to perform tasks and activities. As a child's *bones* and *muscles* grow and develop, his or her muscular co-ordination will also increase. Growth and development is rapid during the first year of life and then steady throughout the childhood years. During *puberty*, there is a sharp increase in the growth of secondary sexual characteristics. Following late teens and early adult life, growth begins to slow down. Progress should be monitored from the day that a baby is born. A child's height and weight may be regularly checked by the local *primary health care team*. (See *centile charts*.)

physical play: a type of activity which stimulates a child's physical growth and *muscle* control. Physical play encourages co-ordination and movement which develops gross motor skills. Gross motor skills involve limb movements which use the large *muscles* of the body. Such movements include running, walking, skipping and jumping. There are various groups which promote physical play and related activities, such as Tumble Tots and Jungle Gyms. (See *play, outdoor play*.)

Physically Handicapped and Able Bodied (PHAB) is a voluntary organisation which integrates people with and without *physical disabilities*. Their aim is to promote and encourage everyone, whether they have physical disabilities or not, to share activities together. One of the functions of the organisation is to arrange holidays. They view this as an excellent example of bringing both disabled and able bodied people together on equal terms.

(For further information contact PHAB, Summit House, Wandle Road, Croydon CR0 1DF, Surrey.)

physiology: the science which is the study of the functions of the various parts of the body. (See *anatomy*.)

physiotherapist: a qualified professional who treats disorders with physical means. These include methods such as the application of heat, *ultrasound*, electro-therapy, massage and manipulation to help individuals maintain and develop movement and *mobility*. Such methods can assist in rehabilitating patients. Physiotherapists may work in the *NHS*, or in the *independent sector*. They train for three years to achieve qualified status.

(For further information contact the Chartered Society of Physiotherapy, 14 Bedford Row, London WC1R 4ED.)

Piaget's view of play is a theory which supports the view that *play* reinforces a child's cognitive or learning experience. Early sensory–motor co-ordination may help children to understand the *symbolic* world in which they live, thus encouraging co-operation, and co-operative play. At each stage of Piaget's theory, *imagination* is to be encouraged by parents, teachers and others. *Toys* and *games* should develop problem solving skills, muscle development, *hand and eye co-ordination*. Play develops and enhances a child's learning. (See Table on facing page.)

Piaget's three stages

Stage	Age	Development
Stage 1 Sensori–motor stage	0–2 years	The developing child uses its senses to discover the world around him/her. *cont.* Senses such as sight, hearing, touch, taste and smell. As an example, a baby will often put objects in its mouth.
Stage 2 Pre-operational stage	2–7 years	During this stage the child is developing different skills such as hand–eye-co-ordination and problem solving. Children learn through their imagination and 'let's pretend play'. Language development enhances this stage.
Stage 3 Concrete operations stage	7 years and over	The child develops skills which involve working with rules, sharing responsibilities with others and taking turns.

pictogram: a method of presenting data collected from *research*. The results are illustrated using a *bar chart* with the length of the bar modified to show a line of pictures or images.

Pictogram: the number of children who went to see Santa Claus in various department stores on December 22

Allders

Hamlins

Debenhams

Bentalls

Littlewoods

John Lewis

Peter Jones

Harrods

Each child's face represents 20 children

pie chart: a method of presenting data collected from research. A full circle is drawn. The relative quantities of different data alternatives are represented as sectors of the circle. The sectors vary in size according to the frequency of the results. By this means the results of *quantitative research* can be shown in an easily understandable way.

pituitary gland is a small *gland* situated at the base of the *brain*. It is attached to the hypothalmus by a short stem. It is called the 'master gland' because its secretions affect the functions of all the other endocrine glands. It has two lobes which are the:

- Anterior lobe – produces the growth hormone, prolactin follicle stimulating hormone, and thyroid-stimulating hormone, adrenocorticotropic hormone, ACTH (see *endocrine system*).
- Posterior lobe – produces antidiuretic hormone and oxytocin.

placenta: the mass of *tissue* which develops within the *uterus* of a *pregnant* woman. It contains *blood* vessels. *Oxygen* and nutrients are passed from the mother into the developing foetus. Waste product and *carbon dioxide* are passed from the foetus into the mother's blood supply to be excreted. The blood supply from the mother runs alongside the blood supply from the foetus, i.e. maternal and foetal blood supplies are different.

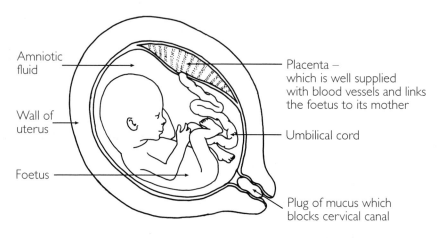

Amniotic fluid

Wall of uterus

Foetus

Placenta – which is well supplied with blood vessels and links the foetus to its mother

Umbilical cord

Plug of mucus which blocks cervical canal

A developing foetus and placenta

plasma is a straw coloured fluid in the blood which contains 90 per cent *water*. Plasma also contains the following:

- proteins such as fibrinogen (aids *blood clotting*), serum albumin (absorbs materials in the blood, serum globulin (antibodies)
- prothombin which is an enzyme which aids blood clotting
- inorganic materials such as chlorides and phosphates
- digested *food* in the form of glucose and *amino acids*
- nitrogenous wastes as a result of metabolism in the tissues.

platelets are tiny structures found in blood *plasma*. They are irregularly shaped and colourless. They are produced in the red *bone marrow* and have an important function in *blood clotting*. There are approximately 250,000 per cubic millimetre of *blood*.

Platt Report 1959, Welfare of Children in Hospital: the first report specifically concerned with the needs of children in *hospital*. Platt made recommendations that:

- children be nursed in appropriate units
- children be cared for by qualified paediatric nurses
- families should be involved as much as possible in all aspects of care and in all decisions
- unrestricted visiting should be allowed, together with accommodation for parents

- *play* and educational facilities should be available
- children should be discharged into the community as soon as possible

(HMSO 1959)[50]

Following this report the National Association for the Welfare of Children in Hospital was set up to support children in hospital and their families. This is now called Action for Sick Children.

(For further information contact Action for Sick Children, 360 Kingston Road, Wimbledon Chase, London, SW2 8LX.)

play is the activity through which children discover the world around them. It occupies an important part in a child's life. It stimulates physical, intellectual, emotional, social and cultural development. It promotes a child's ability to learn and develop different skills, such as *hand–eye co-ordination*. Play helps a child relate to other children through talking, sharing and taking turns. Making and building objects gives a child a sense of achievement and therefore helps them to develop a positive *self-esteem*.

There are several types of play which include:

- *physical play*
- play with different natural materials such as sand, water, dough clay and wood
- construction play with blocks, building bricks and kits
- creative play such as painting and collage
- imaginative play, involving drama, acting out and role modelling
- *music and singing* and *storytelling*.

Play has different stages such as:

- solitary play – a baby will play on its own
- parallel play – the small child sits or stands next to another child. Children will play alongside, but do not interact with each other.
- co-operative play – the child seeks out the company of other children. They play various games and carry out activities together.
- *games* with rules – the children work with guidelines or rules making games more complicated. (See *Piaget's view of play*.)

play buses are special vehicles converted to accommodate toys and equipment for a small playgroup or *parent and toddler group*. They often operate where there is no permanent *play* provision or where outdoor play is restricted, for example, in inner city areas.

play therapy: the way in which *play* is utilised as a form of treatment in order to support a child. This may take different forms such as:

- supporting treatment for a child with a physical disorder – gentle physical *exercise* may be the ideal follow-up treatment following a leg operation, for example playing a stretching *game* can be a means whereby a child has fun during their exercises.
- relief of pain – providing different and stimulating activities can help support a child who is in pain either from their condition or following an operation

- a method of diagnosing a child's *behaviour* problem – a child may display what they are secretly worried about; this is frequently used when *child abuse* is suspected when the child is given different toys to play with, including anatomically correct dolls
- a form of treatment – when the child has a lot of frustrated or pent up feelings; play can be a satisfactory way of releasing these feelings.

playgroups offer care and education, either on a session or full day basis, to children under *school* age. They can be run privately as small businesses or as registered educational charities. An increasing number are opening for longer hours and taking younger children in response to demand. Most playgroups can cater for children with *special needs*. Most playleaders are trained by the Early Years Alliance, formerly the Pre-school Playgroup Association, and many have, in addition, teacher or nursery nurse qualifications. Most playgroups offer parents opportunities to become involved and take some responsibility for the care and early education offered. Playgroups are now more commonly known as pre-school groups.

playworkers are individuals who are either trained or experienced in the area of children's *play*. They form part of a team which provides opportunities for children's play in different childcare settings. They work closely with youth workers but are usually associated with the age group of children from 3–15 years of age. They are based mainly in adventure playgrounds, play centres, community projects, children's wards in hospitals, *play buses, after school clubs* and holiday play schemes. Play work involves creating a safe and happy *environment* which supports children's *creative, imaginative* and social development.

poisoning occurs when a dangerous *chemical* or substance has been taken into the body causing physical distress and harm. Poisons can enter the body in a number of ways which include:

- eating and swallowing contaminated *foods, drugs* or chemicals
- inhaling, breathing in poisons from the atmosphere, or through vapours and *solvents*
- absorbing poisons such as garden fungicides, through the *skin*
- poison injected into the skin such as from snake bites
- poison produced in the body, i.e. the body has an allergic response to 'toxins' which it produces itself.

police officers are responsible for maintaining law and order and ensuring that the public and their property are protected. They investigate *crimes* and are concerned with crime prevention. They work with other professionals to maintain the *criminal justice system* within the United Kingdom.

polio (poliomyelitis): an infectious *disease* formerly called infantile paralysis, which is caused by a *virus*. After initial flu-like symptoms, the virus can attack the *spinal cord*, causing *muscle* paralysis which can affect any part of the body. The most serious cases are those involving the breathing muscles, when *patients* have to be helped to breathe artificially and even then may die. If the virus attacks the nerves supplying the arms and legs, they can become weak or paralysed. Some people also have back problems. Any of these symptoms can result in permanent disability. Polio can be prevented by *vaccination* followed by a booster vaccination. Medical advice should be sought if visits abroad are planned to countries where polio is still common. Since the introduction of a vaccination programme in the early 1960s, notifications of polio have dropped from over 6000 in 1955 to just three in 1992. It is impossible to estimate how many people in the UK are permanently disabled because of polio, but there are still probably tens of thousands. Most people suffering from the effects of polio can lead reasonably active and independent lives.

(For further information contact the British Polio Fellowship, Ground Floor, Unit A, Eagle Office Centre, The Runway, South Ruislip, Middlesex HA4 6SE.)

pollution: the release of poisonous substances, fluids and vapours into the environment. These can have harmful effects on the soil upsetting natural processes, the atmosphere, rivers and oceans. Substances causing such problems are known as pollutants. Examples of pollution include the accidental release of chemicals as a result of an industrial process.

polysaccharides: *carbohydrates* consisting of many sugar units which are chemically linked or bonded together in long chains. Examples are starch and glycogen. Starch is found in most human *diets*. *Foods* containing starch include bread, potatoes, rice and pasta.

polyunsaturated fats: molecules of *fat* which occur in plant and animal cells. High levels are found in nuts, nut oil and fish. *Diets* containing high proportions of such fats have been linked with low blood *cholesterol* levels in some populations.

pornography: any material which is produced to reveal indecent physical and sexual acts between individuals. This material can take the form of newsletters, books, magazines, films, photographs, internet pages and videos. (See *paedophile*.)

portage is a home teaching programme for children with *special needs* and their parents. Set up in America in the 1960s, it involves a specially trained portage worker who supports the family by:

- carefully explaining developmental areas such as *language*, motor skills, *cognitive* skills, stimulation, self-help and *socialisation*
- working in partnership with the parents to produce a learning programme for the child with a number of tasks to be achieved
- helping the child to achieve the tasks set in the learning programme by breaking them down into smaller and more manageable actions, for example, the task of doing up a button will be broken down into several smaller movements, and over a period of time the child works towards achieving each of these until eventually the task can be completed as a whole. All effort is accompanied by a lot of encouragement and positive reinforcement
- ensuring that tasks are realistic for the child concerned, i.e. that they are not too difficult or too easy
- encouraging the parent to reinforce the task at different times in the week when there is opportunity to sit quietly with the child and to work together.

All successes are carefully recorded and enjoyed by all those involved. The portage scheme can be used with children with a variety of *disabilities*. (See *children with disabilities*.)

post-natal care: care given to a mother and her baby following birth. The *primary health care* team will monitor the progress of the mother and baby.

(For further information contact The Institute of Obstetrics and Gynaecology, Queen Charlotte's Maternity Hospital, Goldhawk Road, London W6.)

post-natal depression: a psychological disorder characterised by the new mother feeling sad, worthless and overwhelmed by motherhood. Mothers with post-natal depression need medical supervision, support and practical help.

post-traumatic stress disorder: an *anxiety* disorder arising from a situation which has occurred in the life of the victim. This can be the result of:

- an *accident* such as a car or train accident
- a frightening event such as a fire or bombing
- being involved in a war or a disaster involving many casualties.

The *victim* suffers persistent recurrence of images, mind pictures and nightmares. This can lead to insomnia, feelings of isolation, loss of concentration and guilt. Victims need support and *counselling* to help them come to terms with these incidents. (See *victim support*.)

posture is the position in which the *muscles* of the body support the *skeleton* when standing, sitting, walking or working. In every muscle there are fibres which are continually contracted to create muscle tension, or muscle tone. Muscle tone is responsible for keeping the muscles ready for immediate contraction and keeping the body in an upright position without conscious thought. Upright posture is maintained by the contraction of both the flexor and extensor muscles holding *bones* and *joints* in position. When the body is held upright with the minimum of muscular effort, the distribution of body weight on the hips and leg bones keeps the body balanced. This is regarded as good posture. Posture can be affected by weight, a poor working environment, inadequate seating or shoes and clothes which do not fit properly. Posture is maintained through *exercise*, well balanced *diet* and a healthy *lifestyle*.

practice nurses are qualified *nurses* who are based at a *GP*'s surgery. Their role includes supporting:

- *elderly* people with *chronic* health problems such as leg ulcers
- patients requiring holiday vaccination programmes
- *health promotion*, e.g. asthma clinics
- *routine* health checks and *immunisations*
- well man and well woman clinics.

pre-coding is a method used to analyse answers provided in a *questionnaire*.

pre-conceptional education is advice to a woman who is preparing to conceive. This involves ensuring that the woman knows about:

- eating a *balanced* and healthy *diet*
- taking a folic acid supplement
- giving up *smoking* cigarettes and not drinking *alcohol*
- not taking any *drugs* or *medicines* which could harm a developing *embryo*.

pregnancy: the period of time, normally 40 weeks, extending from *conception* and the date of the last menstrual period to a baby's *birth*.

(For further information contact the British Pregnancy Advisory Service, Ausy Manor, Wootton Wawen, Solihull, West Midlands B95 6BX.)

prejudice: preconceived ideas about a person based on attitudes and *beliefs* which lead to discriminatory behaviour and practice. (See *attitudes, discrimination.*)

pre-menstrual syndrome: a number of signs and symptoms which may affect a woman about 7–10 days before a period. These include:

- feeling very irritable and tense
- feeling nervous and anxious
- feeling bloated, especially around the abdomen
- headaches
- increased tiredness and lethargy.

Treatment may involve taking oil of evening primrose and vitamin supplements.

pre-natal development is growth of the unborn baby which takes place in the mother's *womb*. The three stages of prenatal development are as follows:

Stage	Pre-natal development
1 Germinal	Following fertilisation, there is rapid cell division
2 Embryonic	The major body systems and organs begin to develop and take shape
3 Foetal	The bone cells appear with rapid growth and changes in body form.

pressure groups are groups who 'lobby' parliament or local government on different issues or areas of concern in society. They are set up to:

- highlight the *needs* of individuals and groups in society
- to investigate ways in which legislation can be introduced to support those whom they represent
- to explore ways of improving services.

Example of pressure groups are *Help the Aged, Child Poverty Action Group.*

pressure points are points in the body where an *artery* crosses a *bone*. In cases of severe bleeding from a limb, indirect pressure can be applied to a pressure point above a bleeding artery. For example, in severe bleeding from a wound in the lower arm, indirect pressure can be applied to the brachial pressure point. (St John Ambulance 1997) (See *pulse* and Figure overleaf.)

preventative care: strategies which are in place to prevent the need for future medical care, e.g. *immunisation.*

Primary Care Act 1997 (National Health Service): an Act of Parliament reviewing the ways in which *primary care* is delivered. The Act made recommendations related to:

- personal medical and dental services
- pharmaceutical and ophthalmic services
- *NHS* contracts
- medical practices.

(HMSO 1997)[51]

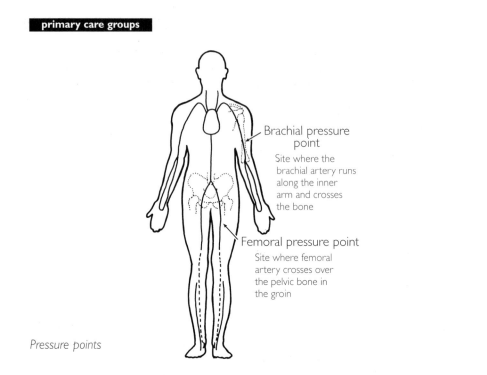

Brachial pressure
point
Site where the
brachial artery runs
along the inner
arm and crosses
the bone

Femoral pressure point
Site where femoral
artery crosses over
the pelvic bone in
the groin

Pressure points

primary care groups are groups of professional carers such as *GPs* and *nurses* working together in a locality. These were set up under *NHS* reforms in 1997. The functions of primary care groups are:

- to contribute to the *health authority's health improvement programmes* on health and healthcare, helping to ensure that they reflect the needs of the local community and the experience of patients
- to promote the health of the local population
- to commission health services in their area from the relevant *NHS trusts* within the framework of the health improvement programmes
- to monitor performance against the *service agreements* they have with the NHS trusts
- to develop primary care by means of joint working across practices, skills sharing and deployment of resources
- to integrate primary and community health services in working more closely with social services on both planning and delivery (attention focussed on child health or rehabilitation where responsibilities are split within the health service and where liaison with *local authorities* is often poor).

(HMSO 1997)[61]

primary health care team: the health professionals who care for individuals in the community. They usually include *GPs, health visitors,* community *nurses, midwives, dentists, pharmacists, optometrists* and *ophthalmic* medical practitioners.

privacy: one of the principal needs of a *patient* or *client* who is being looked after by health or social care workers. Clients may occasionally need to be alone and to have some time to sort out their affairs. Some clients wish to retain some *information* which is private to them. Patients and clients often need privacy when they are being toiletted. If it is impossible for the client to be left alone, then carers should make sure that the client is covered and that the toilet door is closed. Carers should be sensitive to the fact that privacy is a way in which clients can retain some of their own personal *identity*.

private sector: consists of organisations set up to provide health, education and social care services 'at a price'. They are income generating and profit making services and can include:

- public and independent *schools*
- health insurance companies
- some *hospitals*
- childcare providers
- private care homes and hostels
- *complementary and alternative medicine*
- some *screening* services.

(See *independent sector.*)

Probation Service: an agency in the *criminal justice system*. Established in 1907, it has a supervisory role representing the authority of the court and at the same time offering individual or group work programmes to help offenders to redirect their lives. *Probation officers* provide *information* to the court by means of pre-sentence reports, supervise offenders on court orders in the community, and provide care for offenders in custody and supervise those on release. The Probation Service has an important role to play in preparing parole reports on those prisoners who have served over four years of imprisonment and in subsequently supervising their period on parole license. The Probation Service also works with children and families in the family courts. Its main tasks are to:

- protect the public from risk of harm
- prevent the individual from reoffending
- assist with the successful reintegration of the offender into the community.

proteins: important substances required by the body to support almost all its functions. Proteins contain the elements *carbon, hydrogen, oxygen*, nitrogen, phosphorous, and sulphur. The units from which protein molecules are built are called amino acids. There are 21 different *amino acids* present in the human body. The amino acids are linked together by peptide bonds to form long chain molecules. The shape of the chain and the sequence in which the amino acids are linked together determines the function of the protein. Protein is an essential part of a healthy diet and is used to promote growth and to replace and repair body cells and tissues. The main source of protein is found in meat, dairy produce, fish, nuts and in smaller quantities, vegetables (particularly some cereals and beans).

providers deliver health and social care services for a fee. They form part of the *internal market*. Following recent reforms in the NHS announced in December 1997, the internal market is being replaced by *integrated care*.

psychiatric service: the branch of the health service which specialises in the detection, diagnosis and *treatment* of *mental disorders*.

psychiatrist: a qualified *doctor* who has chosen to specialise in the area of *mental health*. Psychiatrists work with people suffering from *mental illness* and those with *learning disabilities*. They often work in a team of other professionals including *psychologists* and *occupational therapists*.

psychologist: a professional trained to observe and interpret both normal and abnormal human behaviour. A psychologist has specialist training following the completion of a psychology degree. They can work as:

- clinical psychologists – dealing with *patients* in the treatment of *mental health disorders*
- *educational psychologists* – supporting the emotional needs and problems of children and young people up to the age of 19 years
- occupational psychologists – advising organisations on their different job training needs
- criminological and legal psychologists – in prisons, special *hospitals*, youth custody centres and secure units.

puberty: changes which occur in the body during the teenage years. Young people develop secondary sexual characteristics due to the release of certain *hormones* into the blood stream. (See *adolescence*.)

Secondary sexual characteristics which develop in males and females during puberty

Males	Females
Growth spurt	Growth spurt
Hair growth on chest, in the axilla and on the pubic areas	Hair growth in the axilla and on the pubic areas
Shoulders broaden and hips narrow	Development of breasts
	Hips broaden and body curves occur
Enlargement of penis, scrotum and testes	Menstruation or period commences
Can perform an erection of the penis and ejaculation of sperm	

public health: the maintenance of *health* in society. This involves a number of regulations relating to social, political, economic and environmental hazards. Public health is monitored by *environmental health officers* and the *Health and Safety Executive*. Different legislation supports its requirements and procedures. Each *health authority* has a public health department responsible for monitoring the well-being of the local population. They are also responsible for making decisions with regard to the treatment and prevention of infectious diseases.

pulse: rhythm produced by the regular pumping of *blood* by the *heart*. The pulse can be taken by placing a finger on the spots where an artery crosses the bone (see *pressure points*), for instance in the wrist, the groin and the neck. The normal pulse rate for an adult is approximately 70–80 beats per minute. It is faster in a baby or child, usually between 100–120 beats per minute. The pulse is usually recorded at the wrist (the radial pulse) or at the neck (the carotid pulse) when an emergency arises.

purchasers are organisations with the responsibility to buy health and social care services. They form part of the *internal market*. Following *NHS* reforms 1997 the internal market is being replaced by *integrated care*.

Q

Qualifications and Curriculum Authority (QCA): a government organisation set up in October 1997. It merged with the School Curriculum Assessment Authority (SCAA) and the National Council for Vocational Qualifications (NCVQ) to oversee the nation's level of attainment in Education and Training. QCA works with the Department of Education and Employment to ensure that the curriculum and qualifications available to children and adults are of a high standard and that they contribute effectively to the nation's education training programme.

By its review of curriculum QCA defines the structure and content of teaching and learning to enable all pupils to develop and demonstrate their knowledge, skills and understanding

Through the development and management of the assessment system QCA enables schools to demonstrate their contribution to national and local targets

As the regulatory body for public examinations and publicly funded qualifications QCA takes the lead in designing and developing a national framework of qualifications

One of a number of bodies committed to enhancing quality in education, QCA aims to help raise national standards of achievement.

qualitative data: information which cannot be recorded in numerical form. The *data* collected relates to the *views, attitudes* and *values* of the respondent. Qualitative data is usually collected through *interviews*. It can also be gathered in other ways, e.g. from secondary sources of *information.*

quality assurance: a framework of standards set up to maintain a professional service in health and social care services. Examples are written into the *Patient's Charter* and *NHS performance.*

quality of life: the daily way of living which is created by the *client, patient* and *service users* and their carers. It relates to the physical, psychological, social and spiritual *well-being* of the individual. *Carers* have a vital role to play in ensuring the quality of life for their clients in terms of physical care, emotional support, social contact and the provision of interesting and stimulating activities to promote *cognitive development.*

quantitative data: *information* which can be collated in numerical form. The *data* is recorded in the form of graphs and *charts.*

quarantine is the separation from others of people who have an *infectious disease.* Patients are isolated for a few days longer than the incubation period of the disease. (See *methicillin-resistant Staphylococcus aureus.*)

questioning: a procedure which involves asking people questions on a specific topic or subject. Its aim is to ensure that the questions asked are suitable to obtain objective answers and to provide the researcher or carer with the required *information.* There are different types of questions which can be asked. They include:

- opinion or attitude questions – those which ask about the respondent's beliefs, values and attitudes

- closed questions – those which have a single or a fixed set of answers
- open questions – those which, when asked, enable the respondents to answer in their own words, the questions reflect views, opinions and can be a means whereby qualitative research is collected
- probes – a form of questioning designed to extract more detailed information from the respondent; they can be used to deal with response problems and can be used to clarify an answer
- prompts – a statement which aids questioning techniques; the researcher may repeat questions in order to reinforce the respondent's understanding of what is required in the answer.

Questioning is used in many different aspects of *caring*, e.g. as part of the *care planning* process.

questionnaire: a list of questions which is used to collect *data*. Questions in a questionnaire should:

- be structured in such a way that the researcher gains the *information* required
- be ordered so that they reflect the breadth of the research
- be short and to the point
- have coded responses in place (see *semantic differential scale*)
- be reviewed to ensure that there is limited or no *bias* in the wording
- not be embarrassing or intrusive.

The questions used can be open or closed. Questionnaires can take a number of forms:

- Self-completion in a given situation. The questionnaire is completed and returned immediately.
- Postal questionnaires. The returns on these are often slow, making it an inefficient way of achieving results.
- Part of a simplified interview technique where the researcher ticks off answers for the respondent.

Questionnaires are a means whereby large numbers of individuals can be given an opportunity to participate in a research project.

Pros and Cons of questionnaires:

Pros

- cheaper than other methods
- generally quicker than other methods
- avoids the problems of interviewer bias
- with postal questionnaires people can take their time and consult documents to clarify answers.

Cons

- non-response (people may not respond to the questionnaire through lack of time or through disinterest); a response rate of only 3–4 per cent is common for most postal questionnaires
- questions may not be easily understood, lacking clear written instructions

- answers have to be accepted as final since no opportunity arises to probe beyond the response given
- postal questionnaires are not a useful method when spontaneous answers are required
- there is no opportunity for observation.

quota sampling: a *sampling method* where a specific selection of people in the population is chosen for use in a research project. This ensures that targeted groups of people are involved in the research representing appropriate categories by *age, race, class* and *gender.* Interviewers are given lists of people to interview from each category.

R

race is a broad term given to individuals and groups who are identified by their *culture* and ethnic grouping. This may include sharing similar biological features such as *skin* colour and hair type. These days, ethnic grouping is a term which is also used. The focus for *ethnic groups* tends to be on cultural similarity rather than on a set of physical features.

Race Relations Act 1976: an Act of Parliament which makes it illegal to discriminate against anyone on the grounds of their colour, race, nationality or ethnic origin. The Act is enforced in two ways:

- If a person is discriminated against on racial grounds they can go to a county court. If the alleged *discrimination* is in the field of employment then they can also go to an *industrial tribunal.*
- The Act also formed the *Commission for Racial Equality* which, in certain circumstances, can assist those who feel they have been discriminated against. The Commission can also carry out formal investigations into organisations where unlawful discrimination is suspected of being practised, in some circumstances without even receiving a complaint.

racism: *discrimination* and unfair treatment on the basis of *race.* It can take the form of:

- racist language where name calling can be upsetting and destructive to the self-esteem of the person concerned
- behaviour which involves ignoring another person; this can create embarrassment (see *discrimination*)
- rejection in terms of employment. For instance, individuals from certain racial groups may apply for advertised jobs and then be told that vacancies have been filled even though the potential employer continues to advertise.

radiation is a phenomenon involving the emission of particles or waves. There are different types of radiation:

- Alpha (α) particles – positively charged particles ejected from radioactive nuclei. They are relatively heavy and have a low penetrating power.
- Beta (β) particles – negatively charged particles (electrons) ejected from radioactive nuclei. They are very small and are usually ejected at greater speeds than alpha particles, and so have greater penetrating power.
- Gamma (γ) rays – electromagnetic waves. These rays have the highest penetrating power.

Radiation can damage the functioning of cells. It can damage the *bone marrow, ovaries,* testes, a developing *foetus, skin* and can cause hair loss or baldness. Damage depends on the amount and type of radiation received; it can also depend on the age of the subject involved. Children and a developing foetus are more at risk because of their rapid rate of *growth* and *development.* (See *radiotherapy, X-rays.*)

radiographers: specially trained, but not medically qualified professionals who work in *multidisciplinary teams* led by radiologists. They mainly work in *hospitals* as:

- diagnostic radiographers – carrying out a range of procedures such as using *X-rays, computerised axial tomography* (CAT) scans, *ultrasound and magnetic resonance imaging (MRI)*
- therapeutic radiographers – administering radiation treatment to *patients* as prescribed by the *doctor.*

Training as a radiographer usually involves three years full-time study at degree level.

radiologist: the trained *doctor* who works in the radiology department of a *hospital.*

radiology: methods of detecting or treating *disease* using radiation. It can involve the use of *X-rays* for diagnosis such as radiodiagnosis or diagnostic radiology and treatment (radiotherapy) but also incorporates many other methods of diagnostic imaging and treatment. The two separate branches of the speciality are now called:

- clinical radiology – involves patients undergoing X-rays including *CAT* scans and other diagnostic procedures such as *ultra-sound* and *magnetic resonance imaging* (MRI)
- clinical oncology – involves patients undergoing ionising radiation treatment mainly for *malignant* disease (i.e. X-rays, radium and other medical methods).

radiotherapy: a method of treating malignant *disease* such as *cancer* or *tumours* using radiation. *X-rays* are intensified and their beams are directed onto the area where *treatment* is required. In some diseases radium needles or rods are inserted into the tumour or the area of disease. Another treatment using radium involves the patient drinking radioactive liquid. The side effects of radiotherapy include nausea, sickness and hair loss.

ranking: a method applied in research with regard to *data* collection. Ranking is used in the recording of the results of *questionnaires* when the researcher wants to measure the degree of the respondents' *attitudes, views* and *beliefs.*

rape: sexual intercourse with another person who is an unwilling partner. This often involves the use of physical force. Help and support can be obtained from the Rape Crisis Centre. To find the nearest centre ring 0171-837-1600.

rating scale: a method used to record answers to closed questions when collecting results for research. The respondents indicate their opinion by choosing the appropriate scale point. (See *semantic differential scale.*)

rationale: the reason for any form of research or investigation. In health and social care there are many subjects which can be researched.

rationing of care is the way in which care is prioritised with regard to the allocation of health and social care services. This has caused a debate about which client group should be prioritised. In the past, the government has reduced resources in one area to put resources into another, for example, reviewing the growing health needs of *elderly people* and prioritising on *health promotion* for younger people. At the same time expensive drugs may be restricted. In some cases *GPs* supporting the prescription of interferon for a patient, to sustain remission from certain types of *cancer,* have had to obtain special permission from the *health authority.*

reception classes in infant and primary schools: the first stage of *statutory* education for young children. Although children are not obliged to start *school* until the term after their fifth birthday, many local education authorities admit children into the reception class in the year following their fourth birthday. However staffing, equipment and curriculum are usually more appropriate to children aged five or over. Policies vary between authorities; it has become commonplace for children to be admitted as 'rising fives' in the term they become five, but the trend is now towards a once-yearly admission, thus bringing in younger four-year-olds.

recommended dietary allowance (RDA): the suggested average daily intake of a nutrient for healthy people in a population. (See *Committee on Medical Aspects of Food Policy*.)

records are the way in which *information* is maintained about individual patients, *clients* and *service users*. Any records which are kept may take the form of:

- hand written notes – reports stored in a filing system
- computerised records – letters and reports written and stored on a hard or floppy disc.

Whatever form of recording is used, access to information and confidentiality is protected by legislation. (See *Access to Personal Files Act*.) In addition to this, the right of access to these files is also protected. (See *Access to Medical Records Act*.) Records should be therefore maintained in a secure place; they are legal documents and can be used in court.

recovery position is the position in which a person is placed when they are unconscious. This position prevents the tongue from blocking the throat and, because the head is slightly lower than the rest of the body, it allows liquid to drain away from the mouth and reduces the risk of the casualty inhaling the stomach contents. The head, neck and back are kept aligned, while the bent limbs keep the body propped in a comfortable and secure position. (St John Ambulance 1997) Placing the unconscious person in the recovery position is usually carried out by a trained First Aider. For health and social care students, learning about first aid is an important health and safety requirement which will enhance their care practice.

red blood cells (erythrocytes) are cells produced in the red *bone marrow* in the long *bones* and the ribs, vertebrae and the skull. The red pigment in the cells is called *haemoglobin*. Red cells remain functional for approximately 120 days. When they die they are broken down in the *spleen*. They are biconcave in shape and carry *oxygen* and some *carbon dioxide* in the haemoglobin. The average person has a million red cells per cubic millimetre of blood.

referral to health care services: the means whereby a person has an appointment arranged for medical treatment or therapy. This can include:

- Professional referral. Every person should be registered with a *GP*. When there is a health need which requires hospital treatment, the GP refers the patient to a hospital consultant or specialist, e.g. a child with persistent earache and *ear* discharge will be passed on to a specialist for examination.
- Self-referral – the person refers him/herself, for example by making an appointment with the *dentist*.

- Compulsory referral – when a person's life is in danger, or they are a danger to others but refuse to accept treatment, they can be detained under legislation (*The Mental Health Act 1983*).
- Referral by others – the person is referred to the service by another person, e.g. a neighbour may be concerned about the way a child is being treated at home. If the neighbour contacts social services to report this they have then referred the child to social services.
- Emergency referral – referral following an *accident*. If the patient is taken to *hospital* in an ambulance, the hospital staff will decide when the patient reaches hospital, whether or not to admit the patient. Being taken to hospital in the ambulance is a way of referring the patient to the hospital service.

reflex action is a simple act of behaviour in which a stimulus provokes a response. The response is usually specific and short-lived.

reflex actions of the newborn: a number of automatic movements which are present in the first weeks of a baby's life. These movements include:

- Sucking – when anything is placed in the baby's *mouth* it will immediately start sucking and swallowing.
- Grasp or palmar and plantar reflex – when an object is placed on the palm of the baby's hand its fingers will grip it firmly. Similarly, if an object is placed on the sole of the foot, the toes will curl around it.
- Moro or startle reflex – the way in which a baby will jerk in response to a sudden noise.
- Stepping reflex – when the baby is held upright on a flat surface, it will make stepping movements with its feet.
- Rooting reflex – when the side of the baby's cheek is stroked, it moves its head towards the movement as if looking for a nipple.

(See *newborn baby* and Figure on next page.)

In addition, a newborn baby will communicate by crying, waving its arms and legs and turning its head from side to side.

After about three months these reflexes disappear and are replaced by more conscious and controlled movements. As a baby grows and develops many different skills and responses have to be learned.

reflexes are the involuntary *motor neurone* responses to a stimulus, e.g. the act of sneezing in response to pollen or dust. (See Figure on next page.)

reflexology: an alternative form of treatment involving foot *massage* which can have a profound effect on the entire person. According to the principles of reflexology, the feet are a map of the body and dysfunction in any area of the body can be reflected there.

regional health authorities: see *health authorities*.

Registrar General's classification of occupations: a method of social classification which stratifies the population according to their paid employment. Occupational groups are used as the basis for deciding class membership. There are five class groups in the scale (see *social class*).

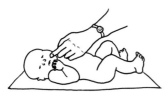

Sucking reflex

Stepping/
walking
reflex

Grasp (palmar and plantar) reflex

Moro/startle reflex

Rooting reflex

The reflex actions of the newborn

Stages of how a reflex works

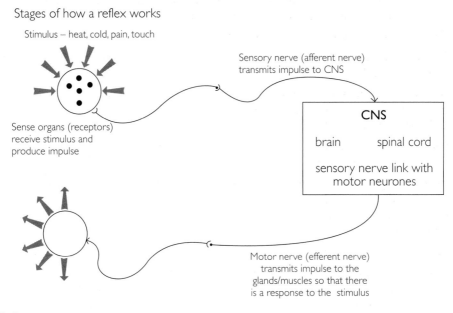

Stimulus – heat, cold, pain, touch

Sensory nerve (afferent nerve)
transmits impulse to CNS

Sense organs (receptors)
receive stimulus and
produce impulse

CNS

brain   spinal cord

sensory nerve link with
motor neurones

Motor nerve (efferent nerve)
transmits impulse to the
glands/muscles so that there
is a response to the stimulus

Reflex

Registrar general's index

Social class	Title	Occupation examples
Class 1	Professional	Doctor, solicitor, university lecturer, accountant
Class 2	Managerial/ technician	Teacher, farmer, nurse, office manager
Class 3A	Skilled non-manual worker	Cashier, police officer, sales representatives, administration clerk
Class 3B	Skilled manual worker	Cook, butcher, electrician, bricklayer
Class 4	Semi-skilled manual	Traffic warden, post office worker, bus conductor
Class 5	Unskilled manual	Porter, window cleaner, labourer

Regulations For Reporting of Injuries, Diseases and Dangerous Occurrences (RIDDOR) 1985 are regulations concerned with recording and reporting *accidents* and ill-health at work. When more than ten employees are based in the place of work, there must be an *accident book* to record:

- accidents
- sickness which may have been caused by work
- dangerous occurrences and 'near misses'.

Employers must report to the *Health and Safety Executive* or to the *environmental health* department of the *local authority* whenever the following events occur:

- fatal accidents
- a major injury or condition requiring medical treatment
- dangerous occurrences
- accidents causing incapacity for more than three days
- some work-related *diseases*
- gas incidents.

Many serious accidents and dangerous occurrences must be reported immediately, and a written report provided within seven days.

There are special forms which must be completed when diseases occur. There are 28 categories of reportable diseases including *poisoning, skin* and *lung* diseases.

Trade union safety representatives must have access to all information relating to all such problems in the workplace. The Employment Medical Advisory Service (EMAS), which is part of the Health and Safety Executive, gives *advice* and *information* on the reporting of diseases. In addition to these procedures, legislation exists designed to record and control diseases which are not necessarily linked to the place of work. Diagnosed cases of HIV and *AIDS* are reported in anonymous returns to the Centre of Communicable Diseases which is attached to the *Department of Health*. This centre is responsible for keeping statistics on HIV, *AIDS* and other diseases.

rehabilitation: the development of procedures and a *care plan* which support *clients* or *patients* after any *accident*, surgery or any other form of medical treatment. Examples include:

- *Physiotherapy* – if the person has suffered injury to a limb or part of the body in an accident, he/she will need physiotherapy and support in order to restore normal health and function. However, if full recovery is not possible, then they will be encouraged to organise their life to achieve as much independence as possible.
- *Occupational therapy* – when a person suffers from *depression*, for instance, they should be encouraged to pick up the threads of their life again. They may attend day centres, go shopping, learn to make decisions and, if possible, return to *work*.
- Counselling therapy – following a disaster such as a fire, a person may need *counselling* to help them come to terms with what has happened.

Rehabilitation is an important part of any person's recovery as it is essential that the person learns to adapt and function again as an active member in society. This involves them being entitled to their own *rights and choices*. (See *activities of daily living*.)

Rehabilitation of Offenders Act 1974: an Act of Parliament which allows, in certain circumstances, the conviction of offenders to become 'spent', that is the conviction need not be disclosed when applying for *jobs*. However, when applying for work in certain caring professions in *private, statutory* or *voluntary* agencies, particularly those involving children, all convictions must be disclosed. (See *Sex Offenders Act 1997*.) The type of conviction which may become spent and the relevant time limits vary both in terms of the offence and the sentence given to the offender. The legislation seeks to remove 'previous offence *discrimination*'.

relationships: links and associations with others within the framework of society. These can include:

- Biological relationships – links with family, e.g. in family life they are important because they provide opportunities for individuals to learn about relating to others. It is where a child is loved and can learn to love in return. Family life should be a secure place for a child to develop physically, emotionally, socially, intellectually and culturally.
- Social relationships – links with friends and peers. The ability to build and maintain friendships is an important aspect of an individual's life. It provides opportunities to give and receive mutual support.
- Formal working relationships within education and employment. The relationship between a manager and employee, or between a child and teacher is not the same as that in a social or biological relationship. Learning and working together assists individuals to develop and mature.
- Sexual relationships – links involving a physical attraction for another person. Developing a close and intimate relationship should be a satisfying experience for those involved.
- *Caring relationships* – links supporting others either as a professional or *informal carer*.

Relationships are a major focus in the life of any individual. The ability to build positive relationships is closely linked to *self-esteem*. Every type has a code of *behaviour* attached. When this code is broken or violated, the relationship bonds are often broken and in some cases the damage is irreparable, for example, in some cases of child abuse. There are several organisations which offer support with regard to relationships.

RELATE is a confidential counselling service for people with relationship difficulties. (For further information contact RELATE, Herbert Gray College, Little Church Street, Rugby, Warwickshire CV21 3AP.)

relaxation techniques are used to reduce tension and stress in the body. There are a variety of methods such as:

- breathing *exercises*, creating even and controlled breathing which relaxes and calms the body
- forms of *muscle* relaxation exercises, such as tightening the muscles and then gently letting each muscle relax and extend
- lying in a candle lit room on a comfortable bed listening to quiet music
- using different lights and imagery to create a sense of peace and relaxation
- meditation
- yoga and specialised exercise programmes which are learned and practised
- different leisure pursuits
- a *massage* with soothing oils.

religion is regarded as a system of beliefs. Different religions have varying views on acts and displays of worship. Acknowledging an individual's personal beliefs and religious views is a key requirement in caring for people. (See *care value base*.)

remedial massage: an alternative form of *treatment* which can remedy specific acute and chronic conditions such as frozen shoulder, neck pain and migraine headaches. (See *massage*.)

reminiscence: sessions set up for *elderly people* which include discussion and information sharing. This usually involves sharing memorabilia from the past. In order to stimulate memory and discussion the group leader may produce a reminiscence box containing a number of items such as old pictures, coins and artefacts.

research is a systematic investigation of a subject which involves gathering *data*, analysing results, drawing conclusions, writing reports and making recommendations. The purpose of research is to:

- review existing knowledge
- describe a situation or problem
- give an explanation of a situation
- gain a deeper understanding of a subject.

In research there are various methods of enquiry. These are investigative procedures relating to a variety of disciplines within the natural, behavioural and social sciences.

The stages in the research process include:

- define the problem – selection of topic
- review the literature – familiarisation with existing research
- formulate a hypothesis – what do you intend to test?
- select a research method
- carry out research
- interpret the results
- report the research findings – conclusion with recommendations.

research methods: methods used to conduct research include:

- experiments
- *questionnaires*
- *interviews*
- *observations.*

residential home: provides accommodation and personal care in a home for a range of client groups. There are usually no professional medical staff employed in the home but a *GP* or *doctor* is on call should the need arise. These homes are registered by the *local authority*. The care given in these homes is called residential care. (See *Home Life 1984.*)

resourcing of services: the methods used to ensure that adequate financial and human resources are available to the different health and social care services.

respect is a caring quality in which a person is given and is seen to be given their rights. It includes:

- ensuring that the *client* has the *privacy* and space they need
- *listening* to the client, their requests, their conversation
- allowing the client the right to their personal beliefs
- retaining a client's right to *confidentiality.*

respiratory system: the system responsible for *breathing*. Respiration consists of two processes, external respiration and internal respiration.

External respiration (*gaseous exchange*) involves:

- Taking air into the *lungs*. The *oxygen* from the *air passes* into the *blood* capillaries lining the lungs.
- Expelling *carbon dioxide* from the body. The carbon dioxide from the cells passes out of the blood capillaries lining the lungs and is breathed out.

Internal respiration involves:

- The release of energy through the breakdown of food. Oxygen is used in this process and carbon dioxide released.

The component parts of the human respiratory system are:

- Larynx. The 'voice box' at the top of the trachea. It contains the vocal cords – two pieces of *tissue* folding inwards from the trachea lining and attached to plates of *cartilage*. The opening between the cords is called the glottis. During speech, *muscles* pull the cartilage plates (and the cords) together, and air passing out through the cords makes them vibrate, producing sounds.
- Trachea or windpipe. The main tube through which air passes on its way to and from the lungs.
- Bronchi (singular bronchus). The main tubes into which the trachea divides. The first two branches are the right and left primary bronchi. Each carries air into a lung, alongside a pulmonary artery bringing blood in. They then branch into secondary bronchi, tertiary bronchi and bronchioles, all accompanied by blood vessels, both branching from the pulmonary artery and merging to form pulmonary veins.

- Lungs. The two main breathing organs, inside which gases are exchanged. The lungs contain many tubes (bronchi and bronchioles) and air sacs (*alveoli*).
- Bronchioles. The millions of tiny tubes in the lungs, all accompanied by blood vessels. They branch off tertiary bronchi and have smaller branches called terminal bronchioles, each one ending in a cluster of alveoli.
- Alveoli (singular alveolus). Millions of tiny sacs attached to terminal bronchioles. They are surrounded by *capillaries* (tiny blood vessels) whose blood is rich in carbon dioxide. The blood passes out through the capillary walls and in through the alveoli. The oxygen breathed into the alveoli passes into the capillaries, which then begin to merge together (eventually forming pulmonary veins). (See *mechanisms of breathing*.)
- Pleura or pleural membrane. A layer of tissue surrounding each lung and lining the chest cavity (thorax). Between the two layers of pleura there is a space (pleural cavity) which contains fluid. The pleura and fluid-filled cavity make up a cushioning pleural sac.
- *Diaphragm.* A sheet of muscular tissue which separates the chest from the lower body, or *abdomen*. At rest, it lies in an arched position, forced up by the abdomen wall below it.

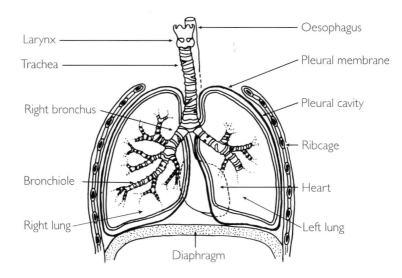

Lungs

respite care: provides a service which offers regular breaks to *carers*. This is a valuable means of support for carers who are looking after relatives or friends on a long-term basis. Since the implementation of the *Carers (Recognition and Services) Act 1995* the value of respite care has been highlighted. It can take the form of:

- the *client* being cared for in a residential setting for one or two weeks so that the carer can take a holiday
- a professional or volunteer carer taking over for short periods so that the carer has some free time
- *day centre* care.

(See *caring for the carers, young carers*.)

respondent: the individual who participates in a project by answering questions in an interview or by filling in a questionnaire.

rest home: residential care which is available usually for elderly people who do not require nursing care. The home is registered with the Local Authority and the care is given by care assistants who are not necessarily qualified.

resuscitation: see *ABC of resuscitation*.

rhesus factor in blood describes a method of *blood grouping*. The rhesus factor is named after the rhesus monkey in which it was originally discovered. Approximately 85 per cent of humans have rhesus factor in their blood. Such individuals are termed rhesus positive. The remaining 15 per cent of humans do not have this factor and are rhesus negative. Rhesus negative patients cannot receive rhesus positive blood. Rhesus factor is inherited.

rhesus factor and childbirth: the rhesus factor can cause problems during *pregnancy* for about one in every 300 mothers. This can happen when the mother is rhesus negative and the father is rhesus positive. The baby may inherit the gene for rhesus positive blood from the father. This can place the mother at risk if some of the baby's blood seeps into hers. The mother and baby have to be carefully monitored. The danger period is usually at the birth of a second rhesus positive child, when antibodies produced by the mother to the rhesus positive blood of the first child can leak into the circulation of the second child causing damage.

rights and choices: see *care value base*.

risk: the way in which a *client* or *carer* can be exposed to harm from others or from their *care environment*.

risk assessment: the procedure which examines a *care* setting for potential *risks* and hazards to *service users* and their *carers*. Following this the areas of concern are recorded and addressed.

risk management involves identifying health and safety hazards in order to implement strategies to eliminate and prevent such risks. Risk management involves:

- identifying a risk
- assessing the extent of the risk
- adopting methods and strategies to control the risk
- providing finances to address any change or adaptation to equipment and property.

role: the behaviour adopted by individuals when they are interacting in social situations. People learn their roles through the *socialisation* process and may play many different roles throughout their lives. Examples include *nurse*, father, *police* officer.

role model: an individual whose behaviour may be copied or aspired to. Young individuals in particular model their *behaviour* on the adults around them. When working with children, adults should develop their *communication* and interpersonal skills in such a way as to show their concern and respect for others, irrespective of different racial or ethical background. Also they should demonstrate sensitivity to different needs, and should develop their listening skills, as a way of helping young children to learn to listen. A positive, encouraging, interested and stimulating adult role model can be a key person in a child's personal development.

role-play: a learning method used by students in *education* or training. It involves the student taking a part and acting it out in a given situation. Other students observe the role play and give feedback in the session. Role-play is also used by children in different ways as they develop their imagination.

routines are periods of time or methods of working which ensure that the overall care of *clients, patients* or *service users* is fully catered for. They will involve:

- times for getting up and going to bed
- meal times including *food* preparation, service and *feeding*
- personal hygiene, changing clothes, *bathing*, washing, toileting times
- recreation and leisure activities.

Routines are part of *care* practice because they can create a sense of security. Also if several workers are involved in caring for a large number of clients, each carer will have roles and responsibilities to maintain a routine.

Royal Association for Disability and Rehabilitation (RADAR): a national voluntary organisation which is run by, and works with, the physically disabled. It acts as a *pressure group* to improve the environment for disabled people, campaigning for their rights and needs, and challenging negative attitudes and stereotypes. RADAR is particularly involved with issues surrounding civil rights, social services, social security, employment, education, housing and *mobility*. (See *disability*.)

(For further information contact RADAR, 12 City Forum, 250 City Road, London EC1V 8AF.)

Royal College of Nursing: a professional organisation for *nurses*. It is run by nurses for nurses. The role of the college is to:

- contribute to the development of nursing practice and standards of care
- provide education and resources for nurses.

(For further information contact the Royal College of Nursing, 20 Cavendish Square, London W1M OAB.)

Royal Commission for Long-term Care: a government committee set up in 1998 to look at:

- establishing *values* with regard to the system of long-term care
- reviewing aspects of *residential care*
- reviewing hospital care and *rehabilitation*
- devising a fair system of paying for care.

Royal National Institute for the Blind: a voluntary organisation which provides national services for blind and partially sighted people. This includes people with sight problems such as elderly people with cataracts. The RNIB offers an information service in all matters relating to eye health and blindness.

(For further information contact the Royal National Institute for the Blind, 224 Great Portland Street, London W1N 6AA.)

Royal National Institute for the Deaf is concerned with the needs and problems of people of all ages suffering varying degrees of hearing loss.

(For further information contact the Royal National Institute for the Deaf, 105 Gower Street, London WC1E 6AH.)

Royal School for the Blind: see *SeeABILITY*.

Royal Society for the Prevention of Accidents (RoSPA): a professional *organisation* and registered *charity*. Its basic aim is helping to save lives and reducing the number of injuries from *accidents* of all kinds. Accidents have been identified as a *national health target* in the latest government health initiatives. RoSPA's accident prevention activities include safety on the road, at work, in the home, at leisure, on and in the water and safety education for the young. There is a growing volume of *legislation* in the UK designed to promote *safety*. The government makes grants towards specific areas of RoSPA's activities which include:

- Road safety – road accidents kill an average of 4000 people every year in Great Britain. Total road injuries total about 310,000 each year. RoSPA is tackling this problem in a number of ways. It campaigned actively for the compulsory wearing of seatbelts, and it was one of the Society's past presidents, Lord Nugent of Guildford, who successfully tabled the amendment on seatbelt legislation for inclusion in the Transport Bill.
- Home and leisure safety – home accidents are the hidden problem of the safety world. Every year, they kill about 4000 people and cause a further 2.9 million people to seek hospital treatment for injuries. Almost half of the injury victims are children. RoSPA is helping prevent home accidents by alerting people to danger spots in the home through publicity and education. It helps and advises all the local government bodies that promote home safety.
- Occupational safety and health – about 500 people die each year from accidents in and around the workplace. A further 1.6 million people have to attend hospital for treatment. RoSPA combats this tragic toll through education, training schemes and specialist conferences. Courses are held at RoSPA's HQ, at its training centre in Acocks Green, Birmingham, or on companies' own premises. Awards are made to firms which have achieved outstanding successes in industrial safety. Three specialist monthly journals are published on occupational safety and health topics.
- Safety education – basically all RoSPA's work is safety education. However, a special effort is made in schools through the production of a large quantity of material specifically designed to teach children from an early age how they can avoid accidents in all environments.

(For further information contact RoSPA, Cannon House, Priory Queensway, Birmingham B4 6BS.)

safety: *safety procedures* are taken into account to protect *clients, patients* and *service users* from harm. It is one of the most important issues for carers working in health and social care. Clients need to feel physically safe and secure in their care settings. Safety procedures are strategies for providing and maintaining a safe environment. If procedures are to be effective, all workers, managers and clients should be aware of them and understand how they work. They should be written down so that there is no misunderstanding about what is expected. *Carers,* other workers and clients need to be informed when they are changed. There is a variety of working procedures which can be developed in the range of *care settings.* These are closely related to the *health and safety* of both the clients and the workers involved. Examples of such procedures include:

- Checking the care setting and carrying out a *risk* assessment. Once a setting is deemed safe, then procedures are put in place to ensure regular monitoring and maintenance with regard to health and safety.
- Checking that any equipment or *toys* which are being used have been manufactured and installed safely.
- Maintaining records with regard to staff, clients, equipment and the different resources used in the care setting.
- Supervising activities and staff–client ratios.
- Ensuring *fire drills*, evacuation procedures and *first aid* are regularly practised.
- Transporting clients in vehicles, travel arrangements and outings.
- Ensuring that all procedures comply with health and safety regulations written into legislation such as the *Health and Safety at Work Act, Children Act.*

safety marks: see *marks of safety.*

salivary glands are responsible for secreting saliva into the *mouth.* Saliva prepares food for *digestion.* Whenever *food* is smelled or tasted then saliva is poured into the mouth. It is mixed with the food and aids digestion. It contains about 95 per cent *water.* It also contains lubricating mucus and the enzyme salivary amylase, which changes cooked starch into maltose (a disaccharide sugar).

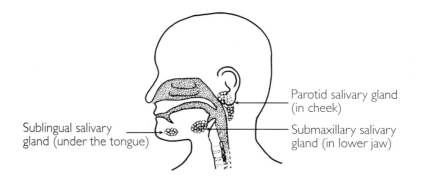

Parotid salivary gland (in cheek)

Sublingual salivary gland (under the tongue)

Submaxillary salivary gland (in lower jaw)

salmonella: a group of *bacteria* which causes certain types of *food poisoning.* Salmonella bacteria are found in raw meat and are destroyed by cooking. Salmonella infection can be caused by:

- Meat, especially poultry, not being thoroughly defrosted. When cooked the temperature inside the meat is not high enough to kill off bacteria and the meat (if eaten) may cause food poisoning. Bacterial toxins reach the intestines of the person eating the contaminated meat and a fever accompanied by vomiting and diarrhoea develops.
- Unwashed hands. Salmonella bacteria on the hands can be transferred to food by the person handling and preparing the food not having washed their hands thoroughly.
- Unhygienic food preparation, i.e. cooking surfaces which are not regularly cleaned allow bacteria to be transferred to cooked meat.

Careful attention to hygiene, food preparation and food storage, is an essential requirement to prevent salmonella infection. (See *Food Hygiene (General) Regulations 1970.*)

salts are ionic compounds containing at least one cation and one anion. The properties of salts are that they:

- are often soluble in *water.*
- have high melting and boiling points
- dissociate into ions in solution and so are electrolytes.

Sodium chloride (NaCl) is the best known salt. Salts have many industrial and domestic uses.

Samaritans: a voluntary organisation which offers a listening and befriending service by telephone. It provides support to those who are suicidal or in despair at any hour of the day or night. This service is available to any member of the general public who wishes to talk about their problems. (See *counselling.*) It is supported by specially trained *volunteers.*

(For further information contact Samaritans, 17 Uxbridge Road, Slough, Berkshire SL1 1SN.)

sample: a group of individuals who are assumed to be representative of the population from which they have been drawn. In research it is not always possible to study the whole population at once and, therefore, a sample is used.

sampling is a process which involves choosing a representative proportion of the population to be studied. It is a widely used procedure in many different types of research. The aim of sampling is to make the chosen group of individuals as representative as possible of the entire population but still manageable in terms of the numbers involved. The conclusions and recommendations drawn from such research can then be applied to the population as a whole. The results are then said to have been 'generalised'. (See *sampling frame, sampling methods.*)

sampling frame: usually a list of people (survey population) from which the sample is drawn. These lists can be drawn from club membership or *school* rolls for example.

sampling methods are ways in which representative samples are selected. There are a variety of methods, such as:

- Random sample – each member of the population being studied stands an equal chance of being selected, e.g. The National Lottery.
- Stratified sample – the composition of the sample reflects the composition of the population, e.g. 48 per cent males and 52 per cent females in the population determines that the sample should itself contain a selection of 48 per cent males and 52 per cent females.
- Quota sample – the researcher chooses a selection of people roughly in proportion to their occurrence in the population, e.g. quota of different age groups.
- Opportunity sample – selecting whoever is available at the time of research.

scabies: an infectious skin disease caused by a parasitic mite. It feeds on skin and burrows in to lay eggs. Mites can transfer from one person to another. Active scabies causes intense scratching. The burrows can be seen clearly between the fingers, on the wrists and can affect the armpit and the groin. Scratching can cause pain, redness and infection. The *treatment* for scabies involves washing all bedding and clothing and applying an anti-parasitic preparation, such as benzyl benzoate, to the skin. To ensure effective elimination of the parasite, the whole family should be treated.

scapegoating: negative views and attitudes which are directed at an individual or a minority group. It is a basis for discrimination with the groups or individuals targeted being blamed for the problems in society, e.g. lone parents are accused of being responsible for some of the discipline problems in society today.

scarlet fever: see *infectious diseases.*

scattergrams: a graphical representation of the correlation between two sets of measurements. These measurements are called variables and the relationship between two variables can be plotted graphically. The more the points on the scattergram are clustered around some definite pattern, the stronger the correlation. In a linear correlation, the points fit along a line. A direction of bottom left to top right represents a positive correlation, while a direction from top left to bottom right indicates a negative correlation.

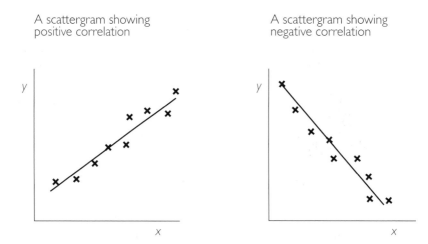

A scattergram showing positive correlation

A scattergram showing negative correlation

schizophrenia a form of severe mental illness. It affects one in a hundred people worldwide. The symptoms can be divided into two groups:

- 'positive symptoms' which include delusions, for instance, when a person believes that they are someone else and suffers hallucinations such as hearing voices and seeing, feeling, tasting or smelling things which are not there.
- 'negative symptoms' such as withdrawal, difficulties in communicating and in expressing emotions.

(For further information contact National Schizophrenia Fellowship, 28 Castle Street, Kingston Upon Thames, Surrey KT1 ISS and the Schizophrenia Association of Great Britain, Bryn Hyfryd, The Crescent, Bangor, Gwynedd LL57 2AG.)

schools: it is a statutory requirement in Britain for all children between the ages of 5–16 years to attend full time education. Children start in primary school in the year that they are 5 years old and change to secondary school at 11 years, or to middle school at 13 years. There are different types of school:

- private or independent – which cater for children up to the age of 16 years; these are fee paying and some are single sex, single faith (Catholic, Church of England or Muslim)
- infant – cater for children from 5–7 years
- junior – cater for children from 7–11 years
- middle – cater for children from 13–16 years
- comprehensive – cater for children of mixed ability between the ages of 11–16 years
- grammar – cater for children between the ages of 11–16 years; children have to pass an entrance exam in order to attend such schools.

SCOPE: a *charity* and voluntary organisation which provides a range of services for people with *cerebral palsy* and their families and *carers*, including *schools, residential care, information* and careers advice. They also offer *counselling*. The monthly newspaper 'Disability Now' provides information relevant to all forms of the disability. A network of local teams provides contact with SCOPE social workers and over 200 local affiliated groups.

(For further information contact SCOPE, 12 Park Crescent, London W1 4EQ.)

Scotland and its parliament: Scotland will have more control over its affairs through the establishment of the Scottish Parliament. Following the White Paper 'Scotland's Parliament', the Scottish Parliament and executive will have responsibilities for various areas such as:

- *health* including the *National Health Service*, public and mental health in Scotland
- *education* and training including pre-5, primary, secondary, further and higher education
- local government, social work and *housing*
- the law and home affairs, including most civil and criminal law and the criminal justice system.

Other aspects of the White Paper include economic development, the environment, sport and art, agriculture, fisheries and forestry. (HMSO 1998)[54]

screening programmes: procedures which are carried out on people in order to look for a specified disease. For example, a woman may attend a *GP's* surgery for a *cervical smear*, when a sample of *cells* is removed from the cervix and sent to a laboratory to be examined for pre-cancerous cells. For a screening programme to succeed the *disease* must exhibit specific characteristics. It must:

- have a high risk of occurrence in the population
- be treatable if detected
- be dangerous if undetected
- be reasonably easy and inexpensive to diagnose at an early stage.

(See also *breast examination, cervical smear.*)

seamless services are the way in which health and social care providers work together in order to meet the care requirements of *clients* or *service users*. (See *continuum of care.*)

Secretary of State for Health: the government minister who is responsible for the provision of health and social care services. The Secretaries of State for Northern Ireland, Scotland and Wales are responsible for health in those areas of the UK.

seeABILITY: (formerly known as The Royal School for the Blind) a charity which supports individuals with *visual impairments* and assists with their education and learning. It is estimated that in Britain today there are over 30,000 people who are blind, visually impaired or have some other visual disability – only 1 per cent of these people are receiving adequate care.

(For further information contact seeABILITY, 56–66 Highlands Road, Leatherhead, Surrey KT22 8NR.)

self-advocacy is the process by which a *service user* speaks on their own behalf. This should be encouraged amongst *clients* and *service users*, particularly those who have *special needs.*

self-confidence: an individual's belief in his or her own ability to achieve something or to cope with a situation. Self-confidence may influence and be influenced by *self-esteem.*

self-disclosure: the way in which individuals reveal intimate *information* about their lives as they build relationships with others. As the client/carer relationship is built up, the *client* may reveal certain details about themselves. It is important for the *carer* to ascertain whether details given in this way are *confidential.*

self-efficacy is the way in which an individual believes in their own ability to carry out tasks and activities, or their belief in their own competence. This is closely linked to a person's thinking or *cognitive* ability, motivation and response to life's challenges.

self-esteem is the view that an individual has of themselves, their own worth and their own identity. Having a positive self-esteem means that an individual is able to identify their strengths and weaknesses and 'feels good about themselves'. Building a positive self-esteem in others is an important requirement in the caring process, and includes:

- effective *communication* skills
- giving praise and encouragement where necessary
- helping individuals to identify their strengths or what they can achieve.

Helping an individual build their self-esteem takes time and is often achieved by building a constructive relationship with the person or child concerned. (See *confidence building, listening skills* and *active listening.*)

self-fulfilling prophecy: when what a person predicts will happen does indeed come to pass. A person's thought processes are activated so that they begin to behave in the predicted way. The prophecy comes to pass because of behaviour which is unconsciously designed to bring it about. Self-fulfilling prophecy can often be built on negative *behaviour,* producing negative reactions which reinforce the behaviour.

self-help: the way in which individuals and groups are encouraged to deal with their feelings and to solve their own problems. This can be achieved through a range of activities such as:

- *counselling* on a one-to-one basis
- co-counselling which involves partnering with another person and sharing experiences
- joining a group, each of whom have been through or are going through a similar process or experience (see *bereavement, support agencies*)
- joining an organisation and working as a *volunteer.*

Self-help is closely related to *empowerment.*

self-perception is the way in which an individual observes their own *behaviour* and makes decisions as a result of that behaviour.

self-referral: a means whereby clients can refer themselves for treatment or therapy. (See *referral systems.*)

semantic differential scale is a rating technique. Such scales explore ways in which people's feelings and views can be measured. *Rating* can take the form of:

- Numerical rating – which may measure answers on a scale from 1–10. For example, 1 can indicate excellence and 10 can indicate low satisfaction or weakness.
- Written or verbal rating – which describes answers using words, such as 'excellent', 'good', 'adequate', 'poor' or 'very poor'.

Such scales are used as a means whereby a researcher can determine the results of *questionnaires* and interviews.

SENCO: *special needs* co-ordinator. (See *statementing.*)

sense organs: parts of the body which contain the sensory *cells.* These include the *eye, ear, skin, tongue* and nose. The cells in these organs are sensitive to stimuli, for instance:

- The sensitive cells of the eyes, i.e. the rods and cones, respond to the stimulus of light.
- The sensitive cells in the taste buds on the surface of the tongue respond to the stimulus of food or substances which enter the mouth. A taste bud is a small round structure on the surface of the tongue which contains a taste cell. When food enters the mouth it mixes with saliva and the presence of food stimulates the taste buds. There are four basic tastes – sweet, sour, salty and bitter. The related taste buds are situated on different areas of the tongue.

- The sensitive cells in the ears, in the organ of corti, respond to the stimulus of sound.
- The sensitive cells in the nerve endings of the skin respond to the stimuli of touch, heat, cold and pain.
- The sensitive cells in the nose respond to the stimulus of smell. The inner lining of the nose is kept moist due to the secretion of mucus. When air enters the nose, the olfactory cells send a message to the *brain* and any changes of smell are interpreted.

sensory disabilities or impairments: disorders or *dysfunctions* which affect the *sense organs* and the *nervous system*, particularly the way in which the body responds to stimuli. These affect sight, hearing, taste, touch and smell.

sensory nerves are responsible for carrying sensory impulses to the *central nervous system*. In the spinal cord the sensory *nerve* links to a motor nerve which transmits the impulse to various *muscles*.

separation is the state of a young child or person who has been taken from their parent or primary care giver. In the young child, this can affect the *bonding* process as the emotional bonds or *attachments* are interrupted. It can also lead to *maternal deprivation* when the child's emotional security and well-being are affected. When a young child is separated from their parents or primary care givers, they experience:

- distress, so that the child may persistently cry, scream and protest.
- despair, when the child begins to feel helpless, become listless, lose interest in their surroundings and fears that the person they love will never return.
- detachment, when the child is convinced that their parent or primary care giver will never return. They try to cope by detaching themselves from the memory of that parent/care giver. Relationships with others are difficult and the child's behaviour can be affected by regular mood swings.

Different researchers such as James and Joyce Robertson, and John *Bowlby*, have worked on theories of attachment and separation and have made recommendations, especially with regard to children in *hospital*. (See *Platt Report*.)

service agreements are written statements of roles and responsibilities between *health authorities, Primary Care Groups* and *NHS trusts* reflecting national standards and targets. (See *national health targets*.)

service requirements: the care requirements which are necessary from a health or social care service to meet the individual needs of a *client* or group of clients.

service specifications: details of the health or social care service which are provided for a *client, patient* or *service user*.

service users are the *clients* or *patients*, who use the health and social care services provided for them. The rights of the service users are published in the *Patient's Charter*.

Sex Discrimination Act 1975: an Act of Parliament which made recommendations with regard to *discrimination*. The Act makes it unlawful to discriminate on the basis of sex/*gender* or marital status in the areas of employment, trade union membership, education, the provision of goods and services and housing and in advertising. Sex *discrimination* can be unfair treatment of women or men, and of single or married people. In employment, the Act applies to recruitment, day-to-day work activities and to dismissal. As with the *Race Relations Act,* discrimination may be direct or indirect. There are several sections of the Act which allow different treatment of men and women under certain circumstances. These include:

- Special positive treatment of women because of *pregnancy* or childbirth.
- Where it is necessary to comply with earlier legislation. An example of both this and the previous provision is the case of a woman who was employed as a driver of a tanker carrying dangerous chemicals. It was discovered that the chemical was dangerous to pregnant women and in order to comply with the *Health and Safety at Work Act,* she was transferred to other driving duties. She complained, but the *industrial tribunal* found that her employer was not guilty of unlawful discrimination on grounds of gender.
- Height requirements for the *police* and prison services. The Metropolitan Police and other forces have now foregone this provision as it tends also to discriminate against ethnic groups where average height is less than for the population as a whole.
- Employment as a minister of *religion.* There was a heated debate in the Church of England in the early 1990s over the ordination of women priests. The Church of England has now agreed to the ordination of women.

(HMSO 1975)[55]. (See *Equal Opportunities Commission.*)

Sex Offenders Act 1997 is an Act of Parliament which requires convicted sex offenders to register with the *police.* It requires that:

- anyone convicted or cautioned for specific sex offences must notify the police of their name, their address and any subsequent changes to these.
- offenders who do not register within 14 days are committing a criminal offence and will face penalties of up to six months in prison and/or a £5000 fine.

The registration requirement is linked to the original sentence received by the offender and is subject to a minimum period of five years for non-custodial sentences and life for custodial sentences of 30 months or more. (HMSO 1997)[56]. (See *Rehabilitation of Offenders Act 1974, paedophiles.*)

sex role stereotyping: the way in which individuals are categorised according to their *gender.* For example, it might be suggested that car mechanics are always male and that cooking, cleaning and washing-up are always carried out by females, or that boys should play football and girls should play with their dolls. Sex role stereotyping is often learned in the home from parents who are their children's role models. Rigid and inflexible attitudes are formed and individuals are expected to play out these roles. These can be reinforced by books, magazines and television programmes. *Equal opportunities* policies are a means whereby these stereotypical roles can be challenged.

sexism is *discrimination* or unfair treatment of an individual on the basis of their gender group. It involves *attitudes, behaviour* and procedures in society which maintain the belief that one gender group is more important in society than the other. It also reinforces *stereotypical* roles and responsibilities of men and women in society. This can take the form of female applicants for jobs not gaining employment in male-dominated sectors. Men and women are still exposed to stereotyping in society as they are expected to behave in a particular way and fulfil certain social roles, although more liberal attitudes have developed in recent years.

sexual intercourse is the sexual contact between two individuals involving insertion of the penis into the *vagina*. This is how human beings reproduce.

sexual maturity: a stage in physical development that results in the ability to reproduce. This is due to different physical changes in the body resulting from the release of *hormones* in both the male and female. (See *adolescence*.)

sexual offences are those acts of sexual indecency which are committed by individuals on others. They include *rape* and sexual *abuse*.

sexually transmitted diseases are passed from one person to another as a result of sexual contact. There are many different such *diseases*.

- Gonorrhoea is caused by *bacteria* which live in the internal linings of the *vagina*. It can affect both males and females who suffer irritation and discharge from the vagina or penis. It may be associated with abdominal discomfort and pain on passing *urine*. Gonorrhoea is treated with a course of antibiotics.
- Genital warts are small lumps found on the male or female genitals, and are caused by a *virus*. The treatment is ointment or cream.
- Genital herpes is caused by a herpes virus. It is treated with ointment or cream.
- Pubic lice are those which live in pubic hair. They are treated with lotions.
- *Hepatitis* B is caused by a virus. It may be spread in other ways in addition to unprotected sex such as by using dirty needles to inject drugs. Treatment includes bed rest and nutritious *food*. There are *vaccinations* available for those at risk, e.g. health care workers.
- Syphilis
- HIV: see *AIDS*.

Treatment of sexually transmitted diseases is important because it can prevent the development of pelvic inflammatory disease which may lead to infertility.

shared use environment: a care setting where the site and premises are shared with other users, for example a church hall which is also used as a *playgroup* during the day, and community centres which provide activities for different *client* groups.

sheath (condom): see *contraception*.

sheltered housing: a type of accommodation for *clients*. It provides an alternative to *residential care* for the elderly and for disabled clients and includes:

- Independent accommodation which is usually grouped together on one site. The accommodation has an alarm which clients can ring if they need help or feel unwell.
- The employment of a resident warden who supports the clients and is available in emergencies. The client's alarm bell alerts the warden.
- The provision of a degree of *independence*. The elderly person still lives in their own home but opportunities for social contact are available.

Many sheltered housing sites have communal facilities such as a large lounge with a television where residents can hold meetings, parties, dances, courses and keep fit, or just pop in for a chat.

Sheridan, Mary: a *doctor* who worked with children and who wrote about child development. Her book 'From Birth to Five Years – Children's Development Progress' has been used as an aid to improve the clinical guidance and upbringing of children. It was Mary Sheridan who introduced the concept of stages in a child's development, which she divided into four categories:

- Posture and large movement – control of large *muscles* and how a child co-ordinates body movement.
- Vision and fine movement – eye movement and the use of fine muscle control such as *hand–eye co-ordination.*
- Hearing and speech – how a child understands sound and interprets it through speech/*language development*
- Social behaviour and *play* – ways in which a child learns social and self-help skills and builds relationships with others.

These categories help childcare professionals to understand the way in which children acquire various skills throughout the first five years of life.

shock: an adverse reaction to a situation, *accident* or disorder which causes a sudden drop in *blood pressure.* This drop in blood pressure could be due to bleeding, *heart attack,* severe *infection* in the body, reaction to *medicines* or even, bad news of an unexpected nature which causes a physical reaction. Whatever the reason, the *signs and symptoms* are the same and they include:

- a fast but weak *pulse*
- discolouration of the *skin,* resulting in a grey/blue pallor with bluish lips
- cold and clammy skin with sweating
- weakness and dizziness
- feeling sick
- fast and shallow breathing.

During shock a person may become unconscious. It is important to call the ambulance at once and not to leave the person alone. (See *ABC of resuscitation, recovery position.*

siblings are the brothers and sisters within a *family.* Sibling rivalry is often viewed as a feature of the relationship between brothers and sisters who compete for their parents' affection.

sickle-cell disorders are inherited *blood* conditions. These include sickle-cell disease and the carrier state, the sickle cell trait. In Britain the disorder is most common in those of African or Caribbean descent, but it may also occur in people from India, Pakistan, the Middle East or the Eastern Mediterranean. It is estimated that there are approximately 6000 adults and children with sickle-cell disease in Britain at present. Sickle cell disorder is caused by an inherited abnormal *haemoglobin* structure. Haemoglobin is the *protein* which gives the red cells their colour and carries oxygen around the body. With sickle-cell disorders the abnormally formed haemoglobin causes the usually round and pliable cells to become rigid and sickle shaped. This is called 'sickling'. Individuals may inherit this type of haemoglobin from both their parents.

There are a number of haemoglobin types usually known only by a letter of the alphabet. The most common types are called normal haemoglobin (HbA) and sickle haemoglobin (HbS). Signs and symptoms of sickle-cell disorder include painful swelling of the hands and feet, *infection* and anaemia. The illness may cause frequent episodes of pain in the *bones* and *joints,* abdomen and other parts of the body. These episodes of pain are called crises.

(For further information contact Sickle Cell Society, 54 Station Road, London NW10 4UA. Tel: 0181 961 7795/4006.)

sign language: a method of *communication* where the hands are used to convey a message. 'Talking' with the hands is an effective means whereby people with hearing impairments can communicate with others. Maketon is one sign language which is commonly used with and by children. (See *British sign language*.)

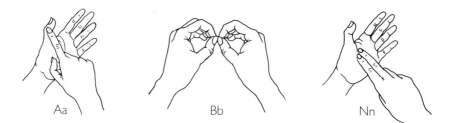

Aa   Bb   Nn

Examples of sign language

signs and symptoms are indications and features of a disease which are normally observed by a *doctor* and are used to help in the diagnosis of a disease. However, they are also those features which are noticed by the individual himself or by others such as *carers* and first aiders.

single unified budget: *funding* which covers *hospital* and community services. This is part of the *NHS* reforms in 1997. (See *NHS: The New NHS – Modern, Dependable*.)

skeletal (striated) muscle is also known as voluntary *muscle*. This type of muscle is attached to the *bone* at a fixed point by means of a *tendon*. Contraction of the muscle results in movement of the *bone*. When viewed under a microscope, the muscle appears striped (striated). These stripes contain bundles of muscle fibres called myofibrils. They run longitudinally and are made up of thick and thin filaments. The thick filaments contain the *protein* myosin. The protein actin can be found in the thin filaments. The filaments work together to produce muscle contractions.

skeleton: the skeleton is a frame of over 200 *bones* which supports and protects the body *organs* (the viscera) and provides a solid base on which the *muscles* can work. The bones include:

- Cranium or skull. A case protecting the *brain* and facial organs. It is made of cranial and facial bones. The upper jaw, for instance, consists of two fused bones called maxillae (sing. maxilla).
- Rib cage. A cage of bones forming the walls of the thorax or chest area. It is made up of 12 pairs of ribs, the thoracic vertebrae and the sternum. The ribs are joined to the sternum by bands of costal cartilage, but only the first

seven pairs join it directly. The last five pairs are false ribs. The top three of these join the sternum indirectly – their costal cartilage joins that of the seventh pair. The bottom two pairs are floating ribs, only attached to the thoracic vertebrae at the back.

- Vertebral column. Also called the spinal column, spine or backbone. It is a flexible chain of 33 *vertebrae* which protects the spinal nerves.

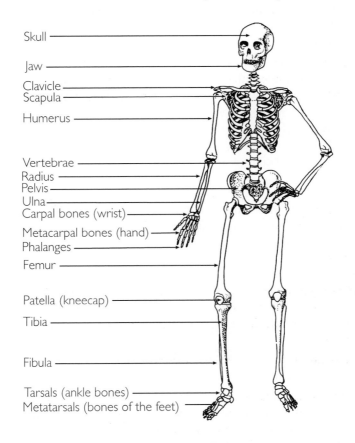

Skull

Jaw

Clavicle
Scapula

Humerus

Vertebrae
Radius
Pelvis
Ulna
Carpal bones (wrist)

Metacarpal bones (hand)
Phalanges

Femur

Patella (kneecap)

Tibia

Fibula

Tarsals (ankle bones)
Metatarsals (bones of the feet)

skin: a protective layer which covers the body and acts as a barrier against *water* loss, *disease* and dirt. It is a waterproof covering which controls the amount of water being lost through evaporation and it also helps to regulate body *temperature*. It is sensitive to touch and contains *nerve* endings. Within it is made *vitamin* D and melanin. There are two main layers to the *skin*, the epidermis and the dermis.

- Epidermis – the outer layer of skin which acts as a form of protection to the tissues underneath. In the epidermis there are several layers of skin cells. The lowest layer is called the germinative layer. There is continuous growth in this layer. As the cells get pushed up to the surface they die because of lack of oxygen and nutrition. The dead skin cells fill with granules of protein called keratin which forms a protective layer. In the germinative layer there are melanocytes which produce the skin pigment (melanin) giving the skin and hair their colour.

- Dermis – the inner layer which contains mainly *connective tissue* fibres, blood vessels, nerves, *glands* and hair roots. In the connective tissue there are elastic and collagen fibres which enable the skin to keep its shape. The *blood* vessels provide *oxygen* and nutrition. The sensory nerve endings are sensitive to touch, heat, cold, pain and pressure. There are five different types of sensory nerve endings in the skin. They are called receptors, and pick up information to relay through the nervous system to the *brain.* The *sweat glands* produce sweat, a watery solution of *salt* and some *urea* which evaporates on the skin thus cooling the body.

Hair follicles provide the means by which a shaft of hair is formed and supported. On either side of the hair follicle there are sebaceous glands which produce an oily fluid called sebum. This spreads over the hair and skin making it supple and waterproof. Excessive sebum causes oily/greasy skin, while insufficient sebum causes dry skin.

The skin regulates body temperature when it produces sweat to cool the body to prevent overheating. Other methods of controlling the skin temperature are dependent on the dilation (vasodilation) and constriction (vasoconstriction) of the blood vessels under the skin surface. During the *ageing* process the skin loses its elasticity and begins to sag and form wrinkles. Skin needs to be washed regularly to prevent a build up of dirt, sweat and loose skin; hygiene is an essential part of caring. *Washing* and *bathing* vulnerable clients, such as the elderly, should be part of a regular *routine.* Young children should be encouraged to wash their hands before meals and after going to the toilet. Teaching *toileting* skills and *hygiene* procedures is an important aspect of working with the disabled. (See *epithelium.*)

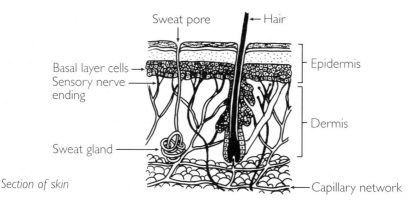

Section of skin

skin sensitivity tests are used in the identification of allergens. Suspected allergens are injected into the *skin* and the extent of the skin reaction is used to indicate sensitivity.

skull: the structure of *bone* which protects and supports the *brain.* (See *skeleton.*)

sleep: a physiological process by which the body alters its state of consciousness within a 24 hour period. Individuals need sleep in order to function efficiently. *Babies* and young children need sleep and rest because it promotes *growth and development.* Different individuals require varying amounts of sleep. Babies, young children and *elderly people* often require a short period of sleep (or nap) during the day. In hot climates there are siestas which are integrated into the daily routine. This gives people time to rest in the afternoon or during the hottest part of the day between noon and 3 pm.

smacking is physical punishment which can take many forms, such as using a hand, stick or strap. Some parents use smacking as a means of control. However, it is never appropriate for childcare workers to smack children in their care. Other strategies should be encouraged such as setting boundaries for *behaviour* with non-physical *discipline.*

smoking is a habit involving tobacco which contain harmful substances such as tar, nicotine and *carbon monoxide*. Nicotine is an addictive substance and it is this part of the cigarette that creates a dependence on smoking. It is absorbed into the bloodstream and affects the body by increasing the heart rate, *blood pressure* and *hormone* production, making smokers vulnerable to heart attack. *Carbon monoxide* combines with *haemoglobin*, the part of the *blood* which carries *oxygen* and reduces the blood's oxygen-carrying capacity. Oxygen is necessary for the healthy function of *tissues* and *organs* in the body. When the oxygen supply is reduced, this can affect growth and bodily function. In order to overcome such a reduction in oxygen, the body produces more haemoglobin. This makes the blood thicker which increases the risk of blood clot or *thrombosis*. If this condition is left untreated, it can lead to such a reduction in circulation in a limb that the only available treatment is the amputation or surgical removal of the limb. Smoking also leads to the deposit of tar on the lungs. The tar clogs up the bronchioles which leads to the narrowing of the breathing passages. This causes breathing problems, coughing and vulnerability to chest infections. For example the cilia in the ciliated epithelium in the *air passages* get clogged up so that mucus is not removed and collects, leading to 'smokers' cough'. The lining of the air passages has degenerated which causes a thickening of lining making breathing difficult.

There is also an increasing debate about passive smoking. This takes place when a non-smoker breathes in the cigarette smoke of others, either in the form of the smoke the smoker has already breathed out or the smoke from the tip of the cigarette. Consequently there is pressure on employers to provide a safe and smoke-free work environment. *Cancer* is the biggest cause of disease leading to early death, in England; it is thought to account for nearly a fifth of all deaths each year. Smoking is the main cause of lung cancer and is linked to heart disease, chronic bronchitis, asthma and cancers of the mouth, bladder, kidney, stomach and pancreas. Mothers who smoke increase the risk of cot death in their babies (see *sudden infant death syndrome* (HMSO 1998)[48]). There is a growing concern about the increase in the numbers of young people who are smoking, particularly girls.

Health education campaigns produce literature to highlight the problems caused by smoking. Action on Smoking and Health provides an information and advice service.

(See Figure on page 266. For further information contact Action on Smoking and Health, 5–11 Mortimer Street, London W1N 7RH.)

smooth muscle is the type of *muscle* found in the walls of the intestinal, genital, urinary and respiratory tracts and in *blood* vessels. Smooth muscles are controlled by the *autonomic nervous system* and *hormones*. The autonomic nervous system has a major role in controlling body movements which require no conscious thought. The muscle cells are spindle-shaped and are organised into bundles of sheets which contract

The health risks of smoking

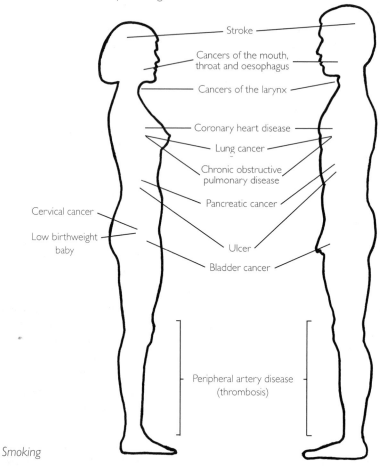

Stroke

Cancers of the mouth, throat and oesophagus

Cancers of the larynx

Coronary heart disease

Lung cancer

Chronic obstructive pulmonary disease

Pancreatic cancer

Cervical cancer

Low birthweight baby

Ulcer

Bladder cancer

Peripheral artery disease (thrombosis)

Smoking

rhythmically. *Peristalsis,* an example of smooth muscle movement, enables *food* to move through the intestinal canal.

social and economic factors are factors which affect how individuals live, work and maintain a healthy lifestyle They are often a cause for concern because of their impact on the *health* and *well-being* of individuals. They include:

- Poverty – people's health is affected by their circumstances, e.g. low income can make it hard to afford to keep a house warm and protect individuals and their families from fire and accidents. There is no money to pay for extras.
- Employment – joblessness has also been linked to poor mental and physical health.

social behaviour is the way a person relates to others. Children should be taught from an early age how to behave with others. They should learn what is acceptable *behaviour* with other children and what is not. Unacceptable behaviour would include biting, swearing and hitting other children. Childcare workers are trained to develop strategies to help children deal with unacceptable behaviour. (See *discipline, tantrums*.)

social care: a type of care which is provided in domicillary, residential and day care settings. It supports the physical, intellectual, emotional, cultural and social needs of the client. Social care should extend a client's contact with others. It also involves sharing *information*, setting up care plans, preparing meals, shopping and some basic cleaning.

Social Chapter is a part of the Maastricht Treaty 1992 which gave the European Union power to enforce social rights with regard to *employment*, working conditions and the rights of workers. This part of the Treaty was signed by the United Kingdom government in 1997.

social class or socio-economic group: a way of differentiating between groups and individuals within society. The *Registrar General's classification* uses professional and employment status as a means by which differences are determined.

(See *Registrar General's classification of occupations and Hall Jones*.)

social exclusion: the way in which an individual or group can become isolated in society. There are a number of factors which can lead to economic and psychological isolation such as inadequate *housing, unemployment* and *health inequalities*.

social policy: the way in which a government introduces legislation and implements policy with regard to issues such as *employment, education, health* and *social care*. It also encompasses the academic study of how different policies are developed and the impact that they have on the life of individuals and society. For example, there have been many changes with regard to the *welfare state* since it was first introduced in 1948.

social role is the way in which *social status* is represented in society. For example, a *nurse* confirms his or her position by wearing a uniform and will be expected to take on the caring nature of a nurse.

social security: financial assistance or *benefits* which are funded by the state. Benefits are managed by the *Benefits Agency* which is part of the *Department of Social Security*. The functioning of the Agency is presently under Government review.

social service inspection units are teams set up within *local authorities* which are responsible for:

- inspecting care provisions registering under the Registered Homes Act 1984
- inspecting childcare provisions registering under the *Children Act 1989*.

Inspections are made of each different provision, but these have not been an annual requirement. The inspection of care provision is currently under review. (See *inspection, Modernising Social Services 1998*).

social services committees are set up by *local authorities* with the responsibility for overseeing local social services policy. Such committees are composed of elected representatives of the local authority. They have a statutory requirement to:

- supervise the work of each *social services department*
- provide local personal social services
- make recommendations with regard to social services
- provide a *community care plan* for the local authority.

social services department: the organisation within each *local authority* which is responsible for personal social services. It is comprised mostly of *social workers* who operate in teams in the care of clients in various categories such as children, *elderly people*, the *mentally ill* and the physically disabled. The local social services department is accountable to the *social services committee*. The work of the social services department is carried out within legislation such as the *Children Act 1989*, the *National Health Service and Community Care Act 1990*, and the *Mental Health Act 1983*.

social status: the position which people hold in society. These positions can be different in various settings or groups such as nurse, hospital doctor or care manager. (See *social role*.)

social stratification: the outcome of dividing the population into layers or strata. Society can be divided on the basis of *class*, income, *race, age* and any other characteristic or grouping by which people can be separated. (See *social class*.)

social support networks: networks including family, friends, partners, relatives and the membership of community groups which offer and provide support for our *self-esteem*. Support is often provided in the context of conversation which permits *self disclosure*, i.e. talking about oneself. (See *networks*.)

social trends: aspects of society which *represent* demographic changes and the effects of change on society. Examples of this are divorce, crime, *poverty, disability* and *dysfunction*. These aspects of society are closely linked to *socio-economic factors*. Social trends are measured through research and statistical information which is publicised annually as a way of monitoring aspects of society and social change. (See *demography*.)

Social Work (Scotland) Act 1986: an Act of Parliament which provides a framework for social work practice in Scotland. (See *foster care*.)

social workers are qualified professionals who operate with individuals and families with different problems within the *voluntary* or *statutory* sector. They help people to come to terms with, or to solve, their problems but their statutory responsibilities, especially in *child protection*, mean they are often viewed as agents of control. Social workers receive professional training which requires them to study all aspects of the principles of social work. Following qualification (usually the Diploma in Social Work), social workers may operate in different areas, which include:

- *advice* and working across the different *client* groups
- children and the child protection team
- youth and community service
- *learning disabilities*
- *mental health*
- elderly.

They are usually employed by *local authority social service departments* and deal with people of all types, ages and backgrounds (see *client classification*). Some may specialise in particular areas such as:

- cases involving young children (including young offenders in the criminal justice system), *adoptions* and fostering arrangements
- supporting those who are mentally or physically ill

- work in *residential homes* with children and young people who cannot live with their natural families
- an increasing amount of *community care* work with elderly and disabled people who might previously have lived in hospitals or residential homes.

socialisation: the lifelong process by which individuals learn about themselves, others and the world around them. It plays an important role in how *attitudes, beliefs* and *values* are developed and personalities are formed and shaped. There are three different types of socialisation:

- primary – the relationships formed in the first few years of life, i.e. within families, with parents, siblings and relatives
- secondary – the relationships formed with friends or peers outside the home
- tertiary – the relationships formed within other formal groups within society.

Socialisation within a group involves relationships between its different members. This may or may not involve rules or codes of behaviour.

society: a group of individuals living together in an organised way.

sociogram: a method used to explore how relationships are determined within group interaction. Group dynamics are observed and a diagram is constructed (see example below) to summarise the information gathered.

Leader speaking to group ·····➤

An example of a sociogram Two way conversation ◄───►

sodium: a *mineral* which is required in small amounts to maintain healthy body function. It is essential for *nerve* and *muscle* development and helps maintain osmotic pressure in the *cells*. The sources of sodium are *salt*, and most other *foods*. The signs and symptoms of sodium deficiency include muscle cramp.

solicitors: law officers who are general legal advisers accessible to the public. They are hired for their services in different legal matters. They can act as advocates and speak on behalf of their *clients* in lower courts. Barristers act as advocates in the high court and are known as 'counsel' for the prosecution or for the defence. Solicitors are the only means of access to barristers.

solubility: if the atoms, molecules or ions of a substance become evenly dispersed (dissolve) in a solute such as *water*, then a solution is formed. If they do not, the mixture is either a colloid, a suspension or a precipitate. Solubility is defined as how well a substance dissolves and it depends on the substance's properties, those of the liquid and other factors such as temperature and pressure.

solvents are liquids that dissolve other substances to form a solution. Some solvents can have a harmful effect on the body; these include butane gas lighter refills, text correction fluids, glues, dry cleaning fluids, aerosols like deodorants or pain relieving sprays, paint thinners or strippers and petrol. In recent years the following facts have been highlighted:

- Solvent misuse is most common amongst youngsters aged from 12 to 16, although younger children may experiment too. It can become fashionable in a small, localised area like a *school* or estate, and then disappear. It seems to go in and out of use and can be a group activity. Of those who start in groups a few who try 'sniffing' may then continue for several years on their own.
- The method of inhalation is usually from a plastic bag which contains the solvent.
- With habitual users there has been a recent trend away from glue onto butane and aerosols. Equally, new users tend to use aerosols rather than glue.
- Effects come on quickly and disappear almost as fast. The experience is like being drunk and users often feel light-headed and dizzy, or dreamy and have hallucinations. Others feel sick and drowsy, and afterwards they can suffer effects similar to a hangover.
- There is an increased chance of accidents happening when 'sniffers' are high on solvents, especially if they are in a dangerous location like a river bank, train line, main road or a high building.
- Solvent misuse to the point of unconsciousness can cause *death* through *choking* on vomit. Death from suffocation is a serious risk if solvents are sniffed in a plastic bag placed over the head.
- Misusing or abusing cigarette lighter refills by clenching the nozzle between the teeth can be almost instantly fatal.
- Potentially, death can occur very rapidly from heart failure as a result of sniffing any of these products.
- Long-term, heavy use, particularly of glue, can damage the *brain*, *liver* and *kidneys*. The young person may have evidence of ulcers around the *mouth*, smell of solvent and may have a flushed face.
- Young people die every week from solvent abuse in the UK.
- Regular use can be habit forming and the addiction can be difficult to break.
- Solvent use is not a criminal offence, but it is illegal for a shopkeeper to sell solvents to anyone under 18 if they suspect such products are intended for abuse. (See *drugs*.)

special care baby unit: a highly specialised team of trained *doctors* and *nurses* working with *babies* who are premature or who experience neo-natal problems and therefore have specific needs such as assistance with breathing. Such babies need individual care often requiring incubators. In addition, other sophisticated equipment may be used to maintain the baby's life.

special health authorities (SHAs) are those authorities who report directly to the Department of Health or to the National Health Service Management Executive. There are three types:

- Non-*hospital* SHAs – these provide a service for the whole NHS which requires some co-ordination at national level. Examples are the NHS Supplies Authority and the *Health Education Authority.*
- Hospital SHAs – a number of specialist postgraduate teaching and research hospitals in London have SHA status. Examples are the Hammersmith, the National Heart and Chest Hospital and the Royal Marsden Hospital.
- Special hospitals – special hospitals are those dealing with the care of seriously disturbed offenders (Rampton, Ashworth and Broadmoor are the special hospitals in England). They form an SHA in their own right – but not all SHAs are special hospitals.

(Department of Health 1993)[46]

special needs: these can be temporary or permanent, short- or long-term. However, there are some special needs which are more permanent and long-term. These are categorised into the following:

- *physical disabilities* affecting motor skills
- chronic illness and terminal disease
- *communication* defects, involving speech and language impairments
- *mental illness*
- *learning disabilities* and difficulties
- sensory impairment or defects such as deafness, blindness and those relating to touch, taste and smell.

(See *Contact a family.*)

special needs and education: children with *special needs* have rights to education which have evolved through different education acts. The most significant change in legislation came in the Education Act 1981 following the *Warnock Report* 1978. The key points raised were as follows:

- children with special needs to be integrated into mainstream *schools* wherever possible
- special educational needs to be more clearly defined. The terms mild, moderate and severe were introduced (see *statementing*).
- a child's individual and specific needs to be part of a continuous assessment process
- a child's abilities to be identified alongside their disabilities
- the term 'specific learning difficulties' (e.g. dyslexia) to be introduced for any child having problems in one area of the school curriculum.

speech therapists are professionals who are trained to help adults and children to overcome language and *communication* problems. Qualified therapists work in a variety of settings which include *hospitals, schools,* community clinics and in private practice (see *language development*). Qualifying to be a speech therapist involves either completing a three/four-year degree course or a two-year post graduate diploma course.

spina bifida is a spinal defect which occurs in early *pregnancy*. It affects development of the unborn baby's spine when one or more of the *vertebrae* fail to close properly, leaving a gap. This means that the *spinal cord* and the *nerves* are likely to be damaged, often resulting in *paralysis* in the area below this point in the spinal cord. It can also impair the way in which the spine develops. Walking can be affected and there can be damage to the *bladder* and bowel causing incontinence. One of the side effects can be *hydrocephalus*. Others include learning and memory difficulties, spatial and perception problems and poor concentration. According to recent research on the prevention of spina bifida, women can reduce the risk by taking 5 mg folic acid daily for at least one month before *conception* and during the first 12 weeks of pregnancy.

(For further information contact ASBAH, Association for Spina Bifida and Hydro-cephalus, 42 Park Road, Peterborough PE1 2UQ.)

spinal cord: the cord of neurons that extends from the *brain* down the *vertebral* canal to the second lumbar vertebra. There are 31 pairs of spinal nerves that leave the spinal cord at different levels to supply various parts of the body. Injury to the spinal cord can be serious and, in some cases, can lead to *paralysis*. (See *nervous system*.)

spiritual health: a person's religious beliefs and cultural identity contribute to his or her health and *well-being*. Spiritual health forms part of *holistic care* revolving around the physical, intellectual, emotional, spiritual, cultural and social develop-ment of the child or person.

spirometry: a test of the body's ventilation capacity with regard to respiration and breathing. A spirometer is the machine used to provide readings which are called spirometer tracings. (See *mechanisms of breathing*.)

spleen: an *organ* situated high up in the *abdomen* against the *diaphragm* on the left side of the body and protected by the ribs. It is a small dark brown organ and is like a fibrous sponge which contains lymphoid *tissue*. It filters *blood* as it passes through. The spleen:

- makes *antibodies* as part of the body defence mechanism
- destroys mature or worn-out red blood cells.

It is important to mention that individuals can function without a spleen because its operations are also carried out in other organs. However, when the spleen is removed individuals are more prone to infection.

squint (strabismus): the uncoordinated action of the *muscles* in the *eye* causing a child to have visual difficulties. A child with a squint is unable to see properly as the two eyes are not able to focus on an objective point. There are two types of squint:

- convergent squint – when the eyes turn inwards
- divergent squint – when the eyes turn outwards.

standard mortality ratio (SMR): a way of comparing mortality rates in differ-ent population groupings. It takes into account the different age structures of the population. The observed number of *deaths* is the actual number of deaths occurring in the geographical area or subgroup of the population. The expected number of deaths is calculated by applying the national age specific mortality rates to the pop-ulation of a health authority area or population sub-group.

The SMR is calculated as:

$$SMR = \frac{\text{Observed number of deaths}}{\text{Expected number of deaths}} \times 100$$

(HMSO 1998)[48]

standard spending assessment is the method used by the government to determine how much funding should be allocated to a *local authority*. A formula is also used to assess how much the authority should spend on their *social care* services.

statementing: an assessment process to determine the specific needs of individual *children with disabilities*. It can be instigated by a local education authority at any time during a child's *school* life from 4 to 18 years of age. Any statementing before the age of four years is organised by the *health authority*. Involved in the process are parents and the education authority who negotiate and agree the relevant education needs of the child. The aims of the process are to identify areas of need and define the resulting educational requirements of the individual. This may require extra resources and facilities to be set up, for example *physiotherapy, speech therapy*, modification of buildings, extra teacher or adult support (see *special needs*). In 1994, *a code of practice* was introduced to give guidance to schools with regard to the statementing process. Following this, schools were expected to identify a member of staff who would take responsibility for special educational needs with the title of Special Educational Needs Co-ordinator (*SENCO*).

There are five stages involved in the statementing process:

- Cause for concern – a class teacher or care worker identifies a cause for concern. This is usually confirmed after systematic recorded observations over a period of time. This concern is shared with the SENCO and the parents.
- Observation and monitoring – an individual education plan is set up with the agreement of the parents and the SENCO, and the child is monitored more closely.
- Outside help – support is given by a professional from outside the school, such as an educational psychologist.
- Procedure for statutory assessment – this should take place within 26 weeks.
- Statement of special education needs is set up – this is a legal document which should describe exactly the child's individual needs, and the relevant support to be given.

(See *special needs and education*.)

states of matter (solids, liquids and gases): solid, liquid and gas can be described as the three states of matter. Kinetic theory explains how a substance changes from one such state to another. These changes are caused by heating and cooling. They include:

- Melting and freezing – when a solid is heated, the particles in the solid gain energy and vibrate faster. After some time they break free from the solid and begin to move freely around each other. The solid is then said to have melted to form a liquid. The *temperature* at which a solid melts is called its melting point.

- Evaporating and boiling – when a liquid is heated the particles gain energy, vibrate and move nearer the surface. Some of the particles near the surface have sufficient energy to be released into the air, so that some of the liquid evaporates to form a gas. The temperature at which evaporation occurs is called the boiling point.
- Evaporation and condensation of water – when water evaporates from liquid into gas, this process uses energy. The amount of energy used is called the latent heat of vaporisation. The reverse process releases energy when molecules condense (come together again as a liquid).(Stockley, Oxlade and Wertheim 1988)[58]

statistics are numerical data which are collected to provide *information*. The use of statistics and the analysis of the information collected with regard to health and social care give indications which can be used in the allocation of resources required for different target areas. Information collected includes:

- the overall state of health of the nation
- *divorce*/remarriage/*family structures*
- *mortality rates*
- the number of children under five in the United Kingdom.

status: a measure of the rank and prestige of a person or group of people. Status can define how people are treated by others and how they see themselves. (See *social class*.)

statutory organisations are health and social care services set up as a requirement by law. They are expected to provide a range of services. These include the *National Health Service* and *social service departments*.

stereotyping: applying a set of presumed attitudes about groups of individuals in society. This relates to the formation of positive and negative *attitudes* which can affect *behaviour* towards a particular group or individual. Stereotyping can be learned by children from their parents. In addition to this, the mass media (i.e. television, newspapers, books, films, games and comics) can reinforce stereotypical attitudes.

stillbirth: the *birth* of a baby showing no signs of life, if it occurs after 24 weeks or more in the mother's *womb*.

stomach: the body's reservoir for *food*. In the stomach the food is churned up by muscular action which changes it into a more liquid form called chyme. The presence of food in the stomach stimulates *glands* in its lining to secrete rennin and pepsin, which react with food and hydrochloric acid (see *digestion*). The walls of the stomach are composed of longitudinal *muscle*, circular muscle, submucosa and mucosa. (See Figure opposite.)

storytelling: telling stories to stimulate interest. Books may or may not be used. Storytelling is a powerful way of influencing children's views about the society in which they live. It can be a means whereby children can develop an interest in books and reading for themselves. Guidelines for the telling of stories are as follows:

- the choice of books or stories is important and should be appropriate to the age of the child
- childcare workers should prepare stories in advance
- the seating in the storytelling area should be comfortable with enough space for numbers of children to sit comfortably

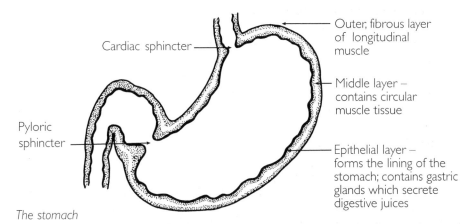

Cardiac sphincter

Outer, fibrous layer of longitudinal muscle

Middle layer – contains circular muscle tissue

Pyloric sphincter

Epithelial layer – forms the lining of the stomach; contains gastric glands which secrete digestive juices

The stomach

- children should be able to see any pictures being used
- stories should be told with enthusiasm, using different voice tone and pitch. *Gestures* should be encouraging and positive
- children should be encouraged to respond to the story with questioning by the storyteller to develop the children's communication skills
- the use of props such as puppets, storyboards and other visual aids can facilitate the storytelling
- songs, rhymes and *creative* activities should be used as a follow-up to the story using the same themes and topics. (See also *play, music and singing*.)

Storytelling is a traditional method of communicating items of interest, family news and images representing a person's culture. People can train to become storytellers enabling them to tell stories in a variety of settings to different age groups.

stress management: strategies used by individuals to cope with the build-up of stress in their lives. (See *relaxation techniques*.)

stress-related illness is any type of illness which is brought on by or made worse by *stress*. Illnesses particularly associated with stress are *heart* disease, *diabetes*, digestive disorders, *skin* disorders and a vulnerability to colds and flu.

stress-response: physical response which supports a person's fight and flight reaction. The stress response may create problems when a person cannot fight or run away or such reactions are inappropriate. A person can become agitated because he or she cannot escape from different problems or situations in their lives. (See *adrenaline*.)

strokes: see *cerebrovascular accident*.

stroke volume: the volume of *blood* which is pumped out from a *ventricle* during each contraction of the *heart*.

substance abuse is misuse of various substances including *alcohol, drugs* and *solvents. Abuse* describes the way in which the substances are taken, causing risk to *health*.

substitute care: a type of child-care which is also known as replacement care. This means that the child is looked after by a *carer* who is not the parent. Substitute care can be provided by *childminders, nannies,* foster parents, *day nurseries, family centres* or *playgroups*. Guidelines for caring for children in different settings are included in the principles and regulations set down in the *Children Act 1989*.

sudden infant death syndrome (cot death): the sudden and unexpected *death* of a *baby* without any obvious or apparent reason. It is a very distressing experience for parents, who need support and *bereavement counselling* to cope with their *grief*. In recent years, cigarette *smoking* in the home has been found to be a high risk factor. These days babies are laid on their back or side, not on their front, to help prevent over-heating. There is currently extensive research being undertaken to find out the reasons why babies die in this way.

(For further information contact the Foundation for the Study of Infant Deaths, 14 Halkin St, London SW1X 7DP.)

sugars: the common name for a group of chemicals known as *carbohydrates*. They are made up of *carbon*, hydrogen and *oxygen*. They are classified according to the number of sugar units which make up their structure.

- monosaccharides (e.g. glucose, fructose, galactose) have one sugar unit
- disaccharides (e.g. sucrose, lactose and maltose) have two sugar units
- polysaccharides are complex carbohydrates, with many sugar molecules which are joined together.

suicide is a voluntary act by an individual to terminate his or her life. Mental illness is not always associated with suicide. There can be other predisposing factors, such as anxiety, severe pain or illness, re-employment, finance, exams, fear of others or an inability to face major decisions. It may be a cry for help which goes wrong, for example, an overdose meant to send a message for help but which leads to the individual's *death*.

supervision orders are procedures managed by *social workers*, who apply to the court for the supervision of a child at risk.

supervision register: a register of vulnerable, mentally ill people in the community. Such individuals are monitored with regard to their ongoing support and care.

support agencies: these are the individual organisations which offer assistance through a variety of methods such as: an *information* service, supplying leaflets, research statistics, videos and advice sessions, *counselling*, telephone helpline, immediate crisis support, local support and self-help groups. (See *network*.)

support groups are available to help individuals through difficult and unsettling situations. They may comprise collections of people who organise themselves to care for each other and to share mutual experiences. They are an essential link for individuals who require positive support during times of crisis. (See *Carers National Association Network, Parents Anonymous*.)

support network: personal or professional contacts within the health and social care sysytem. They consist of a large number of *organisations* set up to provide *information, advice, self-help,* and telephone helplines, which offer individual and group support. They can either be *statutory* or *voluntary organisations*. Examples include *social service departments, Relate* and the *Citizens' Advice Bureaux*. Informal support networks are set up within families and amongst friends and neighbours. Details of such organisations can be found in 'Yellow Pages'. The Citizens' Advice Bureaux can also provide a full list of these organisations.

surgeons: qualified *doctors* who specialise in surgery.

surrogacy: an agreement which involves a childless couple and a woman who is prepared to give *birth* to a *baby* on behalf of the couple. The woman may or may not be impregnated with the husband's sperm. The fertilised ovum (containing the husband's sperm which has fertilised his wife's egg) is inserted into the woman's *womb* by *artificial insemination*. Surrogacy costs are usually between £7000 and £10,000. Any payment made to the surrogate woman is an additional expense. The Surrogacy Act 1985 sets up a legal framework to ban the advertising of commercial surrogacy agents. It also states that any surrogacy contract is unenforceable, so if the woman changes her mind about handing over the baby then there is nothing that the couple can do about it. Surrogacy is a controversial subject, but in some cases it is the only means whereby a couple can have a child of their own.

survey: a set of questions formulated to obtain information from people in their natural environment. It may ask individuals about their attitudes, beliefs, plans, *health* and *work*; in fact any subject can be covered in a survey. The researcher can survey a group of individuals who have undergone certain experiences. The responses obtained constitute the data upon which the research hypothesis is examined. People who are contributing to the survey are called *respondents*. A good example of a survey is the National Census which is conducted every ten years. Before setting up a survey it is necessary for the researcher to ensure the following:

- permission to carry out the study has been given
- a research *hypothesis* is in place
- the size of the *sample* of respondents is appropriate
- the type of sample is relevant
- the *research methods* are effective
- the ways in which the results will be recorded and analysed are agreed.

swallowing: the mechanism involved in the passage of *food* from the *mouth* through the back of the *throat* (the pharynx) into the *oesophagus*. The *epiglottis* is the flap of *cartilage* which covers the windpipe or trachea. When the swallowing reflex is activated the epiglottis automatically covers the trachea to prevent the food being inhaled into the windpipe. Food is pushed through the oesophagus in a process called *peristalsis*. Swallowing is essential for life. The reflex is controlled by the *autonomic nervous system*. The medulla oblongata, situated in the hind *brain*, is that part of the brain responsible for swallowing.

sweat glands are found in the dermis of the *skin*. They produce sweat which contains *water, minerals, salts* and *urea*. The sweat is excreted through the pores of the skin and helps to regulate body *temperature* when it evaporates.

symbolic play: type of play in which a child uses his or her *imagination*. During *play* a child may use one object as a symbol for another. A child may care for a doll, to represent a *baby*. A cardboard box can be used as a hat, while a saucepan and wooden spoon are used as a drum. When the child engages in symbolic play he/she is developing skills which can be used again as they grow older. (See *Piaget's view of play*.)

symbols are signs which represent an object, route or situation and convey a message to the reader. Examples in health and social care include the symbols:

- used in by equal opportunities employers

- used to indicate wheelchair access
- used to indicate that a substance is dangerous – gloves should be worn.

sympathetic nervous system: part of the *autonomic nervous system* which is activated in stressful situations. The sympathetic nervous system stimulates the *adrenal glands* to produce *adrenaline*. The effects of adrenaline are:

- an increased *heart* rate
- increased respiration affecting the breathing rate and its depth (see *mechanisms of breathing*)
- increased sweating.
- a dry *mouth*
- dilated pupils.

synovial joints are types of freely movable *joints* which connect one *bone* to another to form part of the human *skeleton* (see facing page). Such joints are supported by a synovial capsule which is reinforced by bands of elastic fibre called *ligaments*. The ends of the bones are covered with articular *cartilage*. The joint is lined with a membrane called synovial membrane. This is filled with synovial fluid which acts as a lubricant and aids movement. There are various types of synovial joints, such as the hip joint.

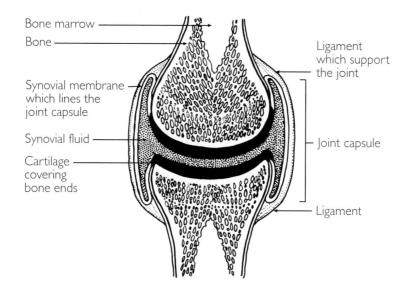

syphilis is a *sexually transmitted disease*. It is caused by *bacteria* which are transmitted during *sexual intercourse*. The symptoms start with a blister which may occur on the penis or in the *vagina*. This is followed by a rash, sore throat and a fever after three to six weeks. As the *disease* progresses, more ulcers occur on the *mouth*, lips or vagina. Left untreated, the bacteria may affect the *heart*, blood vessels and the *brain*. This can lead to general *paralysis* or insanity if the syphilis bacteria severely attack the functioning of the brain. Syphilis is treated by *antibiotics* and the infected person is encouraged to maintain a celibate lifestyle in order to prevent spread of the disease.

T

tabulation: a method using tables to display complex numerical data. A table should be as simple and unambiguous as possible. Tables are used to:

- display a distinct pattern in the figures
- summarise the figures
- provide information
- present collected data in an orderly manner.

All tables should:

- have a title
- include the source of the data
- have column and row headings as brief as possible but clearly labelled
- have units of measurement specified
- have sets of data which are to be compared with each other
- have approximations and omissions from the table explained in footnotes.

tagging is a method of monitoring a *client*. For example, it is used to prevent the *elderly* (when suffering from confusion) from wandering beyond the safe boundaries of their home or residential home. This can involve wearing a safety bracelet or a mobile alarm. This system is still in the initial development stage and is viewed by some as a form of restraint and control which intrudes on the boundary of civil liberties. However, others view the use of safety bracelets as an effective way of monitoring movements of elderly clients and a way in which staff can provide better individual care if their use is integrated into a client's care plan. Electronic tagging is being used in the criminal justice system (presently in pilot schemes) on different groups of offenders.

take-up: the number of people who are claiming *benefit* in comparison to those who are eligible to claim benefit. For example, 98 per cent of those eligible claim family allowance.

tantrums: outbursts of screaming, uncontrollable rage and frustration which can occur in young children. Tantrums are common between the ages of one and three years. Children aged four or five can also behave in this way. Such fits of rage are equally common in boys and girls. Behaviour includes whining, screaming, kicking and punching. A young child may have a temper tantrum because he/she wants to challenge the limits set on their behaviour, but children who are raised in an environment where no boundaries are set are just as likely to have tantrums. (See *challenging behaviour, discipline*.)

target group/audience: a large or small group of individuals who have been identified for a particular purpose. In health education a target group is a collection of individuals who are to be given a specific message. Talks about different aspects of health promotion would be prepared in different ways for different target groups, e.g. a talk about the advantages and disadvantages of breast feeding would be targeted at pre- and post-natal mothers. It is very important that health educators match their oral and visual presentation to the needs of the target group. A formal lecture with many tables and statistics would be unsuitable for a group of primary school children, but would be beneficial to some adults. Leaflets or activity packs which reinforce the message could be more applicable for children or the message may perhaps take the form of a story. The following indications of the nature of the group should be taken into account:

- *age* – different ages and stages *of development*
- *gender* – different information for men and women, i.e. 'well women' and 'well men'
- subject interest – the topic must be applicable to the group concerned
- special needs such as hearing, visual or disability – different methods of communication e.g. blissboards.

taste buds are found on the surface of the *tongue*.

team: a group of individuals who work together for a common purpose. This may be in several ways:

- on a professional basis – a team of *nurses* on a ward
- on a multi-disciplinary basis – different professionals working together in the care of a *client*
- on a learning basis – a group of students on a research topic
- on a leisure or sporting basis – a group of people who meet for leisure pursuits such as swimming, squash, football
- on an educational basis – groups of pupils, students who are academically streamed
- on a competence requirement basis – groups of individuals who work together to achieve certain competencies or skills in the workplace. For example those studying their *national vocational qualifications* in *health care*, *community care* and childcare.

Effective teamwork involves using the skills of each member and ensuring that each person has a function, role and responsibility within the team. It is usual for teams to have a leader who co-ordinates the work carried out by the group. Teams often meet regularly to share information, discuss problems and make decisions. These meetings are often minuted and an agenda or action plan prepared. Written and verbal *communication* between team members is vital, especially when it involves the health and social well-being of service users, clients or patients.

teeth are used to break up *food* in the *mouth* making it easier to swallow. There are four different types of teeth:

- incisors – situated in the front of the mouth. These teeth have chisel-like edges for biting
- canines – pointed so they can be used for tearing off pieces of food
- premolars – have a flatter surface and are used for grinding food into small pieces
- molars – similar to premolars but larger; generally, the upper molars have three roots, the lower molars only two, while the other teeth have a single root.

Teeth develop at any time during the first two years of life. The first set of teeth are called the 'milk' or 'deciduous' teeth. They usually begin to appear when the child is a few months old. There are 20 milk teeth, ten each in the lower and upper jaw, four incisors, two canines and four molars. They will usually be completely formed by the age of three years. Between five and six years these teeth begin to fall out as *permanent* ones come through. There are 32 permanent teeth, 16 each in the lower and upper jaw. These consist of two incisors, one canine, two premolars and three molars on each side of the mouth.

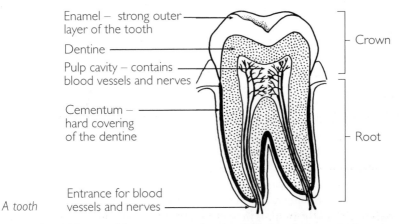

Enamel – strong outer layer of the tooth

Dentine

Pulp cavity – contains blood vessels and nerves

Cementum – hard covering of the dentine

Entrance for blood vessels and nerves

Crown

Root

A tooth

Teeth should be cared for as soon as they begin to break through the gums, so babies should have their teeth cleaned with a soft toothbrush. Toddlers should be encouraged to use a toothbrush to suck and chew on and to watch their older brothers and sisters and parents cleaning their teeth. From an early age cleaning the teeth should become a habit in the morning and last thing at night. A *balanced diet* will encourage healthy teeth and prevent decay. *Calcium, vitamins* and reduced sugar will reinforce healthy teeth because this will discourage the formation of acid on the enamel of the teeth. It is known that bacteria feed on sugar and produce acid which decays teeth. This acid can penetrate the gum and cause decay even before teeth come through. For this reason drinks with reduced sugar content should be given to young children. *Fluoride* in the water supply can also strengthen the enamel of the teeth and prevent decay. Fluoride is also contained in toothpaste. Visiting the *dentist* regularly is important so that teeth can be treated, if necessary, at an early stage. Dental hygiene is vital in caring for people as decaying teeth can be a cause of a general feeling of ill health and bad breath. Poor chewing can result in gum pain and decay. Care workers should ensure, as part of the physical care of their clients, that the client's mouth and teeth are inspected daily and wherever necessary help is given to clean teeth and keep the mouth healthy.

temperament governs an individual's emotional reactions to situations. (See *personality*.)

temperature: a measure of heat. Temperature is measured using a thermometer which can be calibrated to show a number of different temperature scales. (See *clinical thermometer*.)

tendon: a cord which consists of bundles of fibres, responsible for attaching the muscles to the *bone*. Tendons assist muscle movement on a particular area of the bone.

terminal illness is a *disease* or physical disorder which results in *death*, e.g. *patients* who are suffering from advanced *cancer* which has spread to different parts of the body. In terminal illness, individuals need highly specialised care. The basis for this type of caring is compassion, commitment, consistency and the necessary skills to carry out practical tasks and activities. Terminally ill people may have many needs including:

- physical needs, such as help and support with toileting, washing, *bathing* and feeding through the provision of nutritious meals to stimulate their diminishing appetite
- social needs, such as contact with others, conversations and outings with *families* and friends
- emotional needs, such as feeling that they are still loved, that they are not useless and that their lives still have purpose; this is a difficult time for carers who can feel helpless as there is no cure for the illness and often observe the person struggle with pain and despair; *listening* and sharing interesting news and making the person feel that their contribution is important is essential
- spiritual needs, such as facing the issues of life and death, exploring their beliefs and talking about death
- cognitive and intellectual needs, such as *information* sharing; learning new skills could still be helpful to a terminally ill person and the problem solving aspects of dealing with information should be encouraged
- pain control is an important aspect of this type of illness and adequate medical provision should be determined by the *doctor.*

(See *holistic care, palliative care.*)

tertiary care: care which is offered through specialist *hospital* services. Examples include *cancer* hospitals, hospitals offering neurosurgery, and those offering psychiatric treatment and *care.*

tetanus (lockjaw) is a disease caused by the bacterium *Clostridium tetani*. It is found in the earth and enters the body through cuts and scratches. The *incubation period* for tetanus is 4–21 days. It is a disease in which *muscles* of the neck, back and limbs contract and tighten. The muscles of the jaw can lock. Tetanus prevention is an integral part of any *immunisation* programme.

tetraplegia is a disorder, *dysfunction* or *disease* which causes *paralysis* to the four limbs of the body. (See *disability.*)

thalassaemia is an inherited *blood* disorder which is widespread in certain parts of the world such as Mediterranean countries, Africa and Asia. The disorder affects the protein component of *haemoglobin*. There are three classifications:

- minor – the person is a carrier but does not have any *signs and symptoms* themselves
- intermediate – the person has a mild form of the *disease* which may require the occasional *blood transfusion*
- major – the person has other signs and symptoms and the haemoglobin disorder causes *anaemia*, enlargement of the spleen and the *bone marrow* is affected.

The degree to which a person is affected depends on whether one or two parents are carriers. Where the disorder is inherited from one parent, the child usually has no signs and symptoms.

thalidomide: a *drug* which was prescribed for *pregnant* women during 1959–1961 to help their morning sickness. Side effects were found to include severe deformities in developing babies, some being born without fingers, arms or legs.

The New NHS – Modern, Dependable 1997: a government White Paper introduced in 1997 proposing changes to the National Health Service. The principles which underlie the changes are plans to:

- review the *NHS* as a genuinely national service. Patients will get fair *access* to consistently high quality, prompt and accessible services right across the country
- make the delivery of healthcare against these new national standards a matter for local responsibility. Local *doctors* and *nurses*, who are in the best position to know what paients require, will be in the driving seat in shaping services
- get the NHS to work in partnership. By breaking down organisational barriers and forging stronger links with *local authorities*, the needs of the *patient* will be put at the centre of the care process
- drive up efficiency through a more rigorous approach to performance and by cutting bureaucracy, so that all expenditure in the NHS is spent to maximise the care for patients
- shift the focus onto quality of care so that excellence is guaranteed to all patients, and quality becomes the driving force for *decision-making* at every level of the service
- rebuild confidence in the NHS as a public service, accountable to patients, open to the public and shaped by their views. (HMSO 1997)[61]

therapy: a process which is used to help individuals overcome their physical, psychological, social or cognitive difficulties. It can take the form of:

- *counselling*
- *art*/drama/*music* therapy
- light and sound experiences
- physical exercises
- complementary or alternative methods such as *massage* and *aromatherapy*.

thermography measures the amount of heat produced in parts of the body. These measurements are recorded on photographic paper which is sensitive to heat changes. The picture produced is a thermogram, e.g. any area which produces heat will show up as a hot spot. This technique is used to detect *tumours*.

throat (pharynx): the passage which joins the *mouth*, nose, windpipe and the oesophagus.

thrombosis: a blood clot. It is often the result of a disorder which changes some of the liquid form of *blood* into a more solid state. This can lead to a blockage in an *artery* which restricts the blood flow to the *tissue* that it supplies. Examples of thrombosis are *coronary thrombosis*, stroke or *cerebral vascular accident*.

thymus: a *gland* situated in the base of the neck. It lies behind the breast bone and extends to the *thyroid gland*. It develops and grows from infancy and is at its largest during *puberty*. The function of the thymus is to support the *immune* system of the body.

thyroid gland: a *gland* situated in the neck, near the lower part of the larynx where it meets the trachea. It produces a *hormone* called thyroxine which controls the body's *metabolic rate*. This is the rate at which the body releases energy and directly influences the body's level of activity.

Overactive and underactive thyroid

Overactive thyroid	Underactive thyroid
increased metabolic rate	reduction in metabolic rate
raised temperature/sweating	low body temperature
heart damage, fast pulse	slow pulse rate, weight gain,
weight loss, increased appetite	changes in hair and skin,
swelling behind the eyes	stunted growth
swelling of the thyroid gland	

tidal air: the air breathed in and out of the *lungs* during each cycle of breathing.

tidal volume: the amount of air which is breathed in and out during each cycle of breathing or inspiration. It can be measured and assessed. This is particularly important where *clients* or *patients* have breathing problems such as bronchitis or asthma. (See *mechanisms of breathing, spirometry*.)

tissue: a group of *cells* which carry out a particular task, e.g. muscular tissue, nervous tissue, connective tissue. Tissues have various functions:

- they act as a barrier against *infection*
- they enable other materials to be deposited in their matrix in order to carry out specific functions (in the formation of *bone*, calcium is deposited between the bone cells in order to make it strong)
- protection
- support
- they respond to stimuli
- they enable movement to take place
- they increase surface area enabling diffusion to take place
- they allow the diffusion of *nutrients*, gases, *hormones* and other substances to pass through its walls to other tissues and different parts of the body.

Examples of the various types of tissues are:

- *epithelial* – cover or form lining in different parts of the body; glandular tissues which line the spaces in glands and secrete substances into these spaces
- *nervous* – link together and form a network enabling messages or nerve impulses to be sent to all parts of the body
- *connective* – composed of different cells and fibres which support and hold other tissues and organs together, e.g. cartilaginous tissue which supports bones
- muscles.

tongue: a muscular *organ* attached to the floor of the *mouth*. It is covered in mucous membrane and is made up of muscle *fibres* which allow the tongue to move about in several directions. The tongue is covered on its upper surface with tiny projections called papillae. There are also *taste buds*, which are small pores, situated on the surface of the tongue. The functions of the tongue are:

- chewing food so that the food forms a *bolus* or ball
- using muscular actions to push *food* to the back of the *throat* enabling it to be swallowed
- sensitivity to the taste, texture and temperature of the food being eaten
- speech production.

touch: see *sensory organs*.

toy libraries: agencies which lend out or loan selected toys and equipment. Originally established for parents of children with *special needs*, many are now more widely available and some have been set up for *childminders* and playgroups. Some are operated by parents, others by *social service departments, health authorities, schools* and voluntary groups. Many provide an informal setting in which health care and assessment can be carried out.

toys are objects or tools which a child uses for *play* and learning. Toys can range from everyday objects which are found around the house, such as saucepans with lids, empty cereal packets and old clothes, to sophisticated pieces of equipment designed to generate play. Children use different toys at various ages and stages. Toys are important as they give a child something which belongs to them. This is an essential aspect of children developing a sense of identity. Choosing the right toy can be difficult. It is important to allow a child to choose a toy which supports what they like doing and what they are able to do. The health and safety requirements for toys are controlled by toy safety regulations which cover:

- harmful metals including lead
- sharp points and edges
- the eyes of soft toys
- electrical safety
- plastic bags
- flash testing of fur fabric
- cellulose nitrate (a fire hazard)
- harmful metals in pencils
- painting instruments.

The Consumer Protection Act 1987 allows anyone injured by a defective product to claim damages against the manufacturer. Reputable manufacturers, particularly in Britain, work to the British Standard BS 5665. The toys are inspected, and if the inspection is successful, the manufacturer may then put the BS 5665 mark on the packaging.

trade unions: organisations set up to protect and promote the rights of workers or employees. Trade unions are also able to monitor the health and safety conditions under which their members work. They may be affiliated to the Trades Union Congress.

tranquillisers are *drugs* which are used to reduce tension, relieve *anxiety* and make a person feel relaxed and calm. The potential side effects include drowsiness and dependence.

transfer of heat is a process which occurs whenever there is a temperature difference across a region. Heat energy is transferred by conduction, convection or radiation from the hotter to the cooler place. Heat transfer increases the internal energy of the cooler atoms, raising their temperature, and decreases the energy of the hotter atoms, lowering theirs. The process continues until the temperature is the same across the region – a state called thermal equilibrium.

- **Conduction (thermal conduction)** – a process by which heat energy is transferred through solids (and also, to a much lesser extent, in liquids and gases). In good conductors the energy transfer is rapid, due mainly to the movement of free electrons (electrons which can move about), although also by the vibration of atoms.
- **Convection** – a way in which heat energy is transferred in liquids and gases. If a liquid or gas is heated, it expands, becomes less dense and rises. Cooler, denser liquid or gas then sinks to take its place. Thus a convection current is set up.
- **Radiation** – a way in which heat energy is transferred from a hotter to a cooler place without the medium taking any part in the process. This can occur through a vacuum, unlike conduction and convection. The term radiation is also often used to refer to the heat energy itself, otherwise known as radiant heat energy. This takes the form of electromagnetic waves, mainly infra-red radiation. When these waves fall on an object some of their energy is absorbed increasing the object's internal energy and hence its temperature.

Related terms include:

- Insulators – materials in which conduction is slow, such as wood and most liquids and gases. As they do not have free electrons, heat energy is only transferred by the vibration and collision of immediately neighbouring atoms.
- Conductivity (thermal conductivity) – a measure of how good a conductor a material is. The rate of heat energy transfer through an object depends on the conductivity of the material and the temperature gradient (the temperature change with distance along the material). The higher the conductivity and the steeper the gradient, the faster the energy transfer.
- Greenhouse effect – an effect of rising temperature or warming which is produced when radiation is trapped in a closed area, e.g. a greenhouse or the Earth's atmosphere. The objects inside the closed area absorb the sun's radiation and re-emit lower energy radiation which cannot pass back through the layers of glass, or in the atmosphere, of *carbon dioxide*. The level of carbon dioxide is increasing, hence the atmosphere is slowly getting warmer. (Stockley, Oxlade and Wertheim 1988)

transfusion: the procedures used to introduce fluid into a tissue or *blood* vessel in the body. Fluid is transfused when the body's own supply has been diminished due to *accident* or *disease*. An example is a *blood transfusion* where blood is pumped into the body via a blood vessel, usually in the arm.

transitions are *changes* which occur in a person's life. These changes may require a period of adjustment and can relate to many aspects of an individual's life such as *work*, *family* and *lifestyle*.

transplantation ('transplants'): the process by which an *organ* or *tissue* can be transplanted from the body of one person to that of another person. For example, *kidney* transplants, *heart* transplants.

trauma: a physical wound caused by an external force. The term can also be used in a psychological sense (see *post traumatic syndrome*).

treatment: methods used to cure or support a *client*, *patient* or *service user*. Methods of treatment can be either short-term or long-term depending on the condition. Short-term treatment can involve a course of antibiotics for a throat infection, for example. Long-term treatment can involve surgery, different types of *drugs* and physiotherapy for *diseases* such as rheumatoid arthritis. Treatment can be:

- conservative, where different methods are used including bed rest, drugs, alternative therapies or any other procedure which does not involve surgery
- surgical, where different operations are used to treat the condition.

trends in health care: ways in which aspects of health care are changing. The following examples consider various trends:

Social and demographic changes

- Ageing population – people are living longer. This is putting extra demands on health resources particularly as there are fewer in the working population to generate those resources.
- Medical advances – due to more sophisticated methods of treatment lives are being saved which would otherwise have been lost.
- Health care – responds to the requirements of society. Increased homelessness has seen *tuberculosis* return as a significant cause of ill health in the UK.
- Modern lifestyles affect *health* – *alcohol*, *diet*, *smoking*, *exercise*.

Changes in technology

- *Keyhole surgery* – available for many procedures. This has changed the nature of *hospital* care, e.g. day stay rather than a long period as in-patient.
- Diagnostic equipment – *computer axial topography* and *magnetic resonance imaging* scanners, *ultrasound*. Earlier detection of disease allows for more effective treatment.
- Computerisation has improved efficiency of different aspects of care such as *laser* treatments to treat various conditions.

Changes in practice

- *Patient's Charter* puts the emphasis on 'patient-focused care', promoting *patient* choices.
- Nursing techniques which includes *care planning*.

Care in the community

- *Mental Health* – moving long-term patients from large asylums (i.e. psychiatric hospitals) into smaller units of residential care.
- Primary care expansion with some *GPs* running *day surgery.*

triangulation: three or more methods used in one piece of research. This can improve the validity of research. For example, in exploring issues with mature women who are studying nursery nursing, a researcher may use:

- a case study of a particular training centre or college
- both structured and in-depth interviews involving students and lecturers
- questionnaires.

truancy: unauthorised absence from *school* by children of compulsory school age (5–16 years of age). Children stay away from school for a variety of reasons. Under the Education Act 1993, children do not break the law when they 'play truant'; it is the parents who are viewed as committing an offence. *Youth courts* deal with such offences and insist through legislation that parents accept responsibility for their children.

tuberculosis is an *infectious disease* caused by the tubercle bacillus (see *bacteria*). It causes lesions in different parts of the body although in the initial stages of the *disease* the person suffers from a debilitating cough, loss of weight and night sweats. The person often coughs up blood which can be distressing. Treatment involves antibiotics, bed rest and isolation from others during the infectious stages. Recovery can take a number of months.

tumour: a swelling or lump which can occur in different parts of the body. It may contain abnormal *tissue* which has no useful function in the body. A tumour can be:

- benign – the tumour is in a capsule and therefore does not invade or harm the surrounding tissues and organs
- malignant – the tumour is not encapsulated and therefore can invade surrounding tissues and organs causing more tumours to grow and develop.

There are various types of *cancer* which start with one tumour but then affect other parts of the body, e.g. a cancerous tumour of the lung can spread to the ribs or the liver.

twins occur when a woman produces either two eggs at ovulation or one fertilised egg which divides in two and both become implanted in the uterus. If twin eggs are produced and both are fertilised by male sperm, the two embryos grow and develop two individual *foetus*es with the end result of two babies at *birth.*

- Identical twins occur when the one egg divides in two. The babies are born identical with the same physical characteristics.
- Non-identical twins occur when two separate eggs are fertilised. The babies are born with some but not all features and characteristics similar, in the same way as ordinary *siblings.* For example, one baby may have blonde hair and blue eyes while the other baby may have brown hair and brown eyes.

typhoid fever: an infectious disease caused as a result of a person eating or drinking milk or *food* contaminated by *Salmonella typhi.* The disease can be contracted by drinking unclean *water*, particularly water which has been contaminated with sewage. Flies or unhealthy living conditions can also lead to the disease. The disease often thrives in conditions where there are no public health regulations or standards. It can be passed from person to person and individuals can be infected by carriers. Carriers are people who do not themselves have any *signs and symptoms* of the disease but carry the bacteria in their system. Symptoms of the disease are a high temperature or fever with diarrhoea (which may contain blood). At the end of the first week of typhoid fever, a rash may appear on the upper abdomen. The incubation period is from ten to 14 days.

U

ultra-high temperature (UHT): the process of sterilisation of *food* at very high temperatures for short periods. This reduces the chemical changes in food in comparison with other traditional methods whilst extending the length of time that food can be safely kept before being eaten (see *food preservation*).

ultrasound is an imaging technique which displays the body's anatomic features. It is a non-invasive diagnostic and therapeutic process. It produces high frequency sound waves (not audible to the human *ear*) which are directed into the body and generate echoes as they bounce off structures. The resulting pattern of sound reflection is processed by a computer to produce a moving image on a screen or a photograph. Fluid conducts the ultrasound well. It is therefore useful in diagnosing cysts (which are filled with liquid), or in examining other structures which are fluid filled (e.g. observations of the *foetus* in the *amniotic sac*).

under-5s provision: day care facilities which are available for young children under the age of five years. These include *day nurseries, childminders, nursery schools, nursery classes* in primary schools, *nannies, family centres* and *playgroups*. Under the *Children Act 1989* the law requires *local authorities* to ensure that adequate under 5s provision is available.

unemployment is a stage or period in an individual's life when they are without paid work. Individuals can either be viewed as short-term or long-term unemployed. The unemployed are expected to register with the local Department of Social Security. Once registered they are entitled to *job seekers' allowance* and family credit. (See *benefits, worklessness*.)

United Nations Convention – The rights of the child: sets out a number of statements called articles, which describe the rights of all children and young people. The rights include:

- Article 2 – all rights in the convention apply to all children whatever their race, sex, religion, language, disability, opinion or *family* background.
- Article 3 – all decisions which are made affecting children should be in their best interests.
- Article 7 – all children have a right to a name when they are born and to be able to become a citizen of a country.
- Article 16 – all children have the right to personal privacy. This includes not having their personal phone calls intercepted or overheard unless the law allows it.
- Article 19 – all children have the right to be protected from all forms of violence.

(See *National Children's Bureau*.)

(For further information contact the Children's Rights Development Unit, 235 Shaftesbury Avenue, London WC2H 8EL.)

Universal Declaration of Human Rights: declaration of the rights to which every individual in the world is entitled. It was adopted by the General Assembly of the United Nations on 10 December 1948. Parts of the declaration which apply specifically to health and social care include:

- Article 1 – all human beings are born free and equal in dignity and rights. They are endowed with reason and conscience and should act towards one another in a spirit of brotherhood.
- Article 2 – everyone is entitled to all the rights and freedoms set forth in this declaration, without distinction of any kind, such as by *race*, colour, sex, language, religion, political or other opinion, national or social origin, property, birth or other status.
- Article 23 – everyone has the right to *work*, to the free choice of employment, to just and favourable conditions of work and to protection against *unemployment.*
- Article 23 – everyone without any discrimination has the right to equal pay for equal work.

universalism: a framework in society where policies are introduced and implemented in such a way that they are applied equally to all. Universalism was one of the intentions of the *welfare state* when it was set up in 1948 following the *Beveridge Report* in 1942.

urea: a waste product which is produced in the *liver* as a result of the breakdown of *protein*. It is removed by the *kidneys*. If the urea is allowed to accumulate in the *blood*, it can have a harmful effect on the body.

urinary system: the main system of the body involved in excretion. This is a process by which the body gets rid of unwanted substances produced as a result of cellular activity. The *alimentary canal, lungs* and *skin* are also involved in excretion. (See Figure opposite.)

The urinary system is made up of:

- *Kidneys* – two organs at the back of the body, just below the ribs. They are the main organs of excretion, filtering out excretory materials from the *blood* and regulating the level and contents of body fluids. Blood enters a kidney through a renal *artery* and leaves through a renal *vein*.
- Ureters – two tubes which carry urine from the kidneys to the bladder.
- *Bladder* or urinary bladder – a sac which stores urine. Its lining has many folds which flatten out as it fills up, letting it expand. Two muscular rings which are called the internal and external urinary sphincters control the opening from the bladder into the urethra. When the volume of urine gets to a certain level, nerves stimulate the internal sphincter to open, but the external sphincter is under conscious control (except in young children), and can be held closed for longer.
- Urethra – the tube carrying urine from the bladder out of the body (in men, it also carries sperm – see *penis*). The expulsion of urine is called urination or micturition.

urine: a watery fluid which is yellow in colour and is produced by the *kidneys*. It is a waste product formed as a result of various chemical reactions in the body. It consists

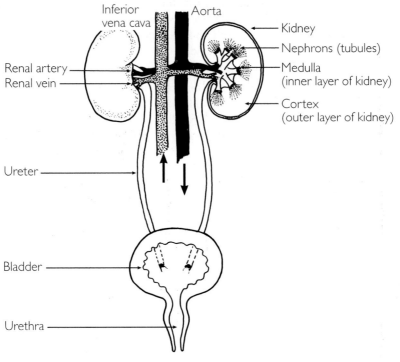

Inferior vena cava
Aorta
Kidney
Nephrons (tubules)
Renal artery
Renal vein
Medulla (inner layer of kidney)
Cortex (outer layer of kidney)
Ureter
Bladder
Urethra

Urinary system

of nitrogenous waste dissolved in *water*. Urine can be analysed chemically to aid the early diagnosis of *disease*. Urine contains water, urea, *salt*, nitrogen compounds such as uric acid and creatinine, hormones and minerals. *Drugs* or *medicine* may appear in urine (e.g. steroids). It can be tested to check for abnormalities or specific conditions, which include:

- sugar – if there is too much sugar in the blood it could indicate *diabetes*
- albumin/protein – when the breakdown of protein or the kidneys may be affected by some disorder or disease
- *pregnancy*.

uterus: see *female reproductive system*.

Utting Report 1997 'People like us': a government report which reviewed the residential care of children. The committee was chaired by Sir William Utting and made recommendations which affect children's homes, boarding *schools* and foster homes. These recommendations, which applied to England and Wales, include:

- developing a residential childcare strategy
- setting up a code of practice for recruiting, selecting, training and supporting *foster carers*
- introducing new legislation requiring *local authorities* to register private foster carers, making unregistered foster care a criminal offence
- extending the *Children Act 1989* to all schools with boarding provision
- defining parental responsibilities and rights in law

- sponsoring an information programme for parents, aimed at reducing risks for children living away from home
- examining the need to strengthen legal protection of agencies communicating information about people unfit to work with children
- ensuring legal protection against abuse is consistent in all settings
- investing all government departments with responsibilities affecting children, to aim to safeguard them and to promote their welfare
- reviewing and re-issuing Children Act guidance on foster care
- recommending new guidelines for local authorities with regard to the supervision of children in care, methods of assessment and meeting the different education requirements
- the health needs of children.

(HMSO 1997)[62]

vaccination: a method of producing *immunity* by injecting dead or weakened pathogens, or closely related micro-organisms into the body in order to stimulate an immune response. It is a means whereby individuals can be protected from the disease or a fatal attack. (See *immunisation*.)

vagina: the lower part of the *female reproductive system*. It is a muscular tube which is lined with mucous membrane. The vagina connects the cervix and the *womb* to the outside of the body.

values form the foundation of an individual's *thoughts*, feelings, *beliefs* and *attitudes*. Values are closely related to moral principles, decision making, attitude formation and *behaviour*. Values are learned during the *socialisation* process, e.g. children learn values through the way they are reared or brought up within their families.

vasectomy: a surgical incision or cut through the vas deferens to prevent male sperm being ejected during ejaculation and intercourse. This is a male form of contraception and family planning.

vegetarians are individuals who do not include meat in their daily *diet*. There are three types of vegetarian:

- Lacto-ovo-vegetarians eat a mixed diet from both plant and animal sources. This includes dairy products and eggs.
- Lacto-vegetarians eat a diet of plant *food* with some milk or dairy products such as cheese. The plant food includes grain, seeds, nuts, fruit and vegetables.
- Vegans eat a diet containing no food from animal sources. This means they only eat plant food such as vegetables, fruit, nuts, seeds and grain.

veins are blood vessels which carry deoxygenated *blood* towards the *heart*, except in the case of pulmonary veins which carry oxygenated blood from the *lungs* to the heart. The walls of veins are much thinner and less muscular than *arteries*. Veins have valves to prevent the backflow of blood.

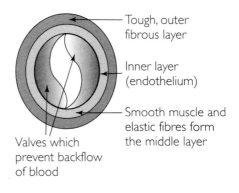

Tough, outer fibrous layer

Inner layer (endothelium)

Smooth muscle and elastic fibres form the middle layer

Valves which prevent backflow of blood

The vein

ventilation: the way in which *air* passes in and out of the respiratory tract. This includes the *gaseous exchange* in the *alveoli* of the *lungs*. Ventilation and the efficient way by which air is breathed in and out of the body are important factors in the general physical health of an individual. When there is a disorder in the ventilation system there are often signs and symptoms such as cyanosis, a bluish tinge to the skin due to the lack of sufficient *oxygen*. (See *mechanisms of breathing, respiratory system.*)

ventricle: a chamber. There are several different types of ventricle in the body. The ventricles of the *heart* are its two lower chambers which pump the *blood* into the main vessel prior to its being distributed to different parts of the body. The ventricles of the brain contain cerebrospinal fluid.

vertebrae: there are 33 of these bones in the backbone. Each vertebra consists of a body and arch enclosing a cavity, which is called the neural canal. The *spinal cord* passes through this canal. The vertebrae protect the spinal cord by providing a bony framework. There are different vertebrae which include:

- seven neck or cervical vertebrae

Neural arch →

Vertebral foramen – (space for spinal cord)

Body of vertebra

Transverse process

- twelve chest or thoracic vertebrae

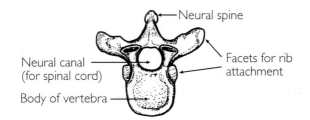

Neural spine

Neural canal (for spinal cord)

Body of vertebra

Facets for rib attachment

- five back or lumbar vertebrae

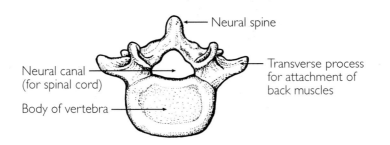

Neural spine

Neural canal (for spinal cord)

Body of vertebra

Transverse process for attachment of back muscles

- five lower back or sacral vertebrae

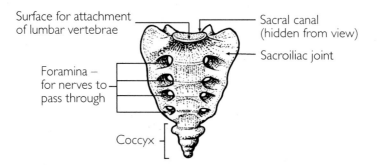

Surface for attachment of lumbar vertebrae

Sacral canal (hidden from view)

Sacroiliac joint

Foramina – for nerves to pass through

Coccyx

- plus the coccyx (the lowest four vertabrae fused together).

victim: a person who has been killed or injured, either in an *accident* or as a result of premeditated action. Health and social care providers are often called upon to assist victims of whatever cause.

Victim Support is a *charity* with volunteer workers who provide counselling to the victims of crime. Individuals are often referred to Victim Support by the *police.*

(For further information contact Victim Support, Cranmer House, 39 Brixton Road, London SW9 6DZ.)

villi: finger-like projections from the surface of membranes. Examples include arachnoid villi in the *brain* and the villi in the lining of the *intestine.* The villi provide a greater surface area for the exchange of *oxygen, carbon dioxide* and *nutrients.*

violence: physical behaviour by an individual which causes hurt or damage to others. This includes physical assault, aggressive behaviour, intimidation, sexual and physical harassment. Violence is often linked with *physical* and sexual *abuse.*

viruses: extremely small infectious agents which are only visible under an electron *microscope.* There are many different types of virus which are harmful to the body and cause *disease.* Viruses reproduce in the body by invading a *cell,* multiplying and causing the cell to burst. An example of a virus is *HIV.*

visual impairments: disorders, *dysfunctions* or *diseases* which affect the *eyes* and the vision of an individual. (See *SeeAbility.*)

(For further information contact The Royal National Institute for the Blind, 224 Great Portland Street, London W1N 6AA.)

vital capacity (of lungs): the maximum volume or amount of air which can be breathed out or expelled by the *lungs* after taking a deep inward breath. It is measured on a *spirometer.* (See *respiration.*)

vitamins are substances which are essential for general health and body growth. They are required in small quantities. When they are not included in a *diet* vitamin *deficiency diseases* may become evident.

Examples of vitamins, their functions and deficiency disorders

Vitamin	Function	Source	Vitamin deficiency disorder
Vitamin A (retinol)	Keeps skin and *bones* healthy, helps to prevent infection	Carrots, milk, fish, oils, green vegetables, liver	Night blindness, lack of resistance to *infection*
Vitamin B1 (thiamin)	Needed for cell metabolism	Peas, beans, yeast, wholemeal bread, nuts	Beri-beri, muscle weakness
Vitamin B2 (riboflavine)	Needed for cell respiration	Liver, milk, eggs, yeast, cheese and green vegetables	Stunted growth, damage to the cornea of eye, inflamed tongue
Vitamin B6 (pyridoxine)	Needed for synthesis of *amino acids*	Potatoes, vegetables, meat, milk	Anaemia
Vitamin B12 (cobalamin)	Needed for formation of red blood cells *protein* and *fat*	Liver, meat, eggs, milk, fish	Macrocytic anaemia, which is a failure to produce haemoglobin in the blood
Vitamin C (ascorbic acid)	Helps *wounds* to heal, necessary for healthy gums and *teeth*	Oranges, lemons, blackcurrants, green vegetables tomatoes, potatoes	Scurvy – a disease which causes gum disease and affects the body's healing process
Vitamin D (calciferol)	Absorption of calcium and phosphorus which is necessary for teeth and bone growth and development	Liver, butter, cheese, eggs and fish	Weak bones – a disease called rickets in children
Vitamin E (tocopherol)	Promotes health anti-oxidant	Vegetables, eggs, butter, fish, meat	Sterility in some animals
Vitamin K (phylloquinone)	Helps the blood clotting process	Liver, butter, cheese, eggs and fish, cabbage, spinach	Slow blood clotting

vocal cords are two folds of *tissue* which protrude from the side of the larynx and vibrate with the passage of air when stimulated by the speech centre in the *brain* to produce sounds that form the voice.

voluntary admission: a procedure which involves a *patient* agreeing that they need psychiatric care and treatment. (See *mental health.*)

voluntary organisations are those health and social care services set up by *charities* to provide services which are free of charge. Voluntary organisations are non-profit making and non-statutory and depend on fund-raising and government grants for their *funding.*

voluntary sector: see *independent sector.*

volunteers: individuals who work within statutory or voluntary organisations without receiving any financial payment. They are often involved with aspects of community work such as dial a ride, working in charity shops and helping out in *day care* centres, or the *Women's Royal Voluntary Service.*

vomiting: a reflex action in which the *stomach* ejects its contents through the mouth. Vomiting is controlled by a centre in the *brain.* Vomiting can be due to:

- stomach infection
- irritation of the stomach lining
- side effects of drugs
- travel sickness
- migraines/headaches
- inner ear disorders
- self-induced (e.g. in bulimia)
- obstruction in gastrointestinal tract.

vulva: the external opening of the *female reproductive system.*

W

Wagner Report 1988 – Residential Care a Positive Choice: a Government report which reviewed the historical development and current use of *residential care*. The report outlined a minimum standard of good practice in residential care and made recommendations. It emphasised the point that 'no one should be required to change their permanent accommodation in order to receive services, which could be made available to them in their own homes' and that 'people who go into residential care should do so by positive choice'. (HMSO 1988)[63] Together with the *Griffiths Report Community Care – Agenda for Action 1988,* the Wagner Report made a valuable contribution to the ideas in the White Paper – *Caring for People 1989* which formed the basis of the *NHS and Community Care Act 1990.*

waiting lists are compiled by health and social care practitioners to control access to their services. Each *client, patient* or *service user* is given an appointment date and time. Under the *Patient's Charter,* the waiting time to see a doctor or consultant is given a maximum limit. The waiting time on the day of the appointment also has a maximum limit. Most health and social care services operate a waiting list of admissions for minor and major surgical operations, treatments and therapies.

Wales (health and social care provision): the arrangements for health and social care in Wales are similar to those in England. The provisions for the NHS and community care and the responsibility for health services in Wales are assigned to the Welsh Office. Following the proposals for a Welsh Assembly presented in the White Paper 'A Voice For Wales', the responsibility for governing Wales would be taken over by such an assembly. Power will be exercised by an executive committee, made up of the leaders of various sub-committees. It will operate in a similar way to the UK cabinet of ministers. The Secretary of State for Wales will still retain powers and duties with regard to a whole range of areas including *education, health, housing* and *social services.*

warmth (interpersonal skills) is an important aspect of human *interaction.* It is a support skill which enables the carer to convey that they are interested and listening with a non-judgmental attitude to their client. It is reinforced with positive *gestures* of eye contact and facial expression. Showing warmth to a *client* can be a factor which contributes to building a positive relationship. (See *confidence building.*)

warmth (physical needs): keeping a *client, patient* or *service user* physically warm. Room temperature should be maintained at approximately 68°F (20°C). It is particularly important for vulnerable clients, such as the elderly and infants, to be kept warm as they can lose body heat very quickly.

Warner Report 1992: a government report which reviewed the selection, development and management of staff who were involved in working with children in residential homes. (HMSO 1992)[64]

Warnock Report 1978: a government report which reviewed the *education* possibilities for children and young people with special needs. It recommended that such children should be integrated into mainstream education, i.e. an ordinary *school* setting. Furthermore, the report recommended that education provision for those with learning difficulties should be extended, with young people being encouraged to take up further and additional education. (HMSO 1978)[65]

waste disposal – disposal of household rubbish: this is known as controlled waste and the *local authority* has the responsibility for collecting such waste through weekly collections.

waste disposal: the result of metabolism taking place in the body due to many chemical reactions. The body has strategies for disposing of the waste products it generates. The two types of waste disposal are termed *excretion* (getting rid of waste products as a result of metabolism) and elimination (egestion). If waste products are not removed quickly enough they have harmful side effects. Through the process of excretion the body gets rid of such substances. This is carried out by the:

- *lungs* – excrete *carbon dioxide* through respiration
- *kidneys* – excrete urea from *digestion* through urination
- *skin* – excretes *water* and *salts* through sweating
- *intestines* – excrete *bile salts* as a result of the breakdown of *haemoglobin*.

Through the process of elimination the body gets rid of waste such as *faeces* at the end of the digestion process. This is called *defaecation*.

water is a compound consisting of hydrogen and *oxygen* (H_2O) which is essential for all forms of life. It can exist as a gas, a liquid or a solid. It is the solvent for most body processes and can react in *cells* through *hydrolysis* and also *condensation*. The properties of water include:

- it is an excellent solvent and can dissolve more biological substances than any other fluid
- it forms 90 per cent of the cell and is the main constituent of the cell cytoplasm
- it acts as a thermal buffer within the body, to prevent it from rapid changes in temperature
- it acts as a lubricant in different parts of the body, e.g. in the air sacs (*alveoli*) which are situated in the *lungs*
- it forms part of a healthy *diet*, hydrating the body and aiding the *digestion* process.

water pollution is caused by chemical and industrial waste which contaminates water supplies, rivers and seas. This includes pollution of *water* supplies by the overuse of fertilisers in *food* production. The control of water pollution is supervised by the Environment Protection Act 1990, the Water Industry Act 1991 and the Water Resources Act 1991. These Acts of Parliament made recommendations which aim at:

- controlling pollution in rivers and the sea (i.e. avoiding the poisoning of water)
- ensuring that water sources are clean for domestic, industrial and agricultural use
- preventing the spread of *disease* through an effective sewage disposal system.

wealth: the total value of possessions held by an individual or a society. It is usually distinguished from income, because wealth can itself be income generating, 'money in the bank' generates interest.

weaning is the process of *feeding* and *diet* change for a *baby*. The initial milk diet is changed to mixed feeding for the older baby. Solids (food other than milk) are introduced at between three and six months. This is usually initiated by a baby who is not satisfied after a milk feed, wakes early for feeds, is miserable or sucks their fists after a feed. There are different theories about what foods should be introduced first, and a vigorous debate surrounding the *carbohydrate, fat* and *sugar* content of baby food. However, there are no strict rules and a suitable mix could be a small amount of baby rice, puréed fruit or vegetables mixed with expressed or formula milk to a semi-liquid consistency.

welfare: actions designed to promote or bring about *well-being*, whether for individuals, groups or entire populations. The term is closely linked to social policy at central or local government level because social policies are the legislative framework through which welfare is delivered. There are four ages of welfare:

- The first age – the poor laws were introduced in England and Wales in 1598 and 1601 as a means of stopping outright destitution.
- The second age – the birth of the welfare state. Alleviating poverty through the introduction of old age pensions in 1908, sickness benefits in 1911 and reforms in 1925 to include women and orphans and to broaden old *age* pension coverage. *Beveridge's* proposals in 1942 led to the introduction of National Insurance. Non-contributory coverage for disabled people regardless of means (i.e. attendance allowance) was introduced in 1971 and a mobility allowance in 1976.
- The third age – this present stage (see *new welfare state*).
- The fourth age – promoting opportunity and developing potential. Welfare 2020 contains plans for on-going reform within the welfare benefit system. (HMSO 1998)[44]

welfare checklist: the seven points which the courts need to consider when there has been an emergency court order under the *Children Act 1989*. The seven points are:

- the child's wishes and feelings, their age and understanding being taken into account
- the physical, emotional and educational needs of the child
- the effect of changing the circumstances of the child
- the age, gender, class, race, culture and religious background of the child
- what harm the child has suffered or is suffering
- the way in which the parents can meet the different needs of the child
- the range of ways in which the court can act under the powers of the Children Act.

welfare contract: a new contract between the citizen and the government based on responsibilities and rights.

Towards a new welfare contract

Duty of the government	Duty of the individual
Provide people with the assistance they need to find work; make work pay	Seek training or work where able to do so

cont.

Support those who are unable to work so they lead a life of dignity and security	Take up the opportunity to be independent if they are able to do so
Assist parents with the cost of raising children	Give support, financial or otherwise, to their children and other family members
Regulate effectively so that people can be confident that private pensions and insurance products are secure	Save for retirement where possible; not to defraud the taxpayer
Relieve poverty in old age where savings are inadequate	
Devise a system that is transparent and open and gets the money to those in need	

Duty of government and citizens alike

To help all individuals and families to realise their full potential and live a dignified life, by promoting economic independence through work, by relieving poverty when it cannot be prevented and by building a strong and cohesive society where rights are matched by responsibilities

(HMSO 1998)[44]

welfare dependency: a situation in which personal or household income is solely dependent on welfare payments, e.g. the state retirement pension or unemployment benefit. People receiving *benefit* are likely to be the poorest in society. The term is particularly associated with the politics of the 'new right', who argue that over generous welfare benefits have made many people too reliant on the state.

welfare provision: the provision of health and social care to all those in need; universal provision. (See *universality*.)

welfare report: a report which has been prepared and written by a member of the *Family Court Welfare Service* or the *social services department* at the request of a court. It considers any matter regarding the welfare of a child within the legislative framework of the *Children Act 1989*. A child's best interests are always taken into account. A welfare report is required when parents are separating and contact with a child is being considered (custody of a child/children, at the direction of the court).

welfare rights: the rights which individuals have in society in terms of access to information and support with regard to *benefits* and financial resources. *Citizens Advice Bureaux,* and *social workers* in this field can also give advice and support in other areas relating to finance, such as debt counselling. The *Child Poverty Action* Group is a pressure group which publishes regular information such as an annual welfare rights handbook.

welfare services are those provided by the state. There are seven areas: *personal social services, health, youth services, social services, housing, education* and *employment.*

welfare state was set up in 1948 following the *Beveridge Report 1942*. It is described as a society in which the state (i.e. government) accepts responsibility for ensuring a minimum standard of living for all people. It is supported by a *benefit* system and associated with a range of *welfare services*.

Welfare to Work: an initiative set up by the Labour Government in 1997 as part of its anti-poverty strategy. It aims to include 250,000 young people (16–25-year-olds) in a 'new deal for young people' by encouraging them off unemployment benefit by the use of four options:

- employment
- training
- voluntary work
- environmental work.

Employers may be offered tax rebates for each unemployed person they take on. This includes all long-term unemployed people, including special groups, lone parents and offenders.

well-being: a positive state of physical, intellectual, emotional and social health. It describes a feeling of being physically well and of psychological contentment.

Welsh Office: the central government department responsible for internal affairs in Wales. The department is presided over by a member of the cabinet who is designated the Secretary of State for Wales.

whistleblowing: a way in which problems and difficulties within organisations are publicised by an individual who is an employee. Whistleblowing was identified in the *Nolan Report 1997*.

white blood cells (leucocytes): these are *cells* produced in the red *bone marrow* and the lymph *glands*. They have nuclei, are colourless and do not contain *haemoglobin*. There are two main types of white cells:

- Granulocytes such as neutrophils, eosinophils and basophils. These are made up of granular cytoplasm and a lobed nucleus. They engulf bacteria and produce anti-histamine and histamine which are released by the body to deal with inflammation.
- Agranulocytes such as monocytes and lymphocytes. They have a spherical or bean-shaped nucleus and no granules in their cytoplasm. They engulf bacteria and produce antibodies.

The number of such cells (4000–10,000 per cubic millimetre of *blood*) is called the white cell count.

Winged Fellowship Trust: an organisation which runs holiday centres for the severely physically disabled, enabling carers to take a break from their duties. The centres are run by a combination of trained staff and volunteers, and 24 hour care is provided. Each centre is fully equipped for the use of disabled people. There is a shop, bar and garden. The Winged Fellowship provides an excellent opportunity for health and social care students to apply for volunteer work and develop their caring skills.

(For further information contact: Winged Fellowship Trust, Angel House, 20–32 Pentonville Road, London N1 9XD.)

'wired for health': access to relevant and appropriate information regarding *health education* on the Internet, particularly for young people and their teachers.

withdrawal symptoms: negative physical or psychological reactions which are experienced by individuals when they suddenly stop taking or reduce the dosage of an addictive *drug*. These include sweating, tremors, *vomiting* and abdominal pain.

womb or uterus: see *female reproductive system*.

Women's Aid Federation: a voluntary agency in the UK for women and children experiencing physical, sexual or emotional abuse in their homes. The Women's Aid Federation of England (WAFE) is a national organisation which supports and resources a network of 214 local projects. Refuges are homes or hostels which offer a safe breathing space where decisions can be made, free from pressure and fear. There are also specialist refuges and services for women and children who face the additional pressures of racism or have specific cultural needs. National Women's Aid Federations operate in Scotland, Wales and Northern Ireland. WAFE represents refuges as well as women and children experiencing domestic violence nationally in England. *Domestic violence* is defined as the physical, emotional or sexual abuse of women and their children in their homes by a person known to them – usually a male partner or ex-partner. Research into domestic violence shows that:

- every year over 50,000 women and children stay in refuges throughout England to escape domestic violence
- over 100,000 women use the services provided nationally and locally by Women's Aid
- 25 per cent of all reported violent crime is 'wife assault'
- nearly 50 per cent of female victims of homicide in England and Wales are killed by a partner or ex-partner
- recent studies have estimated that as many as one in five women experience domestic violence
- today the number of refuges in England is only a third of the number recommended by a government select committee in 1975.

(For further information contact the Women's Aid Federation of England, PO Box 391, Bristol, BS99 7WS.)

Women's movements: groups set up with the aim of removing sexism (discrimination on the basis of *gender*) from society. They work within the agenda of women's rights and *equal opportunities* reinforced by the *Sex Discrimination Act 1975*.

Women's Royal Voluntary Service (WRVS): an organisation which provides practical care and support where it is needed in local *hospitals*, communities and during local emergencies. The WRVS operates in every county, region, major town and city in England, Scotland and Wales. It has three important functions:

- Care in the local *community* – *food* services, *family* support services, home support services for the *elderly*, holidays for disadvantaged children, contact centres, tea bars in prisons and many other projects.
- Care in local hospitals – non-medical assistance for *patients*, enquiry and escort services for hospital visitors, tea bars, shops and the raising and donating of funds to hospitals.

- Care in local emergencies – WRVS emergency service volunteers are present regardless of time or location, to support the *police,* fire and *ambulance services* during incidents such as floods, fires, bomb attacks and accidents. They provide general assistance and refreshments to the rescue teams, clothing and welfare support to victims, families and friends and establish and run rest centres and enquiry points.

(For further information contact: WRVS, Head Office, Milton Hill House, Milton Hill, Abingdon, Oxfordshire OX13 6AF.)

work is a term usually used to describe an adult form of paid employment. At the same time, offering one's services as a volunteer is called voluntary work. Work can also be viewed as an adult form of *play*. However, there is a need to identify the difference between work and *leisure*.

work experience: opportunities for health and social care students to practice theory learned in the classroom, in a *care setting*. In addition to this, it gives students the opportunity to:

- observe experienced and professional carers as they work with *clients*
- meet clients, *patients* or *service users* to develop interpersonal and communication skills
- learn at first-hand how to assess the different needs of clients
- use practical experience to add depth to study and research
- find out about aspects of health and social care; it is often a period when students may decide on their future career.

Work experience is a valuable aspect of any vocational course. It offers crucial features which benefit both the student and the placement organisation. The planning of work experience has the following requirements:

- the dates of the work experience to be negotiated with placements and the tutor or teacher
- students to set up a work experience action plan to ensure practical coverage of units
- students to update their *Curriculum Vitae*
- students to write a letter to the supervisor of the placement enclosing their CV and a supporting statement with regard to their request for work experience.

When students have obtained a placement they should:

- send their CV and supporting statement
- arrange a pre-placement visit
- co-ordinate travel plans
- prepare a *questionnaire* with regard to lunch breaks, starting/finishing time (if different from college hours)
- make sure they have a suitable set of clothes to wear. Short skirts, low cut tops or shorts are usually **not** acceptable. In some work placements, students may be required to wear a uniform
- make sure that they are given suitable tasks and activities to carry out through work experience.

Guidelines – the 'P' laws for students on placement are as follows:

- be **p**unctual – arrive on time
- be **p**repared – problems may arise so be as helpful as possible
- be **p**rofessional – contact college and workplace if you are unwell; if you are anxious or concerned contact your teacher/tutor
- be **p**leasant – communicate with the clients, use your time wisely; co-operate with your colleagues
- be **p**ractical – help with all tasks and activities relating to working with clients and service users.

working class is the position in the social structure which is characterised by those involved in manual work/labour. The numbers in the working class have been declining because manual work is gradually being replaced by machines. (See *social class*.)

Working for Patients (White Paper 1989): a government report which proposed a re-organisation of the *National Health Service*. It made the following recommendations:

- Regional *health authorities* should allocate funds to district health authorities according to population size, local health needs, age distribution and service providers in their particular area.
- *Hospital* trusts should be created within the NHS setting.
- *GP* fundholding should be implemented as a means whereby GPs with over 9000 patients become responsible for their own budgets. They would also be responsible for managing a range of patient care and treatment. A fundholding practice would receive payment from the district health authority.
- The mixed economy of care should be implemented in the form of purchasers and providers – the *internal market.* (HMSO 1989)[66]

This system has since been updated. (See *NHS: The New NHS – Modern, Dependable.*)

Working Together under the Children Act 1989: a document which establishes *inter-agency* co-operation in *child protection*. The document was prepared jointly by the Department of Health, the Home Office, the Department of Education and Science and the Welsh Office.

worklessness: a term in '*New Ambitions For Our Country – A new Contract*' used to describe unemployment. There are three reasons for worklessness:

- a general rise in unemployment, particularly amongst males
- a rise in the number of working men who are not officially unemployed, but are nonetheless out of the labour market or 'economically inactive'
- a growth in households headed by a single adult – often a single parent.

(HMSO 1998)[44]

World Health Organisation (WHO) is a branch of the United Nations. It is affiliated to other worldwide oganisations such as UNICEF. It is concerned with worldwide issues of health and welfare.

wound: damage through accident or injury which causes bleeding. Wounds can either be:

- Surface wounds – bleeding from cuts, grazes caused by damage to the *skin* surface. Treatment involves applying pressure to the area around the wound until the bleeding stops, cleaning the wound with antiseptic and covering the area with a plaster if necessary. In these circumstances the body deals with the bleeding by the action of the surrounding blood supply which constricts, slowing down the bleeding, and by forming a *blood clot*.

- Deep wounds – bleeding which involves the larger blood vessels with blood being pumped out of the body through the cut or wound. This is particularly evident when an *artery* has been affected. The excessive bleeding does not allow blood clotting. Where there is considerable loss of blood, emergency treatment is necessary and medical help should be urgently sought. However, an unqualified person can perform *first aid* which involves lying the injured person down, raising the injured limb or pressing firmly on the affected part and applying pressure to the nearest point of the body where an artery comes to the surface.

In treating wounds and spilt blood, carers should wear gloves whenever possible, as a health and safety precaution.

X

X chromosome: one of the two *chromosomes* which provide the genetic information which determines the sex of an organism. In each cell males have one X and one Y chromosome, females have two X chromosomes.

X-linked recessive gene defects: a defective *gene* which is on the X *chromosome* and affects males with certain forms of *dysfunction, disease* or disorder such as *haemophilia.*

X-ray examination: a method which assists in the diagnosis of a *disease,* disorder or *dysfunction* in the body. When X-rays are directed onto parts of the body they pass through *bone* and *tissue* to different extents to produce an image on a photographic film. X-ray machines are operated by *radiographers. Radiologists* are *doctors* who interpret the X-ray films and make a diagnosis. X-rays are used in *contrast media techniques.*

xenophobia is a fear of foreigners.

XXY syndrome: a *chromosome disorder* also known as Klinefelter's syndrome. It is a condition which affects males who are born with an extra X chromosome. Those suffering with this *disorder* are born with underdeveloped male genitalia and have pronounced female characteristics, such as *breast* development.

XYY syndrome: a *chromosome* disorder caused by there being an extra Y chromosomes in each *cell.* Those who possess this disorder are males who grow to above average in height and have low levels of fertility.

Y

Y chromosome: a sex *chromosome* found only in males.

young carers: children and young people under the age of 16 years who take on the responsibility of caring for a parent or a close member of their *family* with a debilitating *disease* or disorder. The *Carers' National Association* and Community Care Magazine have campaigned for the rights of young carers. In some cases, children forego their schooling and *education* in order to look after a sick relative. The devotion and commitment of these young carers can mean that they live restricted lives and carry heavy 'adult' responsibilities. (See *informal carers, caring for the carer.*)

young offenders' institutions are establishments where young offenders are detained following sentence, usually by a *youth court*. They are taken into youth custody and are allocated a *probation* officer or *social worker* who is likely to visit them regularly until their release.

youth court: a court which was set up under the *Criminal Justice Act 1991*. It replaces the juvenile court for young people and children. It deals with children (under 14 years) and young people (14–18 years).

youth justice teams work with people up to the age of 18 years who are on court orders and also those considered to be 'at risk of custody'. Youth justice teams can comprise *probation officers* and *social workers*, depending upon local arrangements. They are responsible for writing pre-sentence reports for the court. These reports present necessary information about the young person and their offence, and propose a course of action for sentencers to consider. Issues of public protection are now of particular importance.

young offending teams: multi-agency teams set up under the Crime and Disorder Act 1998. The function of these teams is to promote different strategies to support young offenders in the community.

youth service: local authorities employ youth workers to provide a service which aims to encourage the personal development of young people in informal settings called 'youth centres'. It is an opportunity for the local authority to offer a wide range of services for children and young people which include:

- setting up community facilities and groups to provide recreational and educational input
- assisting in the organisation of youth groups and networking with other leaders and groups.

youth workers: those who are trained to work with young people in a variety of ways through the youth service. They may operate as:

- workers who may be based in a youth centre but also spend a proportion of their time talking to young people on the streets
- providers of *advice* and *support* sessions, liaising with other professionals in the care and support of young people and their families.

Z

Zimmer frames are metal frames which give a person necessary support when walking. Zimmer frames have three or four feet, or wheels. Some have attachments for shopping bags and receptacles for carrying items and some fold up for easy carrying in cars and on public transport. They can be purchased or borrowed from *hospitals, voluntary organisations* such as *Age Concern* or the *Disabled Living Foundation*.

zygote: the product of *fertilisation*. The fusion of a male sex cell (the sperm) and the female sex cell (the ovum) produces a zygote. The zygote grows into an *embryo*, which develops into a *foetus*.

ADVANCED HEALTH AND SOCIAL CARE REVISION LISTS FOR UNIT TESTS

The content and focus of the mandatory units have been reviewed in order to identify the key terms for revision.

For end of unit tests look up the following terms, making sure that you understand the text and can memorise the definition.

GNVQ (Advanced) Health and Social care mandatory units (1997–1999)

Unit 1: Equal opportunities and clients' rights

Unit 2: Communicating in health and social care (portfolio assessment only – **no unit test**)

Unit 3: Physical aspects of health

Unit 4: Factors affecting human growth and development

Unit 5: Health, social care and early years services

Unit 6: Planning, health, social care, and early years provision

Unit 7: Educating for health and social well-being

Unit 8: Research perspectives in health and social care

Unit 1: Equal opportunities and clients' rights

Abortion
Access to information
Access to services
Advisory Conciliation and Arbitration
  Service (ACAS)
Advocacy
Ageism
Anti-discrimination policies
Attitudes
Barriers to communication
Behaviour
Beliefs
Bullying
Care value base
Charter standards
Client
Client rights and choices
Codes of Practice
Code of Professional Conduct for
  Nurses, Midwives and Health
  Visitors
Code of Professional Practice for Social
  Workers
Commission for Racial Quality
Community care plans
Complaints and complaints procedures
Confidentiality
Consent
Decision making

Discrimination
Disempowerment
Empowerment
Equal opportunities
Equal Opportunities Commission
Equal opportunities policies
Equity
Ethics
Ethnic group
Ethnic minorities
European Convention on Human
  Rights
European Union
Euthanasia
Homosexuality
Houses of Parliament
Industrial tribunals
Information
Motivation
Northern Ireland health provision
Pressure groups
Resourcing of services
Scotland and its parliament
Self esteem
Self fulfilling prophecy
Stereotyping
Trade unions
Values
Wales (health and social care provision)

Unit 3: Physical aspects of health

Abdomen
Adrenal glands
Adrenaline
Adrenocorticotrophic hormone
Aerobic respiration
Air passages
Alimentary canal
Alveolus
Anaerobic respiration
Angiogram
Aorta
Aortography
Arteries
Arteriole
Arthrography
Audiogram
Autonomic nervous system
Baseline observations
Bile
Blood
Blood cells
Blood pressure
Blood system
Bone
Brain
Capillaries
Cardiac tissue
Cell

Cell cycle
Central nervous system
Charts
Circulatory system
Clinical thermometer
Computer axial tomography
Connective tissues
Contrast media techniques
Digestion
Electrocardiogram
Endocrine system
Epithelial tissues
Glycolysis
Heart
Homeostasis
Immune system
Krebs cycle
Magnetic resonance imaging
Micrograph
Nervous system
Pulse
Respiratory system
Sense organs
Skeleton
Skin
Spirometry
Ultrasound
X-ray examination

Unit 4: Factors affecting human growth and development

Abuse
Adolescence
Adulthood
Advice
Affection
Age
Age profile
Age structure and population
Ageing
Bereavement
Bilingualism
Birth statistics/birth rate
Bonding
British crime survey
Buddies
Change
Child abuse
Citizens Advice Bureau
Classical conditioning
Cognitive ability
Cognitive development
Coping
Counselling
Crime
Culture
Death
Death rate
Defence mechanisms
Demographic trends
Denial
Dependency ratio
Developmental norms
Deviance
Disability
Disease

Divorce
Domestic roles
Domestic violence
Dysfunction
Emotional development
Emotions
Empathy
Environment
Erikson EH
Extroversion
Eysenck's Personality Inventory
Health
Housing
Human growth and development
Identity
Ill health
Income
Infant mortality
Informal care
Inherited disorders
Intellectual development
Introversion
Language development
Life expectancy
Nature–nurture
Physical growth and development
Social and economic factors
Socialisation
Social support network
Suicide

Different organisations which offer
support such as Citizens Advice
Bureau, Relate, Victim Support, Cruse.

Unit 5: Health, social care and early years services

Access to services
Accommodation – in health and social care provision
Administration
Age Classification
Association of Community Health Councils for England and Wales
Benefits
Beveridge Report 1942
Campaigns
Care organisations
Charities
Charter Standards
Classification of care services
Client
Client classification
Collaboration
Community action
Community care
Community care charters
Community care plan
Community health services
Compulsory competitive tendering
Consumers Association
Cost effectiveness
Cost improvement programmes
Council for Voluntary Services

Demographic Characteristics
Dentists
Department of Health
Early Years Services
European Convention on Human Rights
European Union
Fair Employment Commission (Northern Ireland)
Funding
General Social Services Council
Grant maintained status
Health authorities
Health care
Health and social care structures
Hospice
Hospitals
Independent sector
Inter-agency co-operation
Integrated care
National Health Service
Primary care groups
Resourcing of services
Social service committees
Social services departments
Trends in health care
Voluntary organisations

revision lists

Unit 6: Planning, health, social care and early years provision

Activities of daily living
Aids and Adaptations
Approved social worker
Assessment
Attachment within the NHS
Biographical and health data
Care assistants
Care context and care environment
Care management
Care organisation
Care plan
Care planning cycle
Care settings
Carer
Carers National Association
Caring
Caring for the carer
Case conference
Child Health Clinics
Child protection
Combination order
Community drug team
Community health services
Community work

Complementary medicine
Compulsory admission to hospital
Contact order
Contact tracing
Continuum of care
Court of appeal
Court system of England and Wales
Court welfare system
Criminal Courts
Criminal justice system
Criminal proceedings
Crown Prosecution Service
Curfew order
Enablement
GP
Guardian ad litem
Health visitor
Independence
Multi-disciplinary teams
Occupational health nurses
Occupational therapist
Primary health care team
Screening programmes
Young carers

Unit 7: Educating for health and social wellbeing

Addiction
Alcohol
Amphetamines
Atheroma
Balanced diet
Barrier contraceptives
Cancer
Cannabis
Cocaine
Contraceptives
Control of substances hazardous to
  health
Controlled drugs
Coronary heart disease
'Crack'
Crime Prevention

Diet
Drug dependence
Drug misuse
Drugs
Ecstasy
Health
Health action zones
Health education
Health education campaigns
Health and Safety at Work Act 1974
Health and Safety Executive
Health targets
Heroin
Immunisation
Smoking
Target group/audience

Unit 8: Research perspectives in health and social care

Bar chart
Bias
Biased sampling
Bibliography
Case history
Case study
Charts
Cluster sampling
Content analysis
Convenience sampling or non-
  representative sampling
Data
Data analysis
Data collection
Event sampling
Graphs

Hypothesis
Image
Interview
Observation
Pictogram
Qualitative data
Quantitative data
Questionnaire
Rationale
Research
Research methods
Surveys

A list of relevant and updated
legislation and government reports is
included.

References

1. A Voice for Wales (1998), HMSO
2. Abortion Act 1967 (Amendment) (1996), HMSO
3. Access to Health Records Act (1990), HMSO
4. Access to Personal Files Act (1987), HMSO
5. Access to Medical Reports Act (1988), HMSO
6. Agenda for Action (Griffiths Report) (1988), HMSO
7. Association of Community Health Councils (1997), Malnutrition in Hospitals
8. Barclay Report (1982) Social Workers – Their Roles and Tasks, HMSO
9. Beveridge Report (1942), HMSO
10. Black Report (1980), HMSO
11. British Association of Social Workers (1992) 12, Principles of Social Work Practice
12. Care Sector Consortium (1998) National Occupational Standards
13. Caring For People (1989), HMSO
14. Carers (Recognition and Services Act) (1995), HMSO
15. Children Act (1989), HMSO
16. Child Protection For Senior Nurses, Health Visitors and Midwives and their Managers (1992), Department of Health
17. Child Support Act (1991), HMSO
18. Chronically Sick and Disabled Persons Act (1970), HMSO
19. Code of Professional Practice For Nurses, Midwives and Health Visitors (1983), UKCC
20. Community Care (Direct Payments Act) (1996), HMSO
21. Community Care (Residential Accommodation Act) (1998), HMSO
22. Crime and Disorder Bill (1997), HMSO
23. Criminal Justice and Public Order Act (1994), HMSO
24. Crime and Disorder Act (1998)
25. Data Protection Act (1984), HMSO
26. Disability Discrimination Act (1995), HMSO
27. Education Acts (1944) (1997), HMSO
28. Education Reform Acts (1981) (1988), HMSO
29. Equal Pay Act (1970), HMSO
30. Equal Pay Amendment Act (1983), HMSO
31. Excellence in Schools (1997), HMSO
32. Fair Employment Act (Northern Ireland) (1989), HMSO
33. Food Safety Act (1990), HMSO
34. Good Friday Agreement – Northern Ireland (1998), HMSO
35. Health and Safety at Work Act (1974), HMSO
36. Health of the Nation (1992), HMSO
37. Home Life (1984), HMSO
38. Mental Health Act (1983), HMSO
39. Mental Health Act (1984), HMSO
40. Mental Health Patients in the Community (1995), HMSO
41. Mental Incapacity Bill (1995), HMSO
42. Meeting the Childcare Challenge (1998), HMSO

43. Modernising Health and Social Services: National Priorities Guidance (1999–2000, 2001–2002), Department of Health
44. New Ambitions For Our Country – A New Contract For Welfare (1998), HMSO
45. NHS and Community Care Act (1990), HMSO
46. NHS Made Easy (1993), Department of Health
47. Nolan Committee Report (1997), HMSO
48. Our Healthier Nation – A Contract For Health (1998), HMSO
49. Careers Occupational Information Centre (1996), Occupations Crown
50. Platt Report 'Welfare of Children in Hospital' (1959), HMSO
51. Primary Care Act (1997), HMSO
52. Race Relations Act (1976), HMSO
53. Rehabilitation of Offenders Act (1974), HMSO
54. Scotland's Parliament (1998), HMSO
55. Sex Discrimination Act (1975), HMSO
56. Sex Offenders Act (1997), HMSO
57. St John Ambulance (1997) First Aid Manual, Dorling Kindersley
58. Stockley, Oxlade & Wertheim (1998) Usborne Illustrated Dictionary of Science, Usborne
59. Tackling Drugs Together (1995), HMSO
60. Tackling Drugs Together To Build A Better Britain (1998), HMSO
61. The New NHS – Modern, Dependable (1997), HMSO
62. Utting Report 'People Like Us' (1997), HMSO
63. Wagner Report 'Residential Care – Positive Choice' (1988), HMSO
64. Warner Report 'Choosing with Care' (1992), HMSO
65. Warnock Report 'Meeting Special Educational Needs' (1978), HMSO
66. Working for Patients (White Paper 1989), HMSO
67. Working Together Under The Children Act (1989), HMSO

Further Reading

Global Programme in AIDS, The HIV/AIDS Pandemic 1994 Overview – World Heath Organisation, Geneva, Switzerland

Health Provision 1984 –World Health Organisation, Geneva, Switzerland